EDWARD LEAR

Selected Letters

Edward Lear, *c*.1865, by Perret (reproduced by permission of Mrs R. Stileman)

EDWARD LEAR

Selected Letters

Edited by
VIVIEN NOAKES

CLARENDON PRESS · OXFORD
1988

Oxford University Press, Walton Street, Oxford OX2 6DP
Oxford New York Toronto
Delhi Bombay Calcutta Madras Karachi
Petaling Jaya Singapore Hong Kong Tokyo
Nairobi Dar es Salaam Cape Town
Melbourne Auckland
and associated companies in
Berlin Ibadan

Oxford is a trade mark of Oxford University Press

Published in the United States
by Oxford University Press (USA)

British Library Cataloguing in Publication Data
Lear, Edward
Edward Lear: selected letters.—
(Selected letters).
1. Lear, Edward 2. Artists—England—
Biography
I. Title II. Noakes, Vivien III. Series
760'.092'4 ND1942.L37
ISBN 0-19-818601-0

Library of Congress Cataloging in Publication Data
Lear, Edward, 1812-1888.
Selected letters.
1. Lear, Edward, 1812-1888—Correspondence.
2. Poets, English—19th century—Correspondence.
3. Artists—Great Britain—Correspondence.
I. Noakes, Vivien, 1937- · II. Title.
PR4879.L2Z48 1988 760'.092'4 [B] 87-28294
ISBN 0-19-818601-0

Set by Wyvern Typesetting Ltd.
Printed in Great Britain
at the University Printing House, Oxford
by David Stanford
Printer to the University

To Eleanor Garvey

ACKNOWLEDGEMENTS

FOR permission to use letters and illustrations I am most grateful to the Master and Fellows of Balliol College, Oxford; the Beinecke Rare Book and Manuscript Library, Yale University; F. O. Biggins Esq.; the Bodleian Library; the University of British Columbia; the British Library; the Hon. Mrs Alistair Buchan; Cornell University Library; Mrs V. Cumberlege; the Earl of Derby; Maldwin Drummond Esq.; Mrs Alan Edelsten; J. J. Farquharson Esq.; Donald Gallup Esq.; the Glamorgan Archive Service; Diana Holman-Hunt; the Houghton Library, Harvard University; the Huntington Library; the Royal Botanic Gardens, Kew; Major-General Michael Lewis; the John Rylands University Library of Manchester; Henry Martineau Esq.; Dr David Michell; the Trustees of the National Portrait Gallery; The Pierpont Morgan Library, New York; The Ruskin Galleries, Bembridge School, Isle of Wight; Justin Schiller Esq.; the Trustees of the National Museums of Scotland, Edinburgh; the late Edward Selwyn Esq.; the Somerset Record Office, Taunton; the Principal and Fellows of Somerville College, Oxford; Mrs R. Stileman; the Tennyson Research Centre Collection, Lincoln, by courtesy of Lord Tennyson and Lincolnshire Library Service; the Humanities Research Center, the University of Texas at Austin; the Master and Fellows of Trinity College, Cambridge.

For the use of published material I am grateful to the Trustees of Mrs C. H. A. M. Anstruther-Duncan and Penguin Books Ltd. for permission to quote from *Bosh and Nonsense*, and to Macmillan for permission to quote from *The Life and Letters of Sir George Grove* by Charles L. Graves.

For their help in supplying photographs I am indebted to Penguin Books Ltd., Sotheby's, and Thames and Hudson Ltd.

For expert knowledge most generously shared I would like to thank the Hon. Sir Steven Runciman, Alan Downer Esq., Dr Judith Bronkhurst, J. J. Farquharson Esq., Dr Rowena

Fowler, Michael Heseltine of Sotheby's, J. G. Links Esq., Anya Noakes, and Helen Valentine of the Royal Academy Library.

V.N.

CONTENTS

INTRODUCTION

'WHAT my letters are to you I can't say, for I never read them over,—but I believe they would be quite as fit to read 100 years hence as any body else's naughty biography, specially when written off hand as mine are,' Lear wrote to Chichester Fortescue in 1861. Although he imagined his letters being read long after his death, Lear did not write for posterity nor, unlike some more conventional literary figures, did he regard his letters as an art form. They were a communication with his friends, and it is the unselfconscious setting down of his response to what he saw and experienced, his delight in beauty and friendship, his admissions of loneliness and failure, and his frequent lapses into the absurd which give these letters the immediacy of conversation and make them such singular and delightful reading.

The range of his friendship was astonishing. 'What a lot of people of all sorts you know', wrote Fortescue in 1875, and Lear himself tells us that he corresponded with 'every created human being capable of writing ever since the invention of letters . . . with a few exceptions perhaps, such as the prophet Ezekiel, Mary Queen of Scots, and the Venerable Bede'.

Edward Lear was the twentieth of twenty-one children. He was born on 12 May 1812, into a prosperous middle-class family. In 1816 his father suffered a sudden financial collapse, and the family left their elegant home in Highgate for a cramped and dingy house just north of the City. It was either at this time, or possibly from his birth, that he was given into the care of his eldest sister Ann. He had a strange and unhappy childhood overshadowed by illness, but Ann's gentleness and merriment did much to balance his distress. She instilled in Lear a philosophy of pragmatism and a joyful love of the absurd, and the earliest of his surviving letters, written to Ann, show both this and the happy, confident affection he felt towards her.

Although a selection must inevitably reflect something of what the editor considers to be important, significant, or simply delightful to read, in these letters Lear speaks for himself without interpretation, creating a revealing self-portrait. Yet the most extraordinary thing about them is what is not there, for we have a dimension of understanding of Lear which was not available to his correspondents and which makes our reading of these letters even more fascinating. Apart from those who knew him as a child, not one of Lear's friends realized that this humorous, sad, convivial, but lonely man struggled against an illness which he believed might one day destroy his mind and paralyse his body. Lear suffered from epilepsy, with frequent and often violently debilitating attacks. Early in 1878 he wrote in his diary, 'remembering as I well do—all that used to occur from the days I was 6 or 7 years old, it is most wonderful that I exist at all, or that life is ever at all tolerable', and a few weeks before his death, 'It is surprising that I can keep any sort of intellectual life going—all this wretchedness considered.' Then he added, '"We mock them when we do not fear"', for mockery and fear still lingered as the expected response.

In all his known letters there is only one indirect reference to his illness, when in 1832 he tells a childhood friend that he had been 'taken ill—with my old complaint in the head—so much so as to be unable to walk home'. Although he does not write about it, even to Ann, the threat of attacks placed upon him constraints against which he struggled from his childhood and which led him, in his adult years, to find particular pleasure in confronting the physical challenge of often hazardous travel, which was rewarded by the magnificence and beauty such travel opened to him.

As someone whose early years had been dominated by fear and the sense of shame which grew from his condition, Lear responded with happy warmth to children, 'who of all creatures are the most interesting'. He described himself as 'a respectable old cove who is very fond of small children', and his letters to them are uncomplicated fun. With children he was neither patronizing nor sanctimonious. To a day-old child he quoted Sophocles, adding, 'I am sure you will not think me impertinent in translating what he says . . . because there has not been time hitherto to buy you a Greek Dictionary', and he then goes on to congratulate the child 'on coming into a world where if we look for it there is far more good & pleasure than we can use up—even in the longest life'.

In the earliest of his child letters, written when he was 20, he speaks of himself as '3 parts crazy—& wholly affectionate', a role of the gentle clown which he adopted throughout his life. In what he saw as 'this ludicrously whirligig life which one suffers from first and laughs at afterwards', he knew that laughter was a weapon against distress. Writing in 1869 to the American who had just published 'The Owl and the Pussy-cat' he said, 'small as it may be, one does some good by contributing to the laughter of little children, if it is a harmless laughter'. He was the 'old Derry Down Derry, Who loves to see little folks merry', and when *Nonsense Songs, Stories, Botany and Alphabets* was first published in England at the end of 1870 he wrote, 'The critics are very silly to see politics in such bosh: not but that bosh requires a good deal of care, for it is a sine quâ non in writing for children to keep what they have to read perfectly clear & bright, & incapable of any meaning but one of sheer nonsense.'

Lear's pleasure in sharing his nonsense was not restricted to children. When Chichester Fortescue first met Lear in 1845, he described him as 'a delightful companion, full of *nonsense*, puns, riddles, everything in the shape of fun, and *brimming* with intense appreciation of nature as well as history'. Not everyone appreciated Lear's humour. Writing to Fortescue about a visit he had paid to Lord Westbury, Lear said, 'The Chancellor—(I was there Satdy & Sundy—) was delightful: such an abundance of excellent conversation—with a circle, or with me only—one seldom has the luck of getting. He,—Speaking of "undique sequaces"—& "sequax",—& saying—"let us remember the line & go & look for the translation" quoth the Landscape painter in a fit of absurdity—"My Lord I can remember it easily by thinking of wild ducks."—"How of wild Ducks Lear?"—said the Lord C.—— "Because they are *sea-quacks* said I. "Lear" said his Lordship "I abominate the forcible introduction of ridiculous images calculated to distract the mind from what it is contemplating."'

Ridiculous images appear frequently in these letters, particularly from the 1860s onwards, and from the very beginning we see the pleasure that Lear found in words. The earliest letter to have survived, written when he was 13, consists of 110 lines each finishing with a word which ends in -ation. From boyhood he indulged in puns. The spellings he sometimes adopts are not anarchic but are governed by the sound words make, as in 'Whether I shall come to England next year or knot is as yet idden in the mists of the fewcher', or the letter to Lady Wyatt of 16 April 1875 which deals with the problems of preserving mint. The pleasure he derived from their musical quality prompted the creation of nonsense words, and also led to more conventional alliteration, as when he wrote from Corfu to Emily Tennyson, 'Flights of grey gregarious gaggling grisogonous geese adorn the silver shining surface of the softly sounding sea.'

Often it was when he had little news to impart that he lapsed into the absurd. 'I can't say as I knows how to fill this sheet, for there is literally nuffin to say,' he told Fortescue and Lady Waldegrave on Christmas Day 1871, and he went on to write a delightful letter which concludes, 'I think of marrying some domestic henbird & then of building a nest in one of my olive trees, whence I should only descend at remote intervals during the rest of my life.' There is a drawing of Lear and the domestic henbird sitting contentedly in their nest.

There are many drawings in these letters. Some are thumb-nail sketches of views he is planning to paint, but most are self-caricatures of Lear, often with his cat Foss. The earliest self-portrait, drawn in 1831, shows him with a parrot sitting on his head, for it was as an ornithological draughtsman that he began to earn his living. Through the letters we see his developing career from his early days as a natural-history illustrator and the decades of his growing reputation as a landscape painter, to the years of relative failure and professional isolation. There is no philosophical discussion of the artist's role in society, but a great deal about the day-by-day concerns of being a painter. As he approached his fortieth year after a successful decade in Rome, he faced 'the choice of 2 lives:—society—& a half day's work,—pretty pictures—petit maître praise boundless—frequented studio, &c &c—— wound up with vexation of spirit as age comes on that talents have been thrown away. ————or *hard study*—beginning at the root of the matter—the human figure—which to master alone would enable me to carry out the views & feelings of Landscape I know to exist within me.'

In January 1850 he enrolled as a student at the Royal Academy, but his stay there was brief and a mastery of the human form still evaded him, as we can see not only from his subsequent work but also from his correspondence with Lord Derby. Writing in November 1850 about a painting of Athens which Lord Derby had commissioned, Lear proposed that the picture should depict the city at harvest time 'because, as all the threshing is done on the plain—under the Acropolis—the groupes of figures are as *natural*, as they are picturesque in themselves, & indispensable to a good foreground in a large subject'. However, in the next letter he has changed his mind, and now suggests that the time should be 'sunrise or a little after, & I have avoided many figures as solitude & quiet are the prevaling feelings on that side of Athens'. Finally he writes, ten days later, 'In a scene, the chief characteristic of which is excessive solemnity & quiet, it appears to me that all bustle should be sedulously avoided.'

A constantly recurring theme is that of shortage of funds. There were a few years, when he lived in Rome between 1837 and 1848 and for a time after his return to England in 1849, when Lear scarcely worried about money, but throughout the rest of his life financial insecurity determined the decisions he made about his work. When he was 19, the slow paying of the subscribers to his book, *Illustrations of the Family of Psittacidæ, or Parrots*, forced him to abandon the project and work instead for other people. Thirty years later, when he published *Views in the Seven Ionian Islands*, he still lamented the slow paying of fifty of his subscribers 'who naturally think 3 guineas can be nothing, forgetting that 150 guineas are much'. From about the mid-1860s, when his hopes of becoming an established painter began to fade, he became shameless in asking for money in advance on pictures, or in picking up any slight hint of approval for one of his works and writing to the possible buyers to remind them of their interest in it. He knew that his work deserved a wider public and he blamed the dictates of fashion for his lack of success, but although the overtures he made to possible patrons were understandable they were also a mistake. Lord Derby probably summed up the thoughts of others of his contemporaries when he wrote in 1880, 'in the world, where nothing succeeds like success, he has done himself much harm by his perpetual neediness. An artist who is always asking his friends to buy a picture, & often to pay for it in advance, makes outsiders believe that he cannot know his business: which in Lear's case is certainly far from the truth. But he has been out at elbows all his life, & so will remain to the last.' Christie's declined to handle his paintings and he could not afford 'a shining=splendid gallery in Bond St. or elsewhere', but there was nevertheless a steady sale for his work. For a bachelor without dependants his income was quite adequate.

One of the reasons for Lear's constant penury was the amount he spent on travel. From the time he left England for Rome in 1837 until he settled in San Remo in 1870, he seldom stayed more than a few months in one place. As a landscape painter he wished to leave behind 'correct representation of many places little cared for or studied by most painters', but possibly of greater importance in his decision to travel so much was the freedom he experienced on his journeys. 'I loathe London by the time [I] have been here a month,' he wrote to Emily Tennyson in 1865. 'The walking—sketching—exploring—noveltyperceiving & beautyappreciating part of the Landscape painter's life is undoubtedly to be envied:—but then the contrast of the moneytrying to get smokydark London life—fuss—trouble & bustle is wholly odious, & every year more so.' What his friends did not realize was that being on the move helped to reduce the frequency of his epileptic attacks, and although the rigorous journeys sometimes exhausted him, he never felt fitter than when he was travelling.

From his letters we can see the enthusiasm with which he explored new and exciting places. Florence he thought 'a hurly-burly of beauty and wonder' and Rome 'the most delectable of all delightful places'—until he saw Athens, for 'surely never was anything so magnificent as Athens! . . . Poor old scrubby Rome sinks into nothing by the side of such beautiful magnificence.' There are few long descriptive passages about the scenery he passed, for he would have expected his correspondents to see the grandeur and beauty of this in the paintings which he brought home. Instead he writes of an erupting volcano as 'a large snapdragon of plums and lighted Brandy', or tells Ann, 'How the variety of costumes would delight you! As for the priests—they are innumerable—white—

black—piebald—scarlet—cinnamon—purple: round hats—shovel hats—cocked hats—hoods and caps—cardinals with their 3 footmen (for cardinals *never* walk)—white friars with masks, bishops and Monsignori with lilac and red stockings—and indeed thousands on thousands of every description of religious orders.' From Constantinople he describes at length the ceremony of 'foot kissing' which he witnessed in the Sultan's palace, 'I believe the first Christians ever allowed to do so'.

He had been invited to see the ceremony while staying at the British Embassy as the guest of the ambassador, Sir Stratford Canning. Reading these letters one realizes how extensive British influence was at this time, and how valuable it was for a traveller to have a network of acquaintance on which he could draw. In 1831 Lear had gone to live at Knowsley, the home of the Earl of Derby, where he was employed to make drawings of the animals and birds in the menagerie. There he met 'half the fine people of the day', and these became his friends, his patrons, and his hosts. The hospitality he was offered led to contrasting experiences as he travelled. One week he might be eating huge dinners as the guest of the Lord High Commissioner in Corfu, and another he would be sleeping in a simple hut which 'contains no one thing in the world—but you sweep it out & put 2 clean mats on the floor, & there you are established'.

Other rural places were less uncluttered, such as the Han of Tirana which 'was so old & badly put together that one quadrill danced in any room would have made it all powder—& as the boards were about 6 inches asunder—everybody seemed to live in public. But one gets used to odd ways. A mad Dervish was my next neighbour—but he did me no harm. As for the mice & spiders—I kept them off by a mosquito net—*a most invaluable travelling companion here*. But these are trifles which only distract the attention for a few hours—while, during the day everything beautiful & novel is before one.' He was not a reckless traveller, but neither was he a cautious one. In Albania, for example, he reached places in the interior never before visited by an Englishman, and found scenery more dramatic and beautiful than any he had seen. His realization of the rewards which can come from daring to take risks was something he sought to convey to children when he believed his travelling days were over and he began to write his nonsense songs.

The theme of many of his later nonsense songs is the need for an understanding of human frailty, but although he believed that frailty demanded compassion he felt that stupidity did not. In 1856 he wrote to Emily Tennyson, 'you know my exaggerated mode of writing & talking', and nowhere is this more evident than in those letters in which he wrote with passion against organizations which sought to maintain established positions rather than pursue the truth. In this his main target was what he saw as the loveless interpretation of Christ's teaching by some sections of the Church, and the unwillingness of many clerics to look disinterestedly at the new scientific understanding of his day. His outbursts prompted Fortescue to write, 'Don't become a priest against priests, a fanatic against fanatics, or be blind to the practical truths that many of them teach', but though stated with characteristic hyperbole there was justification in most of the criticism Lear made.

For the last part of his life he lived permanently abroad. In those years of 'non=personal=nor=otherwise=than=by= correspondence Communication' he longed for his friends to visit him, and he wrote to tell them so. 'I may hope that you & Ldy Hooker will be afflicted with a transient gleam of Rheumatism, & be obliged to come to Sanremo,' he told Sir Joseph Hooker in 1878. His closest friend, Franklin Lushington, went regularly to stay with him, and others who were wintering close by or travelling in Italy or the south of France would come and visit him. But there were long periods of loneliness, as his letters clearly show. They also show his determination not to give in as he lapses more frequently into nonsense than ever before.

'We kept up till a short time before his death the affectionate regular correspondence we had maintained for many years,' wrote Lushington, 'but by degrees his letters became shorter & showed failure of memory.' His last known letter was written on 29 November 1887, and tells of the death of his much loved cat Foss. Exactly two months later, on 29 January 1888, Lear died in San Remo.

It is now impossible to know how many letters Lear wrote. In

February 1862 he told William Holman Hunt, 'since I arrived here [Corfu] at the end of November 1861—I find I have written exactly 76 letters—so that I really cannot be blamed for indolence, although I am not able to apply often to long epistles.' In 1871 he told Hunt that he had written 408 letters during the previous year. His diaries survive for the last thirty years of his life—from his forty-sixth year—and in these it was his habit to list the letters received and sent, but of the earlier years there is no record. Writing in his memoirs of the time they shared a house in the summer of 1852, Hunt said of Lear: 'In the early morning he occupied himself in a most extensive correspondence; sometimes he would write as many as thirty letters before breakfast.' This frequently quoted figure is misleading; if Lear did write so many letters, they were probably no more than requests for people to subscribe to his *Journals of a Landscape Painter in Southern Calabria*, which were published later that year. We know that, when he was preparing his volume of *Views in the Seven Ionian Islands* in 1863, he wrote 600 letters to possible subscribers, a task he found so overwhelming that he told Fortescue, 'if I were an angel I would immediately moult all my quills for fear of their being used in calligraphy'.

His normal practice was to write his letters early in the morning before settling down to work, or to wait until the light had gone in the evening, for as a painter daylight was precious to him. 'Wrote to Lady Bethell: very hastily—in 25 min.—but I thought, better so, than delay longer,' he wrote in 1860, giving an indication of the time an unhurried letter might take. In 1881 he told Fortescue, 'it is my way to jot down notes of what I want to write, & so—when a time of writing occurs,—to make use of all together.' 'Gnoats for letter to Ld. Carlingford' have survived, as has '4oscue Ye Text=book', jottings to remind him of things to write about. Occasionally he wrote numbered headings down the side of the sheet, each then being developed into a numbered paragraph. Beyond making such notes it seems unlikely that he normally drafted his letters.

To the more urgent letters he would reply almost at once, noting both the receipt and the reply in his diary. Occasionally there would be a long delay before responding, particularly if he were oppressed by what he called his 'morbidnesses', for 'unless

I am in a (comparatively) lively mood I do not like writing', he told Fortescue in 1868, 'there is no sense in boring one's friends with details of irretrievable glumpiness, & yet one is indisposed for any fictitious luminous gilding'.

In order to persuade himself to write letters when he did not feel like it, he might use one of two devices. In September 1873, he told Fortescue, 'I have behaved like a brute about writing,—always promising myself a quiet day for letters not immediately pressing—with an addressed envelope staring at me reproachfully, a dodge I learnt from you.' At other times he would write his address, the date, and the salutation on a sheet of paper, which again would regard him reproachfully until he continued with the task.

The letters have been transcribed from the originals, except in those cases where the original manuscript no longer survives or has gone through the sale rooms and cannot at the moment be traced. All such letters, where the original was not available for checking, have been marked in the List of Letters with an asterisk. Lear's letters to Ann, for example, are known to have existed in South Africa in the late 1930s, when they were in the possession of Eleanor Bowen née Gillies, the great granddaughter of Lear's sister Sarah. They have since disappeared although, strangely, two manuscript letters written by Lear to Ann, and noted as missing from the collection by Mrs Bowen, were bought in a south London bookshop during the Second World War and are now in a private collection in America. Most fortunately, Mrs Bowen arranged to have typed copies made of the letters in her possession and these she distributed to other members of the family. A single set of the typed copies has survived, and although this is not complete—there is, for example, a large gap from November 1838 to August 1844— they cover the years from 1837, when Lear left England for Rome, until shortly before Ann's death in 1861. A few transcripts of letters to Ann dating from the late 1820s, also copied by Mrs Bowen, have survived from another source.

In a handwritten note, Mrs Bowen speaks of the care she has taken that the transcripts should be as accurate as possible. In editing these for publication I have tacitly corrected obvious spelling or typing mistakes, leaving anything which may have been Lear's own eccentricity. In a few places I have changed the transcribed word for another almost identically written word which I feel should have been the correct transcription—these are placed in square brackets.

In all other cases Lear's spelling has been left untouched, except for his use of 'th' for 'the' and 'tht' for 'that', indications of the speed at which he often wrote; it was felt that to reproduce these would have been pedantic and intrusive. [*sic*] has been used only where it is felt necessary to confirm that the spelling is Lear's.

Nowhere is his characteristic inconsistency of spelling more apparent than in place-names. These he would often write as they sounded with little regard for accuracy or uniformity, so that within a few lines he wrote both 'Aboo Simbel' and 'Abou Simbel'. The names are recognizable even though they are irregular, and they have not been changed.

Long text has been broken into paragraphs, as has the text in some other manuscript letters where Lear filled densely written pages without a break. Characters written above the line have been lowered on to it. His punctuation, with its characteristic use of dashes of varying lengths and frequent and often multiple underlinings, has been reproduced (single underlinings as italics, double underlinings as small capitals, triple underlinings as capitals, with subsequent underlinings reproduced beneath), apart from double inverted commas, which have been rendered as single.

Lear frequently illustrated his letters, and where the manuscript survives these drawings have all been reproduced. When the letters to Ann were transcribed, Mrs Bowen made copies of the many drawings which illustrate them, adding, 'I have tried to copy the sketches exactly—even to the smudges.' Those referred to in the text have been reproduced from Mrs Bowen's copies, but those to which no reference is made have been omitted.

The letters are all printed unabridged, with the exception of one to which was attached a four-page postscript written from a different address and on a different date and whose contents did not relate to what had gone before; this was adjudged to be a separate letter. The layout of the valedictions has been standardized, and a vertical rule used to indicate the change of line in the manuscripts. Square brackets have been used to indicate editorial insertions, including translation of foreign passages, and points of ellipsis within square brackets ([. . .]) indicate an illegible word or words.

In annotating the letters I have identified the people to whom Lear refers wherever this is possible. Paintings or publications to which he refers have also been identified, and some explanation given of points he is discussing which might otherwise be obscure. Where there is no annotation in a place where this might seem necessary, the Index may supply an earlier, annotated reference or act as a source of cross-reference.

LIST OF LETTERS

An asterisk (*) indicates letters of which the original manuscript has disappeared and where text has been taken from a transcript.

CHRONOLOGY

1812	Birth of Edward Lear in Highgate, 12 May.
c.1826	Begins to earn his living as an artist.
1830	Starts work on *Illustrations of the Family of Psittacidæ, or Parrots*, June. First two folios published, November.
1831	Earliest drawing for Lord Stanley at Knowsley. Collaboration with John Gould begins.
or 1832	Visits Amsterdam, Rotterdam, Berne, and Berlin with Gould.
1835	Travels to Ireland with Edward Stanley, Bishop of Norwich, and his son Arthur Penrhyn Stanley, July–August. His interest turns to landscape painting.
1836	Walking tour in the Lake District, August–October. His eyesight and general health deteriorate.
1837	Sets out for Rome travelling via Belgium, Luxemburg, Germany, and Switzerland, July. Reaches Rome, December.
1838	Travels to southern Italy, May–August. Earliest oil painting, June.
1839	Walking tour towards Florence, May–October.
1841	Returns to England, spring. Publication of *Views in Rome and its Environs*. Visits Scotland, September. Returns to Rome, December.
1842	Visits Sicily, April–May, and the Abruzzi, July–October.
1843	Returns to the Abruzzi, September–October.
1845	Meets Chichester Fortescue, April. Returns to England, May.
1846	Publication of *Illustrated Excursions in Italy* (2 vols.). Publication of first edition of *A Book of Nonsense*, using the pseudonym Derry Down Derry. Publication of *Gleanings from the Menagerie and Aviary at Knowsley Hall*. Gives a series of twelve drawing lessons to Queen Victoria. Returns to Rome, December.
1847	Visits Sicily and southern Calabria and witnesses outbursts of revolution, May–October.

1848 Meets Thomas Baring, later Lord Northbrook, February. The state of Italy becomes more unsettled, and Lear leaves Rome, April. Travels via Malta to Corfu and the Ionian Islands, April–May. Visits Athens, Marathon, Thermopylae, and Thebes, where he is taken ill, June–July. Arrives in Constantinople, August. Travels across Greece and into Albania, September–December. Returns to Malta, and meets Franklin Lushington, December.

1849 Travels to Cairo, Suez, and Sinai, January–February. Returns to Malta, then sets out for southern Greece with Franklin Lushington, March. Travels in the Morea and visits Janina, Vale of Tempe, and Mount Olympus, March–July. Returns to England, July. Attends Sass's School of Art to prepare drawings for entrance to the Royal Academy Schools, November–December.

1850 Accepted as a probationer, January, and as a full student, April. First picture accepted by Royal Academy. By November he is working on his own again.

1851 Publication of *Journals of a Landscape Painter in Albania, &c.* Meets Alfred and Emily Tennyson.

1852 Introduced to Holman Hunt, who offers to teach him his own methods of painting, early summer. Lives with Hunt at Clive Vale, Hastings, and meets other members of the Pre-Raphaelite Brotherhood, July–December. He begins to gain confidence in oil painting, and conceives the plan of illustrating Tennyson's poems. Publication of *Journals of a Landscape Painter in Southern Calabria*.

1853 Publication of the first of his musical settings of Tennyson's poems. Unable to cope any longer with the damp English weather, he leaves to spend the winter in Egypt, December.

1854 Travels up the Nile as far as the first cataract, January–March. Returns to England, then visits Switzerland, August–October.

1855 Publication of second edition of *A Book of Nonsense*. Accompanies Lushington to Corfu for the winter. Spending most of his time alone, he becomes lonely and depressed.

1856 Employs Giorgio Cocali, April. Travels via Albania and Greece to Mount Athos and Troy, August–October.

1857	Visits Albania, April. Returns to London for the summer, May, and to Corfu for the winter, November.
1858	Travels to Bethlehem, Hebron, Petra, the Dead Sea, Jerusalem, and Lebanon, March–June. Returns to England, August. Decides to winter in Rome, November.
1859	Returns to England in May, and spends most of the summer at St Leonards. Returns to Rome, December.
1860	To England, May. Begins work on large oil paintings of the *Cedars of Lebanon* and *Masada* at Oatlands Park Hotel, October.
1861	His sister Ann becomes ill, and dies on 11 March. Visits Florence, May–August. *Cedars of Lebanon* exhibited in Liverpool and receives favourable reviews, September. Returns to winter again in Corfu, November. Publication of third edition of *A Book of Nonsense* under his own name, December.
1862	*Cedars of Lebanon* exhibited in the Great International Exhibition, March, but hung very high and not well received. Returns to England, May. Leaves England for Corfu, November. Despite the increasing sales of the last ten years, he now realizes that his chances of becoming established are diminishing, and he works on his first group of Tyrants.
1863	Visits the other Ionian islands, April–May. Returns to England, June. Publication of *Views in the Seven Ionian Islands*, December.
1864	Returns to Corfu, January. The island is ceded to the Greeks and he leaves for Athens and Crete, April. In London, June–November. Decides to winter in southern France and leaves England. Finds rooms in Nice, November.
1865	Writes the first of his Nonsense stories, *The History of the Seven Families of the Lake Pipple-Popple*, February. Returns to England, April. Lady Waldegrave commissions a painting of Venice, and he travels there, November. Decides to winter in Malta, December.
1866	Returns to England, April. Contemplates proposing marriage to Gussie Bethell, November. To Egypt, and travels down the Nile as far as Wadi Halfa, December–March.

1867   Visits Gaza and Jerusalem, then returns to England via
        Ravenna, June. Leaves to winter in Cannes, November.
        Writes the first of his Nonsense songs, 'The Owl and the
        Pussy-cat', December. The *Cedars of Lebanon* sold to
        Louisa, Lady Ashburton for £200, less than a third of its
        original price.

1868   Travels in Corsica, May–June, then returns to England
        until December. Leaves for Cannes, December.

1869   In Paris, working on plates for his book on Corsica,
        June–July. In London until December, when he returns
        to Cannes. *Journal of a Landscape Painter in Corsica*, the last
        of his travel books, published December.

1870   Decides to settle, and buys land in San Remo, March.
        Summer in Certosa del Pesio. *Nonsense Songs, Stories,
        Botany and Alphabets* published, December.

1871   Moves into Villa Emily, March. *More Nonsense* pub-
        lished, December.

1872   Spends the summer in England, June–October. Sets out
        for India, but turns back at Suez, October. Foss arrives,
        November.

1873   Leaves for India, October. Arrives Bombay, November.

1874   Travels in India and Ceylon.

1875   Leaves India, January. Summer in England, June–
        September.

1876   His last Nonsense book, *Laughable Lyrics*, published
        December.

1877   England, May–September. Brief visit to Corfu to see
        Giorgio who is ill, September.

1878   Summer, Monte Generoso, Switzerland. The land
        below his house is cleared for building, October.

1879   Lady Waldegrave dies, July. Summer, Monte Generoso.

1880   Buys new land for building, February. Last visit to
        England, April–August; Varese, Monte Generoso,
        September–October.

1881   Summer on Monte Generoso. Moves into Villa Tenny-
        son, October.

1882   Summer in Monte Generoso.

1883   Summer in Monte Generoso. Giorgio Cocali dies,
        August.

1884   Villa Emily sold, February. Summer in Recoaro.

1885   Summer in Brianza.

1886   Spends some weeks in bed with bronchitis, January–April. John Ruskin places him at the head of his list of favourite authors in the *Pall Mall Gazette*, February. Makes final repayment of debt for building Villa Tennyson, March.

1887   Abandons Tennyson project as a failure. Foss dies, November.

1888   Dies in San Remo, 29 January.

BIOGRAPHICAL REGISTER OF CORRESPONDENTS AND PERSONS FREQUENTLY CITED

(these are listed under the name which Lear most frequently used)

ABERDARE. See Bruce, Henry Austin.

BARING, EVELYN (1841–1917). The first Earl of Cromer (cr. 1901). He was ADC to Sir Henry Storks, High Commissioner for the Ionian Islands, when Lear first met him in Corfu at the end of 1863. In 1872 he was appointed secretary to his cousin Lord Northbrook (q.v.), a position he held when Lear travelled to India in 1873 as Northbrook's guest. In 1883 he was appointed HM's Agent and Consul-General to Egypt with plenipotentiary powers. A group of twenty Nonsense birds drawn by Lear for Cromer's son was published in 1911 in *Queery Leary Nonsense* (and subsequently as *The Lear Coloured Bird Book for Children,* 1912), to which Lord Cromer wrote an Introduction. Speaking of Lear's 'chill penury' he says that 'neither his impecuniosity nor his disappointment could sour his essentially lovable nature, or tinge with the least shade of cynicism a humour, which was above all things kindly and genial'.

BARING, THOMAS GEORGE. See Northbrook, Earl of.

BETHELL, the Hon. AUGUSTA (1838–1931). Known as Gussie. The fourth daughter of Richard Bethell, first Baron Westbury, whom Lear first met in the early 1830s. Diminutive but forceful, she was the only woman whom Lear seriously thought of marrying. In 1874 she married Adamson Parker. He died in 1881. It was for Gussie's nephews and nieces, Violet, Slingsby, Guy, and Lionel—the children of her brother Slingsby—that in 1867 Lear wrote his Nonsense story *The Four Little Children Who Went Round the World.*

BOSWELL, MARY (1796–1861). Lear's sister, the eighth child of Jeremiah and Ann Lear. In 1821 she married Richard Boswell with whom, in 1857, she went to New Zealand to settle with her sister Sarah Street. Soon after the Boswells' arrival, Sarah wrote that Mary and her husband were 'illsuited to New Zealand life'. She died on her way back to England in 1861.

BRUCE, HENRY AUSTIN, MP (1815–95). Secretary of State for the Home Department, 1868–73, Lord President of the Council, 1873–4. Created 1st Lord Aberdare, 1873. Lear first met Henry Bruce in

Rome in the 1840s. He commissioned a number of paintings from Lear, including a large picture of Kinchinjunga (1877).

BURDETT-COUTTS, Baroness (1814–1906). Born Angela Georgina Burdett, she was the granddaughter of the banker Thomas Coutts, and took his name on inheriting his huge fortune on the death of his second wife, the Duchess of St Albans. Called 'the richest heiress in all England', she devoted her life to social entertainment and philanthropy, and received a peerage in 1871.

CARLINGFORD. See Fortescue, Chichester.

COCALI. See Giorgio.

COLLINS, WILKIE (1824–89). The author of mystery stories, including *The Woman in White* (1860) and *The Moonstone* (1868), Wilkie Collins knew Lear from his boyhood. It was at his suggestion that Lear wrote the second part of 'Mr and Mrs Discobbolos'. Although delighted at Collins's success, Lear had reservations about his subject matter, writing in 1885, 'I think ghosts & future states may be & probably are quite realities,—yet I don't like them used as mere talk.'

COOMBE, FANNY, née DREWITT (18?–1857). The Drewitts lived in Peppering House, Burpham, near Arundel, where Lear met her in about 1823. In his boyhood Lear regarded the Drewitts as his second family, and much of his early humorous verse (largely unpublished) was written for Fanny and her sister Eliza. She married George Coombe, and Lear subsequently referred to her as Mrs George. Their daughter Fanny Jane Dolly Coombe married Henry Willett of Brighton; their son Percy Coombe was Lear's godson.

DECIE, NORA (1864–1933) and RUTH (1862–1917). The granddaughters of Mr and Mrs William Prescott (q.v.).

DERBY, the 13th Earl of (1775–1851). Lord Stanley, who succeeded to the earldom in 1834, was an eminent natural historian; he was President of the Linnean Society and of the Zoological Society of London. In 1831 he commissioned Lear to make drawings of the birds and animals in the magnificent private menagerie which he had built up at his home Knowsley Hall, near Liverpool. It was for 'the great-grandchildren, grand-nephews, and grand-nieces of Edward, 13th Earl of Derby' that Lear composed the limericks for *A Book of Nonsense*.

DERBY, the 15th Earl of (1826–93). Grandson of the 13th Earl. A leading politician, Lord Stanley was offered the throne of Greece in 1863, an offer he declined. At Lear's request he commissioned a number of paintings, and helped him during the financial crisis which followed the spoiling of Villa Emily in 1880. At that time he wrote in his diary, 'in the world, where nothing succeeds like success, [Lear] has done himself much harm by his perpetual neediness'.

DREWITT. See Coombe.

DRUMMOND, EDGAR (1825–93). Met Lear in Rome in the winter of 1858–9, and was a member of the banking family with whom Lear banked.

DUNCAN, Lady and Miss ANNA. Lear first met Lady Duncan and her daughter Anna in Rome in the late 1830s or early 1840s. It was probably at this time that he prepared for them two volumes of limericks, published in 1982 as *Bosh and Nonsense*. In April 1848 he was with them again in Malta, and in 1864 in Nice. Anna by this time was chronically ill, and the illustrated letters he prepared for them were an attempt to lighten their 'dreary hard life'.

EDWARDS, AMELIA (1831–92). She was introduced to Lear by Marianne North (q.v.) and was the author of *A Thousand Miles up the Nile* (1877). She bequeathed her library and collection of Egyptian artefacts to University College, London, with funds to found a chair in Egyptology. Lear, who admired her work, sought her advice about the publication of his own Egyptian journals.

EMPSON, CHARLES. Bookseller of Newcastle-upon-Tyne.

FIELDS, JAMES. A partner in the publishing house Fields, Osgood & Co. of Boston, Mass. They published the children's illustrated magazine *Our Young Folks*, in which, in 1870, three of Lear's Nonsense songs—'The Owl and the Pussy-cat', 'The Duck and the Kangaroo', and 'The Daddy Long-legs and the Fly'—were first published.

FORTESCUE, CHICHESTER, Baron CARLINGFORD (1823–98). He met Lear in Rome in 1845, and subsequently became one of his closest friends. Elected MP for Louth 1847–74, he was Chief Secretary for Ireland (1865–6), President of the Board of Trade (1871–4), Lord Privy Seal (1881–5), and President of the Council (1883–5). He was created Baron Carlingford in 1874. In 1871 he married Frances, Lady Waldegrave (q.v.). His letters from Lear were published as *The Letters of Edward Lear* (1907) and *The Later Letters of Edward Lear* (1911).

GIORGIO (1817–83). Lear's servant from 1856 until his death in 1883, and on whom he came to depend for all his domestic arrangements. Giorgio travelled widely with Lear, who wrote of him, 'My poor dear George was ever a semi-civilized Suliot, much like wild Rob Roy or Highlander'. After the death of Giorgio's wife in 1874, Lear gave a home to his three sons; the oldest, Nicola, is buried beside Lear in San Remo.

GLADSTONE, WILLIAM EWART, MP (1809–98). Four times Prime Minister, he was sent to Corfu in 1858 in an unsuccessful attempt to quell agitation among the Greeks for a return to Greek rule; it was at this time that Lear met him. Lear subsequently became a fierce critic of Gladstone, particularly of his policy towards Russia.

GOULD, JOHN (1804–81). A taxidermist, in 1827 appointed Curator and Preserver to the Museum of the Zoological Society of London, working at the Society's museum in Bruton Street. In 1831 he published his first book of ornithological illustrations, *A Century of Birds hitherto unfigured from the Himalaya Mountains*. In the early 1830s Lear travelled with him to Holland, Germany, and Switzerland during the preparation of *The Birds of Europe* (5 vols., 1832–7), to which Lear contributed many of the illustrations. He also worked with Gould on *A Monograph of the Ramphastidæ, or Family of Toucans* (2 vols., 1834). In 1838–40 Gould and his wife Elizabeth (née Coxen) were in Australia preparing *The Birds of Australia* (7 vols., 1840–8). In spite of the agreeable tone of Lear's letters to Gould, their relationship was not altogether a happy one. In 1863 Lear wrote, 'A more singularly offensive mannered man than G. hardly can be: but the queer creature means well, tho's more of an Egotist than can be described.'

GRENFELL, HENRY RIVERSDALE (1824–1902). MP for Stoke on Trent, later Governor of the Bank of England, and a close friend of Chichester Fortescue. In 1862 Lear painted two particularly fine paintings for him, of Philae and Beachy Head.

GROVE, Sir GEORGE (1820–1900). Secretary to the Crystal Palace Company, where he had special responsibility for the development of music. For a time he edited *Macmillans* magazine. He was editor of the *Dictionary of Music and Musicians* (4 vols., 1878–89), and the first Director of the Royal College of Music (1883–94).

HASSALL, Mrs. The wife of Lear's physician in San Remo. He attended Lear at his death, of which Mrs Hassall later wrote, 'It was most peaceful, the good, great heart simply slowly ceasing to beat. We went of course to the funeral. I have never forgotten it, it was all so sad, so lonely. After such a life as Mr. Lear's had been and the immense number of friends he had, there was not one of them able to be with him at the end.'

HOOKER, SIR JOSEPH, FRS (1817–1911). The son of the botanist Sir William Hooker. He was a friend of Darwin, who shared with him his early thoughts on the theory of natural selection, ideas which Hooker's own work on the distribution of species seemed to endorse. He worked with George Bentham on establishing a standard of uniformity in classification. In 1865 he succeeded his father as Director at Kew.

HORNBY, ROBERT A. (1805–57). Of Winwick Hall, Warrington. Son of the Revd J. J. Hornby, vicar of Winwick, and great-nephew of the 12th Earl of Derby. A man of independent means, he helped to support Lear in his journey to Rome in 1837.

HOUGHTON, Lord (1809–85). Richard Monkton Milnes, the poet. A friend of Arthur Hallam and of Tennyson.

HUNT, WILLIAM HOLMAN (1827–1910). With Millais and Dante Gabriel Rossetti, one of the three founding members of the Pre-Raphaelite Brotherhood. Lear was introduced to him by Robert Martineau in 1852, and that summer they worked together at Clive Vale Farm, near Hastings. Hunt instructed Lear in his own methods of painting, and his influence is most clearly seen in Lear's subsequent use of colour. Lear considered himself a second-generation member of the PRB, and he called Hunt 'Daddy' or 'Pa'. Lear and Hunt grumbled together both about the Royal Academy of Arts and about lack of intelligent patronage. In 1881 Hunt wrote to Lear, 'If people who do not labor themselves—who produce no work but only manouvre to make the earnings of those who do create pass thro' their hands, if these would be simply truthful, and thoughtful of others to an honest degree, the difference in the power of producing good work would be infinitely increased because the workers would have so much better a chance from undisturbed ease of mind', thoughts which echoed Lear's own.

JARDINE, Sir WILLIAM, Bt. (1800–74). Published (with Prideaux Selby) *Illustrations of Ornithology*, 2 vols. (1830), the first ornithological work on which Lear was engaged at the age of 16. He edited the series, *The Naturalists' Library* (1833–45), to which Lear contributed plates to *Felinæ* (1834), *Pigeons* (1835), and *Parrots* (1836).

LEAR, ANN (1791–1861). Lear's eldest sister, responsible for his upbringing. She was a gentle, kindly, merry woman of profound and practical Christian belief. After her death Lear wrote, 'Ever all she was to me was good, & what I should have been unless she had been my mother I dare not think.'

LEWIS, Mrs JOHN FREDERICK. Wife of John Frederick Lewis, RA (1805–76). Lewis was a painter, particularly of Arab desert life, whose work Lear consistently admired both as painting and in its interpretation of the places and way of life he depicted.

LUSHINGTON, FRANKLIN (1823–1901). Lear's closest friend and his literary executor. They met in Malta in 1849 where Lushington's brother was Chief Secretary to the government. In the spring of 1849 they travelled together in southern Greece, the happiest and most carefree weeks of Lear's life. Temperamentally however he was withdrawn and taciturn, and the happiness of those weeks never returned. In 1855 Lushington was appointed judge to the Supreme Court of Justice in the Ionian Islands, and Lear went with him to live in Corfu. Lear was godfather to all Lushington's children. After Lear's death, Lushington said of him, 'I have never known a man who deserved more love for his goodness of heart & his determination to do right . . . There never was a more generous or more unselfish soul.' Lear left all his papers to Lushington, who later destroyed almost all of them. His own correspondence with Lear has not survived.

MORIER, DAVID RICHARD (1784–1877). Diplomat and close friend of Stratford Canning with whom Lear first visited Constantinople.

NEWSOM, ELEANOR (1799–1885). Lear's fourth surviving sister. In 1823 she married William Newsom, who worked with the Bank of England. In 1847 they moved to Leatherhead in Surrey, where she lived until her death, the last of Lear's sisters to die.

NORTH, MARIANNE (1830–90). First met Lear when he was living in Hastings in the summer of 1852. She later travelled all over the world making drawings of plants which now fill the North Gallery at Kew Gardens. Her sister Catherine was married to the writer John Addington Symonds with whom, in 1867, Lear composed his *Eclogue*.

NORTHBROOK, the Earl of (1826–1904). Thomas George Baring, to whom he was introduced by Fortescue in 1848, was one of Lear's closest friends. He held various government appointments, including First Lord of the Admiralty (1880–5). From 1872–6 he was Viceroy and Governor-General of India, and between 1873 and 1875 Lear travelled there as his guest. He was perhaps the friend most appreciative of Lear's talents, and when in 1886 Lear gave him several hundred of his travel water-colours, Northbrook prepared seven huge volumes into which was pasted the text of Lear's *Journals of a Landscape Painter in Southern Calabria* with the related preparatory drawings. Almost all Lear's letters to Northbrook, still in existence in the late 1930s, appear now to have been destroyed.

PARKER, the Hon. Mrs AUGUSTA. See Bethell, the Hon. Augusta.

PARKYNS, the Hon. Mrs EMMA (183?–77). Sister of Gussie Bethell (q.v.). In 1854 she married Mansfield Parkyns. During the summer of 1866 she encouraged the match between Lear and Gussie, but by the following year she had changed her mind and discouraged Lear from proposing to her sister.

PRESCOTT, Mrs WILLIAM. Of Clarence Villa, Roehampton. Lear met

William Prescott (1800–65) and his wife (?–1886) in Rome in the winter of 1859–60; he subsequently discovered that Prescott had been Jeremiah Lear's banker during the financial crisis of Lear's boyhood. Their daughter Arabella married Colonel Richard Decie who was part of the garrison in Corfu during Lear's time there.

ROSSETTI, WILLIAM MICHAEL (1829–1919). Brother of Dante Gabriel and Christina Rossetti and the seventh member of the Pre-Raphaelite Brotherhood, to whom he acted as secretary; he was a clerk in the Inland Revenue. In the summer of 1853 he stayed for a time at Clive Vale Farm with Lear and Hunt, and he helped Lear to correct the proofs of the *Journals of a Landscape Painter in Southern Calabria*.

RUSKIN, JOHN (1819–1900). Writer, painter, and social worker; the champion of Turner, in response to whose work he published *Modern Painters*. He was the first to defend the work of the Pre-Raphaelite Brotherhood, forcing the art establishment to take seriously what they were doing.

SELWYN, the Revd E. CARUS (1853–1918). Lear met him at Monte Generoso in the summer of 1880; he was Principal of Liverpool College (1882–7) and Headmaster of Uppingham (1887–1907). He commissioned a number of paintings from Lear, including a small version of the *Cedars of Lebanon*.

STANLEY, Lord (1799–1869). Later 14th Earl of Derby. See also Derby, Earls of.

STUART-WORTLEY, the Hon. Mrs JAMES (?–1900). Lear first met her in Rome in the early 1840s; she was the wife of James Archibald Stuart-Wortley, younger son of Lord Wharncliffe and Solicitor-General under Palmerston. She spent the winter of 1881–2 in San Remo with two of her daughters, Blanche and Katharine.

TENNYSON, EMILY, née SELLWOOD (1813–96). Married Tennyson in 1850. Lear, who met Tennyson through Franklin Lushington in 1851, was devoted to Emily, who, in times of his great loneliness, gave him emotional support. His admiration for Tennyson's work led him to the decision in 1852 to illustrate the Laureate's poems, a plan to which he returned frequently and which eventually occupied the last decade of his life. He set a number of Tennyson's lines to music; of these settings, twelve were published. Tennyson's son Hallam was born in 1852, and Lionel in 1854.

UNDERHILL, F. T. A young painter and engraver who in 1863 helped Lear in the preparation of *Views in the Seven Ionian Islands*. Lear employed Underhill to make engravings of a number of Turner's paintings, and these he hung in the library and his bedroom in San

Remo. In the 1880s Underhill again helped Lear, this time in the unsuccessful preparation of reproductions of the Tennyson illustrations. At his death, Lear left Underhill all his artists' materials.

WALDEGRAVE, Lady (1821–79). Daughter of the distinguished tenor John Braham. She married first, in 1839, John James Waldegrave, illegitimate son of the 6th Earl Waldegrave, and then his half-brother George Edward, the 7th Earl. Her third husband was George Granville Harcourt, eldest son of the Archbishop of York, and in 1871 she married Chichester Fortescue (q.v.), who had been devoted to her for more than twenty years. She commissioned seven paintings from Lear, and her niece Lady Strachey edited the *Letters* and *Later Letters of Edward Lear*, as well as two volumes of Nonsense.

WARD, Mrs RICHARD. Daughter of Sir John Simeon, whom Lear met through Tennyson.

WOOLNER, THOMAS (1825–92). The sculptor, whom Lear met through Holman Hunt in 1852; a member of the Pre-Raphaelite Brotherhood. After a difficult period during which he lived for a time in Australia, Woolner returned to England in 1854. He was elected RA in 1874, and was Professor of Sculpture at the Academy 1877–9. Lear, who considered himself a second-generation member of the PRB, called Woolner 'Uncle'.

WYATT, Sir DIGBY (MATTHEW DIGBY WYATT) (1820–77). Met Lear in Rome in the 1840s. He was an architect, and secretary to the Great International Exhibition of 1851. In 1869 he was appointed the first Slade Professor of Fine Arts in Cambridge.

To Ann Lear

To Miss Lear on her Birthday
17 January 1826

Dear, and very dear relation,
Time, who flies without cessation,—
Who ne'er allows procrastination,—
Who never yields to recubation
Nor ever stops for respiration,°
Has brought again in round rotation,
The once a yearly celebration
Of the day of thy creation,—
When another augmentation
Of a whole year in numeration
Will be joined in annexation
To thy former glomeration
Of five seven-years incalculation.
And in this very blest occasion
A thought had crossed my imagination,
That I 'neath an obligation
To make to thee a presentation,
(So 'tis the custom of our nation)
Of any trifling small donation,
Just to express my gratulation
Because of thy safe peragration
To one more long year's termination;
But having made an indagation°
As to my moneyed situation,
What must have been my indignation
Mortification, and vexation.—
I tell you sans equivocation,
—I found—through dire depauperation,
A want of power—my sweet relation,
To practise my determination!—

So as the fates ordained frustration
I shortly ceased my lamentation
And, though it caused much improbation,

I set to work with resignation
To torture my imagination,
To spin some curious dication
To merit p'raps thine approbation,—
At least to meet thine acceptation,
And—after much deliberation
And 'mongst my thoughts much altercation,
I fixed that every termination
To every line should end in -ation!—
Now—since I've given this explanation,
Deign to receive my salutation
And let me breathe an aspiration
To thee—this day of thy creation.

First then, I wish thee, dear relation,
Many a sweet reduplication
Of this thy natal celebration:
And may'st thou from this first lunation
Unto thy vital termination
Be free from every derogation
By fell disease's contamination,
Whose catalogic calculation
Completely thwarts enumeration,—
Emaciation, fomentation,
With dementation—deplumation,
And many more in computation
For these are but an adumberation:—
—And may'st thou never have occasion
For any surgic operation
Or medical administration,—
Sanguification,—defalcation,—
Cauterization—amputation—
Rhabarbaration—scarification
And more of various designation:—
May'st thou be kept in preservation
From every sort of vitiation
By evils dark depreciation:—
Intoxication—trucidation,—
From Malversation—desecration—
From giving way to execration,
And every sinful machination:—

And in thy daily occupation—
Whether it be discalceation,
Or any other ministration
May'st thou not meet the least frustration;
May'st thou withstand all obtrectation
Thrown out to mar thy reputation;—
May'st thou be free from altercations
Or with thy word or thy relations;—
And (though it wants corroberation,
Yet nor quite void of confirmation,—)
If as report gives intimation
You are about to change your station,
May every peaceful combination
Of bliss await your situation
In matrimonial elevation—
May'st thou be loved with veneration;—
—By none be held in detestation,—
And towards thy life's advesperation,
When most are prone to
Their feeble limbs to desiccation,—
Their strength through years to deliquation,—
Their minds and brains to conquassation,—
Their failing speech to aberration,—
Their wearied taste to nauseation,—
                                    then,
Then, may'st thou,—Oh dear relation,
Always receive refulerlation,—
Thy frame imbibe reanimation,—
Thy reason hold her wonted station
And keep her prudent scintillation,
Till thou descend'st by slow gradation
Unto thy final destination—
The long last home of all creation.
—This is my birthday aspiration;—
—Believe it, ever dear relation
Sincere without exaggeration—
In every individual ation!—
Sanguine—in each anticipation—
And kindly meant in perpetration.
                          17th Jan 1826.
          Finis

To Ann Lear

[In 1822, Lear's sister Sarah married Charles Street, a banker of Arundel. He spent much of his childhood with them in Sussex.]

7 November 1829°

Journal

[*November*] 2nd   Monday evening—took my place—
Went to a dance at 9 o'clock,—
Jigged all the colour out of my face
And reached my lodgings at crow of cock.

[*November*] 3rd   Packed up my luggage till half past four,
Got up at six, and drank some tea,
And set off as cold as the frozen sea,—
Wished goodbye—took my hats and
    umbrella—
And shivered and shook to the White Horse
    cellar.°
Sat on the top of the stage and four—
For Robinson half an hour or more,—
Wrattled and rumbled down the Strand
Where the mudscrapers stood in a dingy
    band,
And rode away from London smoke,
Or ever the light of day had broke.

Chelsea and Fulham and Putney Bridge,—
And Kingston on Thames with its banks of
    sedge,—
Esher and Cobham, how cold they were!—
Oh! it was enough to make anyone swear!
—Thumped my feet till I made them ache,—
Took out provisions, a meal to make,—
Offered a sandwich,—(I had but three,)—
To my neighbour, who sat with a shaky
    knee,
'Sir'—said she with a glutinous grin,
'I'll thank you for *two*, as they seem but
    thin,—

'And shall feel quite glad if you'll give one
   'arter,
'To this here young lady wot's my darter.'—
As good as her word was the brazen wretch,
Down went three sandwiches all at a stretch
—Ripley—Guildford and Godalming too—
Whitley—Northchapel and Chittingfold
   gate,—
Saw us looking as black and blue,
As a spoonful of milk in an empty plate.
After the coach at Petworth ran—
(He and his wife,) a hugy man—
Quite as globose as a harvest moon,°
Up he got, and 'twas B. Colhoun.
—Down Fittleworth Hill we made a dash,
And walked on foot up Bury Hill° side,—
Half hot—half cold—like a luke warm hash,
And as stiff as a lobster's claw—wot's tied.
Arundel town at length reached we,
As early as ten minutes after three.
Went to the Bank: found no one there—
Wanted a dinner—the cupboard was
   bare,—
Set off to Peppering°—Cloky and I—
Over the hard chalk merrily—
Halfway there heard a horrible clack—
—Sister and nephews° coming back—
Couldn't return with them—nonsense
   quite—
So posted away in the dusky light—
And five o'clock it might very well be,
Ere I caught a glimpse of the old Elm tree,
And popped on my friends like a powder
   puff—
Ha—Ha—Ha—! it was merry enough!
Gobbled enough to choke a Goliath—
Drank my tea—and sat by the fire;
Saw the baby—that unique child—
Who squeaked—and stared—and sniffed—
   and smiled;—

Then went to bed with a very good will
And fell asleep ere you'd swallow a pill.

[*November*] 4th   Wednesday, rose before the sun,—
And scrambled away o'er stile and gate,—
Left a note to say where I'd run,—
And got to Arundel—just at eight.
Breakfast over—up the hill,
With Sarah to Brookfield sallied forth,
White frost covering the country still,—
Just like a frozen syllabub froth:
Saw the children—ate some oys—
ters—and went out to see the boys:—
Found them performing sundry strides,—
Some by skates and some by slides,—
Went back, and fixed to come and stay,
On Sunday next, then came away.
Found the wind blew vastly bitterly,—
Called at Lyminster°—John at home,—
Looked at the plates of Rogers' Italy,°—
Talked of reform and Chancellor
    Brougham:°—
Back to Arundel made a run,—
And finished a lunch at half past one:
Out again—and called at Tower
House, and staid for half an hour
Walked again with Sister Sarah,
Through roads which surely never looked
    barer,—
Woods of gloomy and leafless trees,
All in a state of shiver & freeze:
Into the town again and dressed,—
Devoured a dinner with infinite zest:—
Went with the Streets to tea next door,—
Wardropers—Blanches° and two or three
    more;—
Played at Backgammon and Chess with
    James,
—Got beaten, and gammoned at sundry
    games,—

Eat stewed oysters at supper time,—read
Original verses—and went to bed.

[*November*] 5th   Thursday. Breakfasted. Cold again—
Dismal and half inclined to rain,—
Walked with Sarah to Hampton Beach,—
Saw the sea twirl like a vomiting leech,—
Walked up and down by the grumbling tide
Till our noses looked like Capsicums
    dried,—
Half past eleven—left behind,
The soap suddy waves,—and boisterous
    wind,
—After demolishing buns and bread—
And making our visages vulgarly red,—
Called at Brookfield for half a minute,
But didn't go in—for no one was in it,—
Went to Calceto and stayed some time,
With Mrs George°—till one o'clock
    chime,—
Then home again—And calls of course—
And dined upon mutton & capers sauce.
After dinner—popped next door—
And sat a dozen minutes or more,—
Went into Uncle Richard's—at first,—
Just in order to see Miss Hurst,—
But found a lot of people there,—
So stayed—to drive away toothache & care.
—Back then we went then—one & all,
And here Miss Bischoff had a fall.
And then we reached, as we'd designed—
Miss Upperton's—And then we dined,—
And lastly, setting off again,
Just as the day was on the wain,
We got to Arundel at last,
At five o'clock—or rather past.

And thus Ma'am, in these dogg'rel verses
All the remarkable reverses

Of fortune, which we met, as how—
Through our strange wanderings, you
    know—
Conclusion now—by saying that I
Can never forget them certainly,—
And hoping that your wine may be
As good to all infinity
Of time, and that your pears mayn't spoil,—
But multiply—like Widow's oil—
I have a pleasure to sign here,
Myself—Yours most obliged—

                    E. Lear.

    7th November. 1829

To Henry Hinde°

[From 1826 or 1827, Lear had been earning his living as a natural history illustrator. In June 1830, he began work on *Illustrations of the Family of Psittacidæ, or Parrots*, which he financed by subscription. He originally planned to publish fourteen parts, but the slow paying by many of his subscribers and the heavy expenses of printing and hand-colouring forced him to abandon the project early in 1832. John Gould, who was one of the subscribers, used the book as a model for his own subsequent works, to which Lear contributed many of the illustrations. During 1831 Lear also started to work for Lord Stanley.]

                 December 1830

Dear Harry Hind[e],
If you've a mind,—
This evening at eight,
Or hardly so late,
Being at leisure,
With very great pleasure,
I find I can come,
To go with you home;—
(And drink of thy tea,
As I promised to thee:)
—Yet—prithee don't, Harry
By any means tarry

If this evening you should be
Engaged—for that would be,
To me—the huge source
Of a deal of remorse;
For you know, if it won't suit,
I can bring up my flute,°
To skiggle and squeak,
Any night in the week.
—Dask, now, I go to my dinner,
For all day I've been a'—
—way at the West End,
Painting the best end,
Of some vast Parrots
As red as new carrots,—
(They are at the museum,°—
—When you come you shall see 'em,—)
I do the head and neck first;—
—And ever since breakfast,
I've had one bun merely!
So—yours quite sincerely
                    E.L.   December 1830.

To Ann Lear

                                5 April 1831

                    Scrawl

Dear Ann—
   I conjecture you'll like it no worse
If I write you this evening a letter in verse,—
But such an epistle as this, Ma'am, I tell ye—can't
Any how prove either pleasant or elegant,—
For writing by night—I am quite in a flurry
And nervously warm—like a dish of stewed curry.

I left Mrs Street upon yesterday morning,
(If my hand shakes—you'll know it's occasioned by yawning)
And really they used me the whole of the time
With such kindness—it can't be explained in a rhyme!

They stuffed me with puddings—chops—cutlets—and pies,
Wine and cakes (I was going to say up to my eyes
But I thought 'twas so vulgar it lacked this addition
They crammed and they stuffed me, yea, unto repletion.)
Exceedingly careful were they of my health,
And I scarcely left home at all—saving by stealth;
—They never allowed me to walk by the river
For said they—'lest the fogs disagree with your liver!—'
And as for a stroll through a valley—''twere odds
If I went—that I didn't fall over the clods!'
—Might I go and look over the Castle?°—'oh! Sidi
Mahommed!!—Suppose you should hap to grow giddy!
And pitch from the top over turrets and all—
Such a wap! Breaking most of your bones in the fall!—'
So I stayed still at home and worked hard at my drawings,
And looked at the rooks—and sat hearing their cawings,
And walked out a little—a small pit-a-pat—
And endeavoured with heart and with soul to grow fat;
And indeed—just excepting—I sometimes am lame—
I don't seem in health or complexion the same;—
For my face has grown lately considerably fatter—
And has less the appearance of clarified batter,
Than when, so malad, I left London turmoiled,
As pale as a sucking pig recently boiled.

Little Charles—I must say, seems improved on the whole—
But at books he's extremely dull—poor little soul!—
But the other child—Freddie is noon night and morn—
The most horrid young monkey that ever was born—
Such violent passions and tears in an ocean,
He kept the whole house in a constant commotion.

I now an ensconced in my favourite abode—
Which is Peppering, you know—with its sprain-ancle road;°
They are all just as kind as they ever have been—
And the fields are beginning to look very green,
I have never procured yet a teal or a widgeon,
But am drawing a very magnificent pigeon.
And as for my visits I'm going for to eat o—
F a dinner today with my friends at Calceto;

I leave this here place upon Saturday next,
Or on Sunday (I'll try to remember the text!—)
And stay [. . .]

     Peppering, Tuesday, April 5th, 1831.

To Eliza Drewitt

         [1831]

I've just seen Mrs. Hopkins°—and read her the lines,
(And they'll do for the mirror in print she opines;)—
—And so pray keep the book—till you've copied the rhyme,
For I shan't be in want of it now for some time.

—I got home about five oclock yesterday night—
As I fancy too you must have done—while 'twas light;—
For I saw you at Houg[h]ton—(I stood on the ridge,
Upon Bury Hill side,)——and ride over the bridge.

I have sent you these numbers, by Robert°——they'll be
An amusement perhaps to inspect after tea,——
—They are beautiful things—and I think they're not dear—
For both reading—and pictures.——Good Bye—
  Edward Lear——

Ode to the little China-Man

  Who art thou—sweet little China Man?——
   Your name I want to know
  With your lovely face so pale and wan——
   With a high diddle diddledy do.——

Your high cheek bones:——your screwed up mouth,
    How beautiful they be!——
And your eyes that ogle from north to south,
    With a high diddle diddledy dee!——

And your cultivated eyebrows too!——
    That depend from either eye!——
(I'm sure it's a fashion entirely new!)—
    With a high diddle diddledy di!———

(But ev'ry one—(as the Frenchman said)——
    Every one to his way,)———
(When he boiled in a pipkin his grandmother's head,)—
    With a high diddle—diddledy—da!)——

Int'resting Mortal!—Whence art thou?——
    In figure surpassed by few!——
Tell us thy name—is it 'Chum-chu-wow'?—
    With a high diddle diddledy du?——

The little man fetched a sort of a sneer—
    As he made his sage reply——
While he twisted his eyebrow round his ear,
    With a high diddle-diddledy dy.——

'Good folks'———(& he shook his noddle-ding-dong———
    'Its enough for you to know———
That in spite of my eyebrows—two feet long———
    Im Miss Eliza's beau!!'————

                         E Lear.

To Charles Empson

38. Upper North Place. Grays Inn Road | October 1. 1831.
Dear Sir,
    I have just received your parcel—& as it may probably be
some time before I send No. 8.°—(as you wish it, to come with
Mr. Gould's, & he is not yet returned,) I cannot help writing a
long letter by way of answer to several of yours which I have

lately received, although the minute scrawl in which I must set forth my communications, on account of having no foolscap paper—promises small comfort to your eyesight:—besides this—I am in the humour to think on paper just now—so that I shall be copious from choice as well as necessity.—

That which strikes me first as most clamorous for an answer—is your account of a Bookseller having my Parrots in your parts—& selling them for 9/.—I am nearly rude enough to suppose you must have been mistaken—as *only two Booksellers* in town have ever had anything to do with me—Jennings & Chaplin in Cheapside—who bought 3 sets—to send, as they informed me to Russia—whether they thought Russia a synonyme for Durham—I wot not.————and Molteno & Graves—Pall Mall————whose subscribers I know are Lord Wharncliffe—& Mr. Ord (of Cheshire,). How any one could even come in possession of any other copies—is a mystery to me—since I manage every thing myself:—you are my sole distributor of Psittacidæ in the Northern regions & send to all my subscribers thereabouts—excepting Mrs. Brandling of Shotton Hall, & Mrs. Clements of Tadcaster—whose copies I convey by their desire, through Mrs Wentworth.° I always felt it very good of you in forwarding the numbers of my previous Subscribers without any profit, & should certainly feel I was doing the least I could—in allowing you to act solely in those places as my agent—since you have taken much trouble on my account. I should be glad to know when you write—who the 'wretch' may be.— ——— ———

Now about the show-copy————I am sorry it has not been hitherto sent—but its non appearance is not owing to my inattention: I have lately had many sets to colour—& have with difficulty supplied my subscribers as wanted—but my colourer is hard at work & plates—(if not a perfect part,) shall be forwarded.—What do you mean by getting my work into the Literary Society?—Although I am very sensible of your kindness—& am always pleased at being noticed by those sort of communities, yet—the few copies I take off, utterly precludes my disposing of any of them otherwise than by sale—however desirous I may be of honour:—actually—only 175 prints have been taken of each drawing—& when those 175 copies are subscribed for, my work stops—for already the Lithographic plates have been erased!——so you perceive—(110 are sold) I must be anxious to make something of as many of these as possible. My reasons for so soon destroying my drawings were these; though I dare say they don't appear so rational to any one but myself: I was obliged to limit the work—in order to get more subscribers—& to erase the drawings—because the expense is considerable for keeping them on, & I have pretty great difficulty in paying my monthly charges,—for to pay colourer & printer monthly I am obstinately prepossessed—since I had rather be at the bottom of the River Thames—than be one week in debt—be it *never* so small.—For me—who at the age of 14 & a half, was turned out into the world, *literally without a farthing*—& with nought to look to for a living but his own exertions,° you may easily suppose this a necessary prejudice——& indeed—the tardy paying of many of my subscribers—renders it but too difficult to procure food—& pay for publishing, at once.——With Mr. Gould all this is very different—he has sufficient to live on, whether his subscribers pay or not, & can well afford the innumerable little expenses of printing—but for poor I—I have just nine and twenty times resolved to give up Parrots & all—& should certainly have done so—had not my good genius with vast reluctance just 9 and 20 times set me a going again.—Opportet vivere [It is necessary to live]—& so I shall pass on to thank you for your criticisms—the long-billed P[arrakeet]. was taken from—*a stuffed specimen*, which—however I disguise it, hook or by crook—you are sure to find erroneous in some degree:—and it certainly is so—for I am never pleased with a drawing unless I make it from life.——Heaven send you patience, Sir—to read this through!——I am sure both Job & Penelope would have given it up as a lost matter before now.——

I do not think I shall have leisure to draw a bird for the Exhibition—though I should like it: a huge Maccaw is staring me now in the face as much as to say—'finish me'—but I guess the poor animal must remain minus a body & one wing for some time to come.—Here endeth the first letter.—

As a species of entremêt. I apologise for no Autographs having yet fallen in my way—Landseer's° you shall have before long, though.—I will write out my list of subscribers.——Now for the Parcel. I am delighted with the flowers—if you have any more sketches of S. American *trees*–(correct,) they would be invaluable for me—for I often want them to put birds on when I draw for Lord Stanley—which is very frequently.—They shall assuredly be done—& I hope to meet your approbation—but, you have forgotten to specify upon *what sized* paper?—Tell me—in the letter which you wish by and bye sir I propose you shall shortly write to me, in order to certify othersome affairs to my satisfaction.

I am glad you like Mr. Gould:—he has been always very obliging to me—although I never knew him till lately: Mrs. G. appears an exceedingly pleasant & amiable woman. To—'is he at all like you?'——I must say—No——very categorically: setting aside personal appearances—he being stout—& good looking,—& I being ensiform, (speaking botanically,) that is—lanky—& considerably ugly,—we are, as far as I can judge—very opposite.—I believe I am anything but candid: in fact—I am naturally suspicious—& exceedingly reserved, the first good quality arises from my having seen plenty of the evil part of the world from my youth up—the second from being but very little used to company or society—for—excepting Mr. Yarrell°—(whom Mrs. Hewitson & Atkinson know,)—to whom I go to study bones & muscles—I don't know a single person in all London to visit intimately. This is very odd, but no less true.—As for taking any of your lively writings amiss—I should be a very great goose so to do: on the contrary—I laugh sometimes by wholesale at them—& always read them with vast goût.——

Do you know Mr. Sharpe of Bamborough Castle?—I was introduced to him some time back—& he asked me to come there: I should not wonder if I see Northumberland—before you Sir see town:—I am rather interested in the North, & it is droll I should have procured so many subscribers there:—originally—my mother's family was from Durham°—although I am so little of a genealogist that——Farnysyde & Brignall are all I can recollect of their names—& Sunniside of their residence. Pray is there such a place in being now?——At the corner of the paper I shall insert a very accurate portrait of myself—thinking it highly

proper you should have some idea of what sort of a being your
correspondent is, & begging—if you are at all inclined to be
wrathful at my levity to remember that I am only 19 years
old—& am only as merry as I am now about once in 6 weeks.—

You will be pleased to hear I am engaged in a Zoological
Work,° shortly to appear from that society—also in a work on
Tortoises by a very celebrated Zoologist
Thomas Bell°—& a very kind friend to me. I
will send you an India Proof° shortly—though
'tis not much in your way.——Now—you will
think me very stupid; but when I sent last—I
packed up 8 number 7s—promising to send
afterwards the 3 extra sets—(which I am
about to do—) thus making up for 11
subscribers.——Did I—by accident enclose *11* of number 7 for you?—(not including
the Brandlings) X N.B. This is amazingly
like; add only—that both my knees are
fractured from being run over, which has

made them very peculiarly crooked—that my neck is singularly
long, a most elephantine nose—& a disposition to tumble here
& there—owing to being half blind, & and [*sic*] you may very
well imagine my tout ensemble. If I *did* pack up 11 number
7s—I would subtract these from the 3 whole sets I am about to
send off with the number 8s. Pray Sir—as soon as you receive
this—be so kind as to write to me & inform me of this, as well as
of the size you wish the paper for the flowers—Should you come
to town—I am sorry that I cannot offer you a home pro
tempore—pro trumpery indeed it would be, if I did make any
such offer—for unless you occupied the grate as a seat—I see no
probability of your finding any rest consonant with the safety of
my Parrots—seeing, that of the six chairs I possess—5 are at
present occupied with lithographic prints:—the whole of my
exalted & delightful upper tenement in fact overflows with
them, and for the last 12 months I have so moved—thought—
looked at,—& existed among Parrots——that should any
transmigration take place at my decease I am sure my soul
would be very uncomfortable in anything but one of the
Psittacidæ. My Sussex friends always say that I can do nothing
like other people, & consequently—this overgorged—uncouth

& nonsensical scrawl can be properly signed by none but—dear
Sir,

Yours respectfully & obliged,
E. Lear.

Nothing however will give me greater pleasure than to see you
at Gray's Inn Road, in spite of the above sentence, which looks
rather uninviting but was by no means intended as such: before
then I hope to have changed my residence.°

To Fanny Coombe

15 July [1832]

For Miss Fanny Jane Dolly Coombe.

My dear Niece—par adoption°—

I shall not apologize for my departure from established rules
so far as to write to one so very juvenile as yourself,—as,—from
the unusual precocity of talent which you exhibited when but 6
months old I have every reason to conclude you are by this time
able to read writing;—neither shall I excuse myself for quoting
a foreign tongue—since I have little doubt but that if you can
master English—you are equally au fait at French;—nor shall I
offer any extenuation for the bad formation of my letters—for I
write by Candlelight—& in a hurry.——My letter indeed is
addressed to you—solely from a staunch belief that your whole
kindred—friends—connexions—& acquaintances are dead &
departed—& that you,—being the youngest—are the most
likely to have survived so general a wreck——thus my epistle
will prove a species of dead letter—& should by rights have
been preluded by a *dead*ication. Faint hopes—however sometimes reanimate my mentals, & should the sundry folks below
mentioned be still on the earth—I should thank you to convey
their several messages to each, — — which indeed is my
principal reason for troubling you with so many skewers &
pothooks. If you cannot yet speak your ideas—my love—you
can squeak them you know.

Tell your Aunt Eliza—that on the evening before she left
London—I was taken ill—with my old complaint in the
head°—so much so as to be unable to walk home—which

consequently prevented me from meeting her at the Coach on the following morning. By a singular fatality—also—her tortoise died the next day. Thank my friend—your uncle Robert—for his recent letter—dated March 27th.!————Tell him also—that when I ask for beasts or birds—it is only because I feel more pleasure in drawing from those given me by my intimate friends—than I could do from those otherwise come by————not from my being unable to get at specimens.—Having a rather Zoological connexion—& being about to publish British Quadrupeds°—I have now living—2 Hedgehogs, all the sorts of mice—weasels—Bats &c—& every beast requisite except a Pine Marten,—all of which, my dear child—I should be glad to present you with—did I suppose you could make the slightest use of them whatever.

Present my profound respects—to W. Wardroper Esquire—with my best thanks for his friendly communications. I am glad that his Pamphlet—'on curing Dropsy in Gallinaceous animals,'—has so extensive a sale. Pray—my dear—tell the 2 above mentioned friends never to incommode themselves in the least about writing to me, as they are aware how obtuse my feelings are, & that I bear being forgotten with much nonchalance.

Congratulate with Mrs. Street from me,—on her recovery from her fall into the mill-pond—& from the 18 Paralytic strokes with which she was subsequently attacked:—my sister Ann is much gratified with her frequent correspondence in spite of her infirmities.—Should you see John Sayres°—beg as a favour that he will not so continually torment me with graphic attentions.

Tell your papa—that I have been to the Opera & have heard Paganini°—both of which pleasures have greatly contributed to widen the crack which nature had originally made in my brain.

Give my kindest regards & best respects to your Grandpapa and Grandmamma—Father & Mother—Uncle George—and Aunt Eliza—who are not correspondents of mine—ask any body to kiss you for me—& believe me—My dear Dolly— |
Your 3 parts crazy—& wholly affectionate
Uncle Edward.

61. Albany St. Regent Park—July 15.

To Sir William Jardine, Bt.

23. Jany. 1834. 61. Albany Street. Regent's Park
Sir William,

I have this day received a draft for £8.—sent by Mr. Lizars to Messrs. Longman & Rees——£5 of which is the amount of the drawings I did for you—the remaining £3 for Nos. 7—8—9 10—11 & 12 of my Parrots. I should have answered your letter sooner had I not been prevented by illness which even now confines me to my rooms.

I was extremely gratified at finding my drawings had given you satisfaction, as I took every pains with them, & shall endeavour to do so in all you may in future be kind enough to order me to make. The Lagothriæ Humboldtii I will commence as soon as my health will allow of my riding to the Surrey Gardens°—as I hear it is in poor health.

Respecting my Parrots—there is much to say:—no more numbers will be published by me—the 12th—which you have, being the last. Their publication was a speculation which—so far as it made me known & procured me employment in Zoological drawing——answered my expectations——but in matters of money occasioned me considerable loss. I originally intended to have figured all the Psittacidæ—but I stopped in time; neither will there be—(from me) any letterpress.

Concerning the request you make that I would allow these being copied—I have no power either to refuse or comply— since I have sold all right in the volume to Mr. Gould. He purchased of me—the copies left on my hands—and he alone is to be applied to on the point you wish answered.

Supposing Mr. Gould should object to my Psittacidæ being copied,—I believe I may add that from possessing a vast number of sketches from living Parrots I should be able to furnish you with drawings at a rather less charge than that I make for quadrupeds at present. It was my habit, at the time I was publishing—to sketch almost every parrot that came in my way—& I thus obtained many figures of said species. Were there any considerable number required, I would make finished drawings for £1. 0. 0. each, both on account of the references I have by me, & because Parrots are my favourites,

& I can do them with greater facility than any other class of animals: I mention this—because I know that in all periodical works of large expenses—economy of every sort is more or less an object. I might also suggest that by recopying my Parrots—you diminish the chance of a hundred (—most of them zoological people)—of my subscribers purchasing your volume, as they would prefer original figures° to duplicates. I am very anxious to see this publication——and particularly, Sir William, I hope you will clear up several demi-groupes which are at present very obscure—P[sittacidae]. viridis—the Genus Brotogeris—& the white winged Parakeet—Murinus & others are among those I allude to.

I hope I shall not be thought taking too great a liberty in adding what I am about to write—concerning some plates of the Nat. Library already published: a very little extra trouble would remedy a defect which is here frequently noticed in them—particularly by Zoologists—I mean the inequality of colouring in many of the copies—the Sabæus—(Green Monkey) is in some copies—a bright green—in others *nearly wholly* gamboge:—others might be instanced.—A little precision in this colouring would, I feel certain, greatly enhance the value of the work. Another point which I would like the freedom of suggesting, is that the proportion of the animals should if possible be more strictly observed. I am aware that in so small a sized volume this is difficult—but it *may* be done in a great measure:——Simia Sciureus—which is larger than the Ouran Outang will illustrate what I mean. I hope, Sir William, you will not be offended with these remarks—as I submit them to your notice simply from an idea that that [*sic*] their being looked to might be of some benefit to future volumes of your work.

I remain, | Sir William, | Yours obliged & respectfully,
Edward Lear.

61. Abany Street. | Regent's Park.

To the 13th Earl of Derby

28 Southampton Row, Bloomsbury | 2 June, 1836

Zaida (female.[)]]
Yabulla }   are the Giraffes° names.
Selim. } male
Mabrook]

My Lord,

I do not know what to say for myself for having so long delayed sending the drawings which will reach Knowsley about the same time this letter does. I took the sketches very carefully from the living animals, but owing to their not being in a good light, I have had very great trouble in getting the drawings to look satisfactory: even now, only the under side of the Trionyx° is what I really like. The cat° was very difficult to represent, & the Trionyx, although James Hunt held it for me for two whole mornings—not much less so:—I shall be very glad to hear if your Lordship is pleased with them—as I have been very much out of temper with all three at times.

I ought to be able to mention the times for my coming to Knowsley, but I am doing some Lithographic drawings for Mrs. Greville=Howard,° & as she is out of town, & I have promised to do one more on her return, (which will be, I imagine, in about 10 days,) I am not yet my own master. But I grumble at London more & more daily.

Of the giraffes—I dare say your Lordship has been already written to by Mr. Sabine.° I do not for my own part know which is the most picturesque party—the animals themselves or their Keepers the Nubians. I have enclosed the signatures of the three—Abdallah—Carbass—and Omar—(the 4th is of Mons' Tibaut,) that your Lordship may see their writing. All of them are very good tempered men—but the *extreme* crowds of people who flock to see them—discompose them now & then. As for the Giraffes—I never imagined any thing living of such extreme elegance, & I much wish your Lordship could see them. Thomas Landseer implored Mr. Bennett° the other morning not to allow the Giraffes to be *libelled* (by any artist who chose to sketch them[)]. 'The council'—replied the Secretary, 'cannot shelter *themselves* from libels—& their animals cannot expect a higher fate.'— —The Nubians, (according to the regulations of the Musselmann faith—) have a great horror of being drawn—all likenesses or idols being forbidden by their creed. Being at the Gardens, however, the other day with Lady Maria & Sir J. Stanley°—Mr. Wilkinson an Egyptian traveller who was of their party, asked the men from me to allow a sketch to be made of their heads,——but they only consented, on Mr. W's representing that *all* the sin would fall on the *artist*—& *none* on the sitter. Want of time—rather than terror of Mahomet's anger has prevented my profiting by their belief of this—or I should have sent some sketches to your Lordship.

At Cross's garden° there is a 4 horned antelope but—I know of nothing—there or anywhere else of novelty in the bird way.

I was for a day or two at Sheen before Mr. Penrhyn & Lady Charlotte° left for Eastbourne,—& at that time all the family were very well. Begging your Lordship will give my respects to any of my Knowsley friends who may now be staying there, believe me, | My Lord, | Your Lordship's grateful | & respectful
servant,
Edward Lear.

28. Southampton Row. | Bloomsbury. 2d of June. 1836.
I have just arranged to go with Mr. Sabine to pay a visit of a day or two to Mr. Baker°—the gentleman who is going to India. (Himalaya.)

To John Gould

[In the summer of 1836, Lear spent several weeks walking in the Lake District. By now he had decided that he wanted to be a landscape painter.]

Knowsley Hall | 31st. Oct. 1836. | hail—snow—frost—&
desolation.

Dear Gould,

I got your letter last evening, as I was about to write to you: thank you for it:—I wanted to know how you were going on. As for your replying I never expect that, as I know how busy you are always.

Your account of poor Captn. Coxon's° death is sad enough: but I was much surprised at the circumstances under which it occurred. For Mr. Bennett's—I don't remember ever to have been more shocked: even now I have heard no particulars. Independently of his being a good principled & kind hearted man, he was a wonder—inasmuch as he was of the very first who were scientific for science's sake. You especially must feel his loss very much,—& so must Rees. You are very just in your remarks—: sudden deaths make a greater impression than other ones, tho' we ought to know & feel the uncertainty of life continually.

To your numerous enquiries, I must answer rather briefly, for I have so bad a cold as to be half blind: add to which so bad a cough & sore throat, that if they dont go I shall be in town much sooner than I expected. I left Knowsley, (only half my work done,) on the 12 August for a sketching tour, & really it is impossible to tell you *how*, & *how enormously* I have enjoyed the whole Autumn. The counties of Cumberland & Westmorland are superb indeed, & tho' the weather has been miserable, yet I have contrived to walk pretty well over the whole ground, & to sketch a good deal besides. I hope too, I have improved somewhat——(hard if I haven't after slaving as I have done) but you will judge when I get back.

I spent a delightful time at Col: Howard, both going & returning—also at some other subscribers of yours—Messrs. Stanniforth, Bradyll,—&c &c.

I could not go on to Scotland. Bye the bye—on coming here, I found a letter from Lizars,° ordering drawings for a British Ornithology——!!!!!!!!!——but I have written to say I can't set about it *at present*. To say truth, I had rather not at all, for my eyes are so sadly worse, that no bird under an Ostrich shall I soon be able to see to do.

I am staying to finish what I had promised Lord Derby I would do before I went away, & shall, I imagine, be home by the end of November, when I shall be most happy to set about anything you please. 3 parts of yours° are coming to night I believe. How are [*sic*] going on with the Zoo: Soc?—Not very well: I guess:——but I now am more in the dark as to their politics than ever.

Remember me to Mr. Rees: I am going to send him a scrawl.

And to V. Audubon° also if you see him. Mr. Hullmandel° I have written to.

Nothing particularly new here that I remember:—Weasel headed Armadillo, &c &c. I should like to, (but doubt if I can,) bring up the drawings of the last 2 summers with me.—

I have been most extremely well all thro' my excursion—& am now otherwise for the first time. Am glad to hear Mrs. Gould and the children are well:—you don't say if you have been out of town anywhere. Remember me to Mrs. Gould if you please, & believe me, | Dear Gould, | Ever your's sincerely,
Edward Lear.

This place is colder than Kamschatka!

To Ann Lear

[By the summer of 1837, Lear's already bad health had deteriorated, and it was decided that he should travel abroad. With the help of Lord Derby and his cousin Robert Hornby, Lear left England for Rome in July 1837. Ann travelled with him as far as Brussels.]

To Miss Lear, | Chez Mons. Le Harivel, | á côte du collége St. Jean, | Rue de la Poste, Faubourg du Schaerbeck, | Bruxelles, | Belge.

Florence, | 3rd., Nov., 1837.

My dear Ann,

I was delighted to get your letter here yesterday. You are the best of correspondents, and I am so glad to find you are so comfortable and well. Your accounts of Bruxelles and its people very much amuse me, and though by your praises of the Beer there, I fear you have taken to drinking, I rejoice to hear you like the place so much. Mrs. Warner,° I do not expect to hear from till Dec. The Nevills° have by this time got a long letter from me. Your little book I shall unpack tomorrow as many of my things have been untouched hitherto, but here I mean to stay a month or so—for you will be glad to hear of my wonderful doings—5 pupils already°—and my old companion Knighton, (now Sir William) who used to draw at Sass's with me,° besides all the Russells and Tattons° in different hotels close by.

But I will begin to tell you what I have been about. Just after

I last wrote I left Milan with only knapsack and sketch book
and off I set to the town of Como—on the Lake of that name.
There I fell in with Sir W., Lady, and all the Knighton party,
and a famous holiday we had on the beautiful Lake; we went
over the Villa d'Este where Queen Caroline lived so long—it is
a large place—but with no comfort about it—the common
people never speak of her, and are so cautious, that if you ask
questions, they evade them always—. On Saturday Oct. 7th., I
left Como in a steamer and rushed into the uttermost parts of
the lake 50 miles off—at Domaso. You ask about the
language;—nothing but Italian is spoken, but I am already
master of enough to get anything I want. But nothing can give
you an idea of the horror one first feels at Italian village inns;
now I am used to it,—but at starting I thought the huge cold
rooms—stone floors—and open windows—and long passages—abominable. The people of the Como province are poor,
but very honest;—and you soon get used to the barefooted
people who wait on you.

As for scenery—*it was quite beyond anything I had seen*; the dark
blue lake reflects the white houses of Domaso—and over them
enormous Alps, Jiggy-Jaggy—shut out the Italians from
Switzerland. Being resolved to see all the district, I took a boat
quite to the top of the Lake where it is awfully grand—and then
walked to Chiavenna beyond which Switzerland begins.
Chiavenna is just by the Pass of Splugen, and is awfully grand:
some time ago, (in 1680) part of the mountain under which it
stands, fell down plump and killed 500 persons—a whole
village—. After getting some sketches of it, I was glad to
proceed Southward again—along the east side of the lake—a
plan of which I place below—to Colico. I tried to stop at Novate

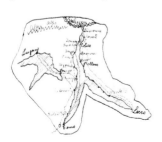

but could not, as all they had to eat
was mutton and goat's flesh, half
putrid, garlic—and dreadfully sour
wine, and although Colico is not over
comfortable, it was a good deal
better. At Bellano there was a better
inn and I stayed 3 days. All this part
of the Lake is magnificent—it is as
narrow as a wide river, so you can see
the hundreds of spires and villages

on the opposite side, while the Alps always form the background. Multitudes of peasants gathering grapes are on every side, and the weather was perfectly charming. All along the road, huge grottoes are cut out of the rock, very cold and dark, but strangely curious, and as you pass through them you see the light like a spot at the other end. From Bellano I walked to Lecco, and on this southern part, olives begin to grow. I think they are very beautiful—more like a huge lavender bush—or a fine gray willow than anything else, and all over little shiny green olives. Lecco is a sweet town—a bustling little port, and the boats on Como, which have red—blue or white sails—are like so many large butterflies. After staying 2 days here, back I rushed again to Colico—and then crossed to Domaso once more—where I stayed prowling about Gravedona for 2 or 3 days—and then walked to Cadenabbia—Dongo—Musso—and Rezzonico are all lovely—and by sunset exquisite, for the Alps are then perfectly pink.

From Cadenabbia, as the weather continued lovely—off I scouted to Lugano—a lake partly in Switzerland and partly in Austrian Lombardy;—if possible it is more beautiful than Como, though very different; for the hills are quite perpendicular to the water, so that you must go in a boat, as there is no road. Up to the top of these mountains there are thick woods, so that as it was now late—all was a mass of crimson and yellow foliage. The city of Lugano, capital of the Swiss Canton—Tessia, is exquisite;—a sort of Paradise in situation in Winter. It seems strange to see day after day—scenes so beautiful, and such variety! At Lugano one is always amused by the figures on the quay—the large mummy-like barrels carrying wine drawn by milk white oxen—rows of women with baskets loaded with immense logs, and Capuchin friars in quantities. However, I had not much time for this lake, so back I trotted to Como, which had now become a sort of old friend.

Unluckily I could not sketch it all as I wished, for on the 21st of Oct. the cold set in so violently that I thought it wiser to go South and accordingly walked from Cadenabbia to the town of Como that day. All this distance is through a wood of olive and chesnut—and you cannot fancy anything so wonderfully beautiful. (I found a bright green Mantis, by the way). And so on the 22nd. I left my dear lake of Como, with a folio full of sketches, and having enjoyed my fortnight beyond description—and back I went to Milan once more. There I found all the Knighton party still, but as all cordons are now taken off the road to Florence°—they started on the 24th. and Mr. Ellis—one of their party—and I—engaged a vetturino for the 26th. A vetturino is a good deal like a hackney coach, and you pay so much (with a written agreement) to be taken where you please and have your meals found you, and lodgings. We paid each 5 napoleons and something to the driver (altogether about £5—) and paid for our breakfasts only; as the master of the conveyance has the right of filling up the vacant seats, you are at the mercy of your fellow passengers for company.

The first day we reached Lodi, during which journey it was quite wet—but all the rest of the days were fine, which was very delightful, as the vetturino not going above 3 or 4 miles an hour, one can always keep up to it by walking. All the roads through Lombardy are very good—but as flat as a pancake; you see nothing but millions of poplars for whole days together! Between the vines or the poplars you perceive peeps of the Tyrol Alps—but in wet weather when one must sit still, I cannot conceive anything more trying than a vetturino journey along Lombardy.

The 2nd. day—or rather evening—we reached Cremona, a handsome town once famous for fiddles. All the Italian towns bear marks of their former grandeur, but in these days, look sadly too large and fine, for their inhabitants. The market places are very curious, the Campanilas or belltowers being of an enormous height—something like this I draw, and really very extraordinary to one who has not heard of them. We used to have but little time to explore the town before supper was ready, and then we were glad to rest, as by 3-30 we were called, to set off at 4 or 5. On the road the vetturino stops for luncheon about 10 or 11 for two hours.

Saturday the 28th. was much the same—a long straight road of poplars—glimpses of the Alps—crossing of the Po—lunching at Bossola—crawling—creeping along behind two other carriages—one of which turned out to contain Mr. Cox° of the Zoological Society and all his family going to Naples—and finally arriving at Mantua by dusk, which we saw but little of.

Sunday the 29th. went in arriving at the Duke of Modena's territories—and breakfasting at Modena, a more lively town than usual. After this—passports,—and customhouses become innumerable as there are so many petty States. Towards evening we arrived at Bologna in the Pope's dominions, whose empire is as full of beggars as Russell Square used to be. Two most curious towers are in this town—immensely high but quite as if they would fall—one is 8 and the other 4 feet out of the perpendicular. Arcades on each side of the streets give the city rather a look of gloom. Here we again fell in with the Knightons, and next morning we all got up at 4 to cross the Apennines which we had seen the evening before, quite a relief after so much flat, as we had gone through. The Pass of the Apennines is quite unlike the Alps, and as we had a most lovely day, I never enjoyed anything so much. Thick woods of oak are on every side, and the road which is very steep and winding, looks quite over all the enormous flat plain of Lombardy;—and in clear weather,—as far as the Alps. Right and left one sees tops with snow, but one only crosses the lowest part, though oxen were necessary to draw up the carriages. You may imagine how beautiful the road looked, with a string of 8 coaches being so pulled up—and all the passengers walking. So much for the loneliness of mountain passes!—at the place we lunched—32 people—all English, sat down together.

As one goes higher and higher, it becomes colder—and near the top we entered Tuscany, stopping for the night at a vile little inn, at Pietramala, for the real inn was of course crammed by the sudden deluge of arrivals. Near this, is a volcano (so called—but really only a burning spring) which Ellis and I took a guide to: it was nearly dark—and over the worst of roads we at last arrived at a black, lonely valley—in the midst of which was, what I can compare only to a large snapdragon of plums and lighted brandy. It has always burned so—and the more rain the better it is. I can hardly call it grand—but it is certainly worth seeing. (I perceive I have missed a day—from Mantua to Carpi—(and so from Carpi to Bologna)—it was nothing but poplars).

On Wed. Nov. 1st. we set off on our last and 7th. day's journey and after a walk (while the vetturino crawled) of 20 miles—we came quite over the Apennines, and, in the most beautiful valley I ever saw—there was Florence! If you look at Claude's pictures° you can exactly understand the scenery—for it is just like it. A complete change takes place in the vegetation; olives and Cypress trees and villages without number succeeding to the rocks of our last day's journey. At last we entered Florence, which is much more magnificent than I looked for. It is all paved, and the houses are enormous and gloomy—like Newgate or the Mansion House—great arched windows and lofty narrow streets. As for the Arno, with its 4 bridges—it is quite beautiful.

As yet, however, I have seen very little of Florence, and what I have seen has quite bewildered me. All the Russells—the Tattons and Knightons are here, and you can imagine how amused I am at seeing cards and notes left as if one were in Sherrard St. still. The best of it is, that I have already procured 4 pupils!!—So that while here I shall be at very little expense. My rooms at this hotel cost 4 pauls daily (2/6)—dinner 5 pauls,—breakfast 2 pauls. It is probable therefore that I may stay here a month or 6 weeks, unless it is too cold (at present it is like May) so as to defer going to Rome until that city is quite purified. Therefore, when you receive this letter, write me another letter—addressed as before—'Poste Restante, Florence'—which must be sent on if I am not here, and consequently you will be a little longer in receiving an answer to it by that delay.

The Piazza Granduca here is overwhelmingly grand—such huge buildings—and gigantic statues—all by first masters such as Michael Angelo etc. etc. The people look like mites walking beneath them. It is quite delightful to have such a companion as Sir. W. Knighton, who knows Arts so well; it is probable I shall be a great deal with him. Lady Knighton (his mother) is a most excellent person, and they are as kind as possible.

I cannot tell you about the galleries—the pictures—the statues—the churches—the tombs of Michael Angelo— Dante—etc. etc. because all this would take so much time, and after all conveys little idea of the place. It is all a hurly-burly of beauty and wonder. The Grand Duke rides about everywhere, and the whole place is like an English watering place, with so many strangers. Robert Hornby writes from Lancashire, all are well. I must now leave off and finish a scrap or two of this letter tomorrow.

4th., Nov., 1837.
The hot roasted chesnuts here are delightful. I eat them perpetual—for to think? for a halfpenny in value one gets about 40 fine, smoking ones!!

(7th., Nov.)
The weather here has set in pretty cold, so I think of going on in about 5 weeks—which will not allow of your letter reaching me here;—direct, therefore your next to 'Poste Restante, Rome'. where my settlement will begin. There is a nice church here. On Sunday, 300 English, besides servants were there!!!!! Every evening, you will be glad to hear is now employed in teaching—and it is delightful, being among so many friends. Mrs. Tatton and all her family, are close by. Mr. Penrhyn's other cousins come next week. The Knightons are all opposite, and the Russells in the same house. Funny enough!—I have a very nice early breakfast, and then at 5 (if I don't dine out) a table d'hote dinner for about 3/– but it is a very good one. Reading over this letter I find I have said things over twice or three times. I have crossed out my address over leaf, knowing how wisely *some people!!* write letters—Now the post is going, I will not keep this longer. Write as soon as you get this and
believe me, | Dear Ann, | Yours affect.,
Edward Lear.

Your letter was a capital long one.

To Ann Lear

Rome, Dec., 14th., 1837.
My dear Ann,
I only received your letter yesterday, although it has been at the Post-Office these 10 days:—but they are sadly careless here, and told me there were none for me: I was getting quite into a fidget about you, though I knew the ways of this part of the world in matters of post delivery. I think the best way of our corresponding will be—for each to write as soon as we receive

the other's letters, and that will make it about a month, more or less by a few days—between our epistles. I am delighted to find you are so well and comfortable, though I do not envy your fogs and gales—not that at Florence I could have laughed at you, for there it is as cold as need be.

At last you see I date from Rome, where I am comfortably settled: but before I describe matters in this most delectable of all delightful places, let me wind up my Florence history—at which city I lingered till the 28th. of Nov. when the cold fairly drove me away. I should not have stayed so long, only I did not like giving up my pupils, and the Knightons and Tattons made the place so comfortable, besides, they still reported that cholera was here—a fib, as one finds now—and all sorts of robberies and murders were represented on the road—all fibs too. During my stay, the weather was afflicting—2 or 3 or 4 pouring days together—(the rain rushing from the spouts like cataracts) and then 1 or 2 or 3 fine days:—these to be sure were most lovely to look at—perfectly bright and cloudless—but colder than I can express. The neighbourhood of the Apennines and their snow, make the wind *dreadfully keen*:—everybody suffers—and chilblains and coughs were universal. All this makes Florence very wholesome for those whose chests can bear it, and one cannot help regretting having left the place—for as far as beauty and gaiety go, the world cannot produce anything prettier than that beautiful city. It is more like a watering place than anything else, and the magnificent bridges (6 close together over the Arno)—and the immense picturesque buildings of the middle ages—the clear lilac mountains all round it—the exquisite walks on every side to hills covered with villages, convents, and cypresses, where you have the whole city beneath you—the bustle of the Grand Duke's court and the fine shops—the endless churches—the Zebra Cathedral of black and white marble—the crowds of towers and steeples—all these make Florence a little Paradise in its way—if it were but hotter.—Oh! how I used to go shivering about!

Just as I was thinking of starting—a most opportune introduction to a sculptor and artist—(Mr. Theed and Mr. Dennew°) led me to join their party to Rome in a vetturino carriage; Mr. T. had a letter to me from Lancashire, and this acquaintance has been of great advantage, as he has shown me no end of kindness and he and Dennew being old residents in Rome, it was a great thing to travel on a road they had been over 12 or 14 times. It is a sadly weary journey! 5 mortal days—from 3 or 4 in the morning—to 5 at night!—crawl—crawl—all up and down hill,—tho' we had such good fun that it seemed short enough. It is a dreary country, as far as Tuscany's frontier, (for though there is a prettier road, we took the shorter one by Sienna). Miles of hills—and plains of mud—vineyards and olive trees—and here and there a village. We had but one day—(fortunately)—very wet—and so were prevented stopping at Sienna, a find old town;—all the rest of the journey was lovely—and we walked often; in the morning we were often alarmed for ourselves—, on account of robbers—but the accounts are all exaggerated after all.

Radicofani—an enormous mountain—visible for two days journey—is the boundary of the Pope's dominion, and on descending the other side one begins to see the sort of country Rome is placed in—lines and lines of blue mountains stretching into the sky—and plains that look as if they extended to Jerusalem. On the 4th. day—you pass a beautiful lake—Bolsena—like a flat blue mirror and then hills after hills bring you slowly to the waste, dreary desert of the Roman Campagna. I fear I cannot make you understand what this strange place is like, but, if you can fancy a whole world rolled out flat—(not flat, but undulating)—and bordered with huge mountains—all barren and a thorough desert, you may form some idea of it. The effect is very wild & melancholy—for you see no towns—only the Dome of St. Peter's—and you wonder at such a vast tract of unpeopled waste.

Meanwhile, the peasants are, beyond everything, picturesque—the huge, crowned hats one has always seen painted—the blue or brown cloaks—always worn like the drapery of the ancient Romans,—the shepherds like satyrs dressed all in goat-skins, and the women, in square, white headdresses—scarlet bodices, and peagreen skirts—all tell you that at length, you are really in Italy. There is nothing very striking in the entry of Rome; it is all modern, and the English and French hotels are all together, fine, square buildings etc. etc.—but all the old part is a good way off. Glad enough we were to arrive! to me it seemed the end of a long journey from last July.

And now, (for you can learn about the antiquities from books) I will describe my lodgings—for good Mr. Theed hunted all over with me—and I was soon settled. They are at No. 39, Via del Babuino (Baboon Street)—very near the gate—*close* to the church and the Piazza di Spagna—The Academy—the eating and coffee houses—all the English and all the artists. I should like, however, that you still address 'Poste Restante—Rome'—as it is safer than to address to lodgings.

My rooms—2—a study and a bedroom, are on the 2nd. floor, about the size of those in Southampton Row,° (but very lofty) and very well furnished;—for these, I only give 10 dollars a month—not £2-10-0—I should not have got them so cheap had not Mr. Theed known the landlady well—who is a very respectable woman. (I forgot to mention how kind the Knightons were on my leaving Florence—one gave me a *hare-skin*—another a bag of gingerbread—a 3rd. a bottle of brandy—a 5th [*sic*] a pound of groats for gruel—a 6th. a box of chocolate—and a 7th. a pair of worsted mittens!—so I was famously set up!—I must mention also that my box which I sent from London full of clothes etc. etc.—was all safe on my arrival here).

I will draw you a plan of my rooms—for I know you will like to understand them. 1. is my bedroom—nicely carpeted—glasses—drawers—curtains, and a nice bed. A;—2—my studio,—also very comfortable. B—the fireplace. C—the window—3 an open gallery by which you go to 4—'the commodité'—(begging your pardon)—5 and 6—are my landlady's rooms, 7 the landing place and 8 the stairs. Everything—washing—boots—etc. etc. are as proper as possible, and a London lodging could not be more agreeable.

At 8 I go to the Cafe, where all the artists breakfast, and have 2 cups of coffee and 2 toasted rolls—for 6½d. and then—I either see sights—make calls—draw out of doors—or, if wet—have models indoors till 4. Then most of the artists walk on the Pincian Mount, (a beautiful garden overlooking all Rome, and from which such sunsets are seen!)—and at 5 we dine very

capitally at a Trattoria or eating house, immediately after which Sir W. Knighton and I walk to the Academy—whence after 2 hours we return home. This is my present routine but there are such multitudes of things to see in Rome that one does not get settled in a hurry, and bye and bye I shall get more into the way of painting more at home, for I have 2 or 3 water coloured drawings ordered already, *so I shall not starve*. Mr. Tatton, my pupil, lodges next door and English are scattered all about the neighbourhood.

Rome is now beginning to look gay and the streets are as full as Regent St. almost—but this is only at a time such as Xmas. or Easter, for usually there is a great dulness observable. The people lounge and sit and swing about and the better orders saunter (for 20 mad bulls would not stir an Italian out of a slow walk!).—and everything but Art and artists—seems stagnant.

How the variety of costumes would delight you! As for priests—they are innumerable—white—black—piebald— scarlet—cinnamon—purple: round hats—shovel hats—cock-ed hats—hoods and caps—cardinals with their 3 footmen (for cardinals *never* walk)—white friars with masks, bishops and Monsignori with lilac and red stockings—and indeed thousands on thousands of every description of religious orders. Just now the town is full of Neapolitan pipers, called Pifferari,—who come at Xmas. to play to the Virgin: they have tall black hats, with peacock's feathers in them—blue or brown cloaks—red waistcoats, and sheepskin's and cord breeches— and they puff at enormous droney bag-pipes all day long to the shrines so constantly seen. I have drawn 2 or 3—and they are most picturesque.

I wish you could see the cattle—! Such beautiful gray sleek monsters! with enormous horns, all tied about with bells and ribbands, and pulling along carts by hundreds; then mules in troops come driving along—and as there are few footpaths— you must keep a good look out. All this is very amusing and delightful, particularly as the climate is so exquisite; you have no idea *how well I have been*;—what will you say to tonight (20th. of Dec.) being the first I have atall wanted a fire through? I assure you all of last week was like June—quite warm with a perfectly cloudless sky—and a sunset of gold; sometimes it has rained a good deal,—but never has there been any of that cutting wind of Florence. I sit and draw all day long in the sun—among the ruins—and often find a cloak too hot.

All the old part of Rome is a good way off our part of the town; if you expected to see a fine collection of splendid antiquities all in a bunch, you would be disappointed; you stumble on pillars—temples—circuses—and tombs—all more or less mixed up with modern buildings; old ruins reroofed— some turned into churches—others barns, or shops; here a row of houses growing out of a Roman foundation—there, a range of columns filled up with bricks, and new windows. Gates— porticos—pillars—arches—pavements—bridges—and statues —all keep you in a state of wonder—but as a whole—they have not an imposing effect. The arches of Titus and Constantine and Severus are the most perfect things—the Coliseum, and some of the gates—and the Pantheon—and by some lights— the melancholy and grandeur of these huge remains are very awful. But as to the *extent* of the ruins, of Rome—noone who does not see them, can form an idea; the palaces and baths of the Emperors—some filled up into convents—some covering acres of ground with masses of ancient walls—the long lines of acqueducts and tombs on the desolate and beautiful Campagna,—and (in the enormous palaces of the modern Capitol and Vatican) the thousands of busts and statues—!—judge how bewildered one's noddle becomes!—for my part, I am taking things very quietly—and like better to poke about over and over again in the Forum, than to hurry with the stream of sight seers all day long.

The Cholera has made immense havoc here—but now, all seems being forgotten; fifteen thousand died—four thousand five hundred orphans are left! Sometimes it carried off whole houses—at others only one or two inmates; the unhealthy often survived; and the stout were victims. Of the surrounding villages, most shut their gates and kept a cordon—but to no purpose; Velletri, alone, opened its gates all the time, and scarcely had any cases of Cholera!—so unaccountable on human principles was the process of the disease! If it should reappear, I shall leave Rome directly—not from fear, but from the disagreeable and awful state everything becomes in. You were partly right about your 'evil eye'—but that suburb of Rome, nobody dreams of going into any more than you would of walking through Field Lane, or St. Giles—notwithstanding a certain female acquaintance of mine° used to frequent 'bandy legged walk'!!

I meant to have written a much longer letter and to have answered yours more fully; but here is the 23rd, and I do not like delaying to send it longer—I have so little time. I gave Mrs. Clark's letter;° they are very well—but that is all I heard—for as they live just opposite me, I did not stretch into acquaintance; indeed, calls and cards, are already as tiresome as in London. Mrs. W[arner]. has not yet written; indeed, you and R. Hornby are my only *regular* writers. From Holloway I heard at Florence; poor Mrs. Nevill was very ill, and should fear, by the way in which Miss N. wrote—too much so to recover. I get sadly melancholy now and then—if I don't get letters. I wish you a very merry Xmas., and happy returns of the 17th. of next month. I shall drink your health in some gruel.

On the 25th. I dine at Mr. Hatfield's!—with several artists; *every Sunday at 6 at Sir W. Knighton's.* I do not think it impossible I may one day fetch you to Rome, for everything is so different to what I had expected,—so—if I were you I would get up my Italian:—I half thought of writing this autumn—but shall now wait and see how cholera goes on,—perhaps another year or two for, if I return to England then, I shall most likely come here again—so much better is my health: today—the windows are open and the sunshine like May. Other folks have sisters and wives and mothers here, so I don't see why I should not too. Meanwhile, write as soon as you receive this, and believe me

ever, | Dear Ann, | Yours sincerely,
Edward Lear.

I like your little book very much and so do the Knighton's— *Never write a <u>WORD</u> of politics in your letters*—your linen belt has been *so useful.* My landlady puts on the buttons etc. *Write my NAME very plainly.*

To the 13th Earl of Derby

Rome. 14th. February. 1838.

My Lord,

My expectations of the arrival of Prince Musignano° have been so useless, that I have at last resolved to write a few lines before his arrival: I know your Lordship would not have imagined I had ever forgotten either yourself or Knowsley, but as Prince M's museum, & the intelligence he might give me concerning anything I might think of sending over° were my great hopes as subjects of interest to write upon, I have delayed thus long:—alas! a horrible paragraph of today's Galignani describes that illustrious & zoological Corsican as dining with Louis Philippe,°—consequently I conclude he does not think of coming to Rome at all.—

In spite of all my researches I have seen very little new in the way of living creatures on my journey here: neither shall I add much to zoological lore in any way. Of little birds there is a great paucity throughout the Continent—such a constant warfare is carried on against the little wretches: neither robins—sparrows—thrushes or any other of the pretty fellows we have so many of, can feel very comfortable in countries where thousands of them are shot for daily food: nor only these,—for having discovered at Lugano that I had been eating a portion of a Jay—I went to the market place to be certain it was not a solitary nastiness,—and there I saw a beautiful variety to 'game'—multitudes of Jays—& Jackdaws included. At Milan there was a sort of a Bird shop—but among several Amazon Parrots & canaries—one Passerine Owl was the only respectable bird—but that was in a bad condition.

I should have mentioned that all through Switzerland I diligently enquired for chamois & marmots, but found none. Of the former I heard afterwards of one for sale when I had left the country,—but usually, the Swiss do not like to part with these things which they keep as pets. (Bye the bye, a cretin, with a huge goître, is at least as good a monster as an Orang,—were it not, being one of our own species, too serious & dreadful a morceau for Zoology.)

To return to Milan,—& to indulge in a little more horror, the skinning of frogs there, (a very popular dish,) is a very odious operation: the market women sit talking in circles, each with her tub of froggies—: & nipping their feet off with little scissors & most adroitly turning off their skins like gloves from an incision they make in the back,—they put the poor little victims in baskets, where, in the spirit of Munchausenism,° they caper & leap about ad libitum just as if nothing had happened. Bah!—But the Milanese have a weakness for clippings & cuttings:—not a cat but hath lost all or part of her tail,° the reason according to the owners, for which embellishing with cuts, is that they will never forsake the house in which they have lost that useful member. Grimalkin is better treated in more northern Lombardy—for about Chiavenna I was amused delightfully by every cat having her ears bored, & little bows—or tassells of blue or pink ribband depending there-from!

I used to like to watch the large bats on Lake Como–: they are very fine fellows, & indulge in beetle catching every twilight, though I never could secure any. I saw a mantis also by the lake one day, & had it been procurable should have saved it for Knowsley: but it was a maternal mantis & not at all fit for being flattened between the leaves of a book. On the road between Milan & Florence, we killed 2 tarantulæ & one scorpion: these with myriads of large locusts in Swiss vallies, & stupendous fleas everywhere conclude my entomological observations.

At Florence, the Grand duke has, (or thinks he has,) a live Zoological collection:—though the inhabitants, an ostrich, a chamois, sundry goats & an infirm wild boar,—looked piteously forlorn & dirty. At Pisa, (which I did not go to,) there are several—(2 or 300 I believe,) camels: they have long existed, & multiply there: also I think at Leghorn:—I do not know why they have not more widely spread throughout Italy.

— —And, now—lastly—from the eternal city—my zoological notes are at a most deplorably low ebb:—my visions of Bustards & porcupines have faded away nearly, & unless Prince Musignano puts me in the way to transplant some Italian beast or bird to Lancashire, I do not know what I shall do.—I have sate & walked on the wild Campagna—& I have looked into holes for porcupines & tortoises—but to no purpose. 2 hares—& one fox have been as yet my only discoveries. Porcupines *are* found however & so are tortoises, but I have seen none yet.

Speaking of bustards, the following anecdote will shew your Lordship that Zoological lore flourisheth vigorously here: at a dinner, (some person having shot a bittern in the morning,)—I heard a confused discussion about bitterns—bustards—& buzzards—&—finally a Mr. Somebody was appealed to, who settled this point by stating confidantly that the 3 terms were precisely synonymous!! I have amused myself by sending Lady Coventry, [(]for it was at her house,) sketches of the injured birds in question.—

I think that the Zoological Society should have a pair of Buffaloes—though by no means are they beasts at all fit for Knowsley:—piggylooking—hideous spectacles they are!—melancholy objects, but very useful: they bring up marble & stone from the river, & you may always see them in the Forum;—in the vast marshes by the Tiber, they abound in great herds, and are there very dangerous & fierce. The Campagna dogs—sheep dogs—also are subject to very un-pleasant ebullitions of ill temper, & it is not at all safe to approach sheep when the shepherds are not with them: 10 or 12 of these brutes, (the *dogs* not the *shepherds*,) devoured a priest some time back———

The flowers & plants in all these places are delightful: &, if your Lordship likes, I will make a dry collection of those found at the Coliseum: cyclamens often grow wild, & on the top of Augustus's palace, (where there is a terrace with the most glorious views,) the wallflowers & violets have been blooming all through the winter, & the aloes & indian figs are in high luxuriance.—

Your Lordship will smile at my catalogue, but I have *often thought of* Knowsley—or rather am seldom without thinking of it, & I as often regret that I cannot do much in the way of increasing its owners amusements. Mr. Baker of Bedford-bury—near Hertford, has been here: (your Lordship may remember him as a friend of Mr. Sabine's, & one, with whom I once imagined I might go out to Himalaya:)—I mention this, because, he has now left on his way to Syria & Jerusalem, & as he is a great collector of seeds—particularly pines,—I fancied that when he returned a communication might be of use to the

Garden at Knowsley: he is a Zoological Member.—On the road near Florence, I overtook Mr. Cox, Mrs. Cox—& all the lesser Coxes—migrating to Naples:—but—here my glimpses, even of Zoological followers, must end.

I would give a great deal to know the state of Knowsley, aviary—roads—&c: I know the 4 end rooms in the gallery have been added to the Museum from Mr. Robert,—but as he is not on the spot, very little more. Captn. Hornby° I see by the gazette is at Woolwich: I have not heard from them a long while: leaving Plymouth must have been a sad blow, & I am sure I felt it by sympathy out here. And now I am going to say, that if ever your Lordship should have a modicum of leisure any account of what is doing at Knowsley would delight me most sincerely: I do not think I ought to have said this either, for I know how little your Lordship likes writing. It is all very beautiful & interesting & wonderful here,—but—it is not England: & I am stupid enough to get into very homesick fits sometimes: I ought to be thankful however that my health is so much better than it ever was. For improvement—I say little as yet: I try hard enough & if improvement in art *must necessarily* follow, I shall be sure to have it:——but I think sometimes, one bird drawing was worth 2 landscapes,—I go on hoping nevertheless, & the continual kindness of my correspondent at Milnthorpe is delightful. Much I should like to know what is thought of his state of health by others. Of Lady Charlotte & Mr. Penrhyn I often rejoice to hear, through the Miss Leysters: Lady C's ice-exploit among the last news. Lady Ellinor° & all besides I trust are well. Lord Stanley's name I see now & then in the papers.—Bishop of Norwich° elected president of the Linnaean!—What does Mr. Lambert say?

I seem to have written the most stupid of letters, & have said no more of cities & countries than if I had been at Hampstead all the time: but as your Lordship must have read 50 better descriptions than I can hope to give I have not put patience to the test. As for Rome, (tho' it is not Knowsley,) it is exquisite: its antiquity part is my sole delight—with its adjacent views:—ceremonies & gaieties I eschew:—indeed the English quarter is as like a London season as may be, & not at all to my taste. Everybody is very kind & agreeable—& the artists & sculptors a very united body of people. Howbeit, numbers

complain of the wet weather, (for it has rained oceans,) & seem
to expect July in January.—To day is the first I have had a fire
all the winter: it has been delightfully close & 'muggy'. We are
now expecting the Carnival on Saturday—& all will be foolery
for a time.

And now, My Lord, I must send my best respects &
remembrances to the very many friends—at—or part of
Knowsley: particularly to those at Woolwich: I fear I have been
a sad correspondent there,—but nonwriting is not forgetful-
ness. And wishing your Lordship a happy new year—believe
me, My Lord, | Ever your Lordships most gratefully | &

respectfully,

Edward Lear.

Ask Mr. Robert for an account of the *Pope's poultry.*

To Ann Lear

Rome, 3rd. May, 1838.

My dear Ann,

See what correspondents we are!—I now begin fortnightly
instead of monthly letters—that is—if they do not cost you too
much. For, now,—as I shall have left Rome,—the *uncertainty* of
the post at Naples they say *is dreadful*—so that the chances are
better with two letters than one. Please always to begin—'I
have received your letter of the—such a date'—& I will do the
same. Perhaps I may sometimes [be] at Amalfi—or Ischia—or
Sorrento—where it may be inconvenient to send for letters but
never mind; we will each write *twice* in the month—without
waiting for each other's epistles—& so we shall get on very well
I dare say. My next letter will be sent off from Naples about the
beginning of June—telling you all about my journey there; I, &
Uwins & Mr. Acland° set off on Saturday—& we are not going
'the Robbing road',—but a long way round—staying some
days at many beautiful places all [of] which I will tell you
about.

I must now describe my dear Tivoli as I promised. First then
you leave Rome at the San Lorenzo gate—& drive for some
time between high ugly narrow high-walled lanes, till you come

to the church of San Lorenzo—a very old one of the time of Constantine; it is very beautiful against the wide sky & mountains. After this about 10 miles of up & down all over the Campagna, I have so often talked of, & which you *must* cross to get away from Rome. All the while you are getting nearer to the Blue mountains, & you see Tivoli perched on a rock a great way up. By degrees the buildings become more distinct & you see quantities of Cypress trees—so black—sprinkled about the town. Nearer still—the Campagna is very rugged & dreary, & you cross a queer sulphur stream as white as milk—& of a hideous smell; but shortly afterwards the country becomes cultivated—& you drive through plantations of olives & figs—& all kinds of grain. Then you reach the Anio or Teverone,—the river which runs through Tivoli, & you cross it on a Roman bridge—with a fine tomb; you know the old Romans always built their tombs by the roadside. These little smudgy scratches will convey some idea.

I must tell you that formerly Tivoli was the fashionable residence of the old Romans; all the rich ancients had villas there. You now pass a vast tract of ruins—Cypresses etc., towers etc.—these are the remains of the Emperor Adrian villa, but I did not see them as I ought to have done. Then you commence a long pull up to the town through the most beautiful olive wood!—such trees!—& every now & then you see bits of the ancient villas—all that is left of once vast buildings—now only a few arches with the curious Roman brick work—covered with large aloes—or roofs of olives. This is a bit. And as you get  higher & higher—such a view as you cannot imagine is seen all over the Campagna with Rome—18 miles off quite on the horizon.

At length you enter the town—a nasty dirty narrow, filthy place like most Italian towns; Elm Street—& Little Turnstile or Middle Row are like its streets—only the houses are very picturesque. The people of Italy hang all sorts of clothes from all their windows, so the towns always look gay. Little Madonnas attached here & there—& now & then a good sized square—& so you ride on to Tivoli to the inn, a beastly place—as you may judge when I tell you there are 16 dogs—10 cats & all sorts of poultry all over the house! One soon gets accustomed however to this—& the dinners are very nice—nice fish & omelettes particularly. Nevertheless 4 of the dogs ate up a large meat pie we had taken—the first day.

In the inn yard is a beautiful ruin of the Sybil's temple—very old, & standing on a great precipice; for Tivoli, as I said, stands on a ledge of rock which projects like a tongue into a long valley,—& as the river comes to Tivoli, it is obliged to tumble, (with such a noise,) *down* the rock before it gets to the valley below,—& it is over this chasm that the temple stands. Much of this river is detained for mills, & it falls in 20 or 30 cascades all down the rock to different parts of the valley—so that such a squashing of water as there is at Tivoli was never heard!— Below this temple are most lovely gardens! which wind down to the very bottom of the chasm—where there are caverns & cascades & rocks—& alleys—& ruins of immense villas more than I can describe to you.

Well now we leave the inn to take a walk; (you must know I spent a whole week at Tivoli) crossing the bridge which joins the tongue of rock to the mainland—we are now on the other side of the river, & we will go round the valley. Such beautiful scenery—more like a dream than reality you cannot conceive! Everywhere vast woods of olives slope down to the valley—& aloes by thousands grow around! Groups of the most picturesque peasantry are always on the road, & in the midst of the vale rises Tivoli itself on its long, narrow rock,—while beyond is still the great Campagna. The little spot A is St. Peter's at Rome, & all between is the wide plain. This is the view from 1 in the little map.

When you turn the corner at 2—then you see a more lovely view still—for the huge ruins of Mæcenas's villa, like the palace of Alladin seems to be quite unreal. It is—(what remains of it,) a pile of beautiful arches—& over these are numerous cascades. In this Paradise of a valley you may wander for days—& every hour see a new view of the town in its

different positions. The one only objection is the incessant uproar of waterfalls.

I must now take you to the Villa d'Este—a scene worth walking to Italy from England—if one could see nothing else. It has struck me more than anything since I left home. You know how magnificent the Roman church used to be; well—about the 16th. century—Cardinal D'Este built this mansion. The house is very grand & simple in form—but it is its situation that so bewilders one. I could not believe I was awake at first. It is raised quite above all Tivoli, at the top of an *extremely* steep hill—*all* of which is turned into one exquisite garden. You come on to the upper terrace & are dumb; the most enormous trees—pines & Cypresses—are beneath you; long walks of gravel, grass & box—formally cut; fountains by hundreds of thousands—terraces; flights of stairs from the villa to the bottom of the hill—& to crown all—the whole Campagna beyond. You proceed down these flights of stairs—& wonder that you have been so deceived on arriving, at the Cypress

trees—which look like giants; they are the largest in the world. From the end of the long valleys you look back—& it is really like magic! I will try to give you a very little idea of this most exquisite of gardens.

No.1. may convey some notion of the place—seen from the end of the long walk; observe the vast height!—& the proportion of the little people! & think how grand these mighty black Cypresses must be! No. 2 shows you the whole house—from another Cypress walk. But this wonderful palace is all quite desolate—nobody has lived in it for a 100 years—& like all palaces in Italy its beauty has a good deal of melancholy with it. Next summer I should like to pass some months at Tivoli—for although I have said so much of it, yet I can assure you that it is impossible to form any idea of the extreme loveliness of the whole environment of the town.

So now I have done with Tivoli. I told you I returned in time for the Holy Week—but I did not like its ceremonies atall; I hate crowds & bustle. The grandest of all is on Thursday at noon when the Pope comes into the great gallery of St. Peter's & the Piattza is full of people kneeling while he blesses them. The illumination also is *wonderful*. About dusk, men (400) are slung by ropes (!!!) all over the dome & colonnades of St. Peter's—where they put little paper lamps in regular places— till the evening grows darker—every line, column, & window becomes gradually marked by dots of light! It has the exact appearance of a transparent church—with light seen through

pricked holes. Imagine a dark sky & my ink dots all light!— about 9 o'clock by an astonishing series of signals—the whole fabric blazes with hundreds of torches; immense iron basins full of oil & shavings are suspended *between* the little lamps, & these all at once burst out into the light! I can only compare it to a stupendous diamond crown in the dark night. It is the most beautiful thing in the world of its sort.

I omit the numerous ceremonies & only pass to the winding up of all the celebrated fireworks at the Castel S. Angelo. This renowned affair is really also beyond belief. This grand castle is

over the Tiber—& joins a bridge, so that when lighted up by the glare of the immense blaze—it is superb to a degree. With a terrific explosion at 9 o'clock—off go the most unaccountable mass of rockets!!!!! You would think all Rome had gone off in one rocket! & as soon as that is over—all the castle is a blue blaze of sparkling festoons—trophies—mottoes etc. etc. This is succeeded by *thousands* of squibs & Catherine wheels—blue lights—& eccentric rockets of uncouth sorts—running fire spitting spouting, spurting—cascades of sparks—columns of yellow balls—globes of crimson sputtering stars—& all this goes fizzing & bouncing about for half an hour!!—till you are nearly deaf & blind & astonished beyond all measure!!!!!!! I am afraid you will laugh at my very bad illustrations but I think they will amuse you.

Since the Holy week everybody has been leaving Rome—for Naples & other places, & now it is very dull indeed—for those who like gaiety. Did I tell you that my friend Sir William Knighton is going to be married? to a Scotch lady.° He returns next winter. There are numbers of nice people here too but to describe is tedious. Mr. Acland who goes with me tomorrow is a friend of the Hornby's.

Believe me, my dear Ann, | Ever yours affect.,
Edward Lear.

To John Gould

107. 2do. Via Felice. Roma. Italia. 17th. Octbr. 1839.
Dear Gould,

Why will you continue to walk topsy-turvy° so long?—for everybody knows, that the people in the Antipodes, being on the other side of the world,—must necessarily have their heads where their heels should be: when you come back you will all be puzzled to walk properly.—I ought to have written to you long before this—but I was always a bad correspondent & idleness—business—& a hot climate combine just now to make me worse than ever. But surely you are still more unconscientious,—for when I DO write, you answer me by a short scrawl—only one word of which out of every 20 can I decipher—& I have kept your last & only epistle to see if I can't sell it as an ancient hieroglyphic:—pray *send*—*but* don't write a reply to *this*:—ask Mrs. Gould to be so kind as to act as your secretary—& dictate as much as you like.—Do not however imagine that I forget you although you are so far off—& topsy turvy to boot:—& if it be any pleasure to be thanked from the other side of the globe, I can assure you I often think of both you & Mrs. Gould & remember many kindnesses of days gone. I am now a days a much happier person than of old—for my health & prospects are all changed for the better—& though I be not yet arrived at that keystone of hope—matrimony, I anticipate firmly the chance of a Mrs. Lear in 40 years hence at least. But I will dismiss my reflexions, which you will wish at Jericho, & scrawl some egotism.—

Up to the spring of 1838 I think I enlightened you as to my doings—& I received your nasty illegible abortion of a note at Naples—whither in company with a friend I had just walked. After that I was taken very ill, & owing to the too fine & sulphurous nature of the air, my cough returned & also spitting of blood, & had I not left the neighbourhood of that filthy old mountain Vesuvius I might have died:—indeed I was never well until I returned to Rome, which soon restored me, & I have reason to be doubly thankful for the friends by whose means I first came here that I am living & in such excellent health at present, for, from many symptoms, I feel sure that I must have followed my sisters—(2 more of whom have died since I left England: there are now only the 4 eldest left:°)—had I not applied in time to the remedy of climate.—

Naples does not please me as a city, altho' no other word but Paradise can be used to express the beauty of its environs, which are unlike any earthly scene beside:—but the town itself is all noise, horror—dirt, heat—& abomination—& I hate it,—nor am I much attached to a sea side residence, not to speak of a beastly volcano whose smokings groanings bumpings thumpings vomitings earthquakings & other eccentricities always annoyed me from morn to night.—I was however most fortunate in witnessing one of the finest irruptions known for many years—a midnight scene I can never forget:—I wonder if you will come ever into these places:—but as you would see no kangaroos or marsupial monkeys about the country, I don't believe you would be pleased.—

In September 1838 I again returned to Rome, staying a little while at Tivoli & the mountains about 40 miles off—scenery all of an exquisite, but different character from the brilliant Neapolitan districts.—All through the winter—(which was a very fine one, though cold,) I was over head & ears in employment: Rome was more crammed than it has been since the days of Titus—& people slept in ovens & pigstyes for want of lodgings—so that what with pupils—(of which I had numbers,) & friends—& drawings indoors & sketchings out of doors—the spring came before one knew where one was. You will lift up your hands & eyes & legs & possibly fall quite off your chair when I tell you that I was enabled to send some of my earnings to my mother & sisters & to put by 100£ besides for the use of the summer!!!——don't go into a fit.——In May— 1839—all the world having forsaken the old lady of Babylon—I went a walking tour towards Florence—& was much pleased thereby—after which, I went to a little town at the top of an high hill, where I have remained—in company with sundry other artists—until yesterday evening, when I returned here for the winter campaign.—

Last summer I commenced oil painting°—but during the winter I had no opportunity of following it up:—this summer however I have pursued it again with a little more success—but am as yet of course a beginner—tho' I hope ultimately to paint some thing or other. It takes a long while to make a painter—even with a good artist's education—but *without* one—it tires the patience of Job:—it is a great thing if one does not go backward.—Meanwhile I am extremely happy—as the hedgehog said when he rolled himself through a thistle- bush——: I am in very nice & comfortable lodgings for a 16 months past—& do not intend to leave them:—I know all the English artists—who are universally kind to me—as well as every body else—& our little supper parties in winter, & our excursions in spring & autumn are very lively & agreeable.

Then the vicinity of the very lovely villas & gardens about Rome makes the whole place a constant source of amusement: —the evening walks among the antique places of this beautiful city—the visits to the Vatican or the galleries of ancient art—or the studios of the moderns:—the days on the campagna round Rome:—the theatres, the games of the people:—the English church regularly on a Sunday:—all these things (though I have jostled them all together helterskelter,) added to the quiet of the place—the unbustling—ancient—dead sort of atmosphere over all persons & streets—& the warm & delightful climate ——all this & a deal more I cannot stuff into my paper—make Rome to me the <u>ONLY</u> delightful metropolis I ever yet saw or resided in.—Nor am I in any hurry to leave it:——I have written to my eldest sister, (who always lived with me in England,)—& she will very possibly join me here next year.—Society is of the best also in Rome—& among many kind friends, Prince Musignano—with all of whose family I am sufficiently intimate—is one of the best. I stay with them at their country place sometimes, & pass very pleasant days there: he has just lost a very sweet daughter, but there are 7 children left still:—just now he is at Pisa, not having yet returned from the Scientific Meeting—about which I can tell you nothing but that very few English were there—& that the Pope would not allow any of his subjects to go there. But I have no doubt you know all about these things better than I can inform you.——

Concerning Zoology—(which I forget fast enough,) I fear I can still less edify you:—bee eaters abound near here—& I told you there were porcupines in my last letter:—I often think of you when I see the large kites & falcons which are so numerous in the mountains where I have been residing.—Do not fancy nevertheless that I should not be much entertained by an account of your novelties abroad, for I still know an Opossum from a Trogon—so pray let me have a very long letter— WRITTEN as I before begged—by Mrs. Gould at your dictation:—& dilate on all your doings—how you pass the days, &c &c &c—is Mrs. Gould's brother° with you?—And how many more children have you; I dare say a great quantity.——

Letters here are one of my great delights:—I hear from all my old friends—excepting I must confess, the Zoologists——from neither Mr. Bell or Mr. Yarrell have I had a syllable. Lady Stanley's sister & Lord Derby's nieces & nephews furnish me with a constant Lancashire Gazette:—poor Lord D. is now as well as he ever can be—that is, in bodily health he is much restored—although his limb remains useless.° He has always been the same uniform patient—& excellent creature throughout the whole illness—& now he is wheeled about constantly or writes all day long:—I still hope he may live many years yet—& I have just now the greatest pleasure in his having received safely some drawings I have been sending him——as well as to all the other kind people by whose good doings I came out here.

I really scarcely know how to fill up this letter with anything that may guarantee your not burning it half read through—for I cannot describe buildings &c &c which you may read about in any book————& the persons here you could scarcely be interest[ed] in—not knowing them—though you may have heard the names of Gibson & Wyatt as sculptors—& Williams as a painter°—:—taking them 'in a lump', it is not possible to find (as far as my opinion goes—) a more good & agreeable set of artists than those of our country residing here—: the French and Germans also are equally pleasant, though one naturally sees less of them. Do tell me if there is any art at all in Sydney—(except portrait painting which I conclude flourishes all over the world:) & what sort of people you are among. An Italian asked me the other day, 'if new Holland were not peopled entirely by the worst criminals sent from home—& if they had not returned one & all to a savage state & run the country naked & bare like Adam & Eve?' I said I imagined not—but I could not convince him that there might be some civilization in the Antipodes.—I heard last from V. Audubon at Edinburgh.——I must conclude from sheer emptiness—so good bye.—My kindest regards to Mrs. Gould & yourself—&
believe me ever— | Dear Gould— | Yr. sincere friend—
Edward Lear.

Address to me exactly as I have written in the bracket at the beginning of this letter:—or send by Mr. Prince° if you think better: I send this to the Zoo: Society—not knowing if the house at Broad Street° be kept up.

To John Gould

107. 2do. V. Felice. Roma. | 27th. Feby. 1841.
My dear Gould,—

I was very glad to get your letter of Feb. 2,—although I knew you were returned & both you & Mrs. Gould in good health:—you are certainly astonishing people, & I as much as any of your friends rejoice at your success.—For all that I am scandalized at your saying nothing about your children, of whom I should have liked to have heard;— —nor do you say anything of an immense letter I sent you out to Sydney: ——neither do I understand how Mrs. Gould could trust you away from her so long—seeing you had not me by your side.°—All this & more I hope, please God, to talk over in less than 3 months in Broad Street, for I fully intend leaving Rome early in May—though I don't yet quite know if I go by Marseilles or by land——since my plans depend partly on those of some of Ld. Derby's family who are here this winter.

What I shall do *in* England I have no idea:—run about upon railroads——& eat beefsteaks.———I am & have been, as you have justly heard—going on very well—which is more than ever I had a right to expect, in spite of your good opinion of me:—I am very glad I took to Landscape—it suits my taste so exactly—& though I am but a mere beginner as yet——still I do hope—by study & staying here to make a decent picture before I die. No early education in art—late attention, & bad eyes—are all against me—but renewed health & the assistance of more kind friends than any mortal ever had I hope will prove the heaviest side of the balance.

I think of publishing some Lithography° on coming to England—to pay expenses &c—but am yet uncertain:—in fact, this English trip upsets me very much, as I am become a hater of moving about—however, I don't think it right to stay away always from one's country. I wish to goodness I could get a wife!—You have no idea how sick I am of living alone!!———
Please make a memorandum of any Lady under 28 who has a little money—can live in Rome—& knows how to cut pencils & make puddings.

My best remembrances to Mr. Rees—Mr. Bell, Mr Yarrell

&c &c: also to C. Hullmandel—to whom I will shortly write. I sent your letter to Prince Canino° & he gave me one of yours to read in return:—your books° are not yet come: I long to see them.

Do you know that foolish & furious old bigot—Waterton,° has been here these 2 winters?—he walked the last 20 miles to Rome BAREFOOT—(*fact*,) & was in bed 6 weeks:—he is very much run after by all silly people, & has entirely demolished all Zoological artists—[(]yourself & Audubon inclusive—) for evermore.——V. Audubon wrote to me the other day: he is married to the sister of John's wife——who I fear is by this time dead———Mr. Vigor's death° shocked me very much—by [*sic*] I have heard no particulars. I am very anxious to see many of my friends—Lord Derby particularly. I hope you will be in town this summer. I hope too you will come to the Florence meeting—& so to Rome—& that you will bring Mrs. Gould also: I should delight in lionizing you in the Campagna—& the beautiful mountains here:—we would certainly take a trip. You would like Prince Canino very much: he is a very good kind man & has the sweetest children you ever beheld—just like so many Napoleons. They have been always excessively kind to me, but I am a sad fellow for disliking '*parties*' & '*society*' & so I see little of them. The wish of my life at present—is, quiet——to live in the country—& paint landscapes——the cutting pencil puddingmaking lady included.— —My very best remembrances to Mrs. Gould: I am really delighted she has been so well in all her travels:—you ought both of you to be very thankful. Love to John Henry—if he recollects me: he & Charley are my only acquaintance—& I have *no idea how many more you have*. If Mrs. Coxon be with you pray give my respects—& remember me to Mr. Prince;——what a valuable right hand he has been to you! Do you ever see Mr. Eyton?°—& now, goodbye—I long to have an immense talk with you. Believe me, Dear Gould, heartily glad of all your success—your

sincere friend.—

Edward Lear

To John Gould

[Shortly after his return to England Lear heard that Gould's wife had died.]

Knowsley Hall. 28th. August. 1841.

Dear Gould,

I have just got your letter—and I think it very kind of you to have written—as I was anxious about you, & have thought a great deal about you. There is always a compensation given by the Almighty for the evils we suffer—if we regard them rightly & such I trust you are enabled to do.—

I have but little to say to you—but I write because you ask me to do so:—my life here is monotonous enough—but such as pleases me more than all the gaiety in the world. Dear Lord Derby is surrounded by his children grandchildren & nephews & nieces & is really happy. He breakfasts with us after prayers:—then about 12 takes a drive with one of his daughters or his son in law or myself:—he takes the greatest interest in all his grounds &c.—He dines in his own room when we lunch—but after our dinner at 7. he sits with us all the evening. I do not perceive the slightest alteration in his mind: his disposition is much softened—& he is kindness & patience itself.—The lot of things is immense here—birds & beasts &c: but I am so thoroughly confined by my Lithography as to have little time to see them.

I shall not be in London yet: I have sent for 4 more stones: & about the 20th. Septbr. I go to Scotland to Lord Breadalbane° & other places.—As soon as ever I return of course I will call on you.

Remember me to Mrs. Coxon, & believe me, dear Gould, |
Yours most sincerely,
Edward Lear.

To the 13th Earl of Derby

107. 2do. Via Felice. Roma. June. 5. 1842.

My Lord,

I am going to write rather a long letter,—but whether your

Lordship will think it tedious or amusing I know not:—only,—now I have just returned from Sicily, I have a little more novelty to talk of so I do not like to let the occasion pass—for my usual monotonous life in Rome is too barren of any interest to write on, and yet I am continually vexed at not writing at all to one who has been the origin of all my present health & prospects.

Since I left England this last time, I have not become so foreignized as before—that is—I hope I am always *an Englishman,*—but I mean that my last summer's pleasures make me a bit doleful now & then, & my greatest delights here are the letters I get from Sheen—Woolwich—or Lancashire. Robert H. is however my great purveyor of news—& even a scrap comes now & then from Marienbad. I have letters from R.A.H. up to the 22d from Coblenz and he is looking forward to his English journey with pleasure.—If I had Aladins lamp—*wouldn't* I go with him!—I sometimes please myself with thinking that I shall not be able to bear exile more than another year—& so that I shall perforce set off for the North—next—or the summer after:—but this I know is wrong, & I ought to remain more settled for a longer time to come. Meantime—I have had out all my old sketches—zoological & all:—& I now & then look at my walk by the boathouse—or at my older acquaintance the Puffin geese—the darling old Spectacle owl°—or the Stanley cranes.°—Even the portraits of half the piggery I have got to console myself with. Had I not been so busy with those Lithographs last year—how much I should have liked to have painted studies of the oaks beyond the Stand hill—& about the Chalnaker!—After all, a day in England is worth a week elsewhere,—though I am not less alive to the beauties of Italy than formerly:———

The Roman season was very dull & stupid this year: everybody was at Naples—for the Roman Lodging keepers have outwitted themselves by doubling their prices. The Society also was not so good as usual—& there were but two Lions, (Lady Charlotte Bury, & Mrs. Trollope,°)—a small quantity for winter consumption. So towards March—as I was rather idle & very homesick,—I thought a tour round Sicily would take up a month's time very improvingly, & accordingly I set off with one of Sir. T. Acland's younger sons—& a nephew of Sir Stamfd. Raffles.° And although from a most wonderful combination of delays & ill fortunes my one month's tour stretched into one of 10 weeks—to the great loss of my time & money—yet I am thankful now that I made it:—since, I look to returning at some future day to various spots in the island of which I should like to make pictures.

Palermo I think pleased me more than any city I ever was in—& we saw enough of it to know it—being there for 3 weeks owing to the illness of one of our party. In a beautiful little plain quite walled in with mountains—and close on the edge of the sea—with two hills like wings forming its harbour—Palermo is as it were shut out from the rest of the world, & is a sort of Naples as to situation, but without the nasty vulgar noisy feeling that odious town always gives me. Close by the Hotel where we lived is the Marina—such a Promenade—!—& the end of that leads you at once to the most quiet of vallies—full of Aloes & Indian fig—where you may walk about & feel a 1000 miles from any city in the world. In that valley took place the Massacre of the French called the Sicilian Vespers in 1213—: & on the opposite side from the Church of S. Spirito where the slaughter began—is the remnant of an old Palace of one of the Saracen Caliphs who was long in Sicily.

—Every spot of this remarkable island has a different sort of historical interest : & either you are taken back to the time of its old Cyclops or Troglodytes—or its splendour under its Greek—& Roman governments—,—or you may ruminate over Gothic & Saracenic vestiges— —or later among German—Norman—Spanish or French ruins—each a monument of some change of destiny to the Sicilians. I confess—since my return here,—the Colosseum & my poor dear Roman Ruins look shockingly vulgar & modern—after the glorious temples of Egesta & Agrigentum & Syracuse—which belonged to very respectable people before Rome was thought of.——

But to return to Palermo—the Palermitans are very nice wellbred people, & much more comme il faut than the Romans—or indeed Italians in general: they are very kind to strangers. The evening is their time for coming out like bats & owls—for, even in March, the noon of Sicily is too hot for comfort. As for the women—perhaps from the remain of Moorish & Spanish customs—they hardly ever come out at all, & a great number of them are nuns—judging by the vast

quantity of grated nunnery windows in the principal streets.—
There is an English church at Palermo—that is—service is
performed by some British clergyman—& the congregation
varies from 40 to 70.—I did not see all the Lions about
Palermo—: even the celebrated dried monks I left unvisited, as
I don't care for such uglinesses. The Cathedral of Monreale, &
the royal chapel at Palermo are perhaps as fine sights as they
can shew a stranger: they were both built by the early Norman
Sovereigns—(1000–1100—) but possibly by Saracenic work-
men—since there is a tinge of Moorish in their designs. Near
the city is a famous hill (—Monte Pellegrini—where Santa
Rosalia the Patroness of Palermo was buried,—)—which
overlooks the whole bay & has a most glorious view. Numbers
of people pilgrimize here on the Saint's day—but we thought
that the crowds could scarcely be greater than those we saw
going up to shoot Quails: we counted 93 donkeys—besides
masses of foot passengers.

The vegetation—directly one is outside the walls,—tells one
of a southern climate more than the costumes of the people—
who might all have been in Liverpool for anything peculiar in
their faces or dress. But the long hedges of aloes—just coming
into bloom—& the fields or hedges on the roadside of the
Cactus Opuntia—has a very original appearance:—I had no
idea that plant—or rather tree grew so large:—it is often as high
as 20—or 30 feet at least,—& when it hangs down from rocks is
very picturesque:—when it grows upright it looks awkward &
as if it didn't know what to do with itself.

The Cattle of Sicily are not so fine a race as their gray Roman
neighbours:—they are red=brown—very large—& with *monstrous* horns. Near Pelligrini is a cave—(which I did not
see)—entirely full of bones of Elephants—generally supposed
to be Antediluvian:—but many, with great probability conjecture them to belong to the Elephants—several 1000 of which
were killed in the war with Amilear—especially as no *tusks* or
teeth are to be found.

While our friend was recovering, Leopold Acland & I went a
journey on the North Coast to Cefalu—& this—though I
cannot describe it,—was the most beautiful scenery for any
extended space I saw while in Sicily. All one's travelling is on
mules—as there are no roads—& walking will not do on

account of the Bridgeless rivers.—From the time we began our
tour round the Island. (29. April,) there was but little striking
scenery, save in spots which were certainly highly magnificent:—all the rest—often toilsome journies of 40 miles a day,
was a succession of Cornfields:—surely we never saw so much
corn in our lives!!—No villages—not even a detached house
greeted one from morn till night—but the towns are very
populous.—

Segeste—the ancient Greek Egesta is now a solitude—one
nearly perfect temple—& a theatre are all left, & the wonder is
why they are not destroyed like the rest of the great city. The
theatre I did not go up to—but the Temple is a mournful thing:
a deep—deep ravine stands below it, & all is as silent as if no
busy life had ever been known there. I long to see Egesta once
more—for Alas! we had but one hour or two there.—
Selinuntium has yet several temples all prostrate:—an earthquake has evidently shaken them down all at once—for the
columns are all fallen outward in the same manner.—
Girgenti—towering over a world of broken edifices is a place to
stay at & marvel. All along the hill of the ancient Agrigentum
ran the old walls cut into tombs—& on the same ridge are
more or less perfect remains of 7. Temples—mostly thrown
down—: one, that of [. . .] Olimpico(?) is of so immense a
size—that a stout man can stand IN the fluting of the
columns!——Girgenti is the most bustling modern town in
Sicily: it exports great quantities of sulphur—Manna—sumach
& other articles.

Sciottino was our next great wonder: a valley near it contains
a most immense mass of rock approachable on one side by a
natural bridge only—or rather being a Peninsula of rock forcing
a stream to flow round it. All this rock—for the space of 2 or 3
miles is perforated with artificial caves—each large enough to
contain 2 or 3—persons,—& cut each with a raised bed or seat
at one side: perhaps they may be 5 feet square on an
average—many larger—& smaller. There are about *3 or 4
thousand* of these caves in the most inaccessible crags—&
tradition calls them the houses of Troglodytes:—other antiqua-
rians say they are tombs—& to this opinion I incline—though
why they should have buried their dead in such places passes all
belief:—how they even formed some of the holes is beyond my

apprehension.—Thus far seems certain: that during the persecutions of the 3d & 4th. centuries by the Roman Emperors,—these caves were used as refuges by the early Christians—for many remains of crosses & other representations of that time character are traceable on the walls of some of these strange places.—I will send your Lordship a little sketch before long—just to give an idea of this most curious place.——

Syracuse delighted us all much, & I think is very beautiful & picturesque. But its great historical interest is the prevailing attraction. Still there are the Quarries where the cruel Government confined & starved the Athenian soldiers:—still are the ancient quarters of the city & its walls, to be traced:—the fountain of Arethusa still bubbles—(though I am sorry to say that the poor old Nymph is turned to a washing fountain—where half the dirty linen of Syracuse is cleaned;)—& the Papyrus still grows in the river Anapus—I think the only place in Europe where it is found. We went up the river, & were charmed by the oriental look of that curious plant which grows to the height of 20 or 30 feet & is wonderfully elegant.—Thus—

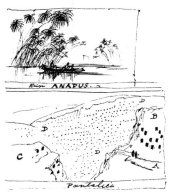

on second thoughts I have added an illustration of Pantalica. A is a path underneath the near rock B—which is full of the caves. C. is also near. DDD. is one enormous perpendicular face of rock—going down in[to] a frightful abyss—covered all over with similar caves.

From Syracuse we went to Catania—a strange city built on the fields of Lava which have destroyed 2 of its predecessor towns. Etna we saw little of for the weather was cloudy.—It smoked now & then & made a growling noise, but it is a quiet creature generally compared to Vesuvius. Unlike that Volcano, its destructive irruptions have seldom come from the top crater of the mountain—but from little craters that form themselves half way down the great hill.—Some of the Ravines at the base of Etna are perhaps the grandest I have ever seen, & I longed to study them for 2 or 3 months.—

Taormina—(the old Taurominium,) was our next halting place:—(I forgot the celebrated Chesnut trees—'dei cento Cavalli' ['of the hundred Horsemen']:—but these were rather disappointing—being I believe a groupe of trees which the poetical mind of the guide chooses to think a single stem.) This city is very interesting from its containing the most perfect remains of a Greek theatre now extant: It looks towards Etna, & the view thence—looking down nearly all the east & S. East coast of Sicily is truly astonishing. Just above Taormina on a perpendicular rock of vast height is a town called Molia— where we had heard that all the babies were tethered to door posts by strings round their waists—for fear of their falling down the precipice:—so we made an excursion there, to see for all or any such babies—but—after diligent search—none were to be found: only—just as we were giving up the scrutiny— Lo!—one solitary piggywiggy—tied by its body—& fallen just 3 feet over the edge of the rock—being the full length of its cord!———From Taormina we came to Messina, & thence to Naples—& so—I—to Rome once more—where I arrived the 26. May. (Passing through Civita Vecchia—I saw Prince Canino for one moment—also passing through but the other way: he seemed occupied about the approaching Italian reunion of science.)—

With regard to Zoology—little struck me in Sicily as very novel:—at Girgenti indeed, I was much delighted by the quantity of that brilliant bird the Roller—which flew like glittering jewels in the morning sun—round & round the old Temples:—I suppose they build there. Some very large Eagles I remarked in lonely places, & numbers of Herons, together with many birds I am too slight on Ornithology to specify at first sight. The butterflies—particularly numbers of Machaon—and Podalirius—were very beautiful—& as for flowers, the whole Island is so enamelled with them that it appears as one great Garden.—

I am now going on to finish some little pictures begun before I left here for Sicily, & when I have finished them, I shall endeavour to get to Frascati or some place near Rome for the hot summer months. Sadly shall I sigh for some English faces, but I shall live upon letters in the place of persons. I should much like to know—when anyone writes from Knowsley—(for

I dare not ask your Lordship—(knowing how much you always have on hand)—for a letter,—though it would please me more than I can express,) to learn if the green plot before the Stillroom window & up to the trees by the Chapel, is yet turned into a Flower garden:—and if my unprincipled friend the Chough is still alive & proceeding in his old habits.—I do hope this long scrawl will not have tired your Lordship—but I have written it in order to amuse, & therefore I know its tediousness will be forgiven. Please to give my best respects & remembrances to all my kind Lancashire friends, & to say to Lady Charlotte that I am now going on with her sketch.—

Wishing your Lordship a long long continuance of the health you now have—, believe me, | My Lord, | Ever your Lordship's, | Most gratefully & respectfully,

Edward Lear.

To John Gould

107. Via Felice. Roma. | August 12. 1844

Dear Gould,

I often think I am very wrong in not having ever written to you since I left England, so I am determined to send you a scrawl now:—and I shall hope you will find time to send half a page to an old friend who very frequently thinks of you.—(Now for goodness sake—don't send a letter written thus—

because you know I *can't* read it:—but a FEW LINES to say how you are—& what your several children are doing, would much please me: little Henry must be growing a great boy now.—Is Mrs. Coxon still living & with you?—If so—pray make my remembrances & respects.—

————It is next to impossible for me to send *you* any interesting news in a letter from Italy: you know how little I see or hear of Zoology here:—for all that, as I sit in the chesnut groves of Licenza & see the bright yellow Orioles in numbers about me,——or the Rollers in the vallies of Galera—or the poor dear BeeEaters—(Merops—) (which are greatly perse-

cuted by the peasants—on account of the bees,) about Ostia &
Ardea,—I often think of my Natural=Historical days. I don't
think you would find anything much *new* here, but if you would
ever take a run hither, I would promise you to go with you
either into the Marshes—(where, in winter are immensities of
wild fowl,) or into the Sabine Hills—for fish—(which *they say*
exist—but—whip me if I ever TASTE anything but a horrid
Barbel:—perhaps a trout once a year.)—

Last year I made wonderful expeditions°—(for I must tell you
I am *unexpectedly* become a tolerable Horseman,) to the region of
the Lake of Fucino & the Adriatic, & saw more of that country
(by knowing the Language & mixing with the people,) than
any Englishman has ever yet done—near as those places are to
Rome. I observed—as I crossed the Lake of Fucino—(the
largest in South Italy–50 miles in circumference—) numbers of
Cormorants—& a sort of Gull I could not make out. They say
the whole Lake is *covered* with birds in winter,—& this I am
inclined to credit—because all the quantities of queer looking
'covies' or 'flights' of birds who pass the Campagna in Decbr. &
Jany—always make their way straight toward Fucino. There
are a good many Eagles in the higher Apennines:—(I went up
(!!) to Gran Sasso—(the highest) 9980 feet high.) There are still
wolves,—but gradually getting scarcer, in the forests thereabouts. The oldest people hardly authenticate a bear story—
& although I made very especial enquiries, I could only set
down 2 *real* bears as matter of fact—& those of 15 years ago. I
believe however, that bears do exist over the forests of Picinisco,
only they don't visit the lowlands.—I staid at one place where
there are forests of Oak & beech more than 40 miles round:
Roedeer were there late in the year—but nothing more formid-
able.— ——

And now I must beg you to thank Mr. Yarrell very kindly
from me for a letter I received from him yesterday: will you tell
him it gives me just the information I wanted,—(just like Mr.
Y:—all *clinchers*—not a word too much or too little:——) & has
quite set me at ease about woodcutting°—which I am
convinced *could not be done here.* Poor dear owls of Romans!—why
they cannot yet black shoes or cook a potato.——Believe me,
the modern Romans—(the more that they are prouder than
their ancestors during the Republic——) are somewhat like

Saxons or Normans of the 11th. century—& yet not half so willing to learn.—I see I must go to England for what I want.—Meanwhile there are frightful rumours of War!°—(which greatly disturb our exiled selves.—If such a break-up should come to pass—I go away directly. With all its advantage for a Landscape painter—of which I can never be too sensible—Rome isn't England.—

Mr. Yarrell tells me Mr. Bell has taken Mr. White° of Selbourne's house—a bit of real news which delights me davvero davvero [really truly]. Please do not forget to thank Mr. Yarrell for his kind letter, which, for the present, I thus answer in your's—. Is Mr. Prince well?—Remember me to him. And Mr. Rees?—ditto.— & Mr. Hullmandel—& all friends.

I hope all your little people are well—&, once more saying how glad I should be to have a line from you—or see you—(which were much better—)—believe me—Dear Gould— | Most sincerely your's always,
Edward Lear. (turn over[)]

I will give Mr. Yarrell's message to P. Canino—when he returns: he is at Naples now, & as Giuseppe Buonaparte, Prince Canino's father is just dead—I dare say he will not be back yet awhile.

Please address to me—107. Via Felice. Roma. No end of big bats here in the evening! & such lots of owls! you had better come;—Rome is worth seeing, & I can give you a spare bed if you like to put up with roughness & fleas—& porcupine's flesh & snails for dinner—: good wine though.—Come. I shan't be settled here till the end of October—for I run about out of Rome this hot weather.

To Ann Lear

[In May 1845 Lear returned to England where he stayed until the end of 1846. While in England he published *Illustrated Excursions in Italy*. As a result of the book, Queen Victoria invited Lear to give her a series of twelve drawing lessons.]

Via Felice, Roma, 6th. Feb., 1847.
Dear Ann,

I will begin a paragraph of a new letter, in order to have a part of it finished before your next comes, which I suppose it will be some time next week. You see, I send you a little engraving of the present Pope Pius 9th.; it is really very like him—though perhaps hardly cheerful enough. He is also very florid in complexion. Pray show his portrait to Mr. and Mrs. Arundale.°

Since I wrote last—Feb. 1st.—it has rained almost constantly;—I never knew such a wretched season here. It is impossible to go out to walk,—and bad enough to go out even to dinner or for the evening. If it continues to rain so, I really fear there will be a second inundation before long. Today is the first of Carnival—but of course nothing is going on—it is all mud and water. I had nearly forgotten to tell you a piece of honour which has happened to me—namely, that one of the Queen's Ladies in Waiting who is here, has delivered to me a little print engraved from one of my drawings—of Osborne House,°—at Her Majesty's desire. This is one trait of many that have come under my notice that Queen Victoria has a good memory for any little condescension and kindness. I am really quite pleased with my little engraving, and shall have it placed in a good frame as soon as I can get one made;—you need not however, tell the incident to everybody;—for it would look like boasting upon my part, who have done little enough to deserve so gratifying a notice.

I have been painting since I returned on several pictures.° Two of Mr. Tatton's—small views of the Campagna, I have nearly finished, for one was half done in England. Then I am commencing one of Mrs. Earl's,—one of Dr. Henry's—one of Mr. Carter's—and a big one of my own fancy, destined for nobody in particular. But all this you must not talk about generally—or to the Arundales, because, by good fortune, I have so much more to do than I merit by my actual place in artistic repute, that such success may give rise to complaints from those who are more skilful & yet have little to do. For all this—I get but little, for these pictures are of small price. At present, owing to my expensive journey out, and clothing, and carriage of packages hither, I am very poor. I reckon that I may get £100—or perhaps £120 this year, & that is what I certainly cannot save much out of. You must remember that I work only up to May—& that the summer does not count. Still, that is far cheaper than I could live for in London, where £300 does not seem an overplus.—We must therefore be grateful on account of my publications—whatever trouble they gave me—& (what is done without trouble?—) for through them I laid by a whole £100. And when we consider that eyesight is not of long duration—laying by now is really a necessary duty. This year however, I shall not be able so to do, as you perceive.— Meanwhile I have given 10 dollars to the Irish° & 3 to the church here—& I hope as I live—if I live,—to be able to spare more in proportion every year.—

I am sadly perplexed about my dinners, now that the days are longer, & I rise earlier, so that from 8 till 6 it is too long to go without food. I am thereupon about to make a change,— leaving off eggs for breakfast, & having some luncheon at 12.

I am happy to inform you that the yellow cat whose face was like a frog, is gone away nobody knows where. I have therefore taken a tabby kitten, which is not ugly, but very shy. However, as I mean to educate her carefully, she will I dare say become rational by & bye. She eats macaroni already,—but not if it be more than an inch long. Her name is Birecchino.

Now I shall say good night, as I must go to Lady Gordon's.° The streets are always wet this year but I use strong goloshes.

10th.

I have had quite a cold in my head, & am resolved not to go out atall at night while this weather lasts. It rains faster & faster, I declare—& last night the wind & hail were awful, & I thought all the windows would come in. But today has been perfectly clear & beautiful—the 2nd. fine day only since I have returned. I passed all the morning at the Villa Ludovisci, & the afternoon on the Via Appia. As for the Carnival,—as yet I have seen nothing of it whatever. I give tea parties at home instead of going out;—your kettle holders are very serviceable. I have sent several drawings of their respective towns—churches, etc. to the families I stayed with in the Abruzzi—& every day there come such nice letters from those good people who are quite delighted with these trifling presents. You may imagine I am much pleased. My cat behaves very well. I have given her a wooden easel peg to play with, which amuses her innocent mind but she has contracted a naughty habit of playing with the window curtains, which I do not atall approve, as she tears

them all to pieces. You will be glad to hear I have done the 2
pictures I took out with me partly finished, & have already 2
orders for paintings of similar size.

13th.

Today is really a beautiful day like Thursday, 2 fine days in a
week seems to astonish everybody. Yesterday I received your
last (of Jan. 29th to 30th.)—& so I shall finish this & take it to
the post this morning before the bustle of Carnival commences.
I am extremely glad to hear you are so well & comfortable, &
that the likeness is so satisfactory. I am quite glad you went to
Brighton, for it seems so much better than Richmond for your
health, as well as that the Arundales are very pleasant
acquaintances. I was at the Knights° last evening. The Miss K.
(Miss Isabella) whom you ask after, is always on a sofa—
neither better nor worse;—but her eldest sister is fast declining
in consumption though in no immediate danger. I must now
conclude, or I shall not get this to the post. My cold is better.
Remember me to Mr. H. G. Catt° if you see him. | Ever yours
affect.,
Edward Lear.

To Chichester Fortescue

[By the early months of 1848, as the struggle for Italian unity gained
momentum, Lear was planning to leave Rome. Before returning to
settle in England he decided to travel round the Mediterranean,
making a collection of drawings from which he could later work.
Although by now an experienced landscape draughtsman, he was
largely self-taught and was aware of the limitations imposed on his
work both by technical inadequacies and by his inability to draw the
human form.]

107. 2do. Via Felice. Roma. | Feby. 12. 1848.

Dear Fortescue.

Your letter of Octbr. 25—1847—ought to have been
answered before now—& I have been going to do so ever since I
had it—but I have said to myself—'what's the use of writing
today when you haven't 20 minutes——or today when you've
got the toothache, or today when you're so cross?'—Fortescue
won't thank you for a stupid letter—particularly as his was so
very amusing—so you'd better wait—you had.—And so I

have—till I'm ashamed of the delay—& therefore I'll send off on the 18th—be the letter of what degree of badness it may.

First—glancing over your bi=sheeted epistle——thank you for your introduction to Baring:° he is an extremely luminous & amiable brick, & I like him very much—& I suppose he likes me or he wouldn't take the trouble of knocking me up as he does considering the lot of people he might take to instead.—We have been out once or twice on the Campagna, & go to Mrs. Sartori's° or other evening popular approximations together. He would draw very well—& indeed does,—but has little practice. Altogether he is one of the best specimens of young English here this winter—tho' there is a tolerably good sprinkling of elect & rational beings too.

In fact it is a propitious season: the rumours of distraction prevented a many nasty vulgar people from coming, & there is really room to move.—Among families, Greys, Herberts—2— Bracebridge, Lindsays, Custs, Dickens's, Hortons & Clives° stand promiscuous; of young ladies Miss W. Horton, & Miss Lindsay are first to my taste—& of married ones—Mrs. S. Herbert & Mrs. Clive—the Lady Woodhouse is admired— though by me not:—she is so like a wren. I'm sure she must turn into a wren when she dies.—The variety of foreign society is delightful—particularly with long names:—e.g. Madame *Pul- its-neck-off*—& Count Bigenouff;—Baron Polysuky—& Monsr. Pig:—I never heard such a list. I am afraid to stand near a door, lest the announced names should make me grin.—Then there is a Ldy. Mary Ross, & a most gigantic daughter—whom the Italians wittily call 'the great Ross-child[']—& her mama— Rosso-antico.—Of young men—Jacson & Clutterbuck, Lord Eastnor: Church°—& your Baring—are the best I know—at least at present. I forgot a divine Mrs. A. Montgomery—a jewel.—I miss the Gordons;—& my old kind friend Ldy. S. Percy° sadly—& somehow—the 6 & 30ness of my sentiments & constitution make me rather graver than of old:—also—the uncertainty of matters here & everywhere, & my now unfixedness of plans, conspire to make me more unstable & ass-like than usual.—John Wynne° neither comes nor writes— what on earth is he doing?—I perfectly agree with you on the remarks you made on the subject of religion, & I do hope my

friend J.W. is not one of the wavering—though I have heard
things now & then to make me rather sad.

And now, regarding yourself,—I heard all about your Greek
tour with interest, & that you were returned *to* England & *for*
Louth°—as you will have found by a disgusting little letter I
sent you at the end of last October. I greatly greatly wish to see
Greece—but how, & when? I wish I could have been there with
you—but that could not be—nor I imagine ever can be now.
The most important part of your letter seems to me that which
gives me news of your being so rich a man:—I can only say I am
sincerely glad of it—& I don't flatter you when I say I believe
you will make as good a use of your money as anybody.—Tell
me—for I hope you will write to me soon—where is your new
estate in Ireland——, & what is it & the house like?—Any
trees?— —May you live as long as your kind old Uncle say
I.———I long also to know how you like your new parliamentary life:—(do you know a friend of mine—Bonham Carter—
M.P. for Winchester?—(This reminds me of—'Have you been
in India?'—'Yes'—'O then do you know my friend Mr.
Jones?—))— —So pray let me hear from you.—Scott I find
has returned to England—I wonder if he got a letter from
me.—Now I am at the end of replying to your letter—& a very
jolly one it is.—So I must een turn over another stone as the
sandpiper said when he was a looking for vermicules.—

You ask what I am about:—making of little paintings—one
for Ld. Canning &c &c:—& one of a bigger growth for Ld.
Ward.° But I am in a disturbidous state along of my being
undecided as to how I shall go on with art—knowing that figure
drawing is that which I know least of & yet is the 'crown & roof
of things'.—Sometimes I plan working hard all this spring &
summer at figure drawing——sometimes I think if the
Neapolitans are all still—of going down to Apulia & Calabria
& so working out by degrees the whole of the Kingdm. of
Naples, which I have already made such efforts to illustrate. I
told you in my last, how I only *did* one of 3 provinces of
Calabria, & how disgusted I was at being obliged to return.—

Then I have a plan yet of going to Bowen° at Corfu, & then
Archipelago or Greecewards–(Greece however is in a very un-
travellable state just now,) should the state of Italy prevent my
remaining in it for the summer.—But, whether I stop here to

draw figure,—or whether I go to Apulia & Calabria, or whether I

Archipela go—

$$\left\{ \begin{array}{ll} \text{—V.A.} & \text{Archipelago} \\ \text{—P.} & \text{Archipelawent} \\ \text{—P.P.} & \text{Archipelagone} \end{array} \right\} \begin{array}{l} \text{or whatever I do} \\ \text{—I strongly} \end{array}$$

long to go to Egypt for the next winter as ever is—if so be as I can find a sufficiency of tin to allow of my passing 4 or 5 months there. I am quite crazy about Memphis & On & Isis & crocodiles & opthalmia & nubians—& simooms & sorcerers, & sphingidæ.—Seriously—the contemplation of Egypt must fill the mind—the Artistic mind I mean—with great food for the rumination of long years. I have a strong wish also to see Syria —& Asia Minor & all sorts of grisogonous places—but—but— who can tell?—Are you likely to come out again—? I suppose not—tho' I see perpetual members out here as if they didn't feel parliament a bore at all.—Tell me if there would be a chance of you for Egypt—from Octobr. to March?—O. mi. I! that would be too jolly to be possible.—I write to J. Battersby & Clowes° for the same score—but I doubt if anybody will come.—You see therefore in how noxious a state of knownothingatallabout- whatoneisgoingtodo-ness I am in.—Yet this is clear:—the days of possible Lotos=eating are diminishing—& by the time I am 40 I would f[ain] be in England once more.—

But a truce to [grow]lings & reflections.——(While I now write [. . .] & Ld. Grosvenor come in. Baring says I am to give his love to you & to ask you, 'if you aint ashamed of Mr. Hale?'————)—I should have told you that Bowen has written to me in the kindest possible manner—asking me to go & stay with him at Corfu—& I shall regret if I can't do so. I wish to goodness I were a polypus, & could cut myself in six bits.

You will always be doing me a kindness by 'sending' me such good griffins as Baring:—if you know of any Egypt hunters don't forget to tell me—if so be we be of suitable 'spheres'.— The 'sphere' general of Rome this year is political—there is no end to reports. What do you think of the Sicilians? Brave fellows are they not?—Those humbug Neapolitans don't deserve as much as the Palermitans anyhow.

Tell me how Simeon° is when you write. I heard from R. Sumner a little while back. Address to me here—107. V.

Felici—for I shall be here through March anyhow. After all when I think of the additional lot of things you must have to do & think of it will be good natured of you to write at all.

Bye the bye I have asked Baring to pay me 20 Dollars from you—for the book you had: don't you know you were to pay me at Syracuse.— —And now good bye:—*I wish you were downstairs in that little room.*—

Believe me, | Dear Fortescue — | Your's most sincerely,
Edward Lear.

To Ann Lear

University Corfu, 19th April, 1848.

My dear Ann,

How delighted I was to get your letter here—2 hours after I came on shore this very morning. To tell you the truth, your epistle has been under my bed for 4 nights—though I could not read it—nor did I know it was there, though I guessed as much; for you must know I came here by the mail packet steamer from Malta—& as there was a great hole in the cabin just under the little nook where I rolled about for 4 nights & 3 days— containing all the letters etc.—I thought once or twice there might be one from you among them, & so it has turned out. And what a cheap one! It only cost 3d!!! With it came one from Robert Hornby, & one from W. Nevill;—both very satisfac- tory—yours is dated March 28th—& you had only then received mine of the 18th when I supposed I should go by Spoleto; but I wrote on the *28th* to tell you my change of plan, owing to the non-continuance of the Trieste steamers to Corfu—& how I was obliged to go by Naples & Malta. Again, I wrote last Thursday—April 13th—from Malta—so, though I fear I have put you to a good deal of expense, you will have known all about me. I was very fearful of your being alarmed, so you must excuse my fussiness.

I left Valetta on the evening of the 15th, at 5 p.m.—I cannot remember to have left any place with so much regret after so short a stay in it. Such extreme kindness I received is wonderful to think of. But I could not live at Malta—there is hardly a bit of green in the whole island—a hot sand stone, walls, & bright white houses are all you can see from the highest places, excepting little stupid trees here & there like rubbishy tufts of black worsted. The harbours are very interesting, but I don't love the water well enough to be always boating—nor can I draw ships well enough to portray such scenes characteristically. The street scenery—so white, so bright, so clean, so balconied, is really beautiful—but there the charm ends. The tapestry in the old palace is worth a visit; I never saw such anywhere; the Armoury too is fine.

On the Sat (15th.) our very merry Naples passenger party dispersed—never most probably to meet all again. Two Sykes go to India for 5 years, their father to Germany; Col. Lockyer remained at Malta, I to Corfu, & the Webbs & Ramsays to England—& so much for Malta & Valetta.

The wind was atrociously high—but the sky bright, when we left the harbour in the War steamer Volcano; very soon, as you may suppose, I was in bed—but I *dined* first, I did—& capitally, & I am sure that made me less ill. There was amiable Lady & Miss Duncan° on board, & a Miss Burgoyne—but everybody went to bed. The steamer was most *perfectly comfortable*. Well, all Sunday, & the night following—& Monday 17th—the swell was odious, & I never got up. Monday evening it became still all at once among the Ionian isles—& a lovely evening we had—full moon. Cephalonia & Zante are charming. Next morning, 18th, we were at Patras, (a round about voyage, but the mails are so taken,) & then, passing Missolonghi, where Lord Byron died,° we came to Ithaca, Ulysses's island—& later to Leucadia whence Sappho leaped into the sea.

About 3 this morning—(19th) am—we anchored in the beautiful Paradise of Corfu bay, & here I am, in the most perfect library possible, with a bedroom to match, looking out on the calmest of seas, with long lines of wooded hill fringed with Cypresses & dotted with villas running down into the water. These rooms are in the University & belong to my very kind friend Mr. Bowen; whom I dare say you never heard of before—nor have I known him long—but he, being an intimate of Fortescue, Wynne, etc. etc., & others of my old friends, & hearing that I was coming to Corfu—wrote to me in the kindest manner & put these rooms & his servant at my disposal—be he here or not. Unfortunately, he is not here, having left 4 days ago only; but, as he is gone to Cephalonia, I am going off next Saturday in the Ionian steamer to catch him, & shall then have the opportunity of seeing Zante etc. in his company—a great advantage as he is Rector of the college here, & has office over all the Ionian islands. So you see I fall on my legs again don't I? I ought really to be most thankful for the number of friends I find. No sooner am I here than the Lord High Commissioner asks me to dinner, so there I dined today—& here come 2 more invitations! Gracious! I had need have as many heads as a hydra to eat all.

Being now most comfortably settled—(my room looks like one at Knowsley or anywhere.) I must tell you a little of the place. (And please preserve my letters now as I have very little time for journal, & may want them some day.)

Corfu—the island, is as you may see by the map—very long & narrow & close to the coast of Albania. The city was Venetian until 1780—but it has little to recommend it—narrow streets & poky houses. But nearest the sea, there is the most beautiful esplanade in the world—(on one corner of which I now look.) On the farther side is the magnificent palace of the Viceroy, (now Lord Seaton°—) & beyond is the double crowned Citadel—very picturesque—as you may recollect from the panorama, which I am so glad you have seen. This afternoon I have been wandering all about & nothing can be more lovely than the views; I never saw any more enchanting. The extreme gardeny verdure—the fine olives, cypresses, almonds, & oranges, make the landscape so rich—& the Albanian mountains are wonderfully fine. All the villages seem clean & white, with here & there a palm tree overtopping them. The women wear duck, black or blue, with a red handkerchief about the head; the men—the lower orders that is, mostly red cap[e]s—& a duck full Turkish trousers. Here & there you see an Albanian all red & white—with a full white petticoat like a doll's—& a sheepskin over his shoulder. Then you meet some of the priests—who wear flowing black robes & beards. Mixed with them are the English soldiers & naval officers, & the upper class of Corfiotes who dress as we do; so that the mixture is very picturesque.

You ask what language they speak; Greek is the national tongue; but they speak just as much Italian—for the Venetians ruled them for so long a time. Many of the tradesmen speak English. It is astonishing how little accommodation for strangers there is here; the only hotel is quite full, & poor Lady Duncan is in a wretched lodging. As for me I should have been very badly off, had it not been for my kind host. What with sea sickness & no sleep for 4 days I am so sleepy I don't know what to do, & wish I were going to bed instead of dining out;—for all that I must now go & dress. I wish you could see the sunset & sea; it reminds me of old days of Amalfi or Sorrento. I must look over your letter again tomorrow, to answer it more.

20th. Today is gloomy & cold; the climate of Corfu is very variable I believe. Last evening I dined at Lord Seaton's—the Lord High Commissioner. He is a very agreeable & kind person. Today I have taken my place for Zante—& I shall not write again till I return here—early in May. I should like to get drawings of Ithaca etc. first. I am very glad you seem so well & that you are going to Chester; when there, walk round the ramparts—but not LATE, as it is rather a notoriously incorrect place for ladies to walk in; the view is very pretty. From Wrexham to Llangollen is very pretty I believe—(for it was nearly dark when I came by,) but I am sure you will like Llangollen itself, though not so pretty as formerly. I will tell you where there is a very pretty place for a short stay—Chepstow— or Ross; I forget if you have ever seen the Wye. The Roman bank *did* stop, but went on again—I had no money there. All the money I have out of England—about £150—is here in this very room but in the shape of dollars. It is very difficult to manage money for travelling in these places. However, it seems, excepting actual conveyance money from place to place I am not to be at much expense just now. How I wish someone would pay my way to Palestine; I should like to see Jerusalem of all things. In my next I will give you an account of Cephalonia, Zante, Ithaca, & Leucadia, (or Santa Maura,) all which I hope to see. I have sent to Drummond's a little box for you; it contains a Malta filigree brooch—(a Maltese cross in shape) & a little handkerchief pin for yourself, & one of those little pins for Sarah, Mary, Eleanor, Harriett,—Mrs. W. Nevill, & Mrs. B. Hunt—if you will be so kind as to send them at any time. I will also put you to the expense of sending the 3 *letters* below to their destination; I cannot afford now to write so much, as to

either posting or time. Turn over. You see I have written an order for the little box on Drummond's—but, as Mr. Webb, to whom I entrusted it may not be in London before the beginning of June, it is of no use to call for it yet awhile. The sun is coming out—good-bye! Write, c/o G. F. Bowen Esq.—University, Corfù—as before—when you get this. | And believe me, dear Ann, | Ever affect. yours
Edward Lear.

Please cut out the 3 epistles carefully, & snip off the numbers,—having put them in envelopes, thus addressed. For A—G. Cartwright Esq., Cliff Cottage, Lymeregis, Dorsetshire—for B.—B. Husey Hunt° Esq., 2, New Inn Chambers, St. Clements, Strand.—and for C.—W. Nevill Esq. Maiden Lane, Gresham St., St. Martin's le Grand. The addresses are as big as the letters. Excuse this trouble.

To Ann Lear

Athens!!! 3! June, 1848.

My dear Ann,
    As there will soon be an opportunity of sending to England, I will write to you directly though the letter will not be long. You will wonder at seeing by the address where I have got to—& still more when I tell you where I am going. But you will be immensely pleased,——particularly at the manner in which I have the astonishing good fortune to travel.
    You must know then that Lady Canning, the wife of Sir Stratford Canning° our Ambassador in Turkey—has often asked me—(once in Genoa—8 years ago, & twice since in England,) to go & see her at Constantinople—which I was obliged to her for doing, but thought I had as much chance of visiting the moon. Now since I wrote on the 22nd. May I had resolved to make a little tour to the south end of Corfù—& did so from the 26th to the 29th, when I meant to return & wait for the next Malta steamer which should bring Lord Eastnor to make some tour—or perhaps Wilmot-Horton° would then have been able to go somewhere—or if not, I should then have decided to go alone for a little while, as I already know enough

Greek to ask for all I want. But the 29th. was a very hot day, &
though I had fixed on going to a little village San Mattia to
sleep, yet I was lazy, & at the top of the hill I debated for 5
minutes whether I should or not. At last my indolence
prevailed, & I determined to go back to Gasturi for the night &
return to Corfù on the 30th as I had first intended. But before I
got to the corner of the Gasturi road I sate down to sketch, & lo!
who should come by with a great train—but all Lord Seaton's
people—& Sir S. & Lady Canning to my infinite surprise. They
were on their way from England straight to Constantinople &
were to remain a week at Athens besides.—Nothing would
serve kind Lady Canning but my coming with the Embassy—
so Lady Seaton whirled me off to dinner—the next day I packed
up—& on the 30th I was actually bag & baggage in the private
steamer conveying His Excellency to the Grand Sultan!!! Did
you ever hear such a funny affair, so evidently without my own
will almost?—Of course everybody congratulated me very
much. Just think:—I am always with this most delightful
family—or the secretary Lord Augustus Loftus—I am at no
expense—see the finest scenery in the agreeablest way, & shall
have advantages at Constantinople none but the Ambassador's
friends or family could ever hope for.

You know Sir Stratford Canning is considered as one of the
very first living diplomatists & has been for ages in Turkey
managing Eastern affairs; he is besides a most cultivated &
amiable person, & thus this journey is in all respects very
desirable for 'your Son'. Lady Canning is goodness itself & so
are the 3 daughters.

Well—on Wed. the 31st. I said good-bye to Corfù for the
present—& was sorry to do so—. The extreme kindness I have
received there—not only from Bowen with whom I stayed, but
from all the officers & the Lord High Commissioner's family,
will always make me look back to the time I passed there with
pleasure. Besides, it is really a Paradise.

We went on board the Antelope man of war steamer—about
3 p.m., with royal salutes fired from the Citadel when Sir S. C.
left shore.—an honour I confess, I should always like to
dispense with. All night we had a most pleasant passage—for
the vessel is the nicest I was ever in—& such champagne
dinners—& what not, as were endless to tell. Early on the first

we were off Patras—& they went ashore—but I preferred staying on board. The scenery of the gulph of Lepanto is very fine, & Mt. Parnassus was still covered with snow. About 6 we landed at Vostizza—where crowds of the people came down to see 'o Kureis Sir Canning,' as they call Sir Stratford, who having been so many years known to them by his negotiations with the Turks etc. on their account is much liked by all the Greeks.

You can have no idea atall of the beauty of the dresses; all the men wear the full white muslin kilt, but the jackets, leggings & ornaments are really surprising for richness & variety. Think of the women with rose coloured velvet jackets with 2 inch gold trimmings—& long crimson & black cap[e]s. They are also most beautiful. We went into one house, where they gave us preserves & water & coffee. They seemed very nice people.

Towards night we reached Lutraki, on the west side of the Isthmus of Corinth.—On the morning of the 2nd. we crossed to Corinth, which stands above the shore at the foot of the enormous rock where the Citadel formerly stood. The interest of these places is extreme; you know St. Paul lived (a tent-maker) here for 18 months—& to this we owe his epistles. Of the very renowned Greek city there is now nothing but one ruin—viz—7 pillars of a very old temple—supposed to be 2,500 years old at least. Neither is there anything but a mass of brick work left to speak of the Roman days of empire over this celebrated place. Throngs of people came round us in the same variegated dresses when we reached the town—now a scattered dirty place, & here we got horses & proceeded to ascend the Acropolis; a very long affair. The summit commands a wonderful view of part of Greece—but it is a mere heap of desolation. It has been so continually destroyed—by Turks etc. etc. that only the walls are standing. We came down again by 2 p.m.—& hiring 2 carriages & 8 riding horses—off we set—Lord Augustus & I riding after the vehicles;—but as I had only one stirrup, & he had 2 of rope, & his servant none—we did not look very grand as the Ambassador's suite. 7 miles brought us across the Isthmus leaving to the right Cenchrea, where St. Paul made the vow. Here we found another war steamer sent to meet us, & thus 5 hours more steam brought us by 9 o'clock to Piræus, & so by 11 to a comfortable hotel at Athens.

June 3rd., 1848. I have risen as early as I could this morning, & surely never was anything so magnificent as Athens!—far more than I could have had any idea of. The beauty of the temples I well knew from endless drawings—but the immense sweep of plain with exquisitely formed mountains down to the sea—& the manner in which that huge mass of rock—the Acropolis—stands above the modern town with its glittering white marble ruins against the deep blue sky is quite beyond my expectations. The town is all new—but the poorer part of it, what with awnings, & bazaars & figures of all possible kinds is most picturesque. There are some very good shops, & a sort of air of progress about the whole place. The weather is getting rather hot. Today we are going to dine at Sir Edmund Lyons'—our minister here.

Sunday, June 4th. Yesterday afternoon we all went to the Acropolis—which is really the most astonishing monument of a great people I have yet seen. Poor old scrubby Rome sinks into nothing by the side of such beautiful magnificence. No words can give any idea of the appearance of such a vast mass of gigantic ruins all of dazzling white marble, of the most exquisite proportions—& overlooking such splendid tracts of landscape. It is difficult to keep away from that part of the city, but unfortunately we are at the other end. The King's palace is a very ugly affair—though built of white marble also.

I find another acquaintance, Mr. Church, nephew of General Church, who will probably go to Constantinople, & return with me. He tells me all the reports of disturbances in Greece, are nonsense, as he has *just been all round it.*

I wish you could think of writing a note to Mrs. Arundale, to thank her husband for a little book he gave me on the Antiquities of Athens, which is perfectly invaluable here. I dare say we shall be here all through this week; we are not to live in Constantinople, but in a palace at Therapia on the Bosphorus. Don't you long to have a letter from me full of Turks & crescents & minarets?— —I fear I give you a good deal of trouble when I ask you to send all the accompanying bits of intelligence to their respective addresses in envelopes;—only take care you don't send the wrong one to various owners. Please also send this to R. A. Hornby, Esq., Winwick Hall, Warrington, Lancashire; he may not get the one I write him, & I would not lose the chance of amusing him, if ever so little. Today we are going to church, so I leave off.

8th June——the church is a very nice little building & very nicely managed. Mr. Hill, the clergyman, is an excellent man, & Mrs. H. is celebrated for having managed to get up schools among the Greeks where a vast number of children are educated. We do not yet know when we shall leave Athens— but I believe on the 12th or 16th at furthest; so you had better write to me as before—only—(Poste Restante Corfù) for I shall hardly perhaps get any letters in time to Turkey. But if you don't mind, write one also addressed—'Care of His Excellency, Sir Stratford Canning, Ambassador Extraordinary, Constanti-nople' and I may chance to get it. But don't forget to write ALSO to Corfù—as I may perhaps miss it. I fear I have given you an immensity of trouble to cut out all those little letters & put them in the envelopes, (besides the expense). You see each is numbered, with its address attached to a slip of writing belonging to a corresponding number. Pray excuse my being so tiresome.

Today—8th—has been extremely hot. There is *no* shade whatever—no, not a bush, near Athens—& as the roads are very dusty it is not an agreeable residence. The King wears the full Greek dress & rides about often with the Queen. I wish you could see the temple of the Parthenon, or the Acropolis by sunset—I really never saw anything so wonderful. Most of the columns being rusty with age the whole mass becomes like gold & ivory—& the polished white marble pavement is literally blue from the reflection of the sky. You walk about in a wilderness of broken columns—friezes etc. etc. Owls, the bird of Minerva, are extremely common, & come & sit very near me when I draw. I am arranging with Mr. Church to start from Constantinople about the 20th or 25th July—but I will write before that. The hotels here are tolerably good—very clean, but *extremely* dear—& all the little comforts of dear old Italy—the ice, fruits, etc. etc. are quite unknown, though the climate is infinitely hotter. I shall get you something Turkish from Constantinople you may be sure. It is a 2 days' voyage from here, (by the same Antelope steamer) & all among the islands—very pretty I am told.

I hope you will enjoy your summer—& that you will get into

North Wales. I really should not be much surprised if I were to come to England before Xmas.—though I would rather wait till the spring, on account of climate. The Areopagus—or Mars hill, where St. Paul spoke—(Acts 17th.)—is a long ridge of rock below the Acropolis—& was once the centre of the town— though now only inhabited by sheep & goats. A flight of steps leads to the top & these St. Paul must have ascended—as there is no other way up; the Acropolis, with its temples must have looked much then as it now does, & perhaps no spot in Europe is more interesting. I have written a long & shambly letter—but cannot read it over.

Ever my dear Ann, | Yours most affect.,
Edward Lear.

Please keep my letters for the present—after Mr. Hornby returns it.

To Ann Lear

[Lear did not immediately travel to Constantinople. Instead he decided to tour Greece with Church and go on to Turkey later. They left Athens towards the end of June, but the tour was brought to an abrupt end when Lear became ill at Thebes.]

Hotel D'Orient, Athens. | July 19th., 1848.

Dear Ann,

The uncertain chances of getting letters while travelling in this helter skelter way!!!—I wish now I had asked you to write here instead of to Corfù—whereas I am not now going to Corfù atall again, & I have ordered all my letters to be sent on to Constantinople. *As soon as ever* you get this—write directly to me at H.E. Sir Stratford Canning etc H.B.M. Ambassador Extraordinary, Therapia, Constantinople.—& I shall get it there—for I am going to stay quietly with them for a month. You need not be atall alarmed about *fires*, or *cholera*, both of which you may read of in the papers; Therapia is on the Bosphorus—& far away from the city. I will write to you directly I get there.

I am here now, having been for some days ill at Thebes, & had I not had the best possible doctor, & the kindest possible nurse in a friend,° I might have been badly off—but I was brought here, & am rapidly recovering. It was partly fever occasioned by a combination of circumstances, & partly a regular want of a cleaning out & doctoring, after some months of either too good living, or irregular fatigue. I have reason to be very thankful that I am so well, & really, everybody is as kind to me as if I were their son; books, jelly, porter, & visits continual from all the English residents, particularly our Minister & his lady Sir Edmund & Lady Lyons.

I must now tell you something of my last tour,—which I took with a friend, Church,—a most kind & agreeable as well as learned companion. He is besides, a good Greek linguist, & nephew of General Sir R. Church, who was & is one of the great Athenian senators, & movers of the new country. We first went to Marathon, which you know, is one of the famous places in the world, as that where the Athenians defeated the Persians under Xerxes. The place like all such in Greece is quite unchanged by time, & the exact points of the battle are as exactly to be followed as those of Waterloo. A vast Tumulus still marks the site of the buried Persians.

All Greece, you must know, is *most thinly* inhabited,—& for a whole day you may only meet a few peasants. This is the way of travelling. We hire a man who undertakes to do *everything* for a certain sum a day; he finds us horses & has others for our baggage, & for his cooking utensils & for provisions & for beds: we were in all 7 horses. We start at sunrise after a good breakfast of coffee & eggs—& we travel till 10. Then we halt at some village, or near a fountain, & a tent is pitched, & in about 2 hours a most capital dinner—soup & 3 courses—is set forth!!—so you see there is not much hardship. Then we go on till at dusk we reach some village when any house does for our night's dwelling—for little iron bedsteads with mattresses are put up directly, & on these a large muslin bag tied to the ceiling, into which I creep by a hole which is tied up directly I am in it, so that no creature gets in & one sleeps soundly in a room full of vermin. I thought I should have laughed all night long the first time I crept into this strange bag, but soon grew used to it. In the morning—all is packed up & off we go again.

We went from the ruins of Rhammus, all along the coast to Oropo & so to Chalcis, that famous old city in the island of

Euboea or Negropont. (Have you a map of Greece?) Chalcis
delighted me, as being full of old Turkish houses & minarets,
the first I had seen—; you have no idea of the picturesqueness of
the people. Every group makes one stare & wonder. The houses
are very full of bowwindows & lattices, but the town is very
wretched. All the great towns—except 3 or 4—are *quite*
new—having been destroyed by either Turks or Greeks, or both
over & over again, in the last war.° They are built on no plan &
look very mean & scattered.

From Chalcis we made a tour of a week all over Euboea: no
such beautiful scenery can be found anywhere as the forests:
you ride for days & days through whispering woods of bright
green pine,—the odour of which is delightful & the branches
are full of bright blue rollers. It is more like a very magnificent
English park than anything else I can compare it to. The
peasants—few as they are, are most obliging simple creatures.
The men wear a plain tunic, but the women dress very prettily.
They bind the head with a yellow handkerchief; but plait the
long hair, & then tie it on to still longer plaits of silk or horse
hair till it ends in bunches of silk with silver tags; in some
villages they string cowrie shells all down these long tails, which
are confined by a girdle. The dress is a shift with prettily
embroidered sleeves or skirt, in pink or black—& over that a
coarse vest also braided with dark braid. The girdle completes
all. This is the general peasant female dress throughout Greece
as far as I have seen.

From Euboea we crossed to Lamia—or Zeitun as the Turks
called it; the last town of the Turkish frontier, & very Turkey in
its appearance. I wish you could see it. The strangest feature of
the place is the *immense* number of storks it contains. Every
house has one or more, some 8 or 10 nests, & the minarets—
(now only ruins) & other ruined houses are all alive with them.
The clatter they make with their bills is most curious, & make
you fancy all the town are playing at backgammon.

From Lamia we came to the celebrated pass of Thermopylae
where the few Spartans withstood so many Persians. This place
is more altered—for the sea has receded, & there is now a good
broad pass. But the scenery is most majestic—thickly wooded
rocks rising nearly perpendicularly over your head. There is
nothing very interesting from that part till we got to Thebes,

that once great Grecian city—now a mere collection of modern houses rising from heaps on heaps of ruins. Its situation—& the view over its vast plain to Mounts Parnassus & Helicon, are most surprisingly beautiful. However, it was here that I was taken so unwell, & I returned to Athens without going on to Delphi at present. I have made many drawings of great value—& hope my time & money are well spent in ensuring me a stock of classical subjects for future paintings. Whether or not you will see me in England before Xmas. is I think rather doubtful—I almost dread a winter so immediately after this warm summer; perhaps it would be better to winter at Malta—& come back early in spring. I have no thoughts whatever of going to Italy any more. But of this—time enough. My present plan is evidently plain before me.

I long to get your letter at Constantinople—so pray write directly. Perhaps this will be the best address—Edward Lear Esq., c/o Lady Canning, British Embassy, Therapia, Constantinople.—yes—that is best! & now my dear Ann, good-bye. I hope you are well. | Ever affect. yours
Edward Lear.

Send this to R. A. Hornby Esq., Winwick Hall, Warrington, Lancashire & he will send it back to you.

To Chichester Fortescue

Therapia. 25. August. 1848. Ugh!
Dear Fortescue,

Your kind letter—just exactly though what I expected,—came today—much sooner than I anticipated: many many thanks my dear fellow—& I hope I may be able to use the assistance.° I will go to Hanson's—(if I can) next week, & insert the result before the letter flits. Alas! of *my*self I can give you but a most flaccid account—greatly to be summed up in the word 'bed—'—but not wholly so. However, I have known perfect health for 11 years thank God, & if the tables are turned I must not be ungrateful: indeed I have been able to suck a large lesson of patience out of my 2 months compulsory idleness—& I hope I may be like any Lamb if ever we meet again. I continued to recover after I wrote to you—(20th. July) & left Athens in good spirits & pretty strong—(i:e—I was able to walk as far as the Acropolis slowly & with a stick,) on the 27th.—& to Alexandræ. There I speedily fell ill again but differently:— yet—when I got to Constple. I was obliged to be taken up to the Hotel in a sedan chair: (bye the bye, I was in a horrid funk—for the motion of the vehicle made me vomit horribly out of window, & the Turks scowled at me as if they thought I did it on purpose.)—

Well—after 2 days I went up to the Embassy here, & was instantly put to bed with Erysipelas & fever—& did not emerge on the banks of the Bosphorus till about August 13, & then very feebly. Since then I went ahead—but on 21—22—23d—I had bad fever fits from not minding diet—: today, as 2 days have gone & the enemy comes not again—I have hope & am an hungered. Hunger!—did you ever have a fever? No considera- tion of morality or sentiment or fear of punishmt. would prevent my devouring any small child who entered this room now. I have eaten every thing in it but a wax candle & a bad lemon.—

This house is detached from the big Embassy Palace—& is habited by Attachés—& though Lady Canning is as kind as 70 mothers to me, yet I see little of them. Breakfast sometimes, Dinner with their lunch, & home here by sunset, whereas they dine at 8. But could I look out on any scene of beauty, my lot—(which remains thus till Sept 9th.) would be luminous.— bless you! the Bosphorus—hereabouts at least——is the ghastliest humbug going!——Compare the straits of Menai or Southampton Water or the Thames to it!——It has neither form of hill—nor character of any possible kind in its detail. A vile towing path is the only walk here—or a great pull up a bare

down.—Of course——sun & climate make any place lovely— —& thus, all the praises of this farfamed place I believe savour of picnics &c &c. However I have seen but little of it so I will not go on—but lest you think ennui or illness disgust me—let me say, that Thebes & Athens shed a memory of divinest beauty over much worse & more tedious sufferings than those I have

endured here which indeed are nought but weariness now.—
My plans are these. If strong enough, I mean to try to do Mt.
Athos by going to Salonica on the 9th. Sept. & returning here,
(i.e. Constpl.) in a fortnight:—(I fear I *must* give up Albania for
prudence's sake just now as help is so remote:)——then to
Athens, doing filthy quarantine at Syra.—

26th.—I cannot but think that Greece has been most
imperfectly illustrated: the detached views of Athens &c—in
various tours excepted—(N.B. I *don't* except that vile squash of
Captn. Devereux's.°) Wordsworth's popular vol:° is all too
much for effect & has not much character I think I recollect.
Williams' Greece° I cannot recall—. But the vast yet beautifully simply sweeping lines of the hills have hardly been
represented I fancy—nor the primitive dry foregrounds of Elgin
marble peasants &c. What do you think of a huge work (if I can
do all Greece—) of the Morea & alltogether?—But my main
object in seeing Greece was improvement in sheer pure
Landscape—(hang Ruskin,)—& some of that I feel I have got
already.

What to do my dear Fortescue when I return to England
!!??¿—¿¡!—(expressive of indelible doubt, wonder, & ignorance.) *London* must be the place—& then comes the choice of 2
lives:—society—& half day's work,—pretty pictures—petit
maître praise boundless—frequented studio—&c &c—
—wound up with vexation of spirit as age comes on that talents
have been thrown away.——————or——*hard study*—beginning at the root of the matter—the human figure—which to
master alone would enable me to carry out the views & feelings
of Landscape I know to exist within me. Alas! if real art is a
student, I know no more than a child—an infant—a foetus:—
how could I—I have had myself to thank for all education—& a
vortex of society hath eaten my time.—So you see I must choose
one or other—& with my many friends it will go hard at 36 to
retire—please God I live—for 8 or 10 years——*but*——if I
did——*wouldn't* the 'Lear's' sell in your grandchildren's
time!—But enough of this—& self.

Grandchildren make me think of Baring's marriage°—which
I am so really glad to hear of, & shall write to him by this
post:—that goodnatured fellow wrote to me from England—
which I wonder anyone does—so busy as you all must be there.

I sincerely wish him a long career of happiness—but I trust you will soon follow his Example, & I keep a expecting of it.—I must leave off.

12. Sept. 1848. Salonica.

I have but a minute to say I have received the 50£ safely—with many thanks—that I got better fast & finally recovered at Therapia, that I came to Pera on the 3d Sept & lionized Constapl. for a week hard—that I set off on the 9th by a steamer, & going to meet Church at Dardenelle—that C. never came, & that I find all this country shut up, & am obliged to give up Athos & change my route entirely—setting off by Jenidze to Monastir & Ochrida tomorrow morng—& so I trust *down* to Yanina—& that I am in gt haste yours most sincerely,

Edward Lear.

To Ann Lear

Therapia, | Aug., 27th., 1848.

My dear Ann,

Here I am still you see—patience! I get better & stronger every day—& Lady Canning feeds me & spoils me in the kindest way possible. The weather has changed today—& is very stormy & windy; the waves of the Bosphorus are quite frightful & come bundling after one another up to the very door quite unpleasantly,—it has rained a great deal. I walked yesterday to Buyukdere 2 or 3 miles off, & was not atall tired; there is a meadow there with 7 huge plane trees growing in a clump—used for tents & picknicks in their shade; they are called the brothers. You see the opening of the Black sea, with the Genoese Castle at one end of the Asian promontory, but—barring the blue sea & white ships & the sky etc.—there is nothing very interesting in the view to one who has known so much exquisite scenery as I have. The walks are sadly monotonous about Therapia, which is reckoned one of the least pretty parts of the Straits; a paved towing path runs between the houses & the sea, & behind these are gardens & hills.—But no oriental trees or vegetation; you would think yourself anywhere in England, only the pretty church spires & village smoke etc. etc.—are wanting. You see I can tell you but little about the Bosphorus—& still less about the great city itself—nor shall I probably do or be able to do so after all. Of course these things are a privation & disappointment to me—but I manage to be patient as well as I can. When at Constantinople I don't think I shall move about much, at least if it be hot—but before I close this letter I will tell you all I can. I mean to get you a Brusa silk dress—which is a famous manufacture near here: they are strong & wash well: also a scarf, & a beady bag—all Turkey material— I do certainly long to be out of this land—& most dislike the thought of the 14 days quarantine. But we shall see.—

Here comes a letter from you—from Corfù—dated July 18th. As yet you did not know I had been ill. Before I leave here—(5th or 9th of Sept. I hope) I hope to get another letter. I am glad you are well, & that all liked the foolish little Malta filigree pins; I could send nothing better. I wonder what seaside you will go to. Have you ever seen Dartmoor?—I know it to be very beautiful, but can't answer for its quiet. I wrote to you from here on the 20th of this month: I hope you got it. Never mind what you read of 'disturbances' in Greece: they are all fibs—those reports: futile fibs. All the rest of your letter is very interesting, but I must keep room in this so leave off comments. I hope to go up to Pèra before many days are over, & shall write an account of all I see—for, I mean to use my short time as fully as possible. My friend Church is staying here 3 days to my great pleasure.

Aug. 31st. 1848. I have some more to tell you worth writing—& I will trouble you to send a letter to Mr. R. A. Hornby Esq., Winwick Hall, Warrington, Lancashire, who will send it back as before—: I can't find time to write twice what I now begin. First though let me tell you that I am immensely stronger & better—indeed quite well now; the weather is again delightful—. Monday the 28th I took a long walk, but Tuesday, the first day of the Bairam or 3 day's fête after the 28 days' fast—is the subject of this page.

On returning to Monday evening—Lady Canning told me that they were all going to Constantinople in their own steamer—to see the Sultan go in procession to & from the Mosque of St. Sophia—& also that they were permitted (I believe the first Christians ever allowed to do so) to see the great ceremony of 'foot kissing' in the second court of the Sergalio. If I could rise at 4 I would go too—& so I determined to try.

Before 5 next morning—(30th) we were all on board—& the Bosphorus—which I have quite changed my opinion about— really was delightful. I only saw it before when so ill I could not admire anything—but now the hills covered with pine & cypress—& the innumerable villas & palaces on the water's edge quite delight me. As we came near the city—it is astonishing what a beautiful effect all the snow white domes & minarets have rising from the water; there can be no place so strange & lovely. We were stunned by salutes of cannon on arriving, & too glad to get on shore—where 6 guards met us—& our own 2—made a fierce party. The Ambassador's family never move out without one of these guards—Kivass—a state of magnificence—rather tiresome than otherwise.

Constantinople is much more oriental in character than Pèra the Frank quarter, & the costumes are more picturesque. The streets are narrow—but far cleaner than I had expected. We walked up—& just outside the Seraglio walls some beautiful groves of cypress pleased me greatly. The enormous pile of building called 'Seraglio' is the work of hundreds of years—& many Caliphs—it stands where the old Byzantium Emperors had their palace. First we entered the court no 1. where a double line of military were drawn up in order from the gate to the Mosque, & that of the 2nd. court. All around were immense numbers of horses & grooms; the dressings & housings of the horses rich beyond description. We had only just time to rush up into a room close to the gate the Sultan returns by, when the procession began; I was close to the window & saw everything capitally.

First came scores & scores & scores of officers of state— generals etc. etc. on superb horses—whose hangings of velvet & gold beat anything I ever saw. The generals themselves are in modern uniform—but with many jewels. Pages & grooms— (who spoil the effect of the procession by not keeping in line, as the horses prance about,) walk by each horse,—& at intervals walk Masters of Ceremonies in scarlet & gold. After this lasted a long time—there was a space—& then came 2 by 2 on horse back—all the Pashas—: (there is a great silence in all this—& it is very like a funeral for solemnity.) The Pashas have a magnificent bunch of diamonds in their scarlet caps—& their blue uniform is most richly embroidered in gold. It is very interesting to see many well known persons—such as Rifat Pasha—Halil Pasha—the [. . . . . .]—& above all Reschid Pasha the present Grand Vizier–who rode last of all.

A long space followed. Then 3 fine horses—all strapped with gold & silver—then a long space again—& a dead silence; & lastly—surrounded by scarlet & gold dressed guards, with halberts or pikes, & carrying most wonderous crescent like plumes of green & white feathers—rode the Grand Seignor himself as if he were in a grove of beautiful birds. I can't say much for His Sublimity's appearance. He is about 25—of a mild—but worn out look—as if he cared for nothing or nobody. Wrapped in long blue cloak—he looked positively shabby.—A great shout from all the troops announced his passage—& then all was still again—he himself notices nobody; it is not etiquette.

We then descended & followed the procession with a vast crowd—& so to the 2nd. court—a great space surrounded by various strange & fine buildings—one a Kiosk or villa— opposite the dark entrance to which troops were drawn in a half moon. On the threshold, was a throne of gold tissue—& all around were the infinity of Pashas, generals, etc. etc.—whose horses were all left outside the court. We got an elevated place & saw it all distinctly. The chief Emir—next in blood to the Sultan's family—clad in green from top to toe—came before the throne—& offered incense—(after we had waited an hour or more though) & then he stood there like a statue.

Presently the music struck up, & the Sultan dashed out of the dark Kiosk, & sat down on the throne, but rose again instantly & stood upright. Then the green man rushed towards him & went down on the ground—& so he did 3 times; then reading a line or 2 from the Koran off he went & down sat the Sultan, surrounded by innumerable officers & only distinguishable by a high feather in his cap & a mass of diamonds. After that for a mortal hour or more filed away the Pashas & generals & colonels—in a most endless circle. The first kissed his foot while he stood; the second rank he sat down to & the last only threw some dust on their heads.

When this was all over (& I was glad it was) the Ulema or Priesthood passed in review; these were very interesting from the costumes of the orders. First, the Sheikh-Ul-Islam—the head of the religion—in white & gold robes—& such a big green turban! He made a dash at the Sultan (who stood,) like the Emir & fell apoplectically at his feet 3 times—going out afterwards sideways like a crab. Then came endless grass green robed priests with white & gold turbans; these the Sultan received sitting. Next, gray priests—& then purple—& lastly blue. After all these other inferior officers passed by—till the Sultan rose, & shot into the Kiosk all of a sudden, & the troops roared out Allah something. It was over. The Sultan never moved a muscle of his face or a limb—like an automaton he was. I never saw so grand a spectacle for novelty—& magnificence. You know how I dislike these shows usually—but this I would not have lost—as it gave one a wonderful idea of the Barbaric despot sort of thing one has read of from a child. Sir S. Canning however, tells me there is no splendour now compared with that of former days.

We were all glad to get back to the boat & the steamer & lunch. The party went on shore—but I remained on board, as that was a good day's work for me. At 4 they came back, & we dined, & by 6-30 we were all back at Therapia. I can't tell when I passed so delightful & novel a day—& after a long illness, one is so thankful for a change.

There have been 2 more fires since I wrote; they only burn the houses, & it seems no life is ever lost.—Tomorrow Sept. 1st.—I leave this kind family & go to Pèra, to lionise the city a little, though I shall be very careful of fatigue. Next Sat. week—the 9th.—I propose going with Church to Salonica, & Mt. Athos—a most curious place I have long wished to see—& I shall send a letter here for you, to be forwarded. Afterwards if I am strong, I may go to Athens by Thessaly, & Epirus & Acharnania—or I may return here & go straight in a steamer. So, do not write here any more—but Post Restante—Athenès. But I would not write before the first week in Oct.—because you see I cannot get it before I go to Athens myself, & it is no good to leave it at the post office so long. Nor can you, after my Salonica letter—hear from me for a good bit.—If I should have any return of fever, I should come back here, & write; but if you do not hear you will conclude I am well—only out of the pale of post offices.

I must leave off. Possibly I will write before the 9th. if I can. |

Ever yours affect.,

Edward Lear.

To Ann Lear

[Lear left Constantinople on 9 Sept. intending to meet Church and go with him to Mount Athos. Travelling with a servant, Giorgio, he landed at Salonica but found the city cut off because of cholera. The only road open was north-west into Macedonia and, unable to make contact with Church, he decided to cross Greece and visit Albania.]

Scutari, (in Albania) Oct., 21st., 1848.

My dear Ann,

This is not Scutari of Constantinople as you may at first suppose—but in Albania—& a very different place; I arrived at it this afternoon, & it is the farthest point of my journey, whence, in a few days—I hope to return southwards. I say 'in a few days' because I cannot stir till this rain which set in this morning is over—when the weather will probably be quite clear again.

I wrote to you from Monastir in Macedonia, & I sent the letter to Lady Canning—so I hope you got it; it replied to your 2 of July 18th. & Aug. 8th.—& contained an account of my tour from Salonica up to the 19th.—from the 12th. Pray mention all the dates of letters you get from me. Meanwhile, supposing you received my last duly, I will proceed, though I fear I can give you but very little idea of the novelty & beauty of the scenes I have gone through—which have delighted me immensely & I have often wished you could see me for a moment or 2. I wish you would get a map of Turkey in Europe & Greece; the former would include all Albania, & show you my whereabouts; I think the society for universal knowledge has these maps very cheap—1d. each if I don't mistake.

But to take up my story from Monastir, I obtained several drawings of the streets, mosques etc. in that beautiful place—but I could only do so by having a police from the Pasha at my disposal, who frowned & whipped & kicked away the multitude who thronged to see what I was about—very naturally. Monastir was too cold to please me—& the high mountain immediately above it was already covered with snow.

On the 20th. we started early, thinking to make 2 days of it to Ochrida—but on arriving at Resne—there was nothing to draw worth a long delay—so we went on. The road lies or rises up a monstrous mountain, Mt. Petrina—& is like a cork screw—among forests of beech, for more than 3 hours, by which time you are looking over endless forests on the lake of Resne—a perfectly beautiful scene—but which there was no time to draw.—Soon we began the descent toward the lake of Ochrida—a vast sheet of water glittering far below, & whose oval outline is only broken by the fort & town of Ochrida on a little promontory—where we arrived at sunset, & were housed in the Han (or Khan as you would call it.)—the best there, but bad was the best.

The 21st. I passed in sketching the castle—& environs of the town—& in paying a visit to Sherrif Bey—the great man of the place to whom I had a letter. This was the first Turkish visit I had paid—but having read a description beforehand° of such formalities, I knew exactly all about it; only, the squatting annoyed me dreadfully. Until today—(3rd. Oct.) I have never seen a chair or table since I left Salonica—& have had to do everything on the ground, which is to me, perfectly dreadful.

The Bey had about 8 servants in waiting—& the usual routine of pipes & coffee was gone through; many persons were in waiting on the divans, & the richness of the dresses is really astonishing—all gold & crimson—scarcely any blue. But as Ochrida is an exceedingly out of the way place & as they are very violent Mahometans, I was here obliged to take to wearing the Fez or red cap—by means of which one may pass along the streets unnoticed; while a hat is a signal for stones & sticks. So you may fancy me so.—if you please. The few women whom one sees in these places are closely veiled like those in Constantinople—(excepting always the Xtians.—who are here very few—) & when any of the ladies of the Turks move from one place to another, they are carried in a sort of van or cart—hung round with carpets, & drawn by buffaloes—& guarded as if they were all gold.

There fell a little rain on the 21st., & I was afraid of a change of weather—but the 22nd. was cloudless so I ordered horses & made a day in the same mountain—Petrina—we crossed on the 20th. & the scenery of which I much wanted to draw. We took up a large cold salmon trout—(the fish of Ochrida are admirable.) & had a very fine day.

On the 24th. we were off early from Ochrida—as soon as I have got what I consider most worth drawing, I am too glad to go from these places—for the Hans, have little close rooms— only refreshed by thorough draughts—& generally dark—so one is out of them all day as much as possible. For the same reason, unless I am in some hotel, I travel on Sundays, as the mind is much more at liberty on horse back in a forest, than in a nasty hole, surrounded by staring people—& with disagreeable accompaniments. I must do the Turks justice however, there certainly are not so many vermin as you will find in Italy in similar places—I fear the reason is only that there is less furniture to harbour them—for your Han room contains no one thing in the world—but you sweep it out & put 2 clean mats on the floor, & there you are established. I have a wooden tubby basin with me—& so one manages ablutions as one may.

In Ochrida, as in almost all these places, there is a sort of piazza—where is a fountain & a Mosque—& a most prepost-erously large plane tree that shades numbers of houses;—these spots are really quite beautiful, & I hope one day to show you my drawing of that particular one. One of the most remarkable features in these places is the tameness of the animals;—on the shores of the lake there are literally millions of coots & other water fowl, who never move as you pass close by them—nor does the beautiful white crane—nor the gray falcon—which you may almost take with your hand. In the streets this tame-ness becomes tiresome, & you are obliged to resort to all sorts of finesses to make a good natured buffaloe get out of your way.

The views of lake Ochrida & the plain from the castle are surely most lovely—but I must now go on with our journey. I was glad to look forward to 2 mountain days—as I am now quite strong & well, but had a cold in the head then, from the draughts in that Han. The morning's ride was not atall interesting, & I began to be afraid Albanian scenery was overrated; we passed a very high mountain—but there was so much wood that one saw nothing. At one p.m.—(7 hours from

Ochrida) was stopped at a Han in a valley, & cold mutton & trout were very welcome. We had taken a guard with us from Ochrida—a folly which I wont again submit to, as it is very expensive, & not the least necessary. At 2 o'clock we set off again, & for 4 hours I never saw more magnificent scenery— though it consisted of one huge valley only—(that of the river Scumbin,)—but with such oak woods & infinity of mountains about it that I was delighted. The great feature of this country is its superb foliage. At 6 we got to a very little Han on the mountain; a fire is in the middle of the floor—& the place is very tolerably clean; everybody puts their mat round the room—& after Giorgio had made me some tea & toast, I was soon fast asleep.

Sept 25th.,—this day's march was fatiguing, but of all I ever saw the most stupendously beautiful; it is of no use describing precipices & forests, nor can language give an idea of them; but certainly even in Calabria, I never saw such magnificence. As for the wallnut & chesnut forests—& oak & beech woods—now beginning to be coloured by autumn—they are not to be imagined. Beyond all, the snowy peaks of the Bosniac mountains peeped up. Han from 12 to 2. Immense descent from 3 to 4, & then a long winding gorge by the river. Here some of the baggage came untied, & rolled off—had it been a few steps earlier, into the river it must have gone. Towards sunset, we had reached quite different scenery—a wide plain covered with olives,—& surrounded by low olive coloured hills—with high forms of mountains beyond—against which many a white minaret stood up like silver. This was Elbassan—where we were to pass the night. Alas!!—these places look so beautiful afar off—but are nought within. Elbassan particularly is a disgusting place, though very picturesque; the streets have the oddest look possible, being roofed over with old mats & sometimes vines—so that, except just over the shops or bazaars, they are quite dark. Of the 3 Hans we went into, only one was tolerable, & that had a clean room, but with no windows nor door;—the others, were as is all Elbassan— tumbled down & deserted.

I must tell you that, north of the river Scumbin, we entered a new tribe of Albanians—half Sclavonians by origin; their dress is more rich than even the southerns, as they wear a long crimson vest over the kilt of Fustianello—& over that again a spencer of scarlet trimmed with fur!! & such pistols & boxes as project from their gilt leather belts!

Sept. 26th.—I tried to draw on the ruined ramparts of the town—but was surrounded by hundreds—& as I heard the Dervishes saying—shaitan! shaitan! [devil! devil!]—I was too glad to get to the Han with only a mob & hooting—After that I choose to have a kwass or man of the police—he costs a dollar a day—but it is not possible in the towns to draw without him. There were beautiful studies all round the walls of Elbassan—& I got a great many. From one of the towers, the high top of Mt. Tomerit is seen plainly. But the people of Elbassan were odious, & the town most unclean & horrible—so we left it unregretted.

27th.—was a day of delightful progress all over one big mountain—from which at every step the long long vista of valley & river, ending in that giant—Mt. Tomerit—was really enchanting. From the summit we look north to endless plains & over the town of Tiranna—our dwelling for the night—bright as usual, with mosques & minarets—but we were not to be deceived this time—& verily—the Han of Tiranna was the worst place I ever slept in yet. How people can live in such places I can't imagine. It was so old & badly put together that one quadrill danced in any room would have made it all powder—& as the boards were about 6 inches asunder—everybody seemed to live in public. But one gets used to odd ways. A mad Dervish was my next neighbour—but he did me no harm. As for the mice & spiders—I kept them off by a mosquito net—*a most invaluable travelling companion here.* But these are trifles which only distract the attention for a few hours—while, during the day everything beautiful & novel is before one. The Mosques of Tiranna are its great boast: & really they are like porcelain—so arabesque & ornamented. I have drawn several of the prettiest.

I had a letter to the Bey—a very polite & agreeable man, & as I wish to go by Croia to this place—Scutari—instead of by the direct road—he gave me a letter to his nephew—Ali Bey—lord of that place—for which we started on the 29th. A long plain occupied all the morning to get over & till sunset—(barring time for 2 drawings I made—) we were employed in scaling the oak wooded hills up to Croia—the once famous city of the Greek Scanderbeg—who resisted the Turks for so long a time. But the great fortress has long since been destroyed—though the site of vast rocks yet remains, & is most remarkable. Croia is a charming little town all up in the sky—for such peaks of mountains as are above it, it would be hard to see elsewhere—& it takes a good 4 hours to get up to it. On the highest point is now a beautiful palace belonging to Ali Bey—& there we went. He is a mere lad of 16 or 18—but most good natured & well bred; poor little fellow. The way he showed me the contents of a common writing desk as wonderful curiosities, was droll enough. We could not say a word to each other but through Giorgio—so I drew for him—& amused him immensely by drawing a steam carriage & saying—rattlattle-attle-attle-attle—& a ship-steamer—saying wishwashsquish-squash—at which the poor boy laughed immensely. All this is only odd—because the state & ceremony about him makes such a contrast; when you see old men kneeling, & great brawny fellows looking frightened out of their lives when he speaks, you naturally suppose a superior being is before you—& are amazed to find he is little more instructed than they are. He sent me a supper of 4 dishes—of which Pilas is to my taste only. But I made Giorgio explain that I was used to dress & undress myself—& not to have 10 servants rushing about me continually; so with great difficulty I got them to quit the room.

Next day 29th.—I drew all day long about that exquisite place—& the Bey's house to boot. At 12 I dined with little Ali Bey;—do you know they have precisely the same dinner always; same sour soup—2 same Pilasi—3 same stew—4 same paste & onions—5, same force meat balls. Then away goes the tin table, & cafe is brought. I was horribly awkward at dinner, & could not get the meat & rice such a distance to my mouth; as for cramming one's fingers into the dish I really could *not*. They don't drink atall. I gave Ali Bey a pencil & some needles for his mother, which delighted the poor child. He showed me all the rooms in the Harem, noone being there—so that is an opportunity I may never have again. Here this boy is to live—doing nothing but smoke from morning till night all his life!!—

On the 1st Oct. we left Croia—& the weather looked bad, &

accordingly we had rain till 12—when it cleared up. Once in the plain again—the road was bad, & the scenery pretty—with the high rock of Alessio ever before us—; this we came to about 4—& got a lodging (vicissitudes of travel!) in the most nasty place of a Greek, or rather Albanian Xtian. Opposite is a convent, with a Franciscan friar—& there, as we must return to Alessio we will then go. The scenery of the river Drino is exquisite—up & down.—As for the scenery we passed yesterday—Oct. 2nd.—it seemed delightful—but alas! it poured *all day long*—the first wet day we had all through. But the Consul—(for we have a vice consul here—) found me a very comfortable lodging—so I am once more very well off & slept capitally last night.

My present plan is to stay here 3 or 4 days—& then return to Alessio & so to Durazzo & Berat—& Avlona, from which place—or later from Janina I will write again. I do not now intend to return to Salonica as I see there will not be time. Should I accomplish seeing all the principal places in Albania & should I be enabled to bring all my drawings safely home I shall be in a position to publish an entirely new book.° I want to try to get some of the costumes° here if I can. Meanwhile—I send you some scraps for my friends which I hope you will kindly enclose in envelopes & send for me; I also send you an order of Drummond for £5 which cut off—& get the money—& buy yourself a little map of Turkey in Europe. £1 I should like you to send to Mary° for Xmas with my love.

I think as this letter will be double, I shall send it by Constantinople—& will write hence by Malta to Mr. Hornby, & beg him to enclose you the letter—only don't forget to send it back directly you have done with it. Being in so very remote a place I adopt these double ways of making my friends aware of my whereabouts.

Did I tell you poor Signora Giovanina° was very ill? She is not likely to live—having known here as a landlady & as a most kind good woman for 10 years you may suppose I am extremely sorry to hear this, & from what I hear the next letters must bring tidings of her death. I have asked Mr. Hornby to send you a scrap (added to his letter) for yourself—Do tell me, what became of a painting of yours,—the Indian girls sending the lamps down the river: it was in existence long after we left

Highgate, for I saw it when mother was in the London house° if I remember rightly. Your little book . . .

[*the rest of the letter is lost*]

To the *13th Earl of Derby*

Cairo. Jany. 12. 1849.

My dear Lord,

I received your letter sent to me at Constantinople when I reached Janina—Novbr. 7:—I thought it very good of your Lordship to write me such a long one, & with your usual kindness in every page—I fancied myself back in Lancashire instead of being in the wilds of Albania. I had been thinking of Knowsley more than commonly during my 3 months' tour there—for—from many reasons—Albania is more like a great Zoological Gardens than any country I ever saw:—the first of these reasons is that the Turks never kill any animal if they can help it—(I wish to goodness they would kill their dogs who eat up the calves of one's legs continually,)—& another cause is that the Albanians, ever since the last rebellion have been denied the use of firearms: consequently creatures of all sorts abound & flourish.

Beginning from Salonica, the great plains below Olympus are *full of birds*: Hoopoes—numberless,—Hawks so tame that they allow you to come within 2 or 3 yards of them—eagles & vultures—all sorts of crows in multitudes—pigeons—quails—in fact it is a wide aviary, though I did not see any bird that I did not know.—When I got up to Ochrida—(beyond Monastir,) the White Egret was as common all round the lake as the coot or duck—& just as little alarmed: I should have liked much to have sent one to Knowsley—but I did not know how to get it away, & could I have done so, the Turks there would hardly have allowed me. Buffaloes are used all through Macedonia & Northern Albania—for every kind of labour. Tortoises—(Testuda Græca—) run across your path, by twos & threes. Geese are in countless numbers on every plain & in all the streets of the towns & villages, & make a horrible clamour:—they are taken out daily (like sheep) in the meadows near

Avlona &c with what I call a 'Gooseherd' who watches them all day & returns with them at night. There seem very few insects in all that country—at least in Autumn:—I only saw gnats & spiders: Neither do there seem to be many snakes—for I saw but one in all my rambles.—Farther north, towards the vast Lake of Scodra, great flocks of wildfowl are seen—for at the time I was there—(October 1,) the snow had already fallen on the higher mountains. There are also wolves, jackals, wild boars, & deer in the great forests near those parts—but I don't believe the Mahomedans kill anything but sheep & fowls.

When I was at Avlona, (west coast of Albania—) I went across the salt marshes to see a Convent on the shore—& perceiving an innumerable multitude of odd looking white stones (as I thought)—I rode up to them, when lo! they were all pelicans! & away they flew. They are very shy, & feed on the fish caught in the low pools near the sea, cavities artificaly sunk for salt=making—& for curing the Bottarga or roe of the Mullet. I never was more amused in my life than at seeing so many thousand Pelicans all together—& I greatly wished I could have dispatched some to your Lordship. Perhaps I could have got one of those—but not living—& I knew that it would hardly be worth while to do so if not alive. The whole coast of Albania swarms with all kinds of plovers—ducks—sandpipers, Herons, &c. & in many of the towns there are a great many storks. In Cimarra—(among which fastnesses I am the first Englishman to have penetrated—) I saw nothing zoological but 2 huge eagles who caught up 2 hens daily from the town to the disgust of the gun=less inhabitants. The Dogs of Cimarra are the strongest & fiercest I ever saw. I came to Janina by the 7th. Novbr. & finding a letter from my friend Cross of Redcar,—I set out to meet him at Malta—as Robert will have told your Lordship, as well as the many mishaps which occurred to me by the way.

Finally, I reached Alexandria on the 4th. Jany—& Cairo on the 6th. where I found my friend. This strange place is so remarkable that I cannot describe it,—& Lane's works° give a better account of it than I can. The camels amuse & amaze me: I rode on one—a rehearsal ride—yesterday—& was not uncomfortable: only I wish they would not roar & snarl so. When the beast turned round & opened his mouth, I thought he was going to eat me, & I nearly fell off as fast as I could. They say however that these are only harmless habits. Cross & I set out today for Mount Sinai, & I imagine I shall go on with him to Beïrout, & then, if I can possibly do so—I hope to complete a work on Albania & Thessaly—& return to England in the summer. How glad I shall be.

I dined at Mr. Murray's on Sunday—but have not been there since;—I am here for so short a time & there is so much to see that I never have a moment. The same reason prevents my writing to Robert, so I beg your Lordship will kindly send him this letter—& I will send him one from Suez on my return from Sinai. If I see Gazelles, or any creature I can easily get at, I shall not forget to make myself useful.

I am so glad to hear your Lordship is so well, & I wish you many happy new years—& the same to all my friends at Knowsley. Pray give my respects & remembrances to Lord & Lady Stanley—& to Mr. Penrhyn & Ldy. Charlotte, & at the Parsonage, & to Wyndham Hornby. I hear capital accounts of Mr. & Mrs. Hornby at Winwick—: I wish I had written oftener to Robert, but I find it *very difficult* to *settle* to write: I have however asked my sister to send him the letters I write to her.—

The weather here is always delightful——clear & perfectly bright & mild: I sit with open windows.

If Robert could send me a line to Bëirout—I should hear from him earlier than I otherwise could: I have been sadly annoyed at losing—or rather—at not yet receiving any letters from him. Pray give my love to him. And believe me, | My dear Lord, | Your Lordships most respectfully & gratefully,

Edward Lear.

To Ann Lear

The Desert: outside the walls of Suez. Jany. 16. 1849.
My dear Ann,—

Thus far we have come quite safely & with great pleasure. I wrote to you from Cairo—on the 12th—just before we were going to start, & I told you that I had already tried my camel, which conveyance both Cross & myself found admirably easy

& pleasant. I cannot tell why people write such nonsense about the East as they do: regarding the camel, you have only to sit quite still when it rises, & hold fast by the saddle—& you are lifted up on the long necked monster—& away you go *just as if on a rocking chair.*—But the great beauty of the camelriding is the size of the sort of table you sit on—made up of pillows, & coats, & carpets & saddlebags:—we sit crosslegged—or opposite each other, or we turn round—just as we please, & we lunch or read as quietly as if we were in a room. Nothing can be more charming. As for the camels themselves—I cannot say much for them:—they *are* quite harmless & quiet, but *seem* the most odious beasts—except when they are moving. The sort of horrible way in which they growl & snarl if you only go 6 feet near them—is quite frightful—& if you did not know them—you would suppose they were going to eat you. They do the same to their own masters the Arabs—& appear to have the most unsociable disposition in the world—even among themselves. I give my camel a bunch of green morning & evening—but all attempts at making friends are useless: When I put the vegetable within a yard of him, he yells & grunts as if I were killing him—& after he has taken & eaten it he does just the same.—They all seem to say—'Oh! bother you! can't you let me alone!'———& are certainly uninteresting quadrupeds as to their social qualities.—Their pace is *just* 3 miles an hour—like clockwork: If you try to make them go faster—they growl: if you stop them or try to go slower—they growl also.—They will have their own way. It is a wonderful thing to see the long long strings of these strange creatures crossing the desert—silently striding along—laden with bales of goods. One & all have the same expression—'I am going from Suez to Cairo to please you—but don't speak to me or come near me:—I shall go on well if you let me alone—but if you only look at me I'll growl—'—At night, when our tent is pitched, all the camels stride away—just where they please—looking for little thorny shrubs they feed on—till quite out of sight: but after sunset—when the Arabs call them, they all appear in 2s and threes—& are soon round the tent fires—where they are all tethered & have a lot of beans given them—& there they stay till morning. Most of them make a nasty noise as if they were sick all night long.—At sunrise, they are disturbed to be loaded,

& then the groans & grumblings begin & go on till we are fairly off—generally by 8. or ½ past.

I told you that my friend Cross had prepared everything for our journey,—but you cannot imagine what a delightful little tent we live in: there is room in it for 2 beds,—all our luggage, & a good table—so we seem in a room. Tonight it is raining violently, & we are greatly afraid we shall have the water through: rain is rare here,—but we have a great oilskin to prevent ourselves from being wetted.—Every sort of good thing has been taken for food, & our Dragoman, Ibrahim—is a capital cook.—To day, for instance, we had soup, stewed & roast fowls, & pancakes for dinner:————

—Jany. 17. 1849. I wish you many happy returns of your birthday, my dear Ann, and have risen a little bit earlier to write this on purpose,————because we are going to try this afternoon to see the great caravan of Mecca pilgrims—who should pass the end of the Red Sea about today or tomorrow, & thus perhaps I may have no time for writing.————To return to the Desert ways of travelling,—Cross & I rise about 6, & having made our 'room' ready—we have breakfast a little after 7—coffee, bread & butter, eggs & meat—. After this, the luggage is prepared for the camels—8 of which are for carrying it—The tent is struck—also the little white tent where our Dragoman lives———& in an hour or so—between 8 or 9—we are all away from our last night's abode. At first—all the loaded camels go off—one by one—straggling here & there, & I don't understand why they don't say goodbye to us altogether, for nobody could stop them if they chose to go:—however, though I said they would have their own way—yet I only meant in certain modes of their own—for to do them justice they seem to have some principle of doing their duty within their queer heads—as they are very exact in returning home,—keeping the road &c.—By degrees—they all get together, & the 'Caravan' goes slowly along over the sandy plain.

Cross & I generally walk for an hour or two at first, & he reads some of the Bible:—the desert is delightful to walk on—more like good gravel than sand. In some parts it is perfectly boundless as it were,—in others there are low undulations of sand. Near Suez you see for 2 days—the long ridges of Gebel Ataka, by which Pharaoh thought the Israelites were 'entangled in the land'.—Sometimes we see a few larks—& once a covey of sand partridges: now & then a crow or two—& also a far off vulture in the air—: these, barring some snails are all the live creatures one meets or sees—save camels, camels, camels.—At present there is a very broad track from Caîro to Suèz–formed by 2 parallel heaps of stones—& there are Telegraphs like white watchboxes from hill to hill, with a stationhouse near them, at which, if one had a ticket from the Peninsular & Orientl. Steam compy—one could purchase beer &c—but not *without* that requisite. These symptoms of civilization rather spoil the lonely character of the wide desert—but after today we shall not have even these.—

Well—towards 11—we stop our camels who make a horrible fuss while kneeling—but soon go on quietly, as we walk ahead of our Caravan. Sometimes we try—when mounted—to pat or scratch them—but they invariably turn round their heads & roar & growl as if we were sticking pins into them:—odious beasts:—so we let them have their own sulky way.—Then we go on—sometimes on camels—(& bye the bye we always lunch on bread & cold meat—oranges & brandy & water, on our moving vehicles:—we get them close together, & so pass plates or bread &c—from one to the other,——you couldn't fall off if you tried.)——and sometimes on foot—till about 4 or ½ past, when Ibrahim goes on to look for a smooth place for the tent, & one that is not exposed to the wind—& then all the camels kneel to unload—the house is made up for the night—& we have dinner at 7 or ½ past 6, after which we seldom sit up long as the day has enough work in it, tho' not very fatiguing. The weather is mostly exquisite—more like a *fine* October day in England: bright & clear—& the air quite dry: The sunsets are glorious. Yesterday however it was very windy—with pepperings of rain, & the fine ridge of Gebel Ataka was dim & misty—& so was all the region of Suez: & after I had done writing last night—a sharp shower fell—but fortunately did not last.—& as we were in our oilskins we did not get wet at all. This rain seems very rare. I forgot to tell you that all along the road there are skeletons of camels, more or less white.' And now I think I have given you as clear an account of our desert life as I can.—Yesterday at 12 we came to Suez, & encamped near the walls—by the Red Sea:—Suez itself is a most stupid place, without any interest at all—except you reckon as such the vast English Inn—for the use of the Indian Anglo passengers.—All the country before you reach the Red Sea, is strikingly illustrative of the account given of the flight of the Israelites:——but I must leave off—for it is 6:0'clock. A.M.—& the camels are beginning to growl & yell as if they were all being killed—which only means, they hear the Arabs moving & foresee being loaded.—Of the Arabs, & the Israelites' road,——I will tell you bye & bye:—Good bye:—

Jany. 18. 1849.—I was going to tell you something of the Arabs who are with us: Ibrahim the Dragoman, is a little brown fellow—very sharp & quick, & an excellent cook: his Irish stews—pancakes, & macaroni are undeniable.—Sheik Saleh the head of the Arabs is a mahogany colored man—wrapped up in a blue cloak: the others are all in striped cloths.—2 are 'blacky moors'—(but you know I never liked blackies, though you *did* make me walk round that chimneysweeper 33 years ago.°) Many of the Arabs wrap themselves in white blankets—

 & look very bundly. You must begin at the 14th. Chapter of Exodus to know our route—for we were encamped just where it [is] most probable that the Israelites were—'before Pihiharoth[*sic*]—between Migdol & the sea'—which locality seems very plainly fixed. Because if the multitude came from On—or Succoth—it seems impossible for them to have gone any other way than by Migdol—now Migdola on the way to the 'end of the ridge'—(so Pihiharoth means)—which is now Ataka a long ridge of mountains projecting into the Red Sea—& *round* which there is no pass. There is another theory of their passing the sea—far below Pihiharoth, which would tell just as well for the *land* journey—but as the sea is there *12 or 13 miles* broad, so great a number could not have gone over & have been followed by Pharaoh's army—*all within one night*—the time named by the Scriptures.—Whereas at Suez—the channel is but 2 or 3 miles broad.—

We left Suez yesterday morning, but when we got to the head of the gulph—we found the Pilgrims from Mecca were not expected for some days—so we gave up all idea of waiting for them—& turned south—following the Israelites journey. We saw one large vulture—the only living creature in the day. Towards Evening, we reached the Ajün Mousa—or 'the Wells of Moses'—a place supposed by tradition to have been just stopped at by the Israelites to fill their waterskins—since they are said to have gone '3 days in the Wilderness to (Howara) Mara.'—There was a good deal of spitting rain & cloud all yesterday, but a little nook we stopped at was quiet & pleasant.—To day—18th.—we have come on through a most wide bare desert—& have had a good deal of rain mixed with sand—so that the mountains & the sea have been equally hidden from us. We are now encamped in Wady Wardan—& I hope the tent mayn't fly away before morning—the wind is so high—but it is not cold or wet. Cross is the very essence of kindness to me, & full of care for fear I should be ill—which if good living & comfort can prevent, will surely do so.—I shall now say goodbye—& I don't think I shall go on till the 23rd or 24th when we hope to reach Mount Sinai.

January. 30th. 1849.—You see my dear Ann, that our journey has far advanced, though I have not been able to find time to write you a daily journal—but as I hope to send this from Suez, it must go—though I fear it will have a scanty supply of intelligence as to our late doings—But when I tell you that I have been quite well, & that I have been 3 days at the Convent of Mt. Sinai—that we have had lovely weather always—one day excepting,—that we are now on our return northwards, & that as yet I have been extremely delighted with our expedition—this is I know what you will chiefly desire to learn. This evening I will endeavour to fill up this sheet, & if I have not time to send another, you must put the cause to my being rather sleepy, & to my fingers being now & then a little nipped with cold. 6.A.M

February 1. 1849—On the 19th. January—we encamped near Wady Ghurundel—having passed the well of Bitter water called Howara. The 'Wady' means 'watercourse', & these are very shallow at first—but as we approached the higher mountains—they are torrents in the seasons of rain. There was a little water in Wady Wardan, but all the rest were dry. The scenery became beautiful as we went on.—i.e.—the form &

colors of the mountains on our left—all the rest is sand & rock, but of every variety of shape & tint.

20th.—We got as far as the great Wady Tayibeh, which has a pretty little oasis of palm trees in it. All day long the magnificence of the mountains we were approaching increased, & we saw the great Gebel Serbal, which some have supposed Mt. Sinai—for no good reason that I can find. When we encamp—about 4—or 5—it is very pretty to see all the camels wandering about browsing here & there.

21st—we turned down the Wady to the sea—& a most delightful day we had on the shore: I picked up a shell or two for you—but was much disappointed not to find a whole museum of beautiful concs & volutes. There are none but common little cowries &c &c. In the middle of the day, we left the sea, crossed the plain El Murgha, & encamped for the night in Wady Badera. Here we had fairly entered the mountains, & more magnificent scenes I have never beheld. It is not known how the Israelites came up to Mt. Sinai—but perhaps by Wady Feiran.

22d. The whole day was passed in grand mountain passes, but we had a good deal of rain, in showers & storms. Wady Mokatteb is remarkable for its long rocky sides being inscribed with unknown characters: there are millions of sentences. Many suppose them to have been written by early Xtian pilgrims, & as there are 2 or 3 on the top of Mt. Serbal, this is why they fix on that Mount for Sinai. We encamped at the beginning of Wady Feiran.

23rd. After a long & tedious winding, we entered the great & beautiful Oasis—the centre of Wady Feiran—& the most wonderful & beautiful place I ever saw. There was a city there—Pharan—in all ages—& it is believed to have been the chief city of the Amalekites.—At present there are only Arabs in huts & tents. But the great beauty of the place is that it is filled up with a forest of palmtrees, & that there is a running stream in the centre. I cannot describe the place, as my paper is short—but certainly the world contains not such another for loveliness. Next day, (24th) we got to Wady Solaff—where our Arab Sheikh resides. We went to see his family, &, were present at a curious dance—but I must describe that at some other time. The 25th we crossed a high pass—El Hawy—& came to El Raha, the great plain which universal tradition has affixed as the site of the Israelites Camp, below the immense mountain—called Horeb or Sinai. The excessive & wonderful grandeur of the spot is not to be described, though I hope to shew you drawings of it—: & the adaptation of the whole scene to that recorded in Scripture is equally astonishing. I believe & so does my friend, that Leipsius, Ld Lindsay & others have chosen to fix on other places as Mt. Sinai° solely to be thought the founders of some new theory. As for Moses not being able to get up here or down there, these matter of fact modes of reasoning appear to me as absurd—if not profane—for if the miraculous nature of the whole transaction be granted, surely these quips & quirks are folly at best.—It is sufficient that these mountains have from the earliest known authorities—always been believed as Sinai or Horeb. The convent—a Greek establishmt was built in the 6th. century.—

————3d. February 1849. It is all in vain to attempt long descriptions in a journey of this kind: the half hour after pitching the tent is so completely a busy one—that nothing is done—but making one's bed—washing & SETTLING: then comes dinner—& after that sleepiness—so the letterwriting does not thrive. Today we have come over the desert from Wady Wardan to near Ain Moussa—& we are encamped by the sea: the moon is ¾ full—& the calm of the place is most wonderful. We arrived in time to bathe in the Red Sea—& pick up some shells before sunset.—We go on to Suez tomorrow, & stay there one day to get fresh fowls, a sheep—candles—wine, beer, & vegetables—Then on Tuesday the 6th—we set out afresh across the desert for 8 days to Gaza—& having done Quarantine for 3 or 4 days—we hope [to] be at Jerusalem in 2 or 3 more—i e—about the 22—or 25th. I will write from thence. The weather for the last 10 days has been *most delightful*: bright blue sky—& neither too cold nor too hot. I wish I could write more about the journey—but time & paper are short. You would not know me if you saw me, as I have a beard now as well as mustaches.—It is of no use to write to me, unless you send off a letter <u>DIRECTLY</u> you get this, addressed to me—(Poste restante, or British Consulate—*Beïrout* Syria.—)—This I think I may get, as I shall hardly be at Beïrout before March 20. Cross's dromedary we call 'Dowager'——mine is 'Miss Woolly'.—I wish I had more paper & time. Pray send this to

Robert A. Hornby. Esq.—Winwick Hall, Warrington, Lancashire: he will return it.

My dear Ann, | Yours most affectionately,
Edward Lear.

To Ann Lear

[From Suez, Lear and Cross set out for Gaza, but the weather changed suddenly and Lear decided to turn back. He sailed from Alexandria to Malta where he met Franklin Lushington, whose brother Henry was Chief Secretary to the Government. On 3 Mar. Lear and Lushington left Malta for Greece, landing at Patras.]

Athens, 4th. April, 1849.

Dear Ann,

You will be delighted to know that I have had a most delightful tour so far—having been just 26 days from Patras—(which we left on the 9th.—& whence I wrote to you,) hither. In all this time we have had *but one* wet day & altogether I do not know when I have enjoyed myself so much. My fellow traveller draws as much as I do, & we only complain that the days are too short.

From Patras—9th.—we went first to Vostizza—the road being always by the side of the Gulf of Corinth. Thence, (10th) we turned inland to the convent of Megaspelion—a wondrous place containing 200 or 300 monks—in a large cave. At the time of the revolution it was beseiged by Ibrahim Pasha, but he could not take it; there were then above 5,000 women & children inside it. 11th.—we went on to Kalavryta, & 12th. & 13th. we passed on the lake of Phonìa, where the scenery is more of a Swiss character—all black pines & snow mountains. Of course the places we slept in were sometimes very bad—mere huts—with lambs generally poking about one's bed all night; but our man Andrea makes us a very comfortable supper always—& our beds are put on the floor—, so that we never have any reason to grumble.

14th. & 15th. to Tripolizza—once the capital of the Morea—but now a mere little town; no town in Greece is more than 25 years old, all the old ones having been destroyed in the battles of the revolution. 16th. Karitena—17th. Andrizzena.

The beauty of this part of Greece can hardly be imagined;—all the exquisite plains of the coast are seen through magnificent forests of ilex & oak. At Bassae on the 18th.—we went to the temple of Apollo—perhaps the finest Greek ruin after the Parthenon. I never saw so beautiful a landscape as it forms part of. Then came our one wet day—19th.—but on the 20th. it was fine again, & we got on to Mavromati, where the ruins of old Messene are very fine; all that country is more like a rich English park than anything I can compare it with.

21st. 22n[d] we were on the mountains again—(for each of the old states of Greece is a plain—quite walled in by mountains,) on the 23rd. we reached Sparta.—The modern town seems one of the most [striking] in Greece. The landscape of Sparta is extremely grand,—a wide plain below tremendous mountains—always snow topped. 24th.—Mistra—the remains of a great Venetian town but quite destroyed by the Turks. 25th. & 26th. & 27th.—3 days' journey to Argos— where you know Agamemnon & all those people lived. The plain of Argos is astonishingly beautiful. Ever since the rain of the 19th the ground has become literally COVERED with flowers; I wish you could see them;—sometimes it is quite pink with Hepaticas—scarlet & blue Anemones—Yellow Euphorbia— Cistus—& several hundred kinds of flowers I never saw before make the whole country a garden.

28th. to Nauplia & 29th.; this was the old port of the Argive Greeks, & was made the modern capital when first King Otho came—till Athens became so. 30th. we went to Mycenae— amazing ruins—& on the 31st. came by the temple of Nemea—up to Corinth—where you know I had already been. 3 days thence brought us to Athens, & I really never remember having had so delightful a trip.

We are now going to Egina, & Colonna,—to see the temples—& then return here for 2 days, when we start afresh for Delphi & Parnassus—& hope to be in Patras again by the 22nd. of April. I shall write to you again from that place, & as then, I must lay out my plan for returning home, I shall be able to tell you about when to expect me. I do not like going by Corfu to Trieste—for the stupid war° having burst out again, one may be detained. So I rather think of spending May in Epirus & Thessaly, & crossing to the Dardanelles some time in June,

whence there are always steamers going to Malta,—& so I could get to England early in July,—the voyage at that time not being very bad generally. By missing a boat however one might be easily prevented coming so soon. I do not see that it would be of any use to you or me, that you should write to me just yet, as I cannot fix any place for post; but if you send a letter early in June—(by the 1st. June mail that is—) to Edward Lear Esq., c/o F. Lushington Esq., Malta—I shall get it directly I arrive there. Meanwhile I shall hope to find a letter from you when I reach Patras. My letter is rather a shabby one, but I am obliged to finish it for all that. I hope you are well. Believe me dear Ann,
| Yours most affectionately—
Edward Lear.

To Chichester Fortescue

[Shortly after Lear reached England he heard that Mrs Warner had died, leaving him £500. Now, with some capital behind him, he could go to the Royal Academy and be taught how to paint and how to draw the human form. In the autumn of 1849 he enrolled again at Sass's School of Art to prepare work to submit to the Academy.]

17. Stratford Place. | 20th. Jany. [1850]

Dear Fortescue
What fun!—pretty little dear——!—he got into the Academy°—he did!—yes—so he did.

You will be pleased to hear that the R. Academy have sate on my drawing from the Antique, & that I am a 'probationer'——— & on my trial till April, when the 3 drawings I have to make will be again sate on—& shall be admitted for 10 years as a student or————rejected.———Vedremo quale sarò [we shall see what I shall do].

I tried with 51—little boys:—& 19 of us were admitted. And now I go with a large book and a piece of chalk to school every day like a good little boy.—

Your's affectionately—
Edward Lear.

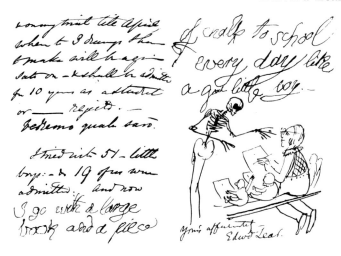

To Lord Stanley

[Lear was too old and too experienced a painter to settle into student life. By Nov. 1850 he was once more on his own.]

17. Stratford Place. | 15. Novbr. 1850.

My Lord,

I was about to write in the course of the week about that which I will presently mention, when, 2 brace of Pheasants having arrived here this morning, I will not lose any time in thanking your Lordship for thinking of me.

The subject I was about to trouble you on, was regarding a

large painting, which Lord Derby most kindly commissioned me to do for him for £100.—Lord Derby left the choice of the subject of the painting entirely to myself, & I have been hesitating for some time between Athens, or Joannina, (the Capital of Epirus in Albania.) either of them being places of great ancient & modern interest (Joannina being Dodona*) which I think is a matter to be considered in a painting of size.

After thinking & turning over some score of sketches, *I* prefer one of Athens—(which includes the Acropolis, Theseium, Areopagus, & Hymettus,)——but, I thought that before I made a little sketch of it to send to Lord Derby, I would ask your Lordship if there were any other subject you would prefer— because I could as easily make a painting of Joannina, or of Parnassus—or of many other places involving classical interest—if you particularly wished me to do so instead of Athens. Of course, it is the nature of even the smallest & most wretched of painters to suppose their works may 'go down to posterity'— which weakness will excuse my making so much fuss about what is not yet commenced.

I shall work at this picture with particular care & pleasure as much from my real desire to please Lord Derby, as that I have often wished to be able to do somewhat to ornament Knowsley, a place, to the owner of which & his family I have so much reason to be grateful.

I was very sorry to have missed your Lordship & Lady Stanley in Lancashire—but I hope to be more fortunate another time.

Pray make my respects & remembrances to Lady Stanley, | & believe me, | My Lord, | Your Lordships obliged,
Edward Lear.

To the 13th Earl of Derby

17. Stratford Place. | Novr. 28. 1850.

My dear Lord,

You will easily have thought that it has been from no want of attention on my part that I have not written since my return to

---

*at least so says Col: Leake,° & he is *the* first authority. Dr. Holland however differs.

town. The very kind letter I had from your Lordship before I left Lancashire would alone have made me anxious to do what would please you—had I not the motive of so many year's kindness & assistance to prompt me so to do.—But I had first to turn in my head about the subject I should choose—& then to arrange about a preliminary Sketch, & these matters have been much deranged by the sudden death of a very old friend—(Mr. Hullmandel—) at whose funeral also I have caught a bad cold—which 'stopped' my eyes for a time.

At last I fixed on 'Athens—during the time of Harvest'—as a subject:—(& before I did so finally—as your Lordship left the choice quite to me—I told Ld. Stanley of my selection—& he also approved of it.)—so that now, the matter will depend on your own approbation—when you see the Sketch—which I will send whenever it is done.—Of course a small design can only give a *general* idea of a large picture: many of the smaller details are always necessarily modified & arranged during the progress of the work————else—painting would be easy work.

But my idea of taking to Harvest time, is I believe a good one: because, as all the threshing is done on the plain—under the Acropolis—the groupes of figures are as *natural*, as they are picturesque in themselves, & indispensable to a good foreground in a large subject. Of course I cannot get this done for next Exhibition—the more that I shall take *immense* pains about it—as I shall do for my own pleasure, & ought to do considering who I do it for.

This leads me to say, that through Windham I have this morning received Fifty Guineas—& I lose no time in thanking your Lordship for so very kindly considering how you could best assist me.—I did not intend to have written until I had been able to forward the sketch—but I now do so at once—& shall send the design before long.

November has been *beautiful* in London:—pray tell Lady Ellinor that I think it is a lovely month—& the *most settled* in the English Autumn. Please to give my remembrances to all my friends at Knowsley————and believe me, | My dear Lord, | Ever
your Lordship's | Gratefully,
Edward Lear.

To the *13th Earl of Derby*

17. Stratford Place. | March. 3. 1851.

My dear Lord,

I hope I have not been thought neglectful in not sending the sketch for your picture earlier—but so many things have postponed my so doing that my own conscience does not upbraid me. First there was the regular darkness & fog-succeeding-fog of November & December & even later:——then there were little things to finish in the way of paintings commenced:—next—there was a good deal of trouble about the little Book I am bringing out°—not to speak of all its 20 illustrations having been finally executed by myself.

After this I became disatisfied [*sic*] with the first view of Athens I had selected—& lastly—having really settled on a view which for a large picture combines excellent requisites, I have arranged, & rearranged, & re-rearranged the subject—till I think it is as right as I can make it—though of course the sketch I send is simply the general effect of light & shade—& the form of the whole. The view is taken from the S. West side of the Acropolis—& commands more features than any other I have—namely—the Acropolis,—& to the right the pillars of the Olympæium with Hymettus beyond:—while to the left are the rocks of the Acropagus, & above them the pointed hill of Lycabettus—with Pentetieus in the extreme distance.

The time is to be sunrise or a little after, & I have avoided many figures as solitude & quiet are the prevaling[*sic*] feelings on that side of Athens. On the Northern—where you have all the modern town—there is so much bustle that the antique character of the place is lost.—I need hardly say—when, after Easter—I commence on the painting, how much I shall endeavour to make it my best. The subject is exactly what I wish to do, & I hope your Lordship will write me word if you like it:—I do not wish for the sketch, as I have made a duplicate. I send also, a 'Plate of Pelicans'—one of the plates illustrative of my new book:—I shall never forget how I laughed, (it was at Avlóna) when I saw all those Pelicans together! I enclose some notices of this little book, & am sure Your Lordship will kindly speak a good word in its favour to anyone who may be

interested in travels & scenery.—Lord & Lady Stanley have
been very kind about it—but I have not yet thanked them as the
last 10 days have been full of all other matters.

Robert wrote to me from Knowsley, & I cant remember
when he has seemed to be so much pleased:—I wish he moved
oftener, as it does him good, & I am hoping that his visit to you
next week will be equally successful.

I hear your Lordship talks of coming to town in May, so that
I trust to see you before I shall have a chance of getting again
into Lancashire. Lady Charlotte I have not seen for some
time—: I was going to Sheen on Sunday, but a violent attack of
cold & Bronchitis which I am now suffering from—prevented
my stirring from my room.

Please remember me to Colonel & Mrs. Stanley—& believe
me, | My dear Lord, | Your Lordship's gratefully | & sincerely,
                                                    Edward Lear

The sketch should be fixed on a sheet of white paper.

To the 13th Earl of Derby

17. Stratford Place. | 13th. March. [1851]

My dear Lord,

I am much obliged by your long letter of this morning:—I
wonder how you find time for so much—knowing as I do how
you have something to do all day long.—I am delighted with
the observations about the Athens sketch:—the remark as to
the small quantity of detail is true—& that I shall have a good
deal of trouble to represent on a large scale the simplicity of the
subject;—nevertheless *that* ought not to prevent my undertak-
ing it. With regard to the great mass of shade—such an extent of
quiet unbroken shadow without detail would not be *tolerable* in
999 subjects out of 1000:—but in the present case there are
certain qualities, which as far as I can judge, will prevent the
effect being liable to objection when finished:—these are, the
PERFECTLY fine forms—namely the Acropolis & its buildings, Lycabettus, & Hymettus:—these are all excellent, & if
one can by skill fasten the eye & mind on them I do not fear the

result. The white marks on the left *do* represent a shepherd & goats, & the light on the right among the rocks is either 1 2 or more figures, according as I may eventually find it necessary to make use of them. In a scene, the chief characteristic of which is excessive solemnity & quiet, it appears to me that all bustle should be sedulously avoided, although one *may* if necessary add what one pleases. Once a month or so, at sunrise I have no doubt a detachment of guards cross that hill of the Musæum to go towards the Piræus: & perhaps once in a year or two some middies° may make a short cut on returning from a ball at Athens—to their ships. But neither of these cases would add to the poetical identity of the place————especially the latter.

I shall therefore, as the subject seems in itself to please your Lordship, commence it after Easter, & if I don't think it feasible I should be sure to change it, as I am determined to make it the best picture I have done.—But I have done a larger effect now (of the same I sent—) in charcoal, & the larger it is the better it looks, because the forms, as I said before, are *so* good, that they can be relied on.

I sent with this a tracing of the subject—which shews the position of the figures better than the Chiaróscuro sketch. It is a great pleasure to find so much interest taken in it.

Please to thank Robert for his letter of today: I am so glad he is at Knowsley.—Wansfell I am sure is not proper for anybody in snow & east winds:—my teeth chatter at the thought.—I am glad to say I am much better, though still confined to the house—& I shall be yet for some time—but my coughing for an hour or so in the morning does not prevent my working at intervals in the day all day long.

Lady Charlotte very kindly came to see me 2 days ago—: I thought her looking very nicely—though she has had——as who has not?—cold.

Believe me, | My dear Lord, | Your Lordships gratefully | &
sincerely,
Edward Lear.

I forgot to thank your Lordship for sending for my book: I hope you will like it.

To Emily Tennyson

[Some time after Lear's return to England, Franklin Lushington introduced him to Alfred and Emily Tennyson.]

17. Stratford Place. Oxford Street. | December. 2. 1851.
My dear Madam,
  It seems rather late in the day to beg you & Tennyson to accept a small 'wedding present'——but on the grounds of the proverb—'never to [*sic*] late to do right'—I shall run the risk of doing so.
  I intended long ago to have done a series of little landscapes illustrative of some of the Poems°—but a thousand things have stepped in between me & my wishes,—so that, (though I hope to do them someday,) my poetic illustrations are for the present laid aside—& the matter of fact ones I shall send you to day must do duty for them in the mean time.
  The two volumes° (which I will forward by rail—) are my own drawings & letterpress relating to some of the Neapolitan provinces, & if you will give them a place on your drawing room table I shall be very much gratified.
  There have been but few weeks or days within the last 8 years, that I have not been more or less in the habit of remembering or reading Tennyson's poetry, & the amount of pleasure derived by me from them has been quite beyond reckoning.—And feeling this I have often thought how ungrateful one habitually becomes, if one does not seek to thank—in some way, however insignificant—the writer from whose mind such daily pleasure has been mixed with our existence.—
  When these superabominable (or infraabominable) fogs and cold are gone by—I shall hope to call at Twickenham, with or without Frank Lushington;—but at present the winter-world of England seems so horrible to me, that I resort to a kind of hybernating tortoise-ship as much as possible.
  Begging you will give my best remembrances to Tennyson, |
        Believe me, | My dear Madam, | Your's sincerely,
                                    Edward Lear.

To Emily Tennyson

[In the summer of 1852 Lear was introduced to William Holman
Hunt, one of the three founding members of the Pre-Raphaelite
Brotherhood, the most exciting and controversial group of painters of
the day. They spent the summer together at Clive Vale Farm near
Hastings.]

Clive Vale Farm, | Fairlight | Hastings. | Tuesday 5th. Oct.
1852.

My dear Mrs. Tennyson,

It was very kind of you to think of asking me for today's
festivity,° and had I been within reach, I should have come with
great pleasure. But I only received your note 5 minutes ago—&
even *could* I have rushed up to Twickenham in time, a friend
being here by appointment would have prevented me. I have
often thought of writing to you lately—& *nearly* came down to
Twickenham last Thursday—: but with all these neglects of
mine I can assure you I was most sincerely glad to hear of your
little boy's birth, and that you and Alfred Tennyson must be so
very happy. I hope he may live to make you both more & more
so every year.—

I was about to write to you as soon as I thought you could
think of any matters beyond the baby, and have been thinking
of a long letter to you on a subject that from time to time has
occupied me for a long while past.

Whereupon I proceed to explain, & if Master Tennyson
disapproves of your attention being taken up by reading—
why—you can easily throw the letter on one side.

I think I once said something about illustrating Tennysons
poems—so far as the Landscape therein set forth admits
of.——Many of the subjects I have arranged——though none
as yet have I thoroughly carried out—which indeed it would
require great time & labour thoroughly to do.—But I have
latterly extracted & placed in a sort of order all the lines which
convey to me in the most decided manner his genius for the
perception of the beautiful in Landscape, & I have divided
them into 'suggestive' and 'Positive': & altogether there are 124
subjects in the 2 volumes. (I have not included the Princess or
In Memoriam.) By 'suggestive' I mean such lines as

'vast images in glittering dawn'——————————
'Hateful is the dark blue sky[']——— —————————

&c &c &c—which are adaptable to any country or a wide scope
of scenery.

By 'positive'——————such as——

——'The lonely *moated grange*[']—————
——'They cut away my tallest *pines*[']——————
——'A huge *crag platform*[']—
——'The balmy moon of blessed *Israel*[']——

&c &c—which indicate perforce certain limits of landscape &
wh: I am possibly more than most in my profession able to
illustrate———— —not—pray understand me—from any other
reason than that I possess a very remarkable collection of
sketches from Nature in such widely separated districts of
Europe—not to say Asia & Africa.

It may seem rather impertinent that I can't help thinking 'no
one could illustrate Tennysons landscape lines & feelings more
aptly than I could do'——————but this very modest assertion
may after all turn out to be groundless inasmuch as my powers
of execution do not at all equal my wishes, or my understanding
of the passages I have alluded to.

My desire has been to shew that Alfred Tennyson's poetry
(with regard to scenes—) is as real & exquisite as it is relatively
to higher & deeper matters:—that his descriptions of certain
spots are as positively true as if drawn from the places
themselves, & that his words have the power of calling up
images as distinct & correct as if they were written from those
images, instead of giving rise to them. If I could prove this at all,
it would be a pleasant carrying out & sealing of his own
words—————

> 'Cleaving—took root & | springing forth anew,
>   Whereer they fell, behold
> Like to the mother plant in semblance grew
>   A flower all gold'————

—a quotation wh: if my illustrations ever 'come to anything' I
would willingly see at the head.—

If you wish, I will send you a list of the quotations I have
made—& I should very much like to hear your & his opinion
about them. I should not like anything of the sort to be done

hastily, & I am sure they had better not be done at all if not *well done*, for if badly executed or ill conceived they will

> '*Un*like the mother plant in semblance grow
>> A flower all mud[']—or all cold—or all anything

else totally disagreeable.—

If I carry out 2 or 3—& could have Tennyson's permission to fill up the whole—I cannot but think that the Engravings from such would make a beautiful edition—& thereby to parody the lines above once more——'might grow

> 'a flower all *tin.*'

But of that there is time enough to think:—nor, if there be any chance of this thought being embodied, should it as yet be buzzed forth—since I should like to produce some actually *good* work before it is noised abroad.

> 'Only to hear were sweet
>> Stretched out beneath the pine,'

& 3 or 4 more, are the subjects I am at all advanced in, but owing to the obvious necessity of working for bread I cannot devote much time to the idea, tho' I should do so were it possible to realize it, as the chance of doing so would give me a spur.

Will you kindly write to me—& tell me if I shall transcribe & send you a list of the quotations, and the subjects I have already chosen?

Now I will make an end at once of this fearful Epistle——— & with best regards to Tennyson, & best wishes for your little boy, | believe me, | Dear Mrs. Tennyson | Your's very sincerely,

Edward Lear.

please excuse this mistakeful letter.
I am becoming a Pre-Raphælite.

To *William Michael Rossetti*

Hastings. | 20 Jany. 1853

My dear Rosetti [*sic*],

I had intended to write to you from Stratford Place, asking you if you had leisure to come & see three pictures—(Venosa,

Reggio, & Thermopylæ—) which I should have liked to show
you as being the result of the inoculatory advices of your friend
Holman Hunt. But the fall of the ceiling of my lodgings put out
all my calculations, & I also thereby lost your address in the
confusion of packing & plaster. I had a few proofs of my
Calabrian Lithographs of which I was going to beg your
acceptance, lest you should think I had forgotten how
goodnaturedly you corrected my proofsheets in the Autumn:—
but this also I must put off till my return to London in
February, which I will send them to you as soon as I get settled.

The larger picture of the three, Thermopylæ, I trust you may
yet see at the British Institution,° to which I have sent
it,—though its being hung at all, or it's being hung well are of
course doubtful. I wish it were not doubtful—for I know it is
quite the best representation of Greek scenery & climate I have
yet painted.

It is difficult for me to say how much I owe to Hunt's
instruction, but I believe the effects thereof will be seen bye &
bye. I suppose you have seen the Fairlight Hill Picture° since it
is finished. In its way it appears to me absolute perfection.

Ora, mi tocca dirvi Addio. O Signore—sa niente se abbia
piovuto quâ in Inghilterra in questi mesi passati?—
È un clima per gli'anatri, per le ranocchi, per gli pesci,—ma
per gli Christiani—no. Io me ne stanco—e quasi quasi
menevado via.

Addio.° [Now, I must bid you farewell. Oh Sir—do you know
anything about whether it has rained there in England in these
past months? | It is a climate fit for ducks, for frogs, for
fishes—but for Christian men—no. I am fed up with it—and I
have half a mind to go away away. | Farewell.]

Your's very truly,
Edward Lear.

To William Holman Hunt

Hastings 9. Feby. [1853]

Dear Hunt,
    I leave here on Friday, & shall be in town on Saty,—my
sister's early quitting England° quite deranging all plans.—I

shall hardly be unpacked or settled before March, owing to the probability of being obliged to go to Devonre. with my eldest sister. &c &c.

I have not got on with the Syracuse° at all lately—there has been NO sun at all—& if you cannot tell me how the shadows of the blessed Jackdaws will fall I dont know what I shall do also the shadows of the 3 blox of stone are too similar in color,—but I dont know how to change them. Altogether I foresee the possibility of this picture being a failure & remaining unfinished, unless you can help me out of the mess.—It has been so completely impossible even to *see* nature lately—much more to paint from it, that the poor beast of painting has not had fair play. This however by no means weakens my faith as to the proper way of painting—had I been really able to follow it out. I shall try to get a small desert piece—Gebel Serbal— perhaps—for the Academy if I have time—but this unlucky moving & N Zealandism at once—quite upset all certainty.

The Thermopylæ is *not* hung well as you thought—but better than not at all. W Rosetti kindly wrote to me that he had seen it, & likes it. I told him that all the praise of colors, & its adaptation was wholly owing to you Sir, Yes sir, you sir——as I shall say to everybody else. Not but that I dare say 99 out of a hundred will blame & not praise the color—how green! how blue! how queer!—

As soon as I can, I will either call or write.

I hope your cold is better,—which is nonsense, for how should it be? This filthy black sky & east wind & cold make me so cross, that if anybody says to me, How do you do?——I answer—Hold your tongue you fool!

Dear Hunt | Your's very sincerely,
Edward Lear.

To William Holman Hunt

Mr. Barham's. Old London Road. | Hastings. | [June 1853]
Dear Daddy—

The Syracuse *is* sold, for £250.——thanks my boy to you. Tell Millais—& W. Rosetti for me.—

I am now going out—to hop on one leg all the way to Hastings.

I'm in such a fuss about S[outh]. Down Sheep,°—& shall now buy a stock of them.

Your's affly
Edward Lear.

Such a letter from Ruskin° yesterday!

To William Holman Hunt

[Although Lear agreed with the Pre-Raphaelite idea of working direct from nature, the practical problems this posed became increasingly burdensome to him. His painting of Bassae was the last on which he worked according to strict Pre-Raphaelite principles.]

Bradgate Arms. Newtown Linford. | near Leicester. | 12. Octr.
[1853]

Dear Hunt—

You rummy old daddy—do you know you have sent me a letter without any signature?—only it ends—'*Dear Lear, I am.*' However there was no mistaking who it came from, & I was right glad to have it. But how did you get my address? I suppose I wrote—but I have been so bewildered by the beastly wet that I hardly know what I do.

Your letter was a comfort even only by taking me out of my present thoughts. 'Tiers, idol tiers'°—can't come out till I come to town, but directly I do, I will have the title done IMMEDIATELY: my coming depends—I believe, on the *weather*!. But of that more anon. (I have often thought [a line and a half deleted by Hunt]. Yet your reflexions are perfectly just & right on the subject, & it seems to me that you are able to turn everything into good. I wish I were younger & bound apprentice for 7 years to you. I think with you that it *is* an artificial lie that a woman should so suffer & lose all, while he who led her to do so encounters no sha[. .] of evil from his acts. 'There's something in this world amiss, shall be unriddled bye & bye. .'—) How & why are you at Egg's?°—I thought he had gone to Italy with Dickens. You are very kind in consoling me about my woes—but I fear they are really very bad.—After I saw you I think, I went to Sussex & saw my poor friend again for I suppose the last time. Returning, I dined at Friths° & met Egg there. I then came here, as I told you, to try at the Bassae°——but in 15 days there have been only 3 fine & one of those Sunday. I began the subject small, (& it really would be wonderfully fine)—but I found my sight quite unequal to the small near foliage. So, when on Sunday week the '*moon changed*' & it seemed '*set in fine for October*', I fetched the big canvass, (from Leicester, where it has been lying,) & set to work with outline at once as I did at the Syracuse last year. Of course the next day, the 4th,—it poured torrents & did so on the 5th. 6—7th—& 8th.—all day long each day. I got oak boughs indoors, but did no good by so doing. On Monday, it was clearer,—i.e. not raining—so I had the canvass carried up & worked some hours.—Yesterday I did so again, but instantly it came down in waterspouts, & nobody coming to me, I absolutely took the 7 foot canvass on my shoulders——& walked off to the inn—a good half mile & more.—Today it rains al solito. I hate giving anything up——it demoralizes one so. If I could only get the *leaves* done, & one little bit of fern, I could get the branches & rocks easily. But the leaves are falling fast. Meanwhile I pen out: & colour old sketches.°

There is no doubt that working large improves me much, & anyhow I *could* not do it small.

F. Lushington comes here—(to Leicester sessions:) on Saturday I believe.—In the meantime, I have the pleasant reflection that by this last year, I had finished & was paid for several paintings, whereas in 1853, I have nothing done— —nor likely to be done. The Hansens° cannot go on much longer, & I must prepare for a break up.—Everything seems odious & perverse, & I see no way through the obscure.

I will write to you again before I come to town, & early in November I hope to see you if not before.——Lord! how I wish I could go back to sloshing & Asphaltism.° What of Millais?° [Do you read Ruskin's [. . . .]]* the eventful associateship draws near.—What is Antony° about?—How is Maddox Brown?° C. Church, (& I hope you & he will meet at my roooms as soon as I get back)——writes——studying Arabic, & very

---

* [This sentence is scored out by Hunt with the comment NO]

wishful to move: he says, will I go up the Blue Nile with him? I think of Athens, Spain, or Malta——if I must give up here:—but it is a wrench I do not like. Nevertheless I have not shaved my upside mouth for a fortnight.° Let me hear from you soon—for I am in the depths of melancholy & exile:—luckily the people are the nicest possible—& the place comfort itself, while all round are the utmost beauties, if only the brutal filth of climate would allow of their being seen. Last Sunday I walked to the Cistercian monastery wh: is well worth a visit: built by

Pugin. Your's affly.

Edward Lear.

Front view   back view

To William Holman Hunt

65. Oxford Terrace. | Hyde Park. | [November 1853]

Dear Hunt,

Frith's address, (wh: I forgot to give you yesterday—) is—

W. Powell Frith, Esq. R.A. | 10 Pembridge Villas | Bayswater.

What a *nice* day it has been!—The songs are gone to Cramers, to be put in hand, & I have begged for Tears idle tears to be the first done & as soon as pozzibull.

I hope you will determine to finish your picture before you start,—for there are many reasons why you should do so. A week, or two, or even a month will not make a difference as to your starting for Egypt so far as season goes,—but it is I think very important for your reputation that you exhibit the Lady of Eyelashes subject as well as the night piece° next year. They are so different that you will gain much by both being seen at once as specimens of what you can do. Pray think over this, & endeavour to complete the subject.

Yours affly,
Edward Lear.

To Ann Lear

[In Dec. 1853, Lear left England for Egypt where he planned to meet with Hunt and Thomas Seddon. Since Hunt was delayed in England, Lear decided to travel up the Nile on his own. After Lear's return to England, Hunt and Seddon travelled on to Jerusalem together.]

17TH. JAN., 1854. | 10 miles from Haon on the Nile.

My dear Ann,

It almost seems absurd to begin another letter to you so soon, seeing I sent one yesterday from Girgeh, but as we are now only 40 miles from Khenneh, (the next post town,) & as I promised to write at every opportunity, I will not lose a single one, although you may possibly get 2 or 3 of my notes all in a lump. But I also particularly wish to write to you this morning, to wish you many happy returns of your birthday, which I did with all my heart when I awoke, & do again now with my pen. I hope you may live to be immensely old, & that I may add to your comfort year by year.

I did not stay [above] half an hour at Girgeh yesterday—only just to put your letter into the post people's care;—I hope they (the letters,) go safely! Girgeh, a large town, is a tumbly down place, & so dusty!!—but I shall see it better in returning; there seem some pretty mosques in it, & as I sailed away, we thought it looked well reflected in the water. But 12 miles beyond, a town called Belliannèh is charming! such exquisite palms,—such curious towers, built for pigeons!!—I hope to draw it on my return.

I think the sunset last night was the most astonishingly beautiful I ever saw;—it is not so much *the sunset* itself,—as the sun here is so very bright;—but the half or $\frac{3}{4}$ of an hour afterwards, which is so amazing. The sky was all in broad stripes of lilac, green, rose, & amber, & it is impossible to describe the effect of this, which only lasts a short time. Before the moon rises—(which here looks *round* like a ball, & not flat

like a plate.) all the sky becomes light, & when it comes above
the mountains, I see to read or draw, just the same as by day!
This morning I have had a delicious walk—through never
ending corn fields; at times the ground was all blue & gray with
CLOUDS of pigeons; & the most beautiful little plovers &
kingfishers hop just before my feet. But what pleased me very
much, was to find a real vulgar old English *toad*! waddling in the
field!—as for crocodiles, none have been seen yet; of course you
know, that *crocodiles* are not dangerous like *alligators*; the
crocodile is very timid, & is only to be seen basking on sand
islands at a distance. The broad-bean fields are a great pleasure
to me now; they are all in full bloom;—the Arab name for beans
is Fool,—& at first the sailors used to puzzle me very much
when they pointed to the fields & said—'fool! fool!'

I am sorry I shall not be able to buy anything today for you
after all—for we shall only stop at Haou, even if we do there; but
I shall not forget the present whenever it turns up. You have no
idea what delicious summer weather it is always! so bright, &
yet with such air!—I shall now leave off, to leave room for
writing more, in case we should not arrive at Kenneh so soon as
we expect.—(Did you go to see the panorama of Mexico in
Leicester Square? do if you didn't)—Goodbye for the present.
10.AM—17th. Jan. 1854.

Evening of Jan. 18th.,—15 miles from Kenneh. Desnée. Here
we are you see, after all not so forward as we thought to be. We
have had no wind today—or only against us, so that we have
been pulled by the rope all day long:—for my part, I find this
very pleasant work, as I live on shore, walking slowly & sitting
on the bank waiting for the boat & there is always something to
look at. Last night, we arrived at one of the most beautiful
places I ever saw—Casr el Saadd. I am quite bewildered when
I think how little people talk of the scenery of the Nile—because
they pass it while sleeping I believe. Imagine immense cliffs,
quite perpendicular about as high as St. Paul's & of yellow
stone—rising from the most exquisite meadows all along the
river! while below them are villages almost hidden in palms. In
returning, I hope to pass a day or 2 at least at Kasr el
Saadd—for it is one of the most beautiful spots in the world.
Tomorrow, I trust to post this at Khenneh, though if the wind is
not fair, I must wait another day. Thebes is still 48 miles

beyond Khenneh, so you may suppose that my curiosity to see it is very great. Good night. Jan. 18th.

I am going to ask if you will kindly send my letters on, addressed to— | Mrs. James Hornby, | Winwick Hall, | Warrington, | Lancashire. I am so vexed at not being able to write to them as much as I would—I cannot write atall when the boat moves, & I am so sleepy after dinner & journal. You know Mr & Mrs. H. are such very kind & old friends that they may see anything I write to you. Just put the letter in an envelope addressed as above & they will be returned to you.

Jan. 19th. Another day of no wind! but we are now only 5 miles from Khenneh, so I shall close at once. Good-bye. |
Believe me, my dear Ann, | Ever yours most affect.,
Edward Lear.

To Ann Lear

Temple of Isis, Philæ. | Feb., 7th., 1854.
My dear Ann,

Tomorrow I set out on *my return*, & I hope to post this letter at Assouàn; I have been here 8 whole days, & am very glad I decided on not going further south, as this most beautiful place alone has enough to occupy an artist for months. We did not bring our boat up here, but, transporting a portion of luggage, beds, cookery things etc. we came here by land,—swept out rooms in the great temple, & have been quite comfortable in them during our stay. 3 or 4 English boats have generally been on the island, so we have had dinner parties, & music every evening nearly. As for me, I have been at work every day throughout the whole daylight hours, & so charming is the place & the climate that I shall be very sorry to leave it. It is impossible to describe the place to you, any further than by saying it is more like a real *fairy island* than anything else I can compare it to. It is very small, & was formerly all covered with temples, of which the ruins of 5 or 6 now only remain. The great T. of Isis, on the terrace of which (A) I am now writing, is so

extremely wonderful that no words can give the least idea of it. The Nile is divided here into several channels, by other rocky islands, & beyond you see the desert & the great granite hills of Assouan. At morning & evening the scene is lovely beyond imagination.—I have done very little in oils, as the colours dry fast, & the sand injures them; water colours also are very difficult to use. But I have made a great many outlines,° & I hope my journeys will eventually prove to have been of great service to me; in health, it certainly has been so already,—as I am now quite strong & well.—

We mean to stay 2 days at Assouàn, which is very beautiful, & then we start down the river slowly, stopping at Kom Ombos, Silsilis, Edfoo, [Esneh], & then at Thebes for some time, whence I shall write to you again. I think we shall get to Thebes about the 20th., & stay 10 or 12 days, so that we shall hardly be in Cairo before March the 25th. or 26th. Then, I do not think it would be prudent to come immediately into the English east winds,—so I shall hardly start before the beginning of April. On this account I hope you will write again on receiving this, & please do not forget to address your letters thus—Edward Lear Esq., c/o Messrs Briggs, Saunders & Co., Cairo, Alexandria. For I have heard that if letters are directed to Cairo *only*, they are not forwarded, & I am quite vexed to think I may lose your letters if they had been so addressed. I hope you are well—& I wish I could send you some of the sunshine & fresh air!!—Please tell the Hansens about me, & let me know how all of them are. It seems to me so stupid to write such a dull letter from such a place as this, but really there is so much to say, that less than 3 volumes would describe nothing, & that is why I suppose I write so badly. Every day brings heaps of people here; some friends of Mr. James Hornby's (Capt. Butler) have been very pleasant society. There are still 9 boats up the river, & 5 or 6 at Assouan, so, as far as English company goes, there is no lack of it. As for Nubians, (for Philæ is in Nubia,) I cannot say they have delighted me;—they are all so saturated with castor oil, that I am literally sick if they come near me—; besides they have rings in their noses. Bah!— —Now I shall leave off till I get to Assouàn,—where I will finish & post this shabby epistle. Dinner is ready, macaroni, turkey, rock pigeons, & pancakes.

Assouàn 9th. Here's a shabby letter! but the post goes out directly, & I do not like to miss it. I shall now come nearer & nearer to you—& am already 7 miles on my way home.

Ever dear Ann, | Yours most affect.,
Edward Lear.

To Ann Lear

[Lear returned to England at the end of Apr. On 1 Aug. he left for a two-month tour of Switzerland.]

Zermatt. Canton Valais, Switzerland. | Aug. 23rd. 1854.

My dear Ann,

You have had letters from me dated from such very queer places that I suppose & hope you may also receive this in due time;—for outlandish as is the village, they say there is a post. I wrote to you last from Thun—about the 10th—just after Bernard Husey Hunt had arrived. I hope you had my letter—pray say if you had. I think I asked you to write to me (this is my address) Hotel Cassino, Imboden, Interlacken, Suisse, & I trust to find a letter there when I return in a few days. If you have not written pray write at once, for I shall be anxious to hear how you are.

Bern. Hunt & I went at once from Thun to Interlacken, & the next day, after the long rains, the weather cleared, & has been *real summer* ever since.—For all that, I have as yet done nothing: Half the month went in travelling, & in waiting for fine weather, & the other half goes in walking & looking about us. I am however, greatly delighted with what I have seen of Switzerland, though I do not think I can ever paint it; to represent it well, it requires more hard labour than the landscape of any country I am acquainted with,—because, though there are not great distances, yet all around one is as it were on perpendicular & in & out surfaces,—filled up with innumerable details, to draw which, requires immense study.

The first day we went to Lauterbrunnen certainly the grandest valley of precipices I ever beheld,—but I still hope to be able to show you somewhat what it is like;—& went on & slept on the Wengen Alps, where I was much pleased. It is the oddest thing to find hotels in all these out of the way places!—with every luxury & comfort.

2nd: day—down to Grindelwald, a wonderful valley with glaciers, which I had never seen before—(they are like madrepore corals—only 15 to 40 miles long, & look as if made of wedding cake—) & then on to Rosenlaui, a most lovely place—the dark pines, the endless green fields, the snow alps, goats, cows, etc. etc. etc.—charming us extremely.

3rd. day (14th) a beautiful walk to the falls of the Reichenbach, up half the Grimsel pass, & to the Falls of the Aar, & hotel at Handek. 4th day (15th) up the rest of the Grimsel, over the top & down to Obergesteln, seeing the astonishing glacier of the Rhone by the way; it is like a ladies' 'goffrée' frill or ruffle—all of ice—20 miles long!—5th day (16th) over the Gries Pass & glacier—like walking on lump sugar—down to Formazza. 6th day (17th) through the valley of Formazza to Crodo & D'Omo d'Ossola—to Pie'di Mulera. I was disappointed with these vallies—as I had seen such lovely ones in Italy south. 7th day (18th) up the valley of Anzasca to the foot of Monte Rosa at Macugnaga. 8th day (19th) over the high pass of Monte Moro to Saas—a walk of great interest. 9th day & 20th through the most magnificent pass of Stalden, & up the valley of St. Nicholas to this place—& on to a hotel on the hill above it. Here we have remained & B. Hunt has left me this morning for England. We have both derived great benefit from the air & walking, & if I do not get any drawing, I shall at least come back better able to bear the winter. This valley is just below the *Matterhorn* an astonishing peak, but I can neither describe it nor draw it at present—the more that while I write, crowds are arriving,—English & American, German, French, Swiss, etc.—& I believe I must wind up my letter. I mean to stay here 2 or 3 or 4 days, & then go by degrees to Interlacken, whence I will write again. I hope to find letters from you there as well as from poor Frank Lushington.° As far as I can see at present, I shall return at the *latest*, early in Oct., unless F. Lushington comes out. I find your *slippers* very useful, & the housewife also. I shall bring you a *fish basket*, a *paper cutter*, a *spoon*, & a pair of *nut crackers*. Love to Ellen, Mary & Harriett, |

Yours very affect.,
Edward Lear.

To Henry Bruce

65. Oxford Terrace. Hyde Park. | 24. Feby. [1855]

My dear Bruce,

I write one line to thank you for your note, & for the cheque for £22 just received. Why what a thoughtful man you are!——You will, I have no doubt like the Licenza, but if you should not, you must be kind enough to tell me, tho' you *have* been & gone & paid for it with so much kind good faith.

But how on earth can you live at 64 Cadogan Pl.?—Why that is Mrs. Brookfields!—Mrs. B. asked me there last Tuesday as ever was.

I can't understand it: and I shall send this to Clapham.

Watts° is a man of whom I never heard any one who knew him speak otherwise than in terms of real liking. I have only met him twice, & those twice at dinners——when I am always in an agony & neither hear see nor understand,—unless I get somewhere where there is no candle in my eyes, nor a dish to carve.° I should really like to meet him at your house some day:—but I shan't be able to get out before May I fear. This cold kills me, & the brutal East wind which is to come is worse to bear.

As you say you have nothing to do, I hope to see you & Mrs. Bruce some day, & you can have folios° ad lib to look over.

Watt's drawings are of the most beautiful I ever saw. But you should not compare me to him, even in joke. We Landskippers are little animals.

O my! ain't it cold! I shall shortly curl up my legs & die like a disastrous old caterpillar.

Someone has just told me there is a rumour of Catania being utterly destroyed.° The Lord forgive me for wishing Bomba had been in it!

Your's sincerely
Edward Lear.

Hic jacet [Here lies]

To Chichester Fortescue

[65 Oxford Terrace, Hyde Park, 1855]

My dear 4oscue,

I came to 'leave a card' on you, as you axed me to the dinner yesterday—so here it is—

I was disgusted at being aperiently so rude to Lady Waldegrave—but I was not well from the East winds, & so completely uncertain whether I had any voice or not, that I thought it better not to sing, than to go to the piano & be obliged to quit it. I felt like a cow who has swallowed a glass bottle—or a boiled weasel—& should probably have made a noise like a dyspeptic mouse in a fit.

But I passed a very pleasant evening, & was delighted with Lady Waldegrave's perfectly natural & kind manner. I should have liked to sit next to you, but I couldn't resist moving up to my next neighbour. I came out purposing to leave cards at Carlton Gardens—so I shall do so, though I know the Lady is out, for I nearly ran under the veels of her Chariot just now:—whereby she made me a bough.

I must add that I think your room looks extremely pretty—& the Pigchr° is stunning as it hangs now. How nicely you have had the 'Morn broadens' done as to frame.—

Your's affly.

Edward Lear.

There was an old man who said, 'How,
shall I flee from this terrible cow?
    I will sit on this stile
    & Continue to smile—
wh: may soften the heart of that cow.

Whats the difference between the Czar & the Times paper?—
One is the type of Despotism the other the despotism of Type.

What is the difference between a hen & a kitchen maid?—
One is a domestic fowl, the other a foul domestic.

Why need you not starve in the Desert? Because you might
eat all the Sand which is there.

Why *are* the sandwiches there? Because there the family of
Ham was *bread & mustard.*

To Emily Tennyson

[In 1855 Franklin Lushington was appointed judge to the Supreme
Court of Justice in the Ionian Islands. His sister Ellen planned to go to
Corfu with him, and Lear too decided to make his winter quarters on
the island.]

Woodbury House. Stoke Newington. | 28. October. 1855.
My dear Mrs. Tennyson,

At times, ever since last Sunday,—I have had reproachful
twinges for never having written to you: but I have never had
real leisure, or, if I had any, I was all jarry & out of tune & you
would not have thanked me for scribbling ever so little. Not but
what I have thought of Faringford [*sic*] at all times & seasons
ever since I left. In the morning I see everything—even to the
plate of Mushrooms: then Hallam & Lionel come in,—& when

they are gone, you, Alfred & Frank begin to talk like Gods together careless of mankind:—& so on, all through the day. According to the morbid nature of the animal, I even complain sometimes that such rare flashes of light as such visits are to me, make the path darker after they are over:—a bright blue & green landscape with purple hills, & winding rivers, & unexplored forests, and airy downs, & trees & birds, & all sorts of calm repose,—————exchanged for a dull dark plain horizonless, pathless, & covered with cloud above, while beneath are brambles & weariness.

I really do believe that I enjoy hardly any one thing on earth while it is present:—always looking back, or frettingly peering into the dim beyond.—With all this, I may say to you & Alfred, that the 3 or 4 days of the 16th–20th. October/55,—were the best I have passed for many a long day.—If I live to grow old, & can hope to exist in England, I *should* like to be somewhere near you in one's later days.—I wish sometimes you could settle near Park House.° Then I might have a room in Boxley, & moon cripply cripply about those hills, & sometimes see by turns Hallam & Lionel's children, & Frank's grandchildren, & so slide pleasantly out of life. Alfred, by that time would have written endlessly, & there would be 6 or 8 thick green volumes of poems. I—possibly,—should be in the workhouse, but I know you would all come & see me.

Now:—I won't write any more nonsense, but be all statistic & beautiful common sense. The sail from Yarmouth to Lymington on the 20th. was most quiet & pleasant, & as successful a boating trip as F's & my last, or previous one, from Lepanto to Patras. At Brockenhurst, FL. went on to the Bouchiers,—I homeward,—or, more truly to speak, to my empty lodgings where 3 chairs the coalscuttle & a table are the prevailing furniture.

Since then, I have been a good deal here,——at the home of very old friends,° (6 miles from town,) the parents of a little my godchild. They are very kind to me always, & are frantic Tennysonians in many ways, one, to be continually forcing me to sing for hours at a time. Other evenings I go to some friends, Beadon° the Police Magistrate, whose house in Stratford Place is always open to me. There one learns that some are born to know sorrows above common comprehension—for their earliest friends are the Bankers Strahan &c—& in their present wretchedness, poor Mrs. S.—(left with 9 children, & by yesterday's verdict,° seeing her husband transported for 14 years,) finds a home. In the daytime I work at the picture of Philæ—which progresses but slowly. My sister Ann comes frequently & sits for 4 or 5 hours.—

I shall hardly get away before the middle of November:—& FL. who writes yesterday,—though he says nothing of any house, alludes to the Cholera having broken out at Corfû. Will this,—I think,—make any difference as to Ellen's going?— Anyhow I do not change my plans.—I have no fear of contagion, but I grieve to believe that the knowledge of that Epidemic being in the Island, will throw one more shade on the solitary pathway at Park House when Frank is gone.

I *must* go down there once more before I go,—if it is only to tell Ellen, (should it be finally decided that she stays) that I go with, & shall [. . . . . . .] her brother. But I shall only walk over from Maidstone, & not stay there. The accounts of Eddie seem no better. Frank himself is certainly *greatly improved* in health:—and if Ellen could but go with him all would seem brighter.

As for me, I have to look forward to a new beginning of life: but it is made much pleasanter than I had believed it possible by help from others, as to commissions for drawings.—

O dear! I can't write any more now for noise. But I will write again ere long.

Kind love to Alfred, & believe me, | Dear Mrs. Tennyson, |

Yours very sincerely,

Edward Lear.

To Ann Lear

Palazzo Curcumelli, Line Wall,— | Corfû. Dec., 13th., 1855.

My dear Ann,

To my very great delight, I found your letter of the 5th when I came in from walking an hour ago. You really MUST be kind enough to write *once* a week—& I will do the same, only, you must also be so kind as to let me repay you for so much expense, since I wish so much for your letters for my own benefit you

see.—I will tell you before I close this why I am particularly
glad to hear from you just now, & why even a single line is
better than none. I am so glad that you got my Dover &
Cologne letters—& that from Trieste also; I wrote rather a long
one from here, & posted it on the 9th, so I hope you will get that
about the 17th or 18th. In it I told of our passage, also very calm
& pleasant, from Trieste to this place, where we arrived on the
morning of the 3rd—& also how difficult it was for me to find
any lodgings, & how I had at last taken those where I am now
writing.

Although there has been a great deal of rain since I came, yet
it has never been cold atall, & *my cough has quite left me*. All those
who pass the hot summer here feel the want of fires, & have
them; but I should not like one at present atall. Nevertheless,
today the wind has changed, & all the heavy clouds are gone, &
the wonderful mountains are as clear as crystal; so I begin to see
the possibility of the weather being colder in Jan.,—Feb.,—
March—April—May;—at the beginning of June I think you
will see me back again in England: And, excepting that my
health is so much better already, you will be surprised to hear
that I have even now several times wished myself back again, or
rather, that I had never come.

Corfù is indeed greatly changed since I was here in 1848. The
war° has filled it with militia instead of regulars as garrison, &
the officers being all wealthy, more or less, bring out their wives
& families, & take houses, so that not a room is to be got but at a
great expense. I find the lodgings I have taken—for £24 for 6
months—the only ones I could get,—very inconvenient in some
respects, though there is a good light. But the worst is, I am so
totally alone—& this is why I hope you will write once a week. I
fear that will not be good for your eyes, but only write a line or 2.
I will also write every week, & your letters will be, I fear, at
present, the only thing I have to look for. £2–10–0 or £3 will be
the utmost expense of this—even if it went on for a year, but you
must let me pay this, & I know you will.

The greatest sadness I have is that I shall hardly see
anything of my friend. Not that his very high position here
would make a difference, but it causes him to be wholly
occupied; so that he rides out only for an hour in the afternoon.
Besides, the house taken for him would not do, so that he still

lives on with Bowen who is now a very great man, & has a splendid palace. In the evenings they go out to various official parties, & would kindly introduce me anywhere, but in the rainy weather, one must have a carriage, & that costs a dollar (5/) each time. Balls there are, 3 times a week, but you know those are not in my way—& besides F.L. & Bowen, I do not know a creature, for I do not reckon the court etiquette of the L.H. Commissioner's Palace. Thus, you see, my dear Ann, I am wholly alone. And as there is no 2 dy. post, no newspaper,—no chance calling,—no daily & hourly invitations,—I sit at home all day, almost unable to paint from very dejection. Nor have I the energy I had in former years, & when I think of the expense I have gone to in sending out all things here & in being obliged to half furnish these empty rooms, I own I am out of spirits enough sometimes. It is better you should know this I think, than that I should sham & tell you I am happy. I suffered much from loneliness in Egypt, but then I had a never ending fund of novelty & excitement which kept much distress at bay. Once or twice, finding I can be of no use to Frank, I have half thought of returning at once, but I think that would be rash & ill judged. If Ellen Lushington had come out° & they had had a home, my days would have gone by in hopes of having someone to speak to in the evening—& some distant resemblance of better hopes might have been looked at, even though I knew they were shadows & not real.—But that was not to be;—so that you see Corfù present & future, is, & is likely to be, pain. Should this not diminish I shall perhaps leave it even earlier, if I could get across to Brindisi, & on to Rome for the spring months. You see now, my dear Ann, how much you may do for me by writing frequently. Certainly I have made a great mistake in coming to settle for months.

My mode of life is as follows. I have bought a comfortable bed. And with a chest of drawers, glass, etc. etc. have fitted up a half bare bedroom. I arise at 7, & Panighiotto, the servant to whom I am to give £1 a month, gets very good coffee, milk, & toast ready. Then, I ought to paint, & do if I can, (having just begun 3 small subjects,) till 12, when Signor Stefanizzi the Greek master comes, & stays till one. I do not make much progress, yet, with the language of course. After that, when it has been wet, I have really hardly known what to do for sheer melancholy sometimes—but generally I have taken long walks—alone always; but that is of less consequence, when among the ever beautiful olives of this exquisite island. A great drawback here is the want of good walks near at hand. Only the Esplanade is there, & that is full of exercising troops, & *endless dogs*—so that I often think you could never stir out here at all. I return at dusk, & a 2/6 dinner is sent from the Mess—rather cold than hot—which I eat up alone,—& then generally go to bed as soon afterwards as I can. This is my usual day. Today is so lovely & bright that I hope to go out to Chinopiastes & draw the view thence from among some immense orange trees, COVERED with golden fruit.

Good-bye, my dearest Ann,—I will write a finish to this, this evening. Pray always say what letters you get, & the day you get them; & tell me all about yourself. My kind love to Mary, Ellen, & Harriett & to Sarah when you write. I am so glad that they are doing well. Alas! I see clouds rising in the north—so I fear my orange trees will not be visited today.

After painting a little at the 3 subjects I have commenced, my Greek master came, & when he went, I set off to Chinopiastes, 5 miles off,—hoping to draw; but the clouds were perverse, & soon began to rain a little, so that I did nothing & I believe it will be best not to think of outdoor work at present any more. The beauty of the villages here, is something not to be described, & I certainly should like to do one or 2 large paintings of Corfu°—for no place in all the world is so lovely I think. The whole island is in undulations from the plain where the city is, to the higher hills on to the west side; & all the space is covered with one immense grove of olive trees—so that you see over a carpet of wood wherever you look; & the higher you go, the more you see, & always the Citadel & the Lake, & then the Straits, with the great Albanian mountains beyond. However, I have to think of Philæ again at present. Noone has called today, so I have literally—(as usual,)—spoken to nobody—excepting my Greek master. Friday evening 14th. Good-night.

Saturday morning, 15th., Dec., I shall finish my letter now, for the post boat comes in & goes out suddenly sometimes, so that this will probably be posted today. Every Saturday I shall send off a letter—but I can imagine that sometimes 2 will reach you at once. It has blown hard all night from the north, & is very chilly this morning. I shall put on warmer clothes. I wish you a most happy Xmas. & New Year. Did I tell you all my first lot of things came safely & I only had to pay 7/ duty? Need is there of saving somehow, for expenses are great here. I hope my next may be a more cheerful letter, but I like to write as I feel.

Ever my dearest Ann, | Yours most affect.,
Edward Lear.

To Emily Tennyson

Quarantine Island, Corfù. October 9, 1856.

My dear Mrs Tennyson,

Another letter from you—& your last unanswered!—But it is not as you say—that I do not write to you; I *do* write—but I destroy what I write:—& that you will say is no better than not writing at all. Forgetting you or Alfred or Faringford is always a fiddlededeeism & impossible.—But this time there is a better chance of a letter going really to the post—for I am just returned from a 2 months' tour to Athos & Troy—& as the idiots here, hearing a report of cholera at Constantinople have put me into the Lazaretto for 5 days, I have a great deal of leisure & quiet, and moreover, thank God, I have come back better in body & mind than I have been since I left England.—But I must tell you that this sheet of paper so addressed & folded, hath travelled with me to Epirus, Thessaly, & Salonica, & all the way to Athos, whence I had intended to send it to you, (& had I gone to the top of the holy mountain I meant to have written a line from it to Alfred,) & after that to Troy: so the very paper has a sort of value on it from its very travels.—

What a place—what a strange place is that Mount Athos!—Apart from the very valuable set of drawings I have brought back, my tour there has been one of the most singular bits of my whole life. Excepting at those Monasteries in Thibet of which Messrs. Huc & Gabet° tell us, there is nothing in the world like the Athos peninsular: for the St. Bernard & St. Gothard monsteries are placed there for a good purpose & do much to benefit others: while at Mt. Athos, many many thousand monks live on through a long long life of mere formal blank. God's world maimed & turned upside down:—God's will laughed at & falsified: nature wounded and trampled on:—that half of our species° which it is the natural & best feeling of mankind to love & esteem most————ignored & forbidden:—this is what I saw at Athos:—& if what I saw be Xtianity, then the sooner it be rooted out, the better for humanity. A Turk with 5 wives, a Jew working hard for little old clo' babies—these I believe to be far nearer what Jesus Christ intended man to become than those foolish & miserable monks,° what tho' they have the name of Christ written on every garment & every wall, & tho they repeat endless parrotprayers daily & nightly.

Do you know the history of Athos—the ancient Acte?—a long mountain narrow peninsular ridge standing up in the sea—joined at one end to the main land by a very narrow isthmus wh: once Xerxes chopped through, & its southern end rising into a pyramid 6700 feet high, strictly the Mount Athos of geography. This peak alone is bare————all the rest of the ridge is a dense world of Ilex, beech, oak, & pine. From Constantine & Justinian, who gave up the whole of Acte to Christian hermits,—to the Byzantine Emperors who added to convents already built, & founded others, and down to Sultans as far as our own day—every ruling power in the East has confirmed this territory to the monks as theirs, on proviso of paying £1500 per ann. to the Porte. So the whole strange place has gradually grown into one large nest of monkery—there being as I saw 20 large monasteries, & perhaps 5 or 600 small-hermitages or chapel=cottages holding 1—2 or more of the fish & water-melon eating, prayermuttering old creatures who vegetate there, or at best, carve little wooden crosses, which I have bought you one to put on some little table on a future day.

I will not weary you by accounts of the mode of government of the monasteries—for I dare say I shall publish my doings some day or other; nor much shall I relate of Karièss the capital of the monks:—nor how my servant° was ill & nearly died: & how I was afterwards very ill:—nor a many other matters. But I can tell you that I never saw any more striking scenes than those forest screens & terrible crags, all lonely lonely lonely: paths thro' them leading to hermitages where these dead men abide,—or to the immense monasteries where many hundred of these living corpses chant prayers nightly & daily: the blue sea dash dash against the hard iron rocks below—& the oak fringed or chesnut covered height above, with always the great peak of Athos towering over all things, & beyond all the island edged horizon of wide ocean.

The Monasteries—the large ones, are like great castles—— fortified with walls & towers: within are courtyards holding churches, clocks, & refectories:—the smaller hermitages often stand in gardens, & are gay without though filthy & mournful within. These, which often are clustered so as to seem like villages,—are perhaps the saddest of all—for you think there must be some child—or a dog—or other life than those gloomy blackclad men:—but no—Tomcats & mules are the only beasts allowed on the holy mountain: & crowing cocks the only birds. I solemnly declare such a perversion of right & nature is enough to madden a wise man——& many of these men are more than half foolish: they murmur & mutter & mop & mow. The greater part are utterly ignorant——& only those who manage the affairs of the convents are atall intelligent. Someday perhaps I shall be able to shew you the views I made of these very strange dwellings.—And so I will say no more of gloomy & terrible Athos.

As I returned hither, I had to wait for a steamer at the Dardanelles—so I gave 3 days to the plain of Troy:—but there—unlike Athos—I must try to go again, for I could not get to Mount Ida, though I tried to do so.—The outlines of the plain & Ida are exquisite & most grand & simple, and all I saw of the site of Ilium delighted me extremely—far beyond what I had expected. I knew also that the scenery of Ida would be wondrously lovely—but the season was so late—& I had no more money—so I came home, leaving Troy to another day. For I have yet to see much of Asia Minor, & Crete, Rhodes, Cyprus and Mitylene—not to speak of Maura & Elis, nor of Lycia & Syria & Jerusalem.

If I am able to leave behind me correct representations of many scenes little cared for or studied by most painters, perhaps I shall have done somewhat; at least, as you have before observed, I certainly give great pleasure to numbers at present, as letters from some to whom I have lately sent drawings of Corfû, confirm. Among my letters are—one from

my dear old friend Mrs. Hornby,—an extract from which I will
by & bye add:—& one from Holman Hunt—very remarkable
& delightful. But, speaking of giving pleasure by paintings, I
am reminded that Sir John Simeon's picture° was done before I
left, though I kept it, that I might finish another—so that seeing
both he might choose one. I shall write to him by this next post,
for I have already begged him kindly to pay for his picture to my
Banker, since I was so short of money at Salonica I did not
know what do do. One of those subjects is Philæ after
Sunset—to illustrate 'I shall see before I die, the Palms and
Temples of the South'.—The other is 'the Crag that fronts the
even, all along the shadowed shore.' This also is in Egypt—&
how I wish you could see them, so that I could hear all the
remarks on both.—

Mrs. Hornby's letter has this; (you know my dear Mr.
Hornby died just before I left England: he was one of the best
men I ever have known:—Mrs. H. one of the most remarkable
and excellent.)—'Tennyson certainly gains in my estimation; I
think in the language of his In Memoriam. I think it belongs to
myself, so *many* of the descriptions seem as if they might have
been written of him I have lost. This has been a long, sad
year—yet I cannot rejoice that it has ended for it seems to make
the gap wider—to have to say—"the year before last" instead of
"last year" '———And how many others feel as she does?—

One would not have expected to find admirers of AT on the
plain of Troy though—yet so it is: tell Alfred that 2 young
ladies, Miss Wood & Miss Ward know Oenone by heart within
sight of Mother Ida, and they are fully aware, (since they go
and live in a tent every summer on Ida—) that the corner of the
platform of Ilion Citadel—i.e. where the citadel once stood—
can be well seen from the mountain above. I hope to go there
next year, & to find the amiable consular family there.

But those who know Alfred's poems most thoroughly are the
2 sisters Cortazzi° in Corfu—particularly the older—Helena.
One evening there was a discussion as to the comparative
superiority of Thackeray or Dickens in drawing female
character:—other writers were also named:—when H. Cortazzi said—'Not one of all those you name could imagine or
describe such a character as the Isabel of Alfred Tennyson!'—
She knows every word of In Memoriam, & indeed all Alfred's

poems—& has translated many into Italian, & set many to music: but in the society of a garrison town you may suppose how few appreciate such talents. And indeed how few of the mass of English ladies—good & amiable as they may be—go one iota beyond the plain housewife everyday thoughts—so that Helena Cortazzi, with her complete knowledge of Italian French & Greek, her poetry & magnificent music, but withal her simple & retiring quiet—is not thought half so much of as that large Miss A.Z. who can only talk English & dance polkas. I believe I have found myself wishing sometimes that I was 20 years younger—& had, I won't say 'more',—but 'any' money.

As regards the future—I believe, but am not sure, that I shall be here all the winter: that depends partly on whether I can make my house comfortable or not. I never passed such a winter as last—of all kind of suffering—but I will not do so again, & if I can't see something like bodily comfort at least, I mean to go to Athens for the winter months—or possibly to Smyrna or Cairo. My dear Daddy Hunt writes that he may perhaps come out—so I shall wait to see what turns up.

I have not got your last letter but one by me—but I will look over this last—(how good of you to write it!) from Builth—Sept. 18th.—I am so glad you enjoy the summer so—& now that the bairns are expanding every succeeding summer & winter will have additional pleasures. I do wish I could be at (or *near*—not *at*) Faringford for a while. There is a little boy in a village not far from Corfu so exactly like Hallam! Have either of the boys any turn for music?—How are Charles Weld° & Mrs Weld? Has Holman Hunt been to see you yet? I think not, as his father, & he himself have been very ill. Venables'° life is a most sad one: nor do I now see any light for him. For the death of poor dear little Eddy boy will cause that of Ellen—& of Emily later. You say—'the accounts of Eddy are beautiful—but of course you know all.'—Indeed I know no more than the barest communication can give me—such as 'things much the same at P[ark]. H[ouse].'—While at Salonica I received 2 letters from F. & in one he was more diffuse, giving me in substance what Venables had written, that he saw no hope, & was very anxious about Ellen, but I have striven so much now for nearly a year to suppose I am believed to take an interest in what goes on, that I take things as they come: & if, after 6 months, I should learn that Eddy & Ellen Lushington were dead—I should try not to feel surprised.

I have returned to Corfû now—much more sound in bodily health & in mental also than I was, & [a line scored through by Lear]. Once, early in the spring, when Eddy was worse, Frank never spoke a word of him for weeks, & when I reproached him he said he was not able to speak on home subjects: this he has repeated more than once,—[another line scored through] The impetuosity of my nature however cannot always be controlled & we have had one or two sad antagonisms—tho we are perhaps better friends afterwards: but our natures are so different, & he is so changed since I first knew him, while I have remained so absurdly the same—(I mean, he has become 70—& I have stuck at 20 or any boy-age all through my life—) that I feel convinced we are best when not with each other.

I remember well how you spoke even of Edmund's reserve: but then Edmd. is so to all—whereas Frank seems to make a rule that the less he likes people the more friendly his manner—& vice versa.—Meanwhile the dear fellow looks as well as even I could wish him, & (when I left in August,) was evidently liking his work better:—I am now sure that the climate may save him from the illness wh: English coughs threaten to him, & I believe that were he married & settled here, such life would be his greatest blessing. But I do not see any chance of that. I shall not be surprised at his resigning at any time—should things be worse at P.H;—but, as I said—I ask no more questions. I will give your messages to him.

But you have puzzled me horribly——& if you find me dreadfully stupid—excuse me on the grounds of my having had a bad fever—& that I have been sojourning with monks & her-mits, whose queer legends did 'all my sense confound'——so that I am, to speak Lancashire——'by common' bewildered just now. Yet here is the paragraph——'*we saw there a Druid's Egg.*'°——May you be forgiven for the frightful confusion of ideas this unhappy sentence has caused me!——Ever since I read it I cannot look at a tree without seeing large nests with Druids sitting in them,—& when Giorgio brought up the breakft. I beheld 3 little Druidini chipping & chirping out of the bursting eggshells.—

I meant to fill up this letter quite full—but I wrote 8 foolscape close pages to dear old sister Ann°—& that has tired me so much. Nevertheless, my Quarantine life is not heavy, & I sit writing all day long. Outside there is a rocky bit of ground, with a few tombs where wretched people have died in sight of their homes——All is still & sunny & beautiful, & I should enjoy sitting on the rocks & dabbling in the water, if the idiotic Quarantine rules did not enjoin a man to follow me every-where—by which severe surveillance they must imply that I can fly away as a bird—since by no other mode—unless I [swam] for many hours—could I reach the city.

I shall now be able to illustrate all the lines of Alfred's little poem to me:°—below is a little scrap giving some idea of the form of Mount Athos. I shall not write more now,—but if I get out before the post goes, I will finish my letter in the town. When will the next poem be out?°—

King Xerxes a dividing the isthmus of Acte, for to let his ships through: Mrs. Xerxes observing the same

13: Octbr: Now what an unjust & beastly Hippopotamus I am!—to have written what I did of Franky overleaf when he wrote to me in the Quarantine—all about Eddy—& himself too! I am a beast & ought to be squashed. Meanwhile we have had a horridodious earthquake: & my old lodgings were so shaken as to be useless. All my things are being moved—& I have taken rooms next door to Frank up here. I never saw him so well—ever since I have known him as he is now—& could he be married, this would after all be the right place for him: & indeed it is—for were he at home his health would suffer.

Worn out by constant importuning I have most unconscien-tiously given these words—'Courage—poor heart of stone—'° to the Miss Cortazzi. I have however told them that Alfred must send me & them 'absolution' so please let me know in your next.—The post of day I fear will not enliven poor Frank.— Meanwhile, with my best love to Alfred, believe me, | Dear Mrs. Tennyson | Your's most sincerely Edward Lear.

14th. I have scratched out some lines—only morbidious—& I repent of morbiddious feelings now—being a better boy than formerly. No letter yesterday—so poor F. is in sad suspense. Say or think what one will, he is the most perfect character I have ever known—& I don't believe there are or will be any other half as good.

To Ann Lear

May 21st. [1857], 7 p.m. | Hotel de la Ville, Trieste.

My dear Ann,

Here I am, where I was just 18 months ago—only then it was very cold, & there was a disagreeable long voyage to be taken in uncertain weather, whereas, it is now very nice & warm, & the voyage is done. F. Lushington & I left Corfû on the 19th. at 11–30—or noon—& the sea was quite like a looking-glass all the way here—& the sky quite cloudless. The steamer also was a new & good one, & if the coals had been better & not so small—which made everything very dirty—the whole voyage would have been faultless. Notwithstanding all that, however, you know I always suffer from the shaking of a steam vessel, & I sometimes think, all the more so when it is calm.

Corfû Citadel was out of sight by one o'clock—& the whole island before sunset. The great Chika mountain of Kimára was most magnificent as we passed underneath it, & before it grew dark I could see the pale long, white heights of Tomohrit beyond Berat. Next morning—Wed.—there was very little to see (all day—) only the 2 islands of Lissa & [. . .]; & today at 12 we came in sight of the lighthouse of Trieste, though we did not get into the harbour before 4. I shall be glad of a quiet dinner & night's rest, I can tell you,—for all the fine voyage. Tomorrow morning at 7, we start in another steamer, for Venice, where you know I have never yet been, & I suppose we shall stay there all Sat. or half of it—going on to Verona for a stay of a few hours. After that we go straight by railway to Milan,—& then by Como over the St. Gothard to the Lake of Lucerne, & to Basle by rail, & rail to Paris, Bologne, & Folkstone. Send a line addressed to me, to '*Post Office, Folkstone,*' as soon as you receive this letter.

You have no idea what a great place, & how busy & fine this
Trieste seems after poor, mean, slow, dirty, uncomfortable,
quoggly, boggly, old Corfû!—such quays! such ships! such fine
wide streets—& such houses. Yet I remember, that after
London & Paris, this same Trieste looked slow & stupid
enough. (I am writing this on your blotting book, & find it very
useful.)

Such a packing up as I had at the last at Condi Terrace! After
the great picture° was packed & set off, which was on the
11th—(at least it sailed on the 11th) I took out all my
rattletraps & put them into the farthest little room, or sent some
to Lushington's next door; & so at the last, all my other rooms
were cleaned & emptied, & I have let them for £2 a month to
some young people—friends of Mrs. Bell's. This lightens my
rent, & is a great comfort to this young couple, who would
otherwise have passed a sad summer in wretched lodgings—for
the badness of houses can be nowhere so vile as in Corfû. After
the Shakespears went away, their rooms were let to some odious
people—who were noisy to a horrible degree; but as I was
mostly out sketching, & as I hope the Shakespears will be back
by next winter, it won't signify I trust.

Corfu was looking more beautiful than I ever saw it just
before I came away; the spring is always the loveliest time
there, & this year there was rain very late, & everything was
green & charming. I have brought your Athos knick-nacks thus
far safely;—& I hope they will arrive so. Also I have with me 2
very tiny tortoises, in an Albanian wooden red box; one belongs
to Lushington, the other I am taking for little Allan Nevill—
poor child. Just now I have let them out for exercise,—& mine
has gone off at a gallop to poke himself into a dark corner; he is
not 2 inches long—& came all the way from Jannina.

I shall keep this letter till I get to Venice, & have it posted on
the day after I get there—i.e.—the 23rd. So I hope you will get
it in time to send a note to Folkstone, where we suppose we shall
be on the 30th. I think of going to Husey Hunt's at Lewes for a
day or 2, till I am sure about rooms etc. etc. in London; that is if
Mrs. Hunt can take me in—which I shall know about at
Folkstone also. Please send this on to Mrs. Hornby, & Mrs.
Empson;° I almost think you had better send me a line *also* to 'B.
Husey Hunt Esq.—*Lewes* Sussex' for fear I should get to &

leave Folkstone before you can write there. I can't write any more—being hungry:—though we have agreed not to dine at the bustling table d'hôte, but to wait till 7–30.—Good-bye for the present.

Sat., 23rd. May, 1857. VENICE. Hotel Europa.
We started from Trieste at 7 yesterday—in a very nice steamer—not over crowded: & the sky & sea were just as obliging—quite clear & calm—& I wish they might chance to be from Boulogne to Folkstone! About 1 p.m. we entered the canals or roads of Venice, & were soon rowed in a Gondola to this hotel. In the afternoon we walked into the Piazza of San Mark—the Cathedral—all about the river Schiavon, Doge's Palace, Ponte Rialto etc. etc.—& dined at 7–30, afterwards smoking a cigar in the Piazza at that hour—9 or 10—full of people—& a band playing—lit up with gas—that is—not the people & the band—but the square generally.

Now, as you will ask me my impressions of Venice, I may as well shock you a good thumping shock at once by saying I don't care a bit for it, & never wish to see it again. Rotterdam & The Hague are 50 times as pretty—(with their green trees & pretty costumes—) barring some of the few buildings here. But those very buildings have been so stuffed & crammed in to my sense since I was a child, that I knew the size, place, colour & effect of all & every one beforehand—& derived no one whit more pleasure from seeing them there, than in any of the many theatre scenes, Dioramas, Panoramas, & all other ramas whatever. Nay—[Stanfield's]—Cook's° & Canaletto's pictures please me far better, inasmuch as I cannot in them smell these most stinking canals.—Ugh! A place whose attributes are those (externally) of mere architecture can be completely portrayed & represented to the mind.—Thousands of descriptions & millions of paintings could not do so with Egypt, Sinai, Greece, Sicily, or Switzerland, because the glories & beauties of nature are in their changes infinite:—here it is wholly otherwise: at least it is so to me.—As for Gondolas—how pleased was I to find I could get from one place to another without going into them!—You know how I hate any sort of boat.—

Well—this morning I suppose I must so far sacrifice to propriety as to go & see some 'pictures.' Very few I intend to see. All the best I know by copies: & looking into the Guide book I see 'This is one of the best specimens of Tintoretto's corrupter style,—or his blue style—or Basano's green style—or somebody else's hoshy boshy lovely beautiful style—all looked on & treated as so many artificialities—, & not the least as more or less representing nature. The presentation of Christ in the Temple—with Venetian Doges & Senator's dresses—& Italian palaces in the background!—fibs is fibs—wrapped up in pretty colour or not.—And besides—looking at pictures wearies me always. It is quite hard work enough to try to make them.° So I shall go & see the portraits of the Doges—& then get away from Venice as soon as I can, thanking my fates I need not come back.

Tonight we shall sleep at *Verona.* The 25th at Milan, stopping quietly at Verona tomorrow, where there is a Colleseum & Romeo & Juliet their Sippilcurs—& what not besides. After that, a diligence takes us over the St. Gothard etc. etc.

Ma'am,—if you happen to observe that this paper hath a crinkly & antique appearance, that is because it fell into the water yesterday as I stepped out of the nasty Gondola. Gondola! forsooth! why can't they call them boats? Rickety old boats? Well—I must put up the tortoises; mine has got himself into the snuffer stand, which is indiscreet & unusual behaviour to say the least—not to speak of the chance of his health being seriously injured by juxtaposition with the candle snuff.

Good-bye, my dear Ann, | Yours affect., ever,
Edward Lear.

I beg you will prepare your mind to see me looking at the very least 66 years old. I wonder if Caroline & the Hon. Mr. Senator Jones° are come yet. I have your Athos beads etc. etc.—all safe as yet—but the hard work is yet to come opening boxes, & diligence packing, thumpy! bumpy!

To Lady Waldegrave

[In 1858 Lady Waldegrave commissioned Lear to make two paintings
of Palestine. One was to be of Jerusalem, the other was not decided. He
left Corfu in Mar., travelling first to Jerusalem, then on to Bethlehem,
Hebron, Petra—where he was attacked and robbed—the Dead Sea,
Beirut, and again to Jerusalem, from where he wrote to Lady
Waldegrave. From the suggestions he made, she chose Masada for the
second painting.]

Damascus. 27th. May. 1858.

My dear Lady Waldegrave,

I had thought of writing to you long ago, to tell you what I
had done by way of trying to fulfil the commissions you kindly
gave me;—but the difficulties of sending anything like a letter
while I am 'on the road' in these countries, are not to be
told.—At least they are great to me,—who am always unable to
write by candlelight;—and the early morning is snatched for
moving forward,—while midday heat & weariness put a veto
on all labour but that of catching & flapping away flies.—And
when in Hotels, (in the very few spots where such houses
exist,)—there are so many things to look after, & to look at, &
so much re=arrangement for the next journey, that the time for
a real sitting down to letterwriting never seems to come.—To
day, the Syrian Haj takes its departure for Mecca, and as there
is no chance of drawing anywhere out of doors, along of the
excitement of the pious Moslem mind, which finds a safety
valve in throwing stones at Nazrãni, I shall remain here & fill a
sheet, if not two, which may reach you to amuse an hour or two
of your leisure some fortnight hence.—

My stay in Jerusalem,—or rather opposite the city,—for I
pitched my tents on the Mt. of Olives when I had ascertained
the point I thought you would like best for your picture,—was
the most complete portion of my tour: i.e. I was able to attend
thoroughly & to the best of ability to what I was doing, in peace
& quiet—whereas much of the rest of my Palestine journey has
been toiled through under far other circumstances.

I first made myself acquainted with the whole circle of the
walls of Jerusalem, and I found that to paint the City as you
wished to have it, at sunset, would not be an easy task, because
of its position. On the West side, you can only see the Jaffa or

Bethlehem gate, & a portion of the walls—*not a bit* of the city itself, & *not a bit* of its more interesting scenery:—so that was out of the question:—the reason of this is that the city slopes down from the west to the east, inasmuch as a line, thus,

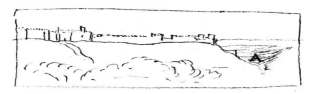

of walls, & the opening (A) of the valley of Hinnom, is all you can perceive. Secondly—on the Northside, you cannot get a good general view of the city anywhere near it, because the slope to the east is so steep, that only the tops of the domes &c are seen, thus;

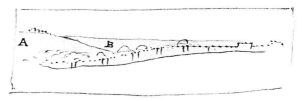

and though you have the Mount of Olives (A)—& the most beautiful line of Moab mountains (B) before you, yet, what I consider one of the most important conditions of Jerusalem, namely, its position on the edge of a ravine——does not appear.—There is however, on the Northside, one of the most famous views of the city—from Scopus, whence Titus first saw it,—& in those days what must it have been!——but that view is so distant and maplike that I did not think you would like it as a picture: moreover being due north, that side of the city only catches a gleam of sun, all the less that the western hills being higher, the real sunset does not affect it at all.—Thirdly—the South side. This is very interesting, as taking in the hill of Zion & the Mosque of David,—with the 2 marquees El Achsar & Omar,—where the temple once stood:—but the line of these wholly shuts out the city itself, and a great portion of the view must be filled by the ground south of the walls, which is wholly devoid of pictorial interest, thus.

There remains then only the Eastside—which is the great & splendid prospect of the whole city, & the only difficulty is to get so little as will go into a moderate form & size, & yet to preserve the chief objects of interest & position, character &c &c.—

—This is the whole form of Jerusalem, and at *sunrise* it presents a really glorious view. But alas! at sunset it is simply one unrelieved surface of houses, because the sun goes down behind the higher western hills A—so that I was in despair about getting such a view as I knew you would like. At length I stumbled on an oblique North=East view, which I mean to paint, & hope will please you. It does not take in the *whole* city but only as it were from the dotted line marked above: but it includes the site of the temple & the 2 domes,—and it shews the ravine of the valley of Jehosaphat, on which the city looks:— and Absalom's pillar—(—if so be it is his pillar—) the village of Siloam, part of Aceldama, & Gethsemane are all included in the landscape. And besides this the sun, at sunset, catches the sides of the larger Eastern buildings, while all the upper part of the city is in shadow;—add to all which there is an unlimited foreground of figs, olives, & pomegranates, not to speak of goats, sheep & huming beings.—The scrawl below will give some idea of what I mean.

S is Siloam. A. Absalom's pillar. Z. the hill of Zion. H the valley of Hinnom. J. ditto of Jehosaphat.—x x x—the hills that stand round about Jerusalem, & which ain't very pretty—but that cannot be helped. This view made a great impression on me as I saw it day after day for 14 or 15 days from the same spot—whence I drew all its details & came to understand its characteristics completely—& I have so many studies of it,—(as well as Photographs which I purchased in order that I might do justice exactly to the scene[)], that I believe I shall make this picture one of the best I have done.—

And now, what shall I say on the subject of the companion painting?—One of the most remarkable, as well as of the most picturesque studies I have obtained is of Sebbeh—or Masada—the history of which you will find in ? Translation of Josephus.° This was one of the places I so much wished to visit, & one which I am so pleased at having drawings of. It is like this somewhat,

only I cannot give here, what only detail & colour can produce,—the great depth of the ravine below. A is the Dead sea:—B is the line of Moab mountains. This scene, as that of the last Jewish struggle for freedom against Rome would I think be a very excellent subject in every way.—But in case you should not like this—there is Hebron, which is very particularly a Hebrew antiquity,—& is besides sufficiently picturesque to form a good picture; though why Abraham chose to live there I cannot think: I found it abominably cold & wet—& besides they threw stones at me whenever I drew, so that I wished the whole population in Abraham's bosom or elsewhere 20 times a day.—

Another subject which is *astonishingly* grand, is Petra. (Not that I can ever see the sketch without feeling my ears tingle at the memory of those filthy Arab savages.) Petra was the capital of the Nabathæan (or Idumæan) Kings, who reigned in Jerusalem as Herods & it was one of them who built Masada. The magnificence of Petra is not to be told,—I mean the magnificence of combined ruin,—splendour of sepulchral architecture and excavated temples,——united to the most romantic mountain or rock scenery & the most beautiful vegetation.—

There is still a subject of interest——the Lebanon cedars——of which I have got very finished drawings: but the Cedars themselves, very solemn & beautiful as they are—stand alone, & do not include other scenery,—so that a picture of the Cedars—will be of the Cedars & nothing else but snow & sheep.

Of these subjects—Masada, Hebron, Petra, & the Cedars, if you will make a choice for your 2d picture, & be so kind as to send me a line to Corfû——I shall be obliged:—for I shall begin your's immediately on my return thither. I am going also to ask you to be so kind as to advance me £50, by paying that sum to my account at Drummond's. (I say 'my account'——conventionally,—really I believe I possess about 2 pounds: but Messrs. Drummonds are used to my ways.) The expenses of this journey have been so much greater than I looked for, that I find myself hardly able to get back to Corfu for want of money which is very disagreeable:—when once there I have much work to do—& shall hope to get on again—but in the meanwhile I shall be obliged if you will place the sum I have asked for at my disposal.—

The worst of all is, that I have not seen Nazareth nor Galilee—& thus I cannot do Ld. Clermont's picture° nor some others I was commissioned to do.—But I begin, finally to decide on returning now,—& if possible on making a 2d visit to Palestine next Spring:—at present the heat is getting too great to allow of my drawing much, & also the country is in such a state that many places can only be visited at the risk of robbery° &c—even if the traveller goes over the ground as rapidly as possible. So travelling,—he may escape outrage—but with me, that mode of progress is useless:—I must stop often, & for a considerable time, so that it is not easy to escape those odious

Arabs. The whole plain of Esdrælon for instance swarms with them, & they attack all passengers. Of known names Ld. Dunglass—Col. Cust, Sir J. Fergusson;—& of unknown names, numbers have been stopped:—and latterly many Americans have been robbed & some murdered, which in one sense is a very good thing, since I do not understand that the American Govt. think proper to uphold the fiction of Turkish renovation, &, instead of being compelled to pooh=pooh the entirely dislocated state of all order in Palestine & Syria, they will it is to be hoped get riled & act accordingly. If it were not shocking, the fate of one large American party near Nazareth is beyond belief absurd:—the Arabs actually went off with all but one large blanket, of which Mr. & Mrs. T. made 2 garments, & therein rode to the town. Some revenge was probably mixed up in this case, on the part of some Arab it is said they had threatened,—for they took every book & drawing, & paper, & even Mrs. Ts. wig & spectacles. Of Dr. Beatie's party, 10 days ago,—the ill fortune was as great or greater:—they were setting out for America, but these animals took all their treasures—not only clothes, but books, collections of plants &c—things of no use to them, but I believe taken as diversions for their nasty little beastly black children.

Of my own mishaps at Petra you perhaps have heard—how above 200 of them came down on me, & everything wh. could be divided they took. My watch they returned to me—but all money, handkerchiefs, knives &c &c—were confiscated. Since then, my 2 muleteers, whom I send by land from Jaffa to Beirut were robbed of their little all by the way—& one might add others,—but cui bono? [who gains by it?]—English people must submit to these things, *because we have* NO INFLUENCE *in Syria or Palestine, nor in the East generally.* I should like to hear of a French party being stopp[ed] or murdered——!!—the Arabs (& Turks) know too well that neither French nor Austrians can be touched with impunity.—

The time is evidently near at hand when all this country will be a field of dispute for Latin & Greek factions once more, & the most miserable Jerusalem once again the bone of contention. If on the one hand the Latin Patriarch is building a great Palace & Convent near Bethlehem, & the Austrians are raising a splendid 'Hospital' (a sort of Knights Templars affair,) in

Jerusalem itself—to be opened by Pius IX it is said,———on the other hand the Russian clergy have constantly increasing influence among the natives, & even just now a particular delegate has come to the 'Holy City' with important powers from Alexander.—In the meantime the 'Protestants' stand alone as a mark for Hebrew & Heathen, Mussulman, Latin, Greek & Armenian, to be found out by all & each as the living Pharisees of the day,—professing a better & simpler form of Christ's religion than their fellow Xtians—yet scandalizing the whole community by their monstrous quarrels: their Consuls & Bishops regarding each other with hatred & each acting to each with open contempt & malignity, while every portion of their resident fellow religionists take one or the other side of faction. And this forsooth at a place of example for Turks & Jews!—this at the very place where he whom they believe the founder of their faith, died!—By Heaven!———if I wished to prevent a Turk, Hebrew, or Heathen from turning Christian, I would send him straight to Jerusalem! I vow I could have turned Jew myself, as one American has actually lately done.—At least the Jews do not lie:—they act according to their belief: & among themselves they are less full of hatred & malice (perhaps—for bye the bye they excommunicated Sir M. Montefiore in 3 synagogues because they said he tried to introduce Xtian modes of life———) than the Xtian community. But these latter, arrogating to themselves as they do all superiority in this & the next life, trample the most sacred doctrines of Christ below their feet daily: 'I say unto you—love one another'—are words which Exeter Hall, or Dr. Philpotts,°—Calvinist or Puseyite— Monophysite Armenian & Copt, or Trinitarian Greek & Latin receive with shouts of ridicule & blasphemous derision.— 'Almost thou persuadest me *not* to be a Xtian', is the inner feeling of the man who goes to 'Holy' City unbiased towards any 'religious' faction:—& it is at least my own deliberate opinion that while the 'Church that is to be' is so far, far removed from the Xtian priesthood & Xtians in a body as it is in South Palestine,—while, in a word Jerusalem is what it is by & through Xtian dogmas & theology,———so long must the religion of Christ be, and most justly, the object of deep hatred & disgust to the Moslem,—of detestation and derision to the Jew.———

From all this mass of squabblepoison let me except the Armenians:—these alone—particularly in Northern Syria seem to think that Christ's doctrines are worth keeping thought of:—as far as I can perceive, they are as much respected for their useful practical lives, as for their uniform peaceful & united disposition of brotherly love one towards another.—

One word about the Jews:—the idea of converting them to Xtianity AT Jerusalem is to the sober observer fully as absurd as

that you should institute a society to convert all the cabbages & strawberries in Covent Garden into pigeon pies and Turkey carpets. I mean that the whole thing is a frantic delusion. Are the Jews fools that they should take up with a religion professing to be one of love & yet bringing forth bitter hatred & persecution?—Have the Jews shown any particular signs of forgetting their country & their ancestral usages, that you should fancy it easier for them to give up those usages in the very centre of that country they have been so long attached to, & for the memory. of which they have borne such & so much misery? Once again the theory of Jew=conversion is utter boshblobberbosh——nothing more nor less.

With all this, & in spite of all this there is enough in Jerusalem to set a man thinking for life—& I am deeply glad I have been there. O my nose! o my eyes! O my feet! how you all suffered in that vile place!—For let me tell you, physically Jerusalem is the foulest & odiousest place on earth. A bitter doleful soul=ague comes over you in its streets—& your memories of its interior are but horrid dreams of squalor & filth—clamour & uneasiness,—hatred & malice & all uncharitableness.—But the outside is full of melancholy glory—: exquisite beauty & a world of past history of all ages:—every point forcing you to think on a vastly dim receding past——or a time of Roman War & splendor—(for Ælia Capitolium was a fine city—) or a smash of Moslem & Crusader years—& the long long dull winter of deep decay through centuries of misrule.—The Arab & his sheep are alone the wanderers on the pleasant vallies & breezy hills round Sion—: the file of slow camels all that brings to mind the commerce of Tyre & other bygone merchandize. Every path leads you to fresh thought:— this takes you to Bethany—lovely now as it ever must have been: quiet still little nook of valley scenery. There is Rephaïm & you see the Philistines crowding over the green plain.— Down that ravine you go to Jericho:—from that point you see the Jordan—& Gilead. There is Anatoth—& beyond all the track of Sennacherib—Mishmash, Giba, Ephraim.—There is the long drawn hill line of Moab. There is Herodion—where the King Tetrarch was buried: below it you see the edge of Bethlehem which he so feared.—That high point is Neby Samwil & beyond it is Ramah.—Close by, the single peak is Gibeah of Saul, where Rizpah watched so long. (Bye the bye that is a 5th. subject to choose from—for I went there on purpose to get that view: & wonderful it is.

A. the Moab hills. B. Dead Sea. C. Jordan.——— And thus—even from one spot of ground, you are full of thought on endless histories & poetries.—I cannot conceive any place on Earth like Jerusalem for astonishing & yet unfailing mines of interest.

—But to leave an endless subject: My stay at Bethlehem delighted me greatly—& I then hoped to have got similar drawings of all the Holy Land.—All the country near it is lovely——and you see Ruth in the fields all day below those dark olives. (This is a 6th. subject—with or without Bethlehem. A. the Moab hills.)———————

Hebron I have already described: & Petra. Next to those I came to the Dead sea—which is a wonder in its way, but the finest part, Ain Gidi, I could not draw well, by reason of more Arab botheration.—Beyond there I saw little else of Southern Palestine——the plain of Jericho, but *not* the Jordan—for there again my beloved Arabs destroyed my peace.—Mar (Deir) Saba—a wonderful monastery—'all as one cut of a Cheshire cheese' as my man said:———the plain of Sharon—& Jaffa:—this was all.—

The last part of my journey, (for I came from Jaffa by sea to Beirūt,) has been of a different kind. All the Lebanon Country is safe & pleasant, & the Maronite Xtians are kindly and respectable critters. But, on the other hand, there wants that indescribable charm—far above & beyond all local beauty & novelty—which the scenery of sublimer Palestine brings to the mind. The higher portions of Lebanon—i.e.—the outer side—recall Etna:—& the stonier & more confined scenes, many a wellknown Cumberland & Westmoreland dell:—the whole plain of CœloSyria, green & lovely as it is, is but Sicilian landscape—or Thessaly on a larger scale.—The interior of Lebanon is however wonderfully fine—: a kind of Orientalized Swiss scenery:—innumerable villages dot the plateaus & edge the rocks which are spread on each side of & rise above dark ravines winding winding downward to the plains of Tripoli & the blue sea. All these I could well have wished to explore & draw, & I might have gone thither had I not become so very unwell from the extreme cold of the upper part of the mountain as to be obliged to return into CœloSyria as soon as I could——having my drawings of the Cedars as a sign of my Lebanon visit.

Next I saw Baalbec.—But I can by no means endorse the enthusiasm of travellers regarding these very grand ruins.

Their immense size, their proportions,—the inimitable labour & exquisite workmanship of their sculptured details, none can fail to be struck with, nor to delight in contemplating. But all the florid ornaments of architecture (Roman withal,) cannot fill up the place of simplicity, nor to me is it possible to see hideous forms of Saracenic walls around & mixed with such remains as those of Baalbec without a feeling of confused dislike of the whole scene—so incomplete & so unimpressive. To my mind the grand & positive=simple Temples of Paestum——the lovely Segesta—the Parthenon & Theseum—& above all, the astonishing singleness of the Egyptian temples are worth heaps of Baalbeks.—Possibly also, the presence of 6 tents full of English travellers,——of a ropedancer from Cairo—with consequent attendant crowds——& of a village full of tiresome begging impical Heliopolitans had somewhat to do with my small love of Baalbek & its neighbourhood. The day's journey thence half way over Anti Lebanon, & the following journey down hither would be of great interest could more time be spent on the way:—but though I have added little to my collection of drawings, the view of this city & its plain is almost a recompense for any trouble.—Imagine 16 worlds full of gardens rolled out flat, with a river & a glittering city in the middle—& you have a sort of idea of what the Damascus pianura is like. I really hope to get a good view of this, but I am sadly put out at losing 2 days by the vagaries of these horrid Musclemen—not to speak of my being lame from a stone thrown at me yesterday. pig!——I shall set off from here [. . .]
29th.—& get to Beirut I hope on June 1:—there, if I ha[. . .] catch the Steamer to Alexda. or Smyrna—as may ha[. . .] that I have done but half 'my mournful task' & [. . .] the money I allotted for the whole—but yet greatly gratifie[. . .] seen & anxious to turn it into substantial kn[. . .] pleasure for the benefit of those who canno[. . .] come to these parts of the world.—

——I feel that as I began my letter with an apology for not having written before,—so, I ought to end it by one for having written so much. But your reading it all or not is optional.

Will you give my remembrances to Mr. Harcourt, & to Mr. Milnes° or anyone who remembers a wandering landskipper.

And hoping to find a line from you at Corfû,—& to hear that you are well, believe me, | My dear Lady Waldegrave, | Your's
sincerely,
Edward Lear.

To Chichester Fortescue

15. Stratford Place. Oxford St.—4th. Novbr. [1859]

O! Mimber for the County Louth
  Residing at Ardee!
Whom I, before I wander South
  Partik'lar wish to see;——

I send you this.—That you may know
  I've left the Sussex shore,
And coming here two days ago
  Do cough for evermore.

Or gasping hard for breath do sit
  Upon a brutal chair,
For to lie down in Asthma fit
  Is what I cannot bear.

Or sometimes sneeze: and always blow
  My well develloped nose.
And altogether never know
  No comfort nor repose.

All through next week I shall be here,
  To work as best I may,
On my last picture, which is near=
  er finished every day.

But after the thirteenth;—(that's Sunday)
  I must—if able—start
(Or on the Tuesday if not Monday,)
  For England's Northern part.

And thence I only come again
  Just to pack up & run
Somewhere where life may less be pain,
  And somewhere where there's sun.

So then I hope to hear your ways
  are bent on English moves
For that I trust once more to gaze
  Upon the friend I loves.

(Alas! Blue Posts° I shall not dare
  to visit e're I go————
Being compulsed to take such care
  Of all the winds as blow.)

But if you are not coming now
  Just write a line to say so–
And I shall still consider how
  Ajoskyboskybayso.

No more my pen: no more my ink:
  No more my rhyme is clear.
So I shall leave off here I think.—
  Your's ever,

                              Edward Lear.

To Chichester Fortescue

                15. Stratford Place. | 9. July [1860]

Dear F.
Washing my rosecoloured flesh and brushing | my beard with
  a hairbrush,————
————Breakfast of tea, bread & butter, at nine | oclock in the
  morning,
Sending my carpetbag onward I reached the | Twickenham
  station,°
(Thanks to the civil domestics of good Lady | Wald.'grave's
  establishment,)

Just as the big buzzing brown booming | bottlegreen
   bumblebizz boiler
Stood on the point of departing for | Richmond & England's
   metropolis.

I say—(and if I ever said anything to the | contrary I hereby
   retract it)——
I say—I took away altogether unconsciously | your borrowed
   white fillagree handkerchief;
After the lapse of a week I will | surely return it,
And then you may either devour it, or keep it, or burn it,——
Just as you please. But remember | I have not forgotten,
After the 26th. day of the month of | the present July—,
That is the time I am booked for | a visit to Nuneham.°

Certain ideas have arisen & flourished | within me,
As to a possible visit to Ireland— | but nobody,
Comes to a positive certainty all in a hurry:
If you are free & in London, next | week shall we dine at the
   Blue Posts?

Both Mrs. Clive & her husband have | written most kindly
Saying the picture delights them | (the Dead Sea) extremely,
   ————

Bother all painting! I wish I'd 200 per annum!
   ——Wouldn't I sell all my colours and | brushes and
   damnable messes!
Over the world I should rove, North South | East & *West*, I
   would———
Marrying a black girl at last, & | slowly preparing to walk into
   Paradise!

A week or a month hence, I will | find time to make a queer
   Alphabet,
All with the letters beversed & | be-aided with pictures,
Which I shall give—(but don't tell | him just yet,) to Charles
   Braham's little one.°
Just only look at the Times of today | for accounts of the
   Lebanon.°

Now I must stop this jaw | & write myself quite simultaneous,
Yours with a l([. . . .]) affection— | the globular foolish
    Topographer.

                                                        E.L.

The Bowl of *Peace*°

To Lady Waldegrave

15. Stratford Place | Thursday [26 July 1860]

Dear Lady Waldegrave,

I have just sent off two boxes and a Neasel which are to go by
the next goods train & to be left at Culham Station° as
addressed. The foolish topografer will follow tomorrow by
the 4.50 express,—& begs it may be fine weather on Saty.
morning.

I am going to ask you if I may divest myself of the duty of
breakfast in the mornings—(save Sunday,) because, as I begin
early, & the effect of light & shade ceases at 11 /2——the
interruption of cleaning & feeding at 10—will just cut up the
best part of my morning. Alas, when in a state of application, or
incubation as it were, I am more or less necessarily disagreable
[*sic*] & absent, & should certainly answer 'Elm trees & bridges',
if they asked me whether I would 'take tea or coffee'.

Directly after I finish my morning work, I should willingly devour a Sandwich, & go across to the Church view, which I shall be able now to see very well, as I can place my canvass on a lofty easel, I myself standing on the green seat, thus—

I shall bring some drawings, but those I will ask you to be kind enough to let me shew you *on Sunday*—as I am anxious to use every minute daylight on Saty for the commencement of the 2 views—& I am unable now from defect of sight to do anything by candle or lamplight.

Believe me, | Your's sincerely,
Edward Lear.

They say that the goods trains go by night, so that the 3 packages—none large—will be at Culham tomorrow early.

To Sir George Grove

[In Sept. 1860 Lear began work on two large uncommissioned paintings with which he hoped to establish his growing reputation— one was of the cedars of Lebanon, the other of Masada. Instead of wintering abroad as he had done for the last five years, he moved into Oatlands Park Hotel, where there were some fine old cedar trees.]

Oatlands Park Hotel, | Walton on Temms, Surrey, | 15 Novr. 1860.

Dear Grove,

I hasten to inform you that in a wood very near here, there are Toadstools of the loveliest and most surprising colour and form:—orbicular, cubicular and squambingular, and I even thought I perceived the very rare Pongchámbinnibóphilos Kakokreasópheros among others a few days back. You have therefore nothing better to do than to come with Penrose° and hunt up and down St. George's Hill for the better carrying out of the useful and beastly branch of science you have felt it your duty to follow. Provided also that you bring your own cooking utensils you may dine off your gatherings though I won't partake of the feast, my stomach being delicate.

Seriously, however, I should indeed like to see both F. Penrose and yourself here:—couldn't you send a line first, and come over to luncheon? though it would be far better if you came and dined and slept and then toadstooled all the next day—back to Sydenham or as you pleased. Saturdays and Sundays are my only insecure days, but those are the days also you would be least likely to think of coming. Daddy Hunt writes to me that he is coming soon:—it would be very nice if we could all combine.

Beside the seedars—you will see 11 other unfinished vorx of art—not to speak of a good many sketches. My life passes daily in a different place, Lebanon, Masada, the Tiber,—the Cervara Quarries,—Philates, Zagori,—Philae,—S. Sabbas,—Damascus, Bethlehem, Beirût, and Interlaken. But I confess that a little more society would sometimes be pleasant—for painting, Greek, music, reading and penning drawings are all used up by the end of the day. Various friends, however, write and come—so I don't complain.

If you let me know—shall I send out and gather toadstools in hampers for you? You can sit and pick them in the large hall.

O! that I could get back to Jerusalem this spring!

Goodbye. | Yours,
Edward Lear.

To Emily Tennyson

Oatlands Parcotel. | Waltonontems. | Surry. | Jany. 14 | 1861.

My dear Mrs. Tennyson,

As you see by the above illustration, I have just sent off my large picture of Masada—one of the strangest=wildest places on earth:—but whether it will be exhibited in the Brit. Institution,° I cannot tell:—one thing is certain, the Artist is just like the portrait above.—

It is much easier to write a little note to mere acquaintanceship, than to sit to write a letter to you & Alfred. The winter=existence in England is to me so profoundly horrible & filthy that I can rarely think on any subject but the black doleful bare trees, the gray woolly sky—the torturing cold to feet & fingers:—the gnawing sureness—(if one thinks at all,) that every moment of the day is a bitter longdrawn year to the majority of people in these isles—(& happily—as the daily Times shews forth—Englishmen & women *do* feel that, and *do* aid to lessen it—) who have no fire no food nor much clothing——vide Coventry—& scores of London districts:— —the reversal of all nature's proprieties, so that people walk on the water, & there isn't any to wash in:—the whitening of the ground & the blackening of the sky:—the starving & deaths of birds:—the columns of deaths in the Newspapers:—the railway & skating accidents 'through the seasonable weather':——all these things vastly disturb me, being in harmony with my own physical suffering,—& to make me see how frightful a calamity winter is in England,—(—& with doubly clear perception that I am in the middle of it,)—and also prevent me from writing or thinking of anything else. We are indeed a great people—*in spite* of our climate. But for those fools and obstinates who speak of LIKING all this filth & horror—forgetting the misery of the poor—I loathe them, one & all:—may the toes of those who lyingly profess to love winter, never be warm! May they cease to know the difference between their toes & their fingers & may both be turned into icicles & afterwards mixed up in icecreams which may they eat, not unaccompanied with fragile biscuits!

My Xmas, & New Year, as I think I wrote to you—were sad enough.° Yet, that the beginning of new life to those who leave this, & who were all wisdom & goodness when here, should be sad at all—is strange:——but that the blank they leave is so terrible.——I also told you of the filthy winter accident here—pipes bursting &c.—(& forsooth these fools overlook their annual frost=misery, or windstorm with wrecks—inundations & drowned harvest, & prate about once in a century earthquakes—or tornadoes!—) & how I had to move into other rooms. There, tho' ill at ease, I have been since I returned from Littlegreen, finishing my Masada: & now I go on to conclude the Cedars, & the remaining 4—Bethlehem, Interlaken, Beirût & Damascus:—but, by Feby—I trust to be at 15 Stratford Pl: once more.

How is John Simeon? Surely the punctilious & pumpsquibilious Pope is a vanishing?° Please God—he & all other impostors may vanish eventually.

What is ⋏ writing? Last night I was a singing 'The Palace of Art'—& many more—till 12.30. Unusual for me: but a clever little Melbourne colonist is very Tennyson=mad, & delights in my singing.—Many friends come to me here:—(I have a Ninstitution concerning them: their bills themselves they pay—: but I give them a bottle of Champagne.)—C. Fortescue 2 days, Cockerell,° H. Hunt, F. Lushington, and James Edwards more than once: & Raleigh (not Sir Walter: for he is dead.—)

Few are here. One Fairie, a friend of Carlyle:—very kind & good, but Scotchy slow—or slowly Scotch. Frank writes, & sends me a ϕotograph of Harry:—wanting sweetness of expression. My evenings—if no friend be here—are dimmydullydillyduffy.—Partly I translate Thousididdles—& so by very slow degrees attain to Greek nollidge.

Partly I play on the hinstrument.—partly I drink tea—&

rush about the room angrily.—In the morning I feed unfortunate birds.

If, (by a naxident—)I sell my 2 large pictures suddingly—I am
off at once to Jerusalem—: but this is hardly likely, & I do not
suppose much I shall leave England before March, then to 'do'
or 'see' parts of Greece never be4 seen—Elis to wit, Crete &
Modon,—Epidaurus—& the river Sticks. If I could get a lot of
spontaneous tumultuous tin, I would go to Ceylon, & for once
& all draw a troppicle seen.

How do you bear this cold weather? Tho' I rather think you
like it, than heat. Do the little fellows thrive with it?

How is the Bastion of Avignon? Abideth Mrs. Cameron°
thereby?

I never see Woolner. It is an uncomfortable country this,
unless one has thousands & fousands & bousands of tin. Gladly
would I leave it—much as I admire & love it. And do not all
who can leave it? If not, why these great & vast colonies?—&
the settlements in all parts of Europe—of wandering AngloSaxons?——Nay. Only 2 kinds of AngloSaxons stay in England.
1st. Those who are wealthy, to whom all countries are alike and
2dy—those who are tied & *cannot* go:—grimly they smile &
say—oh! lovely clime!———cursing & pining away the while
inwardly.

Possibly, gooseberries——when the summer comes—(it
may come in some 3 or 4 years: it didn't at all last
year—)—gooseberries may atone for much evil:—for there are
no gooseberries in the South.

In spite of my sulky letter, I was very thankful for
yours—tho' you maynt think so. Give my kind love to Alfred, &
the 2 boys: & believe me, | Dear Mrs. Tennyson, | Your's
sincerely,
Edward Lear.

I *nearly* came to Freshwater Inn—before I settled here. What sort of place is Appuldurcomb?

To Chichester Fortescue

15. Stratford Place. Oxford Street | Thursday. 7. March | 1861

Dear 40scue,

You will be sorry to hear that my dear sister Ann is extremely ill.——Although she was here last week—as I told you on Sunday—she has had a relapse of her internal complaint & some alarming symptoms are showing themselves. Besides this the poor dear has a dreadful swelling on the back of the neck, wh. continually increases, & which the Doctor fears may turn to Carbuncle. The two illnesses together will I dread be more than at her age she can rally from, nor do I quite think she would undergo any operation, wh. the Doctors hint may be expedient. Her medical man sent for me last night, & I have seen her. Poor dear creature—her sufferings are very sad—yet she is *absolutely* cheerful & tranquil, & speaks of dying as a change about to bring such great delight that she only checks herself for thinking of it too much. She has always been indeed as near Heaven as it was possible to be.

I have written for both my sisters:—the widow° comes today.—

You may suppose I am greatly distressed at this—tho' at present I do not fully realize the whole.

I heard from Ld Clermont today. I had thought it right, as I had before written about that Civitella,—to tell him it was sold.—Sir Francis Goldsmid purchased it on Monday:—for 150 Guineas, wh. you also will be glad to hear.

My plans are of course more than ever uncertain now.

Penrhyn died yesterday morning. Leycester P. wrote to me yesterday—but, altho' I wish to go to the funeral, my sister's state of health may prevent me.

Ld Clermont says he thinks you are overworked: & so do I too—for you were not well at all the other day. Take care, if you find you cannot do so much as you will, to stop in time.—Mrs. Ruxton he says is 'very cheerful, but not so strong as we could wish.'—His writing is so like your's I thought the letter was from you.

Your's affly,
Edw Lear.

To Chichester Fortescue

Monday. [11 March 1861]

Dear Fortescue,

My dear Ann is gone.—she died a little after noon today—in such quiet!

I am going down to Lewes to try to get Husey Hunt, (who is her executor—) to come on Saturday to my darling sisters funeral.—for I shall be so terribly alone.

Yours affly
Edw Lear.

To Chichester Fortescue

Angel Hotel. Lymington. | 18. March 1861

My dear Chichester,

I write this, more to thank you for your's, than for aught else.

I went to Oatlands after the funeral:—but have come today to this place, hoping to get to ATennysons, but there was no steamer.

I am all at sea:—& do not know my way an hour ahead. Wandering about a little may do me some good perhaps.

Your's affectionately,
Edward Lear.

To Emily Tennyson

Corfû. December. 15. 1861

My dear Mrs. Tennyson,

Here I am again in the 'little Isle':—& I had intended to remain so for some weeks longer before I wrote to you, only I cannot withstand the temptation of the chance of hearing from you all the sooner which writing now gives me.

I suppose you have all winter with you: snow, peas-soups, rain hail coalfires plumpudding & chilblains: whereas here, though I confess to a small wood fire, I am writing by an open window, & with the clear mountains perfectly reflected in a mirrorlike sea dotted all over with sparklesailboats, & powdered,——for on each side of the 2 big men of war lying close to my door———with an infinity of white specks——(millions to wit,) of what you might guess to be lotus flowers or sea mushrooms, but in reality they are Seagulls, placidly waiting for their dinners from the big ships' kitchens. I dont remember ever to have seen such a month of purely beautiful weather at this season: day after day the same,——the same rose & crimson evenings, the same lilac & silver mornings. Once only it clouded & was abominably cold for 2 days, & then came pouring rain which everyone said would last 3 months at least———but lo! next morning all was wiped up & smiling once more. However—we must have lots of rain bye and bye of course.—At my first coming, (I arrived on the 19th. Nov.) I was extremely bizzerable here. Apart from F. Lushington being away—& the Reids,° & Edwards & the Cortazzi,——all of wh. facts I was prepared for———there was no one else hardly left in the whole Island, & nobody having been here above 2 or 3 years, nobody cares for nobody: the Boyds° & Loughmans & Pagueneaus being the only vestiges of old Corfu. Then, I could not get lodged—(for of course a large painting room is a sine quâ non—) & I was going on to Athens:—& I got altogether moped & cross & disgusting. Even when, by a lucky chance I popped into the 1st. floor of a new house on the line wall with a *perfect north light*,—I was bored to death by the *noise* of Corfu houses,—wh. are so built that you hear *everything* on all sides & above & below:—people over me gave a ball: people under me had twin babies: people on the left played on 4 violins & a cornet: people on the right have coughs & compose sermons aloud.—So I nearly went mad till by degrees I got furnished & to work,——and such a lot of work as I have cut out might be a proof of complete insanity to those who do not know that unless I work I am wretched. Florence, Turin, Mt. Blanc, the Dead Sea & the Mer de Glace, Spezia & Massa, & Corfús endless

besides Philæs and Olympusses occupy my minutes, & leave
me but little grumbletime, the more that light here is always A
No. 1.——Then, everybody seemed to think I had come here to
amuse them: Everybody asked me to dine or play whist:
everybody 'hoped I would let them sit & look at me
painting.'—The grates wouldn't burn;—the drains *would*
smell. Even the regular & undemonstrative Giorgio was put
out, for his brother (Spiro) was ill, & his youngest boy
also.—And before I could get to work, Xmas English bills
began to come in, & against all this desolation & bother, I had
only better health to put in antagonism,—& hope for the
fewtcher.———But at present I am somewhat livelier. One of
the twin babies is dead—& the other poorly. The violin people
have gone. The people over head are quieter. The grates burn
better & the drains 'smell' better. Spiro & Karalambi the small
are recovering. And as yet there is but little wind & next to no
cold. So, until you hear to the contrary you may suppose I am
progressing.—Aubrey de Vere° is here—he mooneth about
moonily.—Some friends of Mrs. Brookfield (Decie,) also are
here: but I have finally fixed NEVER to dine out except on
Sundays. Frank's successor,° Sir C[harles]. Sargent, seems a
nice fellow—but I eschew intimacies. Bowen's successor°—(—
old Woolff's son—) is also goodnatured. Mess=Dinners
abound, but the Palace is dull—at least after goodnatured
vulgar roaring helterskelter Ldy Young.° En revanche, the
Govnr. is a better Govnr. & hath brains & a will. He has asked
me a 2d time to dine today—& I hope he wont begin to ask me
to dinner often, as I avoid Swells: but I do not know how to
prevent popularity unless I invent some new plan not yet hit
on.—

Meanwhile the island is, if possible lovelier than ever, & I
cannot conceive more fairy=like scenery, or more perfect Greek
landscape.—My life is going to be (by degrees) thus—as far as I
can. Rise at 5 or 6—& do Greek till 8. Bkft. & teach George° till
9. 9 to 4—work hard as possible. 4 to 6. walk: (the sun don't set
till 5 here;) 6.30 dine. 7.30 to 10.30 penning out Topographical
drawings.———If so be I get any tin, I shall devote April &
May, to doing a fresh piece of Peloponnesus illustration—
probably Elis or [. . .] Maura, or Epidavrus, or I might could
would or should go to Crete: but these things depend on other

matters so much, that it is vain to arrange ʙ 4 𝄞.—In June,
I expect I shall be back in England——for the Gt. Exhibition,°
& the showing there of my two large pictures, Corfu &
Lebanon, may do me some good as to commissions.—Whether
I shall go to Palestine in the Autumn, or in the following Spring,
remains also undecided.——

Intanto pray let me hear from you—how you yourself are, &
Alfred & the boys. Is ⋏ writing? Do you hear anything of my
new Book of Nonsense°—price 3/6—coming out by Routledge
& Warne?—Is Sir John Simeon returned? Does Mrs. Cameron
rave?—If ⋏ will come here, I will give him a room between the
babies & the violins, but I have no other.—Does the tutor still
live with you? Do the boys get on? Do they begin Greek?—(wh.
is the foundation of all knowledge & happiness & good on this
world—far beyond cleanliness or Godliness.)—Have you read
A. P. Stanley's Greek Church?° (which is worth its weight in
gold.) What have you to say about Franklin's marriage?°—
'Please say something': (as the old Methodist lady said at the
prayer meeting.) Do you like woodcocks? (they are 4d & 5d a
piece here, & such being the case, might possibly induce you all
to come out directly.) How is poor Mrs. Weld? A brother of
Archie Peel is here—one Major P.° a nice fellow but sickly.
Oranges are a halfpenny a piece—but it is a vergogna [shame]
to gather them they look so lovely. Owls are plentiful. Flights of
grey gregarious gaggling grisogonous geese adorn the silver
shining surface of the softly sounding sea.—We are all talking
about the 'American Outrage'°:——tho' to judge by my letters,
one among us does not think of much anyhow. That however is
a mistake, for I think lots [. . .] nor do I cease to feel my sister's
death at all, & I suppose I never shall now. My love to ⋏ & the
Boys, & wishing you, & them a happy Xmas & New Year,

believe me, | Yours affly,
Edward Lear.

[Written at top left hand of front page] Bp. Heber's widow° still
lingers on here.
[Written at top right of front page] I have decided to go to the
Palace in dirty boots: to eat my fish with my fingers: & to spit in
the tumbler:—on wh. I shall never be asked again.

To Emily Tennyson

Corfu. 16. Feby. | 1862.

My dear Mrs. Tennyson,

The ducklike benevolence with which you have sent me another letter, before I had answered your last!!—and in this one—the dedication verses° by Alfred—which are doubtless among the loveliest & grandest of all he has ever written. As for me, I copied them out at once for Mrs. Decie,—& go about reading them to all who will hear me. They are exquisite.

Do you know, just as you were writing,—I have been going through every one of ⚁'s poems—Princess, Maud Idylls, & all——having lost my former list of Landscape Illustrations,— —in order to get up my ideas on the subject of the Landscapes once more. In all, I have put down 250. In the Poems 153—Princess 24. Tithonus 1, Maud 32. In Memoriam. 23.—Idylls—17.—Shall I ever live to paint them? It is to be doubted. Meanwhile I am working very drudgefully at various necessities, & wish I were a chimneysweeper or a teapot.

Many thanks also for so kindly taking the trouble of writing all the F[ranklin]. L[ushington]. Wedding day description. I too have heard from him at Paris—& a very nice letter. I do hope & think they will be happy, altho' I quite agree with what you wrote in your letter of Decr. 27—as to wishing that there had been 'something new': and also in what you say that in 'good & unselfish things there is always something new[']. Possibly—for they will, I hope, see some society in Norfolk Square,°—this marriage may do much towards openening [*sic*] lights into the too close boskinesses of Park House————for the nieces anyhow will stay there.

I had intended to write you a very long letter, but I have written two, Mammothian in size: & cannot write well any longer. This house too is unquiet—for there is a family named Maud above me—which I wish I could send 'into the Garden' if there were one:—& although one of the twins is dead, yet the other, having I firmly believe swallowed the violin (which has been mute of late,—)—hath a hoarser & catguttier voice than in aforetime. How sorry I am to hear Arthur Stanley is going to meet the Prince of Wales° only at Alexandria! I had so hoped to see him here. Why & how have the Cators changed their names?—Do you mean she is rechristened James—& he Caroline? Of Brookfields° in general; of Mrs. Brookfield in particular: will you cause her to be thanked from me for having made me known to some of her friends here, Lieut. & Mrs. Decie, they are as kind as clever & pleasant, & I dine there happily on Sundays. Only to day I dine at the De Veres, Aubreys brother——which he is at Athens, & the brother is a Major here.—Why does not Mrs. Cameron go to Barbadoes? She should. Perhaps she may. I think I would try to come & live in one of her houses, only you & ⋏ would immediately go & live in Durham.—O my! here the sun is so bright. Only a few—a very few—winter days have happened: then there were storms—thunder & lightning & rorin of the angry Elephants. I do not know if I shall come to England this year. Alfred would not like this place—it is so crowded & small & silly & buzzyfuzzy.° I however who live in a chamber on a wall,— overlooking the sea——seldom go out; or if I do I avoid the Garrison gapings & gawglings & run away to distant olives, & return at dusk. Perhaps—in mid April, I may coast along from here to Arta—& draw coves & harbours.

I read ⋏ to Luard°—a R. Engineer here—& have inoculated several with admiration of what they were before ignorant of. Miss Goldsmid, a sister of Sir F.G. is here, & is a pleasant contrast to the ordinary run of society. How is Miss Simeon? How is Sir John? The death of John Godley° must have been a fresh sadness to him. I wish you & ⋏ could see my views of Corfu & some others I have been doing:—those of Florence, Turin, & Athos, I may perhaps be able to shew you in London——tho' if I get there it will hardly be before the end of June.—I have commission to do 'my spirits falter in the mist'°——& it is to be an English Cliff coast scene. Do you think Freshwater or rather the Needles cliffs would do? I am in a fever to know Dr. Lushington's decision on Dr. Williams' case:° there is very much fermenting in my foolish mind now a days—but I cannot describe it now.

It is nearly afternoon church time, & I must go, & so must close this for the present.

Thank you extremely for the letters & the Dedication. My love to Alfred & the boys: Why are they unwell?

Your's affectionately,
Edward Lear.

Monday. 17th.
After writing this, my dear Geoff Hornby° came & got me out to church, after which we walked up to Ascension, which I wish Alfred & you could see. I think he might come here one day, & abide in a Yacht:—I have this morning got the promise of the 3d floor in this house, whereby I shall be quiet, & have a better view. Have you got one of the new boox of Nonsense?—I desired one to be sent to the boys. Please tell me.

—Well, we came down from Ascension at 5.30—& Geoff went to his ship, & at 6.30 we walked up again to the Casino, & dined with the De Veres who are you know Spring Ricy people.° In the Evening I sang 4 or 5 of ↑'s songs—to their delight. I should tell you that lately a person whom I know & like, has become a widow, & I, wishing to shew sympathy thereat, wrote to her,——half afraid after posting the letter that I had done wrong. Last week came the following message from her———— 'tell Mr. Lear that I thank him for his letter, which was a great pleasure to me:—he always says the right things:—but how should a man who sings as he does not understand the feelings of others?'————O Lawk! aint that pretty? Have you not got a grand good piano yet? Buy Mrs. Cameron's if she Barbadoe-sizes. It is really an awful shame that the P. Laureat[*sic*] hath only an ancient & polykettlejarring instrument° in his house. Neither is it moral, for it sets a bad example to others, & flouts the musicle deities. O dear—I feel so sick! Geoff will have me come on board to dine to day,—& the wind is rising: I declare I won't go if it is rough. Please think of, & suggest various subjects for Alfred to write on. Would William Tell be a possible feasible one?—Sith he always says he must know the scenery of subjex——& surely Grütle would be a wonderful scene—not to speak of all about the Lake, Uri, &c.—Bless me,—this place is in such a fuss! Here's a big man of war—Turk—& a little Turkey steamer besides: I must say I like the Ottoman flag,——the broad & long onecoloured crimsonflashing manyfolded traily fally floating banner, with the Gold Crescent shining out of it. Then there are 2 Greek Steamers, bringing down the 2 sons of old King L. of Bavaria, one of whom is to be the successor of the K. of Greece.° The Greeks don't like having Bavarian Kings. I wish I could send you heaps of Cyclamen—which are all lying so thickly about the trees. Yet see how vicious a practice it be to spell ill,—for perhaps you suppose I mean 'sickly men', & that I am lamenting an unforeseen mortality in the island, & wishing only that I could send the invalids to England. Not at all. I mean the beautiful flowers, I do. Also there are snowdrops & violets & anemones. I suppose Lionel does not like parting with his nurse. Do they get on with their learning well? Does Lionel draw as he used, or Hallam? What are Hallam's specialities?— To go on with the fuss, there are 3 men of war here, & a gunboat—all ours—& a steamer—the Osborne—gone to fetch the Prince of Wales. He is to be here on the 20th or 21st. but nobody knows exactly how or when or where or why or which or whosoever or what. I must go and paint goats,—Bother goats,—& goats' ears & noses. Bother goats' ears & noses.—

――――

To Ruth Decie

15. Stratford Place. Oxfd St. | 9. Sept. 1862

My dear little tiny child,°

You will excuse my familiar mode of addressing you, because, you know,—you have as yet got no Christian name—;—& to say—'my dear Miss Decie' would be as much too formal, as 'my dear Decie' would be too rude. But as your Grandmamma has written to me that you are just born I will write to congratulate you, & possibly this is one of the first letters you have as yet received. One of the old Greek Tragedians° says――――and I am sure you will not think me impertinent in translating what he says— (μὴ φῦναι &c) [not to have been born &c] because there has not been time hitherto to buy you a Greek Dictionary, (& I am sure you cannot read Sophocles without,――besides, the Dictionaries are so fat & heavy I am certain you could not use them comfortably to yourself & your nurse,)—μὴ φῦναι &c—which means 'it is better never to have [been] born at all, or if born,—to die as soon as possible.' But this I wholly dissent from: & on the contrary I congratulate you heartily on coming into a world where if we look for it there is far more good & pleasure than we can use up—even in the longest life. And you in particular will find that you have—all quite without any of your own exertions—a mother & a father,—a grandmother & a grandfather,—some uncles,—an extremely merry brother (who propels himself along the floor like a compasses,) a conservatory & a croquet ground, & a respectable old cove who is very fond of small children & will give you an Alphabet bye & bye.—I therefore advise you to live & laugh as long as you can for your own pleasure, & that of all your belongings.

Please tell your Grandmama that I also wished to stop when the carriage passed but couldn't—& say also, that I will write to her again shortly. And now my dear you have read enough for the present. Good night, & believe me, | Your affte. old friend
Edward Lear.

Give my love to your Papa & Mama.

To Chichester Fortescue

Hastings. 4th. October. 1862.

My dear Fortescue,

'Force majeure' as the French say, has entirely bevagued & bemuddled my plans since I wrote to you from Eastbourne on Friday. For, when I came here I firstly found that no sort of lodging suitable to me could be got—(tho' the place is by no means full,)——because there were only such houses to let as have a southern front light & a dark back room. One or two there are indeed otherwise, but in too remote & exposed situations for me to try on towards the end of October. So I have given up this plan altogether.—And moreover I find that this end of Hastings would be just now to me particularly unpleasant from other reasons—the dominion of my Lady W. & Parsondom° included. So altogether I give it up, & return to London tomorrow morning—Monday: & if you are in town, let me know.

My first act there is to pack & send away all I require at
Corfu. My next to finish Grenfell's pictures, & 4 small ones of
the 10 Guinea institution as soon as I can, & then go South.

What I do with the Cedars° I do not know:—probably make
a great coat of them. To a philosopher, the fate of a picture so
well thought of & containing such high qualities, is funny
enough:—for the act of two Royal Academicians in hanging it
high, condemn it first,—& 2dly the cold blooded criticism of
Tom Taylor in the Times, quasi=approving of its position,
stamps the poor canvass into oblivion still more & I fear,
without remedy.

Notwithstanding which, in 20 more years, I can't see what
difference all that will make to me.

I am still more or less undecided about giving up England
altogether as a residence—until such time—(perhaps never to
come,—) when I can remain in a suitable home so as to study &
paint as I wish uninterruptedly, & with the brains & memories
it has pleased God to give me.

Did I ask you if you had ever read—'Letters from Palmyra',°
& 2 sequels—'Rome' & 'Judæa'?—I am greatly delighted with
the book.

My return to London, will I hope enable me to see you &
some one else at Strawberry Hill before I go.

Your's affectionately,
Edward Lear.

To Mrs Prescott

15 Stratford Pl. | 6. Nov 1862

Dear Mrs. Prescott,

You must have thought it very odd of me, never to have
answered this note. It only came last night—which its
deleterious delay its envellope explain will.

I was very sorry not to see you when you called: I was in the
city. The mouseplate°—(tell Mrs. Decie) is well packed. But
you left nothing for little Mary De Vere.

Tell Wolstenholme° if you please that I got stamped
agreements both from Routledge & from Dalziels:° which
improvement in worldly acuteness I have to thank him for. I

placed the result of the Book of Nonsense in the Funds, & as I went there the whole of Fleet Street & Cheapside were *crowded* with people on foot & driving————so unusual is it for Artists to save money at all! & such sensation does the act occasion!

Thank you for returning my umbrella———I had thought myself relieved of that responsibility.

My kind remembrances to Mr. Prescott, & with many thanks to you & him, & believe me, | Your's sincerely,

Edward Lear.

To Edgar Drummond

[Since Lear's large paintings had not sold and he was now running short of money, he decided to publish a book illustrating the Ionian Islands.]

Corfû. March 23. 1863.

Dear Drummond,

I write a line to send with some money orders I am forwarding to the Bank, & I want to ask you to cause me to be assisted if I get into a dilemma through the tortoise=like payments of my 'constituents'. No less than 289 pounds 8 shillings are just now owing to me by various human beings—whom I am by no means angry with—as they can't tell the bother they occasion me————: nevertheless the bother is a bother—because I am afraid of overdrawing my account—& yet I want to go to Sta. Maura & other places.

What I want to know is, supposing I draw money of which none may be existing,—to the effect of 50 pounds, can I do so without impropriety? I have written to the friends in question, but some are away—some are here or there or nowhere, & although it is more than probable that one or two will pay their tin before long—yet it may so happen that they don't. Look here,——

Chichester Fortescue M P —— 66. 0.0
Stephen Cave Esqr — M P —— 10.10.0
Duke of St. Alban's ———— 60.18.0
Rev. E. Ashton ———— 10.10.0

Henry Grenfell Esqr. M.P —— 68. 0.0
Capt. Lawson ———————— 21. 0.0
Mrs. W. Rawson ————————— 52.10.0

                              £289. 8.0

Q E D. ——————

I really wanted to have gone to Crete, but after all, I have made up my imbecile mind to go & do Paxo, Sta. Maura, & Ithaca—so as to commence producing a work on the Islands when I get to England. Something in that way must be done this summer, before I return here.

How have you & Mrs. Drummond been all the winter? And the invisible babes? I wonder if I shall see them this year. We have had 9 whole weeks of sunshine, & now a sort of muffy puffy weather—with showers. I wish you & Mrs. Drummond could have been here. Yachts have been out here numberless: & swells of the highest order to the extremest extent. Also ships—Marlborough, Chanticleer, Trafalgar, Edgar, Shannon, & what not. I never before knew Corfu so agreeable & lively in every way. What with the excitements about the Greek King, & the Prince of Wales's marriage—(bye the bye the weather changed just as we had bought all our illuminating materials, & we have never been fortunate enough yet to get a fine night,) we have been constantly in a state of amiable intelligence & enthusiasm.

I have done a vast amount of work, principally Watercoloured drawings—many of which I hope to show you on coming to London, which I suppose I shall do before mid June. But I am beginning to be a weary of this double annual journey, & probably shall arrange this year to be longer periods abroad——if so be one lives on for other years.—

                    Believe me, with my kind remembrances to
                    Mrs Drummond,— | Your's sincerely,
                                        Edward Lear.

You may not have heard (it is not generally known,) that I refused the throne of Greece—King Lear the first——on account of the conduct of Goneril & Regan my daughters, wh.

has disturbed me too much to allow of my attention to governing.

To Henry Grenfell

Corfû. 23. March. 1863

My dear Grenfell,

Do not be wrath with me when you perceive this scrap of paper, which its object is to ask you, if you can do so without bother to yourself,——to pay all or a part of the tin—68£ is the whole total,—into my account at Drummonds. I would not make this disgusting request, if it were not that I am in such a horrid mess for want of tin—as I have over 250£ owing to me from one person or another in sums more or less small—but added up they cause me to gnash my teeth. Because why? I have come to a perpetual end of my ready money, all but two pounds——& I have no inkum but what comes from objiks of art——yet meanwhile rent & food must be paid up daily & monthly. I am going—if possible—to see one or two of the islands I have not been to yet, & after that I trust to get to England for 2 or 3 months.—I heard the other day that your 2 pictures are much liked—& I hope you enjoy them & will long continue to do so.

Shall [you] not come out here some day—when Parliament is up? Sir Hy Storks I see more of than formerly, & always like him more. He is particularly goodnatured to me, & continually asks me to dine on Sundays—when he has a quiet little party, & very pleasant society. No end of gigantic swells have been here this winter Dukes, Earls, Barons & what nots. At present the Duchess of Montrose is the most remarkable individual in society—but I can't say I admire her much. Lady Shelley°——to my mind is one of the nicest here.

So——*The* Marriage°—(I don't mean the Prince's) has at length come to pass. I hope C.F. & Ly W. are going to Red House at Easter. They really seem immensely happy—& I think will remain so. But what do you do at 45 without the C.O. Secretary? What of the state of Russ's health & spirits?

Do you see T. G. Baring?—Give my love to him if you do. I wish you would all come out in a Yott. It is a bore not seeing one's friends, for I don't make them easily—i.e. new ones:—one can't at half a hundred year's old. The De Veres—though—Spring Ricical people—are among the nice ones here.—What of Colenso?° Balaam's ass & Elisha's bears & Jonah's whale tremble with anger at his temerity.

> Good bye, | Your's sincerely,
> Edward Lear.

To Chichester Fortescue

15. Stratford Place. Oxford St. | 14. Sept 1863.

My dear Fortescue,

The Member for Louth has not been again: which I am sorry for, for I very seldom see him now.—As for myself I go on grinding on most sadly & painfully, for it is not altogether the physical annoyances of banishment from fresh air & nature combined with many hours daily work of a constrained kind that bothers & depresses me,——but beyond these—the impossibility of getting any compensation=spiritual from the Views I am drawing, since their being all executed reversed° causes them to seem unreal, & without any interest.

You may ask—then why undertake a task so odious?—The reply to which would be, what else could I do?——The remains of my Watercolour gains could not carry me through the winter, & therefore, as ever the case with Artists who have no settled income,——something else was necessary. And as it would be folly to commence more oil works—those I have done being still unsold,——or to begin more Watercolors when there are none to see them,—the Ionian Book was my only apparent open=door of progress—& as I wrote to you before, in many points it would probably be of service.

As to gain however, I half begin to think not. For to make it so, a very large Subscription List would be absolutely requisite,—seeing that the sale of one hundred would do little more than pay the expenses:—and after all it is 6 months' hard work in question,—2 & a half in getting the sketches—as much more in arranging them, & Lithographing.

But when I look over the 600 names I have written out——not more that 100—or 150 of whom would be pretty sure to subscribe, the amount of writing & the vexation of application rather alarms me, & I sometimes think that when the last Lithograph is done I shall sell the whole bodily—ensure myself from loss only——& cut away South. Meantime I do not go out—: slavery becomes bearable as a habit:—but some hours of freedom once a week make all the rest blacker. Besides, I have got back to my Greek a little, & now & then get someone to come & dine with me.

The King of Greece is only just now going away from Denmark it seems,——so he cannot be in Greece till November I imagine. If I hear before I start that there will be a proximate break up in Corfû,° of course it will make the greatest difference to me as to what I take out there. The chances are that I shall give up my rooms there this winter, & go to Athens to look about me, for there probably my next sojourn will be. Next year it is very unlikely that I shall return to England;——Maclean of the Haymarket° wishes to take charge of any drawings I may make for sale, & if I find this plan answer sufficiently to keep me afloat, I shall probably adopt it permanently for the few odd years of life remaining. For the double journey & expense hither brings no reward whatever:—the few friends I care much for, I see only for a few hours, & really don't communicate with as much as when abroad:—the sitting for 6 weeks or 2 months in a room in the chance of purchasers coming is far from pleasant:—& the Country house life is rattling & expensive, (whatever you may think,) & moreover cannot be carried on by those who have ever to work for life. I don't say I shall not come to England again—nor am I a man to do anything quà 'line of life' without well thinking it over:—but at any rate I shall not be here next year.

On this account particularly I should like to get to Dudbrook° on one Saty. before you & Ldy Waldegrave go to Ireland:—the later—the better I should like it. But I am by no means sure I can come at all—for after a week's work I am often really indisposed for anything but walking hard—which one can't do in a house especially at meal time.

I fear the New Zealand bothers° are recommencing & no mistake. The Southern islanders are happy to be out of all that confusion. I have had 2 letters—'North' & 'South', sent me by my sisters this last week, but shocking enough. Bye the bye, one of the oddest feelings I can remember to have encountered came to me by a circumstance last Monday. On the Sunday, I had gone to Highgate Cemetery to see about my dear Sister Ann's grave, & returning, perceived afar, that the old House I was born in°—(its gardens & paddocks were long ago destroyed by new roads & buildings,) was advertised for sale as building materials, 4 houses being to be raised on its site. So the following day I went up there, & all over it: & I can assure you, the annihilation of time which seeing such early=known localities produced was curious, & made me afterwards thoughtful enough. As I stood in various parts of the large empty rooms, I could absolutely hear & see voices & persons, & could—(had I had a pen & ink paper & time,) have written out months & years of life nearly 50 years ago, exactly & positively.

(The old woman who shewed the house seemed horribly puzzled at my knowing all the odd closets & doors &c—& received 2/6 with a mixture of pleasure & fear.) I don't think there's any more to say:—I must go & finish the 7th. Lithograph—wo is me.

My kind remembrances to Lady Waldegrave:— | Your's
affectionately.
Edward Lear.

This work is so filthy too:—I shall never be clean again.— When it is done, I shall sit 10 days in a warm water pot, covered with a covering—& receive my friends—thus

The other day, in Hants,—a country vicar had a new curate. The V. asked some boatmen how they liked his sermon. 'Beautiful Sir—a werry fine sarmin: we was all of us a thinkin of it for hours arterwards'.

—'It was from the words—Mene, mene, tekel &c—wasn't it?'—said the V.

'Yes Sir, it wor:—& I can't tell how many fine things as Mr. A said. Only I says to myself says I when he'd done,—& I says it every day————I wishes to God as I was Tekel Sir!'

To the Rt. Hon. W. E. Gladstone

[This letter is written on the back of a printed notice advertising the forthcoming publication of *Views in the Seven Ionian Islands*, and listing 101 names of those who had already subscribed.]

[October 1863]

Dear Sir,

I hope that the enclosed circular of a work I am about to publish on the 7 Ionian Islands may interest you sufficiently to induce you to subscribe for a copy of it. I have lived there so long, that I may say without impropriety that few artists can have drawn the beautiful scenery there as much & as carefully as I.

I do not know if when you were Lord High Commissioner you saw much of the interior of the Island, though I remember Strahan telling me that he attended you & Mrs. Gladstone to Philates in Albania. And,—but that your time must be very greatly occupied, I would like extremely to shew you drawings of those places some day.

I am very glad to hear that my friend T. Woolner has made a bust of you which is spoken of as excellent. Woolner is so conscientious & thinking a Sculptor that he is certain to be of the first rank if he lives:—or rather—(for he is that now,)——he will be generally allowed to be so.

I remain, | Dear Sir, | Your's obliged,
Edward Lear.

To the: | Rt. Honb. | W. E. Gladstone. M P. &c &c.

To Sir Digby Wyatt

I

O Digby my dear
It is perfectly clear
   That my mind will be horribly vext,
If you happen to write,
By ill, luck to invite
   Me to dinner on Saturday next.

2

For this I should sigh at
That Mrs. T. Wyatt°
  Already has booked me, o dear!
So I could not send answer
To you——'I'm your man, Sir!'——
  —Your loving fat friend,

Edward Lear.

15. Stratford Place. | Saty. 14 | November. 1863.

To Mrs Prescott

15. Stratford Place. Oxford St. | 17. November. 1863

My dear Mrs. Prescott,

Your extremely kind letter came last night, simultaneous
with one from Ld Dudley—& with a visit from Col. Chapman,°
whom I had known long ago in Zante. If you knew how many
such kind letters I have, you would feel how impossible it would
be to reply to them by deputy. I really know you would gladly
help me in writing, & am as much obliged as if you did so:—but
what remains for me to do now is comparatively light work &
can be done 'by degrees', as the man said who threw the
gunpowder into the fire. Yet, with few exceptions the letters I
have to write are to persons who have long known me more or
less, & they require something accordingly personal—a good
bye—or some mention of my own or their belongings—answers
to question &c &c:—a mere dry 'Send your 3. 3 to me & be
bothered'!——would be a very ungracious return for having
good naturely taken a copy of my Views—as many have done
more out of interest in myself than in them. So you see, as the
obstinate spider said when the amiable Bee offered to make part
of his web,—'I *must* do it myself':——though I thank you none
the less for your kindness.

[. . .] is riz suddingly to 323—by a great shower of Liverpool
subscribers this morning. Now—: if I get 330—& all pay—I
shall really clear nearly 500£—& I assure you that such a sum
will perfectly content me:—for I shall be able to put some of it
by—& shall probably get to Palestine, about the Spring, with

the remainder. Thomas Cooper, the little man who keeps the house here, will have plenary powers granted him to issue more volumes, & to collect tin: but as I shall see you again before I go, I will tell you of the progress of events. Meanwhile 4 mortles are a printing off the 21 Lithographs, & others are a doing of the Letterpress, of which the 23 pages are written & delivered to the printer.

Thank you also for your kindness about my 4 offspring,°— but I should like to tell you that they cause me no uneasiness at all. I have had so much good to be thankful for all through my life, that I have got into a habit—or principle—of never regretting matters which can't be altered easily, & more than that, of seeing that they are pleasant, & not the contrary. Physically, being of a restless & fidgetty nature, I have always fought against my mind aiding that tendency, so that literally 'What's the odds so long as you're appy?' is my general phase of feeling. (I cannot, bye the bye, but be amused with one part of your kind theory,—to wit—of Exhibition;—for you do not seem aware that pictures can not be exhibited *twice*—& that as mine have all already been so somewhere or other, your plan falls through fatally. Moreover, there is one of your sentences that made my hair stand on end for four hours, & it was not without the most violent brushing from 2 new brushes that I could calm it to its former position————I mean where you put the words 'Royal Academy' and 'dirty work' into one para-graph!!!!!—This is truly dreadful & I trust you wrote it inadvertiently.) But seriously, when I think how many painters with infinitely greater talents than mine have had to struggle on painfully—(such for instance as Maddox Brown, & for many years, Linnell,)—I think myself well off;—and I know more-over that I have gained immense advantages by the execution of such pictures as the Cedars, & Masada—even if they were to be destroyed tomorrow. Besides, if I were to think about them at all now, it would lead to continual bother:—for example I confess that I have more than once caught myself wishing that Mr. Prescott's portrait were where the side lookingglass is over the chimneypiece at Clarence, & the Masada at the end of the room, where it would seem as if painted apurpose for its position, & would light up beautifully:————but I always quash these ideas as far as I can at once, & aim rather at the view of matters I wrote of above. And again,—today I dine at Holford House—('May Lindsay' of other days wrote me the kindest note—asking me to call there—wh. I did yesterday. Good Gracious! *What* a house!—) where there are 2 walls wholly unfilled & absolutely adapted to either Cedars or Masada. But if I were to allow myself to think of that, I should fidget all dinner time & make myself more disagreeable than I very frequently do. Thus you see, my dear Mrs. Prescott—that I am really very stupidly contented & fillisofical after all:—things must take their chance in the groove we have set them to run in.

E. Wolstenholme & Vincent have just very thoughtfully sent me their subscriptions:—& now that—42 copies are paid for I feel an increasing 42de about the whole affair. The odd plate of the Citadel of Corfu also—(wh. I promised to Frank as I can't do him a bird yet awhile,) is come back from Luard all over warlike names—so that Decie was right in saying L. knew all about it.

I am much pleased with Col. Chapmans's visit last night: he is less altered in appearance & manner than anyone I know in so long as 15 years. And I was delighted at his liking the views in the Book as much, & also by his speaking of the 2 paintings at Clarence°—which bye the bye are another sign to me of the good I get by painting the big pictures.

I send you another—the last list I shall print before the book comes out————but there are 20 names minus.

Some day if————

O gracious grasshoppers————

heres the first page of the Letterpress proofs come in! Now you *can* do me a service by asking Decie if with you—if 'Staff Surgeon Dr. Roberts' is correct—or if it should be Staff Surgeon Roberts MD————or only Staff Surgeon Roberts?

What I was going to say before was—some day please send me Lord Dufferin's address.

Believe me, Dear Mrs. Prescott | Your's sincerely & with
many thanks
Edward Lear.

To William Holman Hunt

15. Stratford Place. Oxford Street. | 31. Decbr. 1863.
My dear old Daddy,

I am pretty nearly on the wing, & not well enough to go & try
if you are in town—tho' I do not suppose you are, & shall send
this to Fairbairn's.° On Monday or Tuesday I hope to cross to
Boulogne, & very glad shall I be to do so, for I am really half
dead or stupid with the constant writing & worry of the last 2
months. And even now I cannot get in 50 subscriptions, so I go
away very paupery, because I put what I could into the Fumms
pa. The same amiable friends who are always saying—'o—it is
so wrong not to put by!—you should sacrifice anything to do
so!'———these   same   friends   individually   say—'o———3
guineas,———what difference can they make?'—& thus it is,
through their consistency that I am minus 157.£. to begin life
with once more in the year 1864.

Happily there seems but one opinion of my book—so that is
some sort of consolation. But as I have a good many little
Commissions for drawings &c I shall not waste more time here,
but go.

I have been thinking more than once over your plans,
& I have come to the conclusion that I hope I may hear
you have taken the Cambridge=Church=decoration=offer.°
I feel, that, (being sure you will make the commission an additional [credit *crossed out*] fame for yourself,) this is a chance for
getting you out of the groove of Dealerism. If you can become
independent of those hedgehogs I should feel truly pleased.
And by what you told me, you will have time to do as you
please great part of the year. Moreover, Cambridge is not
Oxford: & if there were nothing else of good, W. G. Clark° lives
there.

I have often thought of going to live at Cambridge myself:
but that, as many other intentions,—fades away.

Write to me as often as you can; tho' I confess I am a beast at
corresponding now a days.

Goodbye, Daddy; perhaps Daddy I shall be a Water
Baby;°—but anyhow there are very many chances that we meet

no more, for often a man knows his own less or greater chances of life better than his friends.

Ever your's affectionately
Edward Lear.

o pa dont tell the Deelers I said as they woz edgoggs.

To Evelyn Baring

[Corfu. January 1864]

Beneficial & bricklike Baring,

Thank you for your note. I will come to His Excellency tomorry. Meanwhile, please give him the accompanying note & Book, which I hope he & you & Strahan° will like.

Give my love to Strahan. I have some frightful bad books for you both to read.

χαῖρε—φιλέ μου
Ὁ Ὀδοάρδος Λῦαρ

[Goodbye—my friend, | Edwardos Lear.]

To Evelyn Baring

Toosdy | [12 January 1864]

Dear Baring,—

Disgustical to say, I must beg you to thank His Excellency from me, & to relate that I cannot come. I was engaged to dine with the De Vere's, but am too unwell with awful cold in the head & eyes to go out at all.

I have sent for 2 large tablecloths to blow my nose on, having already used up all my handkerchiefs. And altogether I am so unfit for company that I propose getting into a bag and being hung up to a bough of a tree till this tyranny is overpast. Please give the serming I send to His Excellency.

Yours sincerely,
Edward Lear.

To Evelyn Baring

4 February 1864

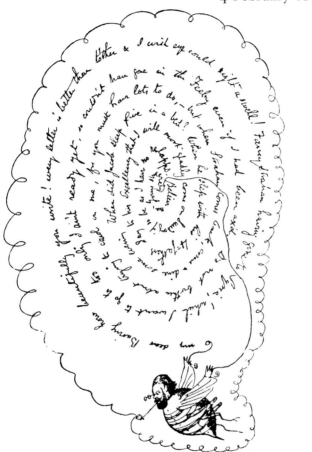

[my dear Baring how beautifully you write! every letter is better than t'other & I wish eye could right as well! Fancy Strahan having gone to Syria! which I want to go to too only I ain't ready yet, so couldn't have gone in the Feeby even if I had been ax'd. Do not bother about trying to cawl on me, for you must have lots to do,—but when Strahan comes back, come & dine some evening. When did Jacob sleep five in a bed? When he slep with his 4=fathers. Say to his Excellency that I will most gladly come on Sunday if so be as I have no relapps. Believe me, Yours sincerely]

To Evelyn Baring

19 February 1864

[Feb. 19. 1864 Dear Baring Please give the encloged noat to Sir Henry—(which I had just written:—& say that I shall have great pleasure in coming on Sunday. I have sent your 2 vols of Hood to Wade Brown.° Many thanks for lending them to me—which they have delighted me eggstreamly Yours sincerely]

To Evelyn Baring

[early 1864]

[deerbaringiphowndacuppelloffotografsthismawningwitchi
sendjoo thereiswunofeechsortsoyookankeepbothifyooliketodoo
soanwenyoo= =haveabetterwunofyourselfletmehavit.

Yossin seerly,
DwdL[ear]]

To Nora Decie

April 3. 1864. Corfu.

My dear Nora,

As it is most probable that you are less occupied than your
mama or grandmama, I have written to you to beg you to tell
them I am on the point of leaving Corfu, & that I am going to
Athens & Candia, & may probably be in England by the end of
June.

Will you say also that I am very sorry not to have been able to
write all the winter, but I I [*sic*] have done the same to
everybody, & I don't think I shall ever write much more. I
passed through Nice on my way hither but only arrived late at

night & set off early next morning, but I wish you could thank Mrs. Riley for her letter—which was very useful. (*Nice* my dear does not mean *nice* (like sugarplums & pudding,) but it is a town chockfull of houses, & it is called *Nice* as if it was written *niece*, which means Frank's daughter's relationship to you, only he has not got any daughters yet.)

Everybody here is packed up & going away, & we are all & every one of us cross & disagreeable & sorry & in a fuss & bothered. I should not however advise you to use the words 'bother' or 'chockfull'—for they are not strictly lady like expressions.

I hope Frank & Ruth are well, & your mother & father: give my love to them, & to your grandmama & grandpapa. Good bye, my dear; I am going to start tomorrow, having sent my luggage away, & intending myself to go by sea, as it is cheaper than going by the steamer. I therefore join Captn. Deverills 3 geese,° & we are going to swim all the way round Cape Matapan & so to the Piræus as fast as we can.

To Henry Bruce

Στράτφορδ Πλαῖς, | 12 Ιουλιου, 1864

Φιλέμου Μπροῦς,

Νὰ λάβῃς πολλὰς εὐχαριστήσεις διὰ τὰς Ἐννήκοντα Λίρας καὶ Δώδεκα σελλίνιας τὰς ὁποίας ἐξεύρω ὅτι ἐπλήροσες εἰς τὸ λογιαρισμόνμου εἰς Δρούμμοντς.

Νὰ φυλάξῃ ὁ Θεὸς ἐσέ καὶ τὴν Κυρίαν Μπροῦς πολλοὺς

χρόνους διὰ νὰ εὐγάλῃς εὐχαρίστησιν χωρὶς τέλος ἀπὸ τὴν Ζωγραφίαν.

Εἶμαι πάντοτε θερμότατος
Ὁ ἰδικός σου φίλος
Ἐδοάρδος Λῦαρ.

[Stratford Place. | 12 July 1864

My dear Bruce,

Many thanks for the ninety pounds twelve shillings which I find you have paid into my account at Drummonds.

May God keep you and Mrs Bruce many years so that you will get endless pleasure from the painting.°

I am always most warmly your own friend
Edwardos Lear]

To Mrs Prescott

15 Stratford Place. | Oxford St. W | July 19./64

Dear Mrs. Prescott,

Supposing you should ever have the ninety ninth part of a minute to spare, you would like to see my new 'Gallery'—on the fust flaw. Also a picture of Florence° which goes away soon. I am sorry to say the Cephalonia (Henry A. Bruce's) is gone.

I have been out of town for some days—very much against my will: my nephew° having died quite suddenly on his return from the Rifle Meeting at Wimbledon. I came back last night from poor Fred's funeral, which, (in the little town where he was Manager of a Joint stock bank,) was almost a public one: the various corps of Volunteers carrying his coffin &c.

Do you hear anything of the De Veres? I wish I knew their address. When do you go to Scotchland? Shall you feed on oatmeal & Haggis continually?

Please give my love to everyone: & believe me, Your's
sincerely,
Edward Lear.

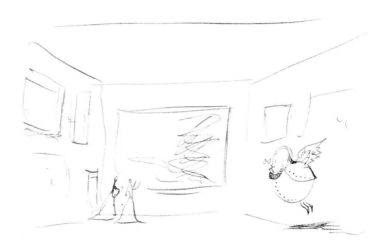

To Mrs Prescott

15 Stratford Place. W. | 12. Oct 1864

My dear Mrs. Prescott,

I thought it very kind of Mr. Prescott to look me up so soon.—I should have written very shortly—believing you would soon return.

Meanwhile, now I know who the grouse came from, accept my best thanks for them:—those birds enlivened the monotony of mutton chops very nicely. But I was not sure who had sent them, for wh. cause I preserved the original label (as see enclosed,) & I meant to wear it with a ribbon round my neck until it caught the eye of the donors whoever they might be. For I thought, if I write to thank anyone for what they have not sent, that would be like asking for other birds, & would altogether be a grouse mistake.

I am (I hope) to come to you on Saty week—the 22—& stay Sunday—a peep at you before I flee away south to

I dont know which—or much care, provided the place begins with a Nem.°

I hope after the 23d that you will come & see 2 pickshiors I have finished.°

Believe me, | Your's sincerely,
Edward Lear.

To Anna Duncan

[Nice] Tuesday 3 January 1865

Dear Miss Duncan,

I disclose the photograph which I hope you will approve of.

I got home very safely last night, and partly this was owing to the care taken of me by two remarkably large & amiable Frogs, whose arms I took, & who saw me down the lane. (You will see a true representation of the fact overleaf.) Nothing could exceed the genteel & intelligent expression of their countenances, except the urbanity of their deportment and the melancholy and oblivious sweetness of their voices. They informed me that they were the parents of nine and forty tadpoles of various ages and talents some of whom were expecting shortly to emigrate to Malvern and Mesopotamia.

Believe me, | Yours sincerely,
Edward Lear.

To Lady Duncan

61. Promenade des Anglais. Nice | 7. Jany 1865

My Dear Lady Duncan,
   You & Miss Duncan will be much pleased to hear what occurred just after you left yesterday, & I am very sorry you had not happened to stay longer. Imagine how much surprised & gratified I was by a visit from the two considerate Frogs, who brought their two Eldest Tadpoles also to see me. On the other page you will see a correct drawing of the interview. Both of these amiable persons were much pleased with my 2 Lamps, which I regret I did not show you, & one of them was so good as to say that if he were able he would have tried to carry one of the Lamps as far as Maison [. . . . .] to let you see it. They did not stay above 20 minutes, as they had a good way to go home, & I was vexed that there was nothing but a piece of cold lamb in the house & some Marsala, both of which they declined, saying

that either Watercresses or small beetles would have been pleasant, but that they were not hungry. I did not quite know at first how to be civil to the Tadpoles, as I found that owing to their long tails they could not sit on chairs as their parents did: I therefore put them into a wash hand basin, & they seemed happy enough.

Such kind attentions from foreign persons quite of a different race, & I may say nature from our own, are certainly most delightful: and none the less so for being so unexpected. The Frogs were as good as to add that had I had any oil paintings they would have been glad to purchase one—but that the damp of their abode would quite efface watercolor art.

Believe me, | Your's sincerely,
Edward Lear.

Exit of Frogs carrying Tadpoles

To William Holman Hunt

61. Promenade des Anglais. | [7 January 1865]

My dear Daddy,

I was very glad to get your letter on my return from Genoa on the last day of 1864:—& also to find one from Fairbairn—containing a long description of the picture, which I am really delighted to know about, & that it pleases them so much, as well as that you yourself like it. I long to see it. I only wish that T.F. & the 2 elder children were in it, but by the time a few more children are born, you will I hope paint another hexafamiliar groupe for them. They deserve to have the best paintings in the world, for their kindness & generosity, & although I liked them before, I now feel them to be still more of an A no 1 lot. I calculate on your not leaving Burton before Feby 1. at soonest—but, as you say—it is better not to calculate or prearrange. About your sleeplessness I don't know how to advise—for you are the exact opposite of me. *I* am wretched unless I can be out before sunrise, but hate night outgoing,—& the long gray cold mornings in London madden me—as do the late hours. But with the wonderfully artificial life English people lead—I see no remedy. I dare say you are right about the Janina,—tho those fields are very marshy:—but, as I said to T.F. my pictures never can be perfect: it is not their nature: they are born with one leg shorter than t'other, or one side of their nose crooked——& so they must die. I sometimes wish I were able to study more & so produce more nature=like work; but the whole groove & tenor of my life is against that, & it is perhaps better to aim at extensive Topographical representation, of a better order than has hitherto been called such, than at producing fewer paintings of a more perfect class. Anyhow, there don't seem any choice just now——& the speculation of 2 floors in Stratford Place must either kill or cure next year I fancy.

One of my aims this winter, was to 'get' all the Corniche—or Riviera di Ponente: & that I have done both ways—with 145 sketches & better health than before—also less abdomen. I now would fain sit down & work at the Palestine, Egyptian, & other drawings for sale in Stratford Place——but some 15 or 20 families bore me out of my life to 'shew drawings'——&

moreover ready cash is wanted: so I have commenced some slight small 5 pound potboilers, wh. I shall mount on white boards, & sell if I can. One was sold yesterday. To get these however, I have to be out all day many days——otherwise the vulgar known subjects of Nice can't be obtained & set before the eyes of the many seductively. You see therefore I am pulling 3 bowstrings——if not 4 or 5: 1st. getting sketches to make drawings from. 2dy. making said drawings: 3dy making drawings for London sale. 4ly. (at night,) penning out Corniche drawings. 5thly. Possibly contriving a Corniche book. 6thly. Foaming with rage when not doing anything else. Most happily the excellent George makes everything as comfortable as possible, but I hate furnished lodgings: the carpets & papers here are so extremely damnable that they resemble large flights of red & blue & green parrots with roses & mustard pots interspersed—so that I had to buy 4£ of brown Holland to cover them up or I should have gone blind or mad. I am bound to say however, the weather *is* wonderful. No fires—except in North rooms—or at night—& a blaze of sun all day. A letter had just now come from my sister Newsom. Another of my nephews is dead—one of the Federals:° he got home on sick leave to Boston—but died in 2 days: his father my brother, dont seem to recover the shock, & I expect to hear of his death. The Confederate brother is not heard of: his son still in prison. Whenever you are inclined, write. I wonder what you will do in the East. Some one said, Dannel in the Lion's den. Of course those legends are very sure of success in multitudinous ways—but I would fain see somewhat of a truer & broader caste of poetry. (So far as popular delight would make success sure—Daniel &c—with Balaam's ass seen thro' a window— Jonah's whale on a distant shore—Elijahs ravens—& the Gadarene piggywiggies—would be a lovely subject.) Have you thought of Jacob or Rebekah—or rather the man sent from Jacob's wife. But you are a far better judge of these things than I. Only some day, before you start, let me know—even if you don't come this way. There is a   every week from here to Genoa:—But be sure   to let me know be- fore you come— —if so be as   you do come.—
  Some one said here ʌ is to be made a baronet.° Is it true?
                                I must leave off. | Your's affly
                                            Edward Lear.

To Emily Tennyson

15. Stratford Place. Oxford St. | W | May 10. 1865

My dear Mrs Tennyson,

A letter of your's—date Apl. 21—should have been answered before now by rights. The Cogoletto° is still here—but if Alfred does not come to town, I will send it—wishing I could bring it. If Watts's portrait of the boys is equally like that of their mother————non dico più [I say no more].

I have opened my Gallery—which contains 138 views—& looks splendifical. About 100 visitors have been as yet—& some drawings have been bought;—nevertheless I am not sanguinary as to my success this year—from various causes:—& if I am not repaid for the great outlay of rooms—fittings up—frames—wintering abroad with double rent—&c &c————I think I shall collapse in the Autumn, & go & live at Parâ on the Amazon. There, & also in the Bush in Australia—(as I heard Mr. Lowe say last night,) are abundance of fat caterpillars highly edible & refreshing————& thus life for its few remaining years, would be cheaply sustained. I should certainly go—if it were not for my one remaining sister;—(the other, of the two still living, I do not reckon—as her real home is in New Zealand—& as her husband now 80 is in a most sadly failing state,—his (& *her*) release cannot be remote. He has the same sad delusions that poor Mr. Prescott had°—& the dreadful amount of anxiety my poor sister has to bear is hardly to be told. This is the 3d case of this miserable nature now known to me, & I have come to the conclusion that nobody ought to marry at all, & that no more people ought ever to be born,—& so we should be gradually extinguified, & the world would be left to triumphant chimpanzees, gorillas, cockroaches & crocodiles:)—but I cannot resolve to do so, that is, to leave England, while she lives; (& after all I may go out of the world first). For even if I get enough tin to cover all expenses, the method of doing so is so harrassing [*sic*] & odious—seeing the vapid nature of swells, & the great amount of writing, & the close confinement to the house,————that I loathe London by the time [I] have been here a month. The walking—sketching—exploring—noveltyperceiving & beautyappreciating part of the Landscape painter's life is undoubtedly to be envied:—but

then the contrast of the moneytrying to get, smokydark London
life—fuss—trouble & bustle is wholly odious, & every year
more so. So you will not be surprised at my going off one day
suddingly to a new life in some other part of the 'Globb' as a
Scotchman said to me.—(Can you imagine anyone saying of
one of my Palestine drawings——'Rachel's Tomb'———'Ah!
poor woman!—I heard Mr. Lear had been staying at Cannes
where she died!'—& another person tells me that he heard 2
visitors disputing over the Motto 'I will see before I die
&c'——as to whether it was in *Jonah*, or Jeremiah!———)
Frank I have not seen more than once:—Holman Hunt
twice;—there is no comfort in London whatever. Woolner I saw
at his own place once.—

I went down on Saty to the poor Prescotts——& saw all of
them. As yet they can hardly realize all the grief. Did you read a
very nice paragraph or article on Mr. Prescott in the Pall Mall
Gazette?—It was written by Mr. Helps. I should like to know
how Alfred likes a Pome or Tragedy by one Mr. Swinburne—
Atalanta in Caledon [*sic*]: I take to it extremely. I wonder if the
boys have gone to school yet. You see Manning succeeds
Wiseman: Protestantism of all sorts—i.e.—daring to think—is
to be considered as one & the same as Democracy, & thinking
this the Aristocracy are to become Papists. It will be time to
make a stand openly before long—against fibs, & bad creeds,
and clerical crookednesses altogether. I think I must have tried
you by this time—so with love to Alfred & the boys, | believe
me, | Your's affectionately,
Edward Lear.

To Edgar Drummond

15 Stratford Place. | W | 11. Sept 1865

Dear Edgar Drummond,

I have sent the queer little toy for your youngest child's
benefit: please give it to Mrs. Drummond for him, & I hope he
has not got one already.

You must screw the screw handle on to the edge of a thin
table——taking care that the strings attached to the weight are
not entangled, but can act freely. Thereupon—[(]the weight
being concealed by the edge of the table,) you must kick or

knock it more or less—& according to such propulsion the remarkable bird will wag his tail & nod his head with vivacity or solemnity forthwith.

Some day if you are passing I think you will like to see 2 (long ago begun) pictures of Corfû & one of Olympus;—also one—not yet quite finished—of the Campagna di Roma—I fancy one of my best.

I have asked your brother Alfred if he will come to me one evening, & later I will write again to you,—but I can't ask both together along of the nature of the Establishmt. here—for as others now dine at home, I am lucky if I can get small arrangements attended to.

Yours sincerely,
Edwd Lear.

I shall have to go out *straight* to Alexandria°—along of Quarantines—I fear.

To Edgar Drummond

15 Stratford Place. | 22 Sept 1866.

My dear Edgar Drummond,

Your last should have been answered before now, only that when there is nothing pleasant to write, the pen is allowed to be unoccupied longer than it ought. The dark weather & constant interruptions have made me far behindhand with my Watercolor drawings, & it will be well into October before I can commence on oil——at a time when short days & darkness increase;—consequently, except to my Sister, & to one old friend who is now poor instead of rich,—I shall be quite unable to move out of London. Nor, even were time not the question, could I well do so in this weather—the constant rain & dampness making me unwell & asthmatic to a degree not pleasant in visitors at country houses. I had occasion, on business, to go to Lewes last week, & have coughed & snuffled ever since.

I do not know if you have much corn—or of other crops: if so I fear you must be suffering.°

Once more it seems my return to the East is jeopardied—for

every place thereabouts seems in a bubbling state not propitious to Topographers. But there is yet time to judge & arrange.

Regarding my pictures, I have (in spite of artistic friends,) returned to my earlier plan of reduction of prices°—viz—

525£ for the Cedars instead of 735£
315£ for the Masada instead of 525£
& 210£ for the Beirut instead of 315£

and this resolution I shall not now change; nor indeed can I do so, as I am speaking of it everywhere. And if you should still wish to possess the Beirūt, altho' it might not be convenient to you to do so by paying for it at once, I want you to know that you may have it—(only giving me a note that it was bought for so much,)——& pay for it AT ANY TIME THAT BEST SUITS YOU—IN PART OR AT ONCE. This I mention because of what you named to me when last here: & you need not answer this now—nor at all if you think proper. I shall have the picture varnished, & there it will be.

The Olympus shall be 'mended'° the very day I get out my oils—i.e—when the last drawing of the 240° is finished. I wrote to you (at Sandbeck I think,) telling you of its safe arrival here.

I am on thorns about Crete—Epirus—Samos &c°—but can get no real information as yet. If I do, on Monday, from Corfù, I will write.

My kind regards to Mrs. Drummond, & believe me, | Your's
sincerely,
Edward Lear.

To Lady Waldegrave

Cairo. March. 9. 1867.

My dear Lady Waldegrave,

I wish I could write you a long letter, but I want to thank you & CF for your help before the mail goes, & there is scanty time & much to do. I came back from having safely performed the first half of my journey—viz——the Nile & Nubia—yesterday, & found your very kind letter, as well as one from Messrs. Drummond, informing me of the payment of One Hundred Pounds which you have so kindly lent me. Conjointly with your aid, assistance also came to me, in more or less degree—from Lord Houghton,° Mrs. Clive, B. Husey=Hunt, T. Fairbairn, John E Cross, F. Lushington & W Langton. I am a queer beast to have so many friends.—

I am so pleased the Venice° is so much liked, but it is quite fit & right that C[hichester]. S[amuel]. P[arkinson]. F[ortescue]. should like it less than your portrait: so long as it ranks next I am well content. I should like to see Richmond's drawing of C. I hope he won't make him clerical & holy & soft, he being neither. What an awfully cold winter you see to have had! & in other respects not a pleasing one—particularly as regards Fenianism.° I hear just now that W. Cranborne, Gen Peel & Ld Carnarvon have left the Govt:—will it break up & cease—or join Gladstone—or what next? I should like to have read C.'s letter°—but I get no sight of papers now—as directly they are devoured, off they go—& no old ones exist. The consul General here—Col. Stanton RE. & Mrs. S—are very good natured, but I am not up—after rising as I do at 5 30 & writing all day—to going into 'society' at 9 or 10.

In a few days I go to Memphis for a day or two—to wind up my Egypshun work—& then I hope to start across what is called the short desert—for Gaza Askalon & Ashdod: & if I chance to find a nosering of Dalilah with Samson's hair set in it, won't I pick it up? Then, after a time & times & half a time at Jerusalem, I trust to go to Nazareth for the scene of M. Milnes' picture. The sea of Galilee,—the City on a hill which cannot be id,—the site of the cursed cursive concurrent pigs,——Endor with or without a witch, & other places are to be visited: if possible——Gilead & Gerarh, & if possibler, Palmyra. Also Canobeẽn & other Lebanon places,—so that from Beirūt I may come back by Carmel &c to Jaffa—& Alexandria, & thence by Italy to England early in July. I hope then that I shall have done with all this part of Asiatic Topography—& that I shall be able to projuice 2 worx—one on Egypt—t'other on Palestine.

Nubia delighted me; it isn't a bit like Egypt, except that theres a river in both. Sad, stern, uncompromising landscape—dark ashypurple lines of hills—piles of granite rocks—fringes of palm—& ever and anon astonishing ruins of oldest Temples:—above all wonderful—Aboo Simbel which took my breath away. The 2d. Cataract also is very interesting—& at Philæ &

Denderah I got new subjects—beside scores & scores of little atomy illustrations all the way up & down the river. An 'American' or Montreal cousin° was with me above Luxor, but he was a fearful bore; of whom it is only necessary to say that he whistled all day aloud—& that he was 'disappointed' in Abou Simbel. You cannot imagine the extent of the American element in travel here! They are as 25 to one English. They go about in dozens & scores—one dragoman to so many—& are a fearful race mostly. One lot of 16—with whom was an acquaintance of my own—came up by steamer—but outvoted my friend, who desired to see the Temple of Abydas,—because 'it was Sunday, & it was wrong to break the Sabbath to inspect a heathen church.' Whereon the Parson who was one of the party preached 3 times that day, & Mr —— my friend shut himself up in a rage. Would it be believed, the same lot, Parson & all, went on arriving at Assoŭan—on a *Sunday* evening—to see some of those poor women whose dances cannot be described, & who only dance them by threats & offers of large sums of money? As all outer adornment of the person—except noserings & necklaces, are dispensed with on these occasions, the swallowing of camels & straining at gnats is finely illustrated. At Luxor I frequently saw Ldy Duff Gordon°—but on my return she had broken a blood vessel—& is now reported very ill indeed. She is doubtless a complete enthusiast, but very clever & agreeable.—I heard there of the death of my poor friend Holman Hunt's wife at Florence—& here I find affecting letters from her sister. Poor Daddy is still at Florence, where some friends take charge of his motherless boy.°—Meanwhile it is getting very hot here, & the flies are becoming most odious & unscrupulous. As a whole the Shepherd's Hotel (or Zech's as it is called now,) is more like a pigstye mixed with a beargarden or a horribly noisy railway station than anything I can compare it to. To add to my difficulty in writing I have a miserable toothache or neuralgia—so I must stop.

My kindest regards to the Mimber, & with many thanks; believe me, | Dear Lady Waldegrave, | Your's sincerely,

Edward Lear.

As I passed Philæ going up—just at sunset, the very same effect of the Duc D'Aumâles picture° was over it.

To the Earl of Northbrook

15 Stratford Place. Oxford St. | 11. Oct 1867

My dear Baring,

I meant to have written a longer letter in answer to your's—for which many thanks,—but I have not time to day. Yet, as Bush the Bookseller° has sent me the enclosed, (you remember telling me to let you know if a copy of my Parrots turned up,) I shall send it on with these few lines.

The 'Psittacidæ' is (tho' I say it) really a beautiful book, & very rare now. (The 1st. Ld Ellesmere told me he had given 6£ at a sale for one—) To those who know anything of the foolish Artist, it is interesting as the first of his published works, & that wh. led to his going to Earl Derby's:—to those who don't, it has interest as being the first book of the kind drawn on stone in England of so large a size, & as one wh. led to all Mr. Gould's improvements—vide that gentlemans Birds of Europe——Toucans & c——many of which the said foolish Artist drew.

I cannot say, being a truthful cove—that I am sorry Mr. Romaine° his nose was by Scamp bebitten: not out of dislike to Mr. Romaine, but that the fact may prove a warning—for snapping dogs are odious to all visitors, tho' they haven't the candiour as I have to say so: moreover if I had only one little girl, I daresay I should let her have 10000 little snapping dogs. In the meantime—if anything goes wrong in the Navy—I shall know to what—Hydrophobia or nervous aberration—to attribute the errors. Who *nose* what may occur? I am more cold & more cross than ever——it's so horridly dark & beastly. My only consolation is to buy toys for Charles Knight's & Holman Hunts children.

Yrs affly
Edwd Lear.

My love & condolences to Sissy.
C. Fortescue was here 2 or 3 days ago: gone back to Chewton.°
And I met Hy Grenfell t'other day.

To Emily Tennyson

[It was only after Lear realized that he would never become one of the established painters of his day that the most important phase of his Nonsense writing began. The first of his Nonsense songs, 'The Owl and the Pussy-cat', was written in Dec. 1867 for the daughter of John Addington Symonds.]

Villa Montâret | 6. Rue St. Honoré, | Cannes. | Alpes
Maritimes.

My dear Mrs. Tennyson,

You see by the above address that I had intended answering yours of last Feby long ago. But a constant lot of worry & occupation made me a very bad letter writer—& consequently the address should now be,

AJACCIO | Corsica. | May 6. 1868

I was so disgusted with furnished lodgings last winter in Cannes that I resolved at length to have a settled place to come to for the winter, & thereupon hired a floor in a new house opposite the sea, & having purchased a sufficiency of pots & pans &c, set up house for the present in the Maison Guichârd—Boulevard l'Imperatrice. How long I shall remain there remains to be seen: anyhow at the beginning of April as I couldn't to back to Palestine, I thought I would 'do' Corsica—& came here with that intent, tho' I doubt if it can be carried out after all as fully as I wished. The J. Symonds° were in the Steamer, at Nice;—but during their stay here he was constantly unwell. They have just been heard of from Pisa—but had a sad journey hence, the carriage having been upset on the way.

I have seen the southern part of the Island pretty thoroughly. Its inner scenery is magnificent–a sort of Alpine character with more southern vegetation impresses you, & the vast pine forests unlike those gloomy dark monotonous firs of the north, are green & varied Pinus Maritima. Every corner of the place not filled up by great Ilex trees & pines & granite rocks, is stuffed with cistus & arubutus, Lauretinus, lent[. . .] & heath: & the remaining space if any, is all cyclamen & violets anemones & asphodels—let alone nightingales & blackbirds.

The people are very unlike Italians in some respects: wanting their vivacity—but with all their intelligence & a shrewdness quasi Scotch. The children are grave & thinking little animals, & one can understand the Napoleon or any other Buonaparte cropping out of such ground. It is curious to see the house N.I. was born in—& to find so many points of Corsica where his history is as it were one with that of the Island. At Porto Vecchio I read 3 of his letters—a place too where there were bundles of others from Paoli. This place is exceedingly beautiful—Ajaccio, I mean: the far mountains are glorious, but the Gulf has not much beauty—it is the tendency of Corsican coastinesses to run out into too long lines. The town is dull—& a kind of vacant dreariness pervades things in general—an impression perhaps assisted by the fact of nearly everyone dressing in black. Less picturesqueness of costume, or good

looks in either sex one rarely sees in 4 weeks of a southern=place=touring. There are people who look forward to Ajaccio becoming a great AngloSaxon winter institution, & already 2 Doctors are frantic about it—& I suppose a high, low, and rich=ulistic parson will soon start churches. A gt Hotel is talked of, but intanto this is a decent one. A Miss Campbell°—a vast & manlike maiden—has been here for months with her singularly ugly female servt—& she roars & raves about Corsica,—goes hither & thither, & is bringing out a book about it. I could well have wished to do the same, could I manage to see the whole place—but I am sorry to say my servant Giorgio has just got an attack of fever—& I can't manage alone, as it is a very rough country to travel in, except for such strong folk as Miss Campbell. It will be a considerable bore to have made the voyage & spent a lot of tin for nothing.

I was very glad to know that you are better in health, & that you have given up answering fooly peoples persecuting painprovoking pages. I wonder what ⋏ will do with his Hebrew: also if Hallam is quite well now, & Lionel also.

Likewise if you are beginning to build in Surrey. I myself, should I build at all have determined to do so in one of the tall Pine trees at Bavella here. Some of them are 140 feet high, & wonderful to see: they end in a flat tuft, & there it is I should build. It would be very grand to look down on the forest & on the hills from that point, but one would have to live wholly on pine seeds, & that sparingly. I find I am getting foolish so will stop.

My love to ⋏ & the boys: I hope to return by mid June to England. | Yrs. affectionately.

Edward Lear.

Your letter was delightful & I have not thanked you enough for it, as it was valuable in many ways. The conventional life of an English Colony like Cannes is terribly tiresome, & I half wish I had not fixed there.

To the Editor of The Times

[published 14 October, 1868]

Sir,—In a notice entitled 'The Brindisi Route' published in *The Times* a few days since, the writer, who dates his letter from the Hôtel d'Orient, complains that there is no decent inn at Brindisi.

Will you permit me to say through *The Times* that there is another and very tolerable inn in that town of which your correspondent was probably not aware—namely, the Hôtel d'Angleterre, kept by Sebastian Gallo. The landlord, who has lived as servant in the families of the late Lord Seaton and of General Sir George Buller, at Corfu, and with the late Captain Murray, Resident of Paxò, is well acquainted with the ways and wants of English families, and his inn may be justly recommended to persons going by the Brindisi route to or from Egypt. I stayed two days at Sebastian's inn last summer, and was made as comfortable in every way as the limited size of the house he then occupied would allow of; he has since moved into one larger.

Allow me to add that for families who do not wish to make the railway journey from Bologna to Brindisi without rest there is an excellent hotel at Rimini, called 'I Tre Re.'

At Ancona (unless there is some new inn) I cannot recommend a halt, but at Bari the 'Risorgimento d'Italia' may very well be made a resting-place, if a break in the journey is necessary. I remain, Sir, your obedient servant,

Edward Lear.

15, Stratford-place, Oxford-Street.

To James Fields

All Letters to Mr. Lear to be addressed thus——

Edward Lear, Esq., | care of Mr. R. J. Bush, | 32, Charing Cross, S.W.

[Langham Hotel, London, W1] 18th. November '69
Dear Mr. Field[s],

I was agreeably surprised at receiving your letter to day;—the un-travelled=across=the=Atlantic mind awakes slowly to the idea of getting news from America so rapidly. I will have your name printed in my list of subscribers, which is to close finally on the 30th. inst. Thank you for interesting yourself about the Corsica book.° I certainly wish it to go ahead, because I hope it may pioneer Crete, Egypt, Palestine & other journals I have kept & illustrated.

Says my publisher, says he,—ask Mr. Field[s] the name of the House in New York, & of their Agent here, so that we may not clash by applying from two sides of the earth to two different booksellers simultageous. Says I, I dare say the agent is Toübner, but I will ask.—And so I do.

Next, will you kindly send, as swiftly as possible, or more swiftly than possible if possible——the name & nature & time or times of your magazine.° For, having been just now at Dr. Lushington's for some days—where billions of that dear old Gentleman's grandchildren have been screaming about the songs I sang,—they all want to know the Magazinious nomenclature, that they may order it 4thwith. Please to write to me at Mr R J. Bush's—as [. . . .] he will know my place of concealment [. . . .] hybernation. I have a story also of the

Lake Pipplepopple & its 7 families°—highly instructive, & wh. I wish I could see you & Mrs. Field[s], & that young Lady, laughing over.

You will I know kindly print my name in full 'Edward Lear'—wh. will, when I get the Magazine, delight my feeble mind, & console me for remaining in this cold foggy place. After all, small as it may be, one does some good by contributing to the laughter of little children, if it is a harmless laughter. There are one or two more poems also waiting for you.

Beyond all satisfaction just now is that of knowing that you & Mrs. Field[s] are so pleased with the 'Morn broadens':° & it is very nice of you to have found time to tell me of your being so. I certainly do hope I may see it & you both [. . . .] Boston one day. If I sent out a scrap of Philæ from Cannes for Mr. Curtis, will you continue to let him receive it?

Mr. Motley has sent me his name, & a very nice note, about my Corsica. So you see I am in a condition of general content.

But oh! is there not a brutal balance to all satisfactions? And are all those I have enumerated to be weighed against my cold fingers, & the normal state of nosefreezing proper to this beastly season of November?

I beg you will give my very kind regards to Mrs. Field[s] & also to Miss Lowell, & believe me, | Dear Mr. Field[s], | Your's
sincerely,
Edward Lear.   in haste.

a 2d letter has just now come, from Mrs. Field[s]. pray thank her

To Thomas Woolner

[Lear had now made the decision to settle permanently abroad. Early in 1870 he bought land in San Remo and began to build.]

Maison Guichârd. Cannes. | May 1. 1870

Dear Woolner,

As I am not likely to see you & Mrs. Woolner this summer, but as I should like to know something of how you all are, I shall send a line or two, in hopes that one day you may post one in return. I have had a long letter from Daddy, date March 15.

The drought in Jerusalem seemed to be about to make it quite uncertain whether he could stay there or not, & he even talks of returning to Cairo or Alexandria. In the last letter I had written to him I find I have knocked my head against a wall; for supposing that he was—as he used to be—of what you & I should call 'advanced or liberal principles' in religious matters, I had spoken about the increase of rationalistic & antimiraculous thought, & hoped his future pictures would point or express such progress. Whereas I find I never made a greater mistake, & that on the contrary, he is becoming a literalist about all biblical lore, & has a holy horror of Darwin, Deutsch, & I suppose of Jowett & A Stanley, tho' he don't name them. You may imagine that I shall nevermore touch on this subject:—meantime, if he should paint Balaams Ass or Gideon's Fleece it will not surp[ris]e [m]e. Of the 2 subjects he now is occupied upon,° he forbids me to tell the nature: perhaps you may know them, but as he discloses them to me on the condition of secrecy I of course am silent: they are not however of the supernatural order, & what I have writte[n] above only is to be applied to future work.

What are you yourself about? & how is Mrs. Woolner, & all your children? also my little brother Cyril, & good Mr. & Mrs. Waugh? Daddy does not mention J. Graham's death°—but I suppose must have heard of it. He tells me Miss Waugh is to be married to her brother's friend Mr. Key. How did you, & how did the friends whose names you so goodnaturedly procured as subscribers,—like my Corsica book? About 80 of those creatures (none of your lot,) have never paid—so at present I am all in the dark as to how accounts may stand.

During the winter I worked fearfully hard to get 2 large pictures done for the Academy°—both Corsican scenes. They have however hung one only—tho' if well hung that is better than that the two should be hung indifferently—besides a little Egyptian bit. The other 3 I sent are at Foord's°—& I think the Bavella might repay you the trouble of looking in, if so be you was a passing of the door, No. 90. Wardour street.

What do you think as I have been & gone & done? I grow so tired of noisy lodgings, & yet am so more & more unable to think of ever wintering in England———& so unable to bear the expense of two houses & two journies annually, that I have

bought a bit of ground at San Remo & am actually building a house there. It was to have been like this—only the Architect wouldn't let me carry out my simple principles of Art. 1—diningroom. 2 Drawingroom. 3 staircase window. 4. hall windows. 5 Street door. 6 & 7. Back & front bells. I regret extremely that I have been prevented from building on this plan.

'My house' will be done in November, & then I shall get all my Stratford Place furniture that remains unsold out by steamer, & what I have here by rail, & so I shall begin life again for the 5th & last time. As I have sold no drawings this winter & have no commissions ahead, I shall endeavour to live upon little Figs in summertime, & on Worms in the winter. I shall have 28 olive trees & a small bed of onions: & a stone terrace, with a gray Parrot & 2 hedgehogs to walk up & down on it by day & by night. Anyhow I shall have a good painting room with an absolute North light, & no chance of its being spoiled——— the room being 32 feet long by 20 broad. I hope some day you, & Mrs. Woolner too may see me there. I can tell you little enough about this place. Arthur Butler° was one of the few people I liked, but he was very unwell often, & I fear caught a bad cold once when on dining with me, he left in the wet. I myself saw hardly anyone, as I was badly laid up on my arrival by bronchitis caught on the road, & could not risk evening air at all. Nor was there much fun in the people who came to my studio, tho numbers *did* come:—yea, even such as Ld & Ldy Westminster, Rothschilds, Raikes[,] Curries, & Mackenzies were among those who passed long time in looking at my drawings,—tho no one bought a pennyworth, nor gave a single commission. It was the fashion, on the contrary, to do 2 things with their money: first to have a bust done by Munro:° 2dly to buy each other's drawings at Church Bazaars. Miss A did a daub, & Lady B bought it for 5£. Lady B did a worse daub: & Miss A bought it for 6£.—As for Munro, when I tell you that he has just gone off to Nice to make a bust of the Gd Duchess of Russia, you may suppose he is not so very bad as I certainly thought him last year. I think I must now stop my rather stupid letter. Kind remembrances to Mrs. Woolner: & to the

Fairbairns[,] E. Wilson,° & others who remember me. | Your's
sincerely,
Edward Lear.

To the 15th Earl of Derby

Certosa del Pesio. Cuneo. Turin. | 26. July. 1870.

My dear Lord,

Although the post is very soon going out I must write a reply
however hasty, to your exceedingly kind letter (date 14th.); it
has only JUST NOW reached me, for things move slowly in this
part of the world, & it must have been many days at Sanremo
though why I cannot tell.

(Before I proceed I must add what may seem all but
incredible——but it is fact however silly. A week (I think) after
I wrote came a large batch of newspapers—a literature I have
had no time to look at for months, owing to my leaving Cannes,
& being very occupied at San Remo. As all the English left these
parts long ago, & as those who write to me assume that I read
the news in papers——I have gone on in thick darkness till that
batch of newspapers came.—In the first I opened to my
surprise I saw the announcement of your marriage on the very
day before I had sent off that letter!—In other earlier papers I
afterwards saw that the future marriage° was announced,—but
that paragraph was my first intelligence of your new life, and
most absurd it seemed that I should have written a letter at a
time when it seemed to me there was every chance of it's being
unread, & hardly any of its being answered!—In this I was
mistaken, and I cannot but think it extremely kind that you
should have given me so much time as you have, when I little
expected even to have a line of reply————as at any other
time I should have done.

As I have said thus much on this subject I know you will
allow me to add that you have my most sincere wishes for your
happiness and for that of the Lady whom you have chosen.)

Now, I will refer to your Lordship's letter. I accept your offer°
with the greatest pleasure—and whether I finish a Corfù or any
other subject depend upon it I will do my utmost to make as

good a picture as I can. It certainly is a curious coincidence that the first oil picture I did (except *one*, belonging to Ld. C[harles]. B[ertie]. Percy,) was for your Grandfather. It is one of 2 small views:°—then the first picture the late Earl bought, was that of the Windsor: and now, the very first work I shall commence when settled at San Remo will be this for yourself of Corfù! I am *extremely pleased*, and quite see that a larger picture would not have been easily possible.—My new painting room at Sanremo will not be ready (I fear) for early work in oil this winter—say at least before February:—but I was about until it be so to do 2 large (for watercolor,) drawings in order to try–(vainly I fear,) to get elected Associate at the Old W/color Society:° The stained paper for these 2 is (I believe) already on its way out, & I have already made the rough designs for the drawings— Montenegro & Corfù——& if when I have done these you should prefer the latter in Watercolor to a similar subject in oil there will be ample time to decide. Perhaps in the meantime I may send a list of subjects of my topographical drawings—such I mean as are of greatest interest of picturesqueness.—

I think I would rather do a picture *purposely* for you, than that you should have any done *formerly*. I wonder which were bought by you at Maclean's: I was not then in England.

I find I am writing more & more badly, as I hear a horrid warning Postman's horn.

Please excuse this scribbling answer to so good & kindly a letter: I did not like to wait till tomorrow.

Accept my best wishes not only for the happiness of your private life but also for that you will, I trust for many years, lead as a statesman.

And believe me, | My dear Lord | Your's sincerely,
Edward Lear

(I am soon returning to San Remo, but cannot get to work till I do—& it is too hot yet to go back. This place is an old Carthusian convent—sold in 1801 by the F[rench].—& now used as a summer pension for Piedmontese families—. Do the Carthusian friars look down on their old gardens & corridors?—& if so, seeing there are 43 ladies, 19 nursery maids and some 50 children in said gardens & galleries——————————————————————— how do they bear the sight?)

To Chichester Fortescue

Certosa del Pesio. | Cuneo. | Turin. | 31st. July 1870

My dear Fortescue,

1. Time of getting his letter
2. Bkft at S Hill
3. CFs & J. Simeons paintings of mine also myladys.
4. FL. and the Essex house.
5. Lord Derby & request
6. War
7. Ld Clermonts letter.
8. George Kokali
9. Ld Granville
10. I. Secretaryship
11. Ireland
12. Valaorites
13. Egyptian journal
14. Child book
15. Certosa life
16. Scenery
17. Topographic life
18. Pictures
19. Piedmontese
20. Counts & Markisses
21 visit to | Turin
22. Things sent for
23. flies
24. Ld Henley
25. C. Simeon
26. C. Roundell
27. Heart disease
28. Sisters.

I was delighted to get your letter date 14th, which came to me on Saturday last—23d. Since when I have jotted down scraps of memoranda to aid me in writing to you when I had a Noppertunity. To day being Sunday, which I show my respect for by wearing a coat with tails & by writing letters instead of Egyptian journal, I can seize the memoranda accordingly. But as I have been writing all day, I am unequal to the task of 'composition' & shall accordingly put down all the notes, & comment upon them just as they come without any order at all. Here goes.

1. Your letter came about noon, just as (2) you must have been holding the breakfast at Strawberry: I should like to have been there. (3) Poor John Simeon! all you say of him is true. I wrote to Lady S to day. He & you have been two of my friends who have done me always justice as to my working conscientiously, & who have always appreciated my work. I should like by degrees to get a set of photographs of all my pictures.° Mylady is another who has been just the same to me: I was reckoning only a few days ago that she has as many as 8 of my works:

29. Congreves.   you 3 or 4 also.
30. Milady.   4d. My f[riend] Lushington has
31. Ld Derby,   very kindly of late got me a
    marriage and letter.   complete Certificate of London
32. Corsica   residence,   Countersigned   by
33. Reviews.   Italian Consul—a necessary form
34. Ld E. Bruce   for getting furniture duty free. He,
35. Holman Hunt   F. Lushington, being now P[olice].
Magistrate in the East of London, has taken a house in the East
county of Essex—he says it belongs to a Rev. Braham. The
name & county set me thinking if it were a brother of Lady
Waldegrave—but I never heard of one: so I have come to the
conclusion that Ward has taken orders. If he preaches like his
French sermon, all his congregation will burst.

(5). You will think this next an odd bit, but I had an
uncontrollable desire to paint one more picture for Knowsley,
so I wrote to Ld Derby that I wished to do so if he would let
me,——knowing how fond of my works he has always been, &
that from a child he knew me. But directly after I sent the letter
I got some papers—where in the very first I saw his
marriage!——& in the next the announcement that it was to take
place. So I set down the letter, wh: must have arrived on the day
after his marriage, as gone to limbo.

6 The War° is a bore. But if F. wants to devour others, I can't
but recollect that P. *did* devour some of Denmark & other
places: So I don't see one is worse than t'other.

7. I have half written a letter to Ld Clermont, as I have done
to everyone who has pictures of mine, about some photographs:
not knowing where he may be I addressed the letter to Carlton
G[ardens].° please let it be forwarded.

8 My good servant Giorgio, who hurt his foot badly on the
Col de Tenda, & had to stay here some time, has gone back to
Corfu. I heard from him yesterday—all safe. But I miss him
here considerably——having to do many things for myself I
now can't well manage. He returns to me in October, early.

9, 10, 11. I had not known of Ld. C[larendo]n's death when I
last wrote, but next day or so I did, & wondered who would fill
Ld. G's place, who I guessed would succeed him. But I cannot
but wonder at your not being moved at present from the I[rish].
S[ecretaryshi]p.—for who on earth could replace you? I do not

see how you can be staccato from Irish affairs for some time, & the next step I fancy would be naturally L[ord]. Lft.——because it would with a Peerage be the just reward of so much work, & to one who is so identified with the island. You could have done the Colonies well I believe—(G.B. will I think be radiant at Ld K[imberley]. being there instead of you,) but the nonpossibility of filling up the I. office at this particular time could not I think be got over. So you see *I* dont look on the matter as a slight, but quite the particular contrary reverse. Why was old Lord H[alifa]x put in again? I suppose some one must have been, & there wasn't much choice.————

12. I see Valaorites is Capo in Greece. I do hope the Greek affair° wont be dropped. Valaorites was always thought a good man by people one thought good & worthy of credit.

13. My only employ here is writing: & I have already written out the 1st. part—(1854) of my Egyptian journals: I believe *you* would like them, as they are photographically minute & truthful. But it will be long before I publish them.°

14 I have also finished (up here) my new Xmas book:° 9 songs——110 'old persons' & other rubbish & fun. All have gone to England to be lithographed.

15. I live the queerest solitary life here, in a company of 70 people. They are—many of them—very nice—but their hours don't suit me, & I HATE LIFE unless I <u>WORK</u> ALWAYS. I rise at 5. Coffee at 6. Write till 10. Bkft at Table d'hote. Walk till 11–30. Write till 6. walk till 8. dine alone. & bed at 10 or 9.30.——

16. The scenery here is of the most remarkably English character as to greenness—but of course the Halps is bigger: I never saw such magnificent trees, such immense slopes of meadows, & such big hills combined together; the Certosa Monastery itself however is a beast to look at.

17. I should certainly like, as I grow old, (if I do at all,—) to work out & complete my topographic life——publishing all my journals illustrated, & illustrative of all my pictures: for after all if a man does *any*thing *all* his life & is not a dawdler,—what he does *must* be worth something—even if only as a lesson of perseverance. I should also like to see a little more of other places yet—but that must be as it may as the little boy said when they told him he musn't [*sic*] swallow the Mustardpot & sugartongs.

18 I am going to do a big 2d Cataracht for next year's Academy—& a big something else for the International——if this War don't spoil all.

19–20. The Piedmontese are really charming people, so simple & kindly. Only I wish they wernt all counts. Who ever heard before of an omnibus stuffed quite full of counts—(8—) & 2 Marquises?.

21. I went to Turin on the 17th: but can't remember why I put that down, as there was nothing to say about it.

22. All my old Stratford Place things are now on their way out by sea.——

23 There are 2 sorts here—fireflies which are delightful & splendid, common flies, which are brutal and oathproducing.

24. So the agreeable Clara Jekyll has become Lady Henley. I met him once at S[trawberry]. Hill. She has written me a very nice letter.

25. If you see Cornwall Simeon, remember me to him.

26 Do you know Charles Roundell,° Sir R. Palmer's cousin? Secy. to Ld Spencer? he is a gt friend of mine, & has 4 of my pictures.

27. I must tell you that I have been, at one time, extremely ill this summer. It is as well that you should know that I am told I have the same complaint of the heart as my father died of quite suddenly. I have had advice about it, & they say I may live *any* time If I *don't run suddenly,* or go *quickly upstairs*: but that if I do I am pretty sure to drop morto. I ran up a little rocky bit near the Tenda, & thought I shouldn't run any more, & the palpitations were so bad that I had to tell Giorgio all about it, as I did not think I should have lived that day through.

28. My sister Ellen at 71. is vastly well. The New Zealander at 77 quite robust, & TALKS of coming over for a trip to see us—viâ Panama!—

29. My friend Congreve°—formerly a Master at Rugby, & for years past settled at S. Remo is in gt affliction, as Mrs. C. is dying of Cancer. His non return to S. Remo is a most serious thing for me—but I can't think of my own bother, as his is so much greater. He takes pupils, & has 4 villas there, wh. I wish to goodness were let to friends of mine for 200£ 120£ 120£ & 72£ all furnished.

[30] Are you & Milady going back to Ireland—& not to

Chewton at all after Pt. ceases to sit?—Give my kindest regards to her. I wish you would both have the rheumatism for a month, & come to the Corniche. Mind if ever you do, go to *Bogge's Hotel de Londres*—close to $\boxed{MY\ PROPERTY.}$

31. Behold, to my utter surprise, a letter HAS come from Lord Derby!——nothing more friendly & kindly could have been written, & with a commission for 100£ to paint a Corfù for him! I am extremely pleased for many reasons. So I begin my San Remo life with the same Knowsley Patronage I began life with at 18 years of age. I had some strong & particular reasons for making the request I did,—& to no one else could I have made it, or would I have made it.

32. You will be glad to hear that Bush's accts. of the Corsica have come in, & that, tho' there are still over 300 copies on sale, I have now no more money to *pay*, but on the contrary 130£ to *receive*: this is not however, *profit*, because my payments of the woodcuts were not made by Bush, but my myself. All truly religious & rightminded people should buy the Corsica for 30/ for wedding & Xmas gifts.

33. I wonder if after the Parliamentary business is over, & newspapers slack, if the Times & the Daily News & Saty. Review could yet put an article on my Corsica in their kollems.

34. If you see Lord Ernest Bruce—who has never paid his subscription, tell him he is a brute. If I had chosen I could have written far otherwise than I did about the Duffer.

35—Holman Hunt writes from Jerusalem: he is getting more & more religious: you & I should say—superstitious:—but don't repeat this.—

There, that's enough & more than enough. If you can't read this, nor Milady either, cut it across diagonally & read it zigzag by the light of 482 lucifer matches.

Your's affectionately
Edward Lear.

Vot a letter!

To Lady Wyatt

San Remo. | Italia. | Decbr. [4 *crossed out*] 11. 1870
My dear Lady Wyatt,

I was extremely glad to get your letter—on the 30th. ult or thereabout, & meant to have written (as you see,) sooner. I am sorry to say your dream has not come true, & I am as likely to live & die alone as ever, & no great matter either. Poor Mr. Congreve has come back—but that does not alter matters as his poor wife's return would have done, & the best half of my neighbour's house is still wanting. His 2 boys however are perfectly nice children. My only remaining fig tree was accidentially smashed by a lad with a ladder, so that figuratively speaking I now cut a figless figure. I think Matt's° wife must be so good a woman that she is seen almost to do him good in the long run: since she knew all 'his history' beforehand, I shall hope so;—for she must be a good little cove. I adjure you not to have any phitzavagew any more: & not to let Digby work too hard. I saw something about him in a paper, & was going to read it but was prevented: either he pulled down a statue of P. Albert° or he didnt. I think you have better even yet buy the 400£. piece of ground above Congreves:—Congreve built 4 houses this summer—& they are all let: & so is Asquasciatis new villa: Nevertheless the place can't help remaining quiet, because not only are there no roads, but no places for roads to go to. At Cannes, such towns as Antibes, Auribeau, Vallauris, Grasse & half a score more necessarily had roads—& villas grew up on those roadsides:—but here, why should there be a road made up a mountain for nothing but the chance of ultimate villa growth? Your brother & Mrs. Nichol[l] have decided wrongly: little Edith would have benefitted by this place—but now she will naturally lose her last year's gain. I see little Congreves, & Isaakes, & Eastons playing all day about,——except for the last week wh. has been cold. But I only took to fires 8 days back—& only one day have been prevented by rain from going out.

A copy of my 'Nonsense Songs &c' has come out, so I hope you & D have seen it: may it bring some tin! For I have but that one commission from Ld Derby, & 2 small fishes beside, &

what I shall do I don't know. I am at work,——*when* I work wh is very irregularly,——on a large W. Color picture of Montenegro: and though parts are done—parts ain't: of wh. anon. I do get the Times regularly—5 days after pufflication: that is I don't: leastways I should: but they don't send it as they ought. No—my white ties are useless—& Digby may buy them cheap: also the tails of my coat. I don't go out at all: coach hire is to be shunned—& besides there is no one to go to, but Ldy K. Shuttleworth,° who asked me to a lunch to meet the Bp of Gibraltar—but I declined for ever & ever. (N B. I heard the lunch was very bad—& there were 11 parsons at it!) There: I have now finished jotting down answers to your's—for which once more thanks: letters are the only solace of my life at present, except sardines & omelettes.

As for my house, the 'Villa Emily', I imagine all the workpeople will be out of it by Decbr. 31. For the last 10 days, Giorgio my old servt & I have worked like slaves at unpacking cases, & strange to say, all my 7,000 drawings are now in their drawers, just as if it were in Stratford Place: the 5 cabinets of drawers being so; in the upper large room A. B is my bedroom.

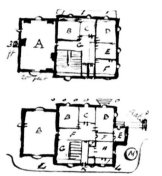

C. dressing room.—D. a book case all round. E & F. your & Digby's rooms when you come—if you can eat boiled mice & stewed spiders. G. is all over parble mavement: & I. I. I. is a barble malcony as looks direct south. A. on the ground floor, is similar to A upstairs. B a sitting or shew room. C. for a servt.—D. dining room with steps out to Terrace o o o. E a portch entrance. F F. parble massage with glass daws. G. an ollow understairs. H. Kitchen. I. Pantry J. china cubbid. K Bakdor. L—paved passage behind house. M. my well. The amount of expense in blinds—irons—railings &c &c grows horrid, & in truth I dont know what I shall do——yet it is absolutely necessary to get these things however trivial in themselves, & also to arrange & plant the garden. Another 100£ or perhaps 150£ will have to go in purchasing 975 metres of ground which have unexpectorally come in to the market, my respected neighbour Bogge of the Londres being about to retire. The building of anything on part of this bit of ground would ruin my property totally,° & a part of it will save me a long quarter of a

mile walk to S. Remo. 1. Congreve villa & ground. 2. Hotel de Londres. 3. My ground & house 4. Hanburys. 5.5. Bogges bits I am going to buy.——I am going to plant a bordure of zrubs 2 metres wide all round 'my property' /////////

Here enter Giorgio with 2 letters: one from poor Mrs. W. Prescott—one from Tom H. Wyatt. So please will you thank him from me first, for I cannot write just yet. I am really glad that he thinks Constance *is* gaining strength; please send my love to her. T. seems happy that Matt is married, and altogether his letter is cheery. I haven't much more time: I began, as I said, 3 large drawings—Montenegro, Gaza, & Corfu. But from various causes, consecutive work in these rooms is impossible, so I undo one day what I do the previous. The Montenegro is a cold and gloomy scene—*as it is intended to be, for it is so in reality:* & I have done one bit of rock so well that you sprain your ankles directly you look at it. In the foreground I had taken a gt deal of pains in a large figure of a Montenegrine, & he was really like life. But some days back as I went into the next room I heard an odd trumpetty noise, and coming back, he had put out his hand, & had taken my pockethandkerchief off the table & was blowing his nose violently! I do not tell you this as anything wonderful, (because you must constantly read of many things more astonishing about Mediumo & St. Rappers,)——but only because I had instantly to sponge out the whole man, for I thought, if he can take up a handkf, he may take up spoons or money. So I killed him, & I wonder where his better part has gone to. O dear! I wish I had done this dreadful drawing! & that I had sold it! I shall do some 3 or 4 small pictures for London Eggzibissions if possible.

Now I must not write any more. I hope Mr. Nicholl & Miss, & your brother Mr N are well. My love to Digby, & wishing you both a happy Xmas & New Year, Believe me, | My dear Lady Wyatt, | Your's sincerely, Edward Lear.

Tell me how you like the Nonsense book. a 4th. Alphabet is coming, & 110 old nonsense persons.

To David Richard Morier

San Remo. | Italia. | January 12. 1871

My dear Mr. Morier,

Your letter of the 6th. came this morning to my great pleasure: & when a person of your age writes *sitch* letters, they ought to be answered directly,—even if the doing so produces only a very stupid reply.

I am so pleased you like my 'Nonsense songs & stories[']: & that all the world is thereby delighted.—And I like to think that if a man ain't able to do any great service to his fellow critters, it is better wie nicht [than nothing] to make half a million of children laugh innocently. I hope Miss Morier liked the flowers: & I hope the household will try the Cookery receipts. While I was up at the Piedmont Certosa, I made at least as much again of this same nonsense——but it is decreed that that is to wait till next Xmas—as the present book is expensive enough for one time. The critics are very silly to see politics in such bosh: not but that bosh requires a good deal of care, for it is a sine quâ non in writing for children to keep what they have to read perfectly clear & bright, & incapable of any meaning but one of sheer nonsense.

Yes. The War *is* a horror.—I am going to turn Moslem as fast as I can, being sick of sham Xtianity, the only religion now rampant.

As for going to *Cannes* I *can't*: so unless Miss Morier comes here, I shall not see her. I can't at all understand why she—(having actually been at San Remo,) chose to go back to that windy cold place—where (so Mrs. Ker° writes to me,) all the flowers are killed by frost—though we have [Daturas] & roses in bloom out of doors.

Not but that we have had a good share of cold, but the position of San Remo guarantees winter being less odious than at Cannes. The truth however of the latter place being preferred is that this is *dull*. There are no peers or peeresses here,—no footmen or swell carriages,——all is quiet & stupid. So if people like to suffer cold & cherish coughs for the sake of fine society,—why should they not? Ἄς κάμουσι ὅπως Θέλουσι [Let them do as they like.]

You say nothing of ὁ Τερρίχιος Ἄμιλτον, [Terrichios Hamilton = Derek Hamilton?]——I hope he is well: please give him my kind remembrances.

My ouss is phinnished:—but I don't inhabit it yet for fear of 'roomatizz' said the Kangaroo.° However, I go there every day, & overlook making of blinds, shelves, κατουρησικά, and all sorts of ἀποκατόματα.° Giorgio the Suliot also goes & picks up my olives;——for, be it known to you I have about 30 trees.

Nevertheless, I am in a werry bad way as regards tin,——having no commissions for pictures or drawings, except one from Lord Derby & 2 small fishes from another friend. After all, if I can't keep warm in my new house I shall sell it, & go to Honolulù. I beg to observe I have got 2 terraces planted with broad beens, & I only wish you were here διὰ νὰ τά φάγης—ταῦτα τά φασούλια. [to eat them—these beans.] Voulez vous be so kind ὅ λα καλὰ χαιρετίσματα [all good wishes] alle Signore Miss Morier e Mrs. Neave [to the Ladies Miss Morier and Mrs Neave]? Goodbye—My dear Mr. Morier, for I am writing by candlelight & can't see. | Your's

affectionately,

Edward Lear.

I'm going to buy a Parrot, to walk on my terrace with,—so.

my new willer.

To Marianne North

Villa Emily. | San Remo. | Italy. | 8. June 1871.
Dear Miss North,

Your letter came yesterday, & I would gladly send you something better than I do,—but nonsense has gone out of me at present—as I have various sadnesses & bothers to write of to England & Cannes, where sundry friends are ill. So I thought the only thing I could hit on——not liking to say I could send nothing——was the actual fact & history of your letter, which I really did send away, (last year I had to pay nearly 2£ for unstamped letters,) & only, on recollecting whose handwriting it was, rushed out to San Remo & reclaimed it by paying one shilling & 2 pence. I doubt however, if your friend will think the drawings worth her keeping. I fancy I have already had the pleasure of making Miss Edwards'° acquaintance (at Mrs. G. Scrivens,°) but I am glad anyhow that you are sending a letter by her, as I shall always be glad to know any friend of yours. I envy you your going to America. I fear I am growing too old for any more travelling.—

What possesses Mrs. J[ohn]. S[ymonds]. to have the measles at this date? I hope Johnnie is better, & wish they would both come & winter here. No, Lady Shuttleworth & Miss Shuttleworth are not here: they have been gone a fortnight. Do I wish they had taken a dreadful howling poodle with them? I do. I am glad you liked my pictures in the R.A.° To days post happily shows me that a Mr. Brooke likes one of them well enough to buy it—wh. is just what suits me, as public Exhibition is all I live by nowadays that travelling purchasers are collapsed & eclipsed by French circumstances.

My kind remembrances to J. & Mrs. J Symonds when you write. Pray forgive me sending you so foolish a contribution, & with my best wishes for your American journey, believe me, |

Your's sincerely,
Edwd Lear.

It is some time since we met, & you may perhaps fancy the likenesses are not good;—but they are so, as you would see if you were here.

Mr. Lear refuses to pay for a Letter insufficiently stamped and sends it away. (Edward Lear. June 7. 1871)

Mr. Lear remembers that the handwriting is Miss North's, and stamps with late remorse & rage. Edward Lear, June 7. 1871

Mr. Lear executes a rapid Stampede to the Post Office.
Edward Lear. June 7. 1871

Mr. Lear delivers an extampary and affecting discourse to
obtain the Letter.   Edwd Lear. June 7. 1871

Mr. Lear stamps and dances for joy on securing Miss North's
letter.   Edward Lear. June 7. 1871

To the Hon. Mrs Emma Parkyns

Villa Emily. San Remo. | Decr. 18. 1871

My dear Mrs. Parkyns,

Half an hour ago came your letter of the 13th. with Gussie's
at the end. I was delighted to see your handwriting because I

had thought you too ill to write.—Eight Daughters?———
—Thats nothing. My mother had 13, & there is a Mr. Leach
here with 14. I laugh heartily at your idea of a son 'spoiling the
set' like 8 blue teacups—with one green. I write at once to wish
you all a happy Xmas & many more such,——& thank you
heartily for your kind wishes. But in spite of your philosophy &
sadness I think you have a better chance of merriment with so
many about you, than I have who live alone, & whose principal
occupation now adays is picking
off Caterpillars from my stocks &
passionflowers. I must however
grant that we DO see the sun—
tho' the winter is pretty sharp.
Since Novr. 27—there has been
no single cloud, & if you could sit
out a doors you might believe it
June,—i.e. if you sit out of the
wind: for the East wind is disgust-
ingly cold here. Unfortunately I

am obliged to sit indoors, & in a room not looking south, in
order to have a good painting light. I am doing a lot of 30£ &
40£ pictures—but with what success I cant tell yet. Some of
those of Egypt would delight M[ansfield]. P[arkyns].° (I've got
lots of beans up if he comes this way in March.) I wish he were
better paid: for he certainly is meritorious & no mistake. You
say nothing of Wally°—: I hope he is going on well. I knew a
Mrs. Craven at Corfù—Clergyman's wife—but I suppose this
was a sister in law.

It is really an immense pleasure to me to know that I amuse
so many people, & I am delighted you like the last book.° I have
written another song lately—'The Yonghy Bonghy Bò' which
is much approved of. Also Mr. & Mrs. Discobolos, & the
[']Scroobious Pip'. I cannot recollect the Polly Pussybite
Story:° is it too long to copy out small,—or too large to be sent
me, as the 4 Children MSS was? I should certainly like it to
come into the next Vol—if I can do another. Meanwhile one on
Egypt is on the stocks, & no end of big awful illustrations of
Tennyson's Landscape poems. The Jumblies I believe, with
you, are real critters.

We aint not got no great lot of society here, but such as there is is good & enough————————Kay Shuttleworths, a'Courts, Congreve & Green, Philip Miles's &c &c. Of course there are plenty more, but I am too old to make new friends, & those I choose to know at all must have some link with others. Do you know I am 6o next May 12th.? Criky!

I think Weybridge is damp if you live by the river: but up near Fox Warren it is dry: Oatlands is good but I suppose all built up now.

My love to Gussie & thank her for her letter. But why does she say my favourite betesnoirs are Clergymen? I am sure I like A. Stanley, & Voysey,° & C. Church, & lots of others. I suppose it was some nasty horrid curate I fancied she was going to marry, though I cant recollect any in particular. Tell her that just after I wrote last, Emilie Barry's turned up. They only staid a few days. I can't say I took particular to him,—he was such a silent cove or swell. Then I got into a scrape by rushing out abusively about Orby Shipley (I called Ritualists miserable Cretins I fear,) before I knew he was a brotherinlaw.

This is a silly letter, but if I dont write at once time goes on so; whereby I shall post it myself 4thwith.

My love to Mansfield & best Xmas wishes to all of you. & believe me, | Dear Mrs. Parkyns, | Your's affectionately,
Edward Lear.

You wouldn't like the water in my well: though I've just bought a filtering or filthying machinery—it aint so good as it was before. I believe its rats & beetles as lives down that well.

To Chichester Fortescue and Lady Waldegrave

Villa Emily. San Remo. | Xmas Day. 1871

As your last letter to me was a joint composition, I shall write a few lines to both at once, just to wish you both a happy Xmas & New Year and many such. I was very glad to hear from you, though I never wonder when I don't, knowing how fully occupied both must be. I can't say as I knows how to fill this sheet, for there is literally nuffin to say, except that barring one day, rain, we have had cloudless days here since Novbr. 26. Up to the 21 inst it was cold in the wind or shade, but June in the shunsine,—but since that day of rain it is quite warm & most lubly for to see. I'm sorry to hear Lady Strachey is so unwell: I often think how nicely her little boy would repeat a poem I have lately made on the Yonghy Bonghy Bò. Mrs. Bruce, I hear from her sister Pamela who is wintering here, is better. I wonder if you have been edified by my 'More Nonsense'—wh. I find is enthusiastically received by the world in general.

I was only away from San Remo a little while in Noctober, going as far as Genoa with Franklin Lushington of Thames P[olice]. Court—who came to stay with me a bit. I told S.P.Q.R F about my visit to Rome, in a letter I wrote last Septbr. (Bye the bye—there is a nelderly Mr. Faithful Fortescue here: is he anybody's uncle or aunt?)

I am bizzy in these short days in working at small pictures in oil,—& what is my spare bedroom in spring or summer I make my painting room now—as it is warmer. San Remo is fullish: Knatchbulls, Philip Miles', Calls, a'Courts, Monteiths, Ldy K. Buchanan & Co——Ldy. Isabella Hope & Co—Pitts, Levern Gowers, Ridley, Galtons & what not—but I see as few people as possible, till I open my studio for Wednesday afternoons, wh. I can't do yet. Have sold one 12£ drawing, as is all I fear I may sell, but nobody kumms. My garden is a great delight, & looking beautiful. Mice are plentiful, & so are green caterpillars; I think of experimenting on both these as objects of Culinary attraction.—Whether I shall come to England next year or knot is as yet idden in the mists of the fewcher. My elth is tolerable, but I am 60 next May, & feel growing old. Going up & down stairs worries me, & I think of marrying some domestic henbird & then of building a nest in one of my olive trees, whence I should only descend at remote intervals during the rest of my life. This is an orfle letter for stupidity—but there is no help for it.

Goodbye, & with every good wish. | Yours affectionately,
Edward Lear.

To Chichester Fortescue

Villa Emily. | Sanremo | 28. Feby. 1872

My dear 40scue,

Your letter of Xmas should by rights have been answered before now——but the short days take up all time in work——& by Lamplight my sight still troubles me too much to allow of much straining it. But though I didn't write I wished Mylady & you a happy New Year, & indeed am very frequently thinking of Strawberry as I am in the 5th. vol of Cunninghams edition of H[orace]. Walpole's letters,° which interest me very much, & give me a very different idea of his character than I had before I read them. Why were all his Curiosities sold? Did Mrs. Damer° sell them? Or the father of Lady Waldegrave's Lord Waldegrave, or he himself, or the Hastings Earl? And was or is there any correct catalogue of the sale & where the objics went to? I remember Lord Derby (13th) buying the basin as drowned the Cat as Gray saw as caught the fish: & Dunn Gardner had a bronze Hostridge. But who had all those wonderful miniatures,—the Benvenuto Cellini Bell &c &c

&c?—There are parts too I can't make out as to the building—the 'chapel with garden'——&c &c. Did Mrs. Clive outlive H.W: which I suppose she was his ladylove.

Yes you have had, have, are having, & are still to have a beeeeeeeestly winter, & are much to be pitted. We aint ad nun atall: & I've never had a fire till the evening in my sitting room—no,—not once. Can't you rush out at Easter? & stay for 3 or 4 days?—You could come in 3—& go back in 3. I could put you up beautifully, & feed you decently,—but I couldnt the Lady—having but one spair bedroom, & no feemel servants. I have got several large drawing boards, which you could use as Boards of trade,° & if you are making Bills, you might put a lot in your trunk & finish them here quite quietly. There ain't a creature here you would know I think——Lord & Ldy Derby are at Nice, & may come here bye & bye;——unless colonially you know Lady Grey who is Sir G. N. Zealand Greys wife or widow. Didnt she marry some one else & keep her own name? I cant help fancying I have heard of her—tho like Belshazzar's dream, don't know what about. A sister of Mrs. Hy Grenfell is here—& one or two nice people besides,—but we are all humdrum middleclass coves & covesses, & no swells. Why dont Ld & Ldy Clermont come out—as he seems so unwell.

I have very kind letters from Northbrook, who is glad to have his children there. I am doing 2 pixtures of the Pirrybids for him. Patronage ain't obundiant at San Remo—but I have a maggrifficent gallery, with 99 water color drawings—not to speak of 5 large oils—of the series illustrative of A Tennyson's pomes—

1 The crag that fronts the evening—all along the shadowed shore.
2 Moonlight on still water between walls &c
3 Tomohrit———
4 The vast Acroceraunian walls.
5 Creamy lines of curvy spray—

none of these however are finished—though visible to the naked eye: nor do I intend to part with any of them.

(In one is a big beech tree, at which all intelligent huming beans say———'Beech!'—when they see it. For all that one forlorn ijiot said—'Is that a *Palm*=tree Sir?'————'No,' replied I quietly————[']it is a Peruvian Brocoli.')

I live very quietly, & fancy my eye getting better now & then, but aint sure. Sometimes I go to church & sit under Mr. Fenton & hear all about that big Fish as Swallowed Jonah. A small walk daily—but this ain't a place for walks. If you come I'll show you the Infant school, & the Municipality, and a Lemon valley, & an oil press, and a Railway Station, and a Sanctuary & several poodles————not to speak of my cat,° who has no end of a tail—because it has been cut off.

My old servant Giorgio is much the regular old clock he has been for 17. years: & is pleased by letters from 2 of his sons once a fortnight. Ask Mylady to lock up the Board of trade for 10 days—& run hither. Only let me know if you are coming & the day.

My dear old kind Dr. Lushington is gone—& half one's old friends. I must say that life becomes werry werry pongdomphious. I heard Lord Strachey is much better———of wh. I am glad. Did you see Charley M. Church when at Chewton.

Is Mylady well? My kind remembrances to her.

I'm doing some drawings for Tozer° of Oxford: did you ever read his capital book————'Highlands of Turkey'?—Do.

Good bye o my board of trade!! O Samuel!!! O Parkinson!!!!

Good bye. Your's affectionately,

Edward Lear.

To Mrs Richard Ward

[In 1871 Lord Northbrook had been appointed Viceroy of India, and he invited Lear to travel there as his guest. In Oct. 1872 Lear set out, but he turned back at Suez. In Oct. 1873 he again left Italy for Bombay, arriving there in Nov.]

Villa Emily. Sanremo | 22. July. 1873

My dear Mrs. Ward,

I meant to have written sooner to thank you for your letter, & to acknowledge the safe arrival of the Checque for 7 *Ginnies*. The sum named vos *Pounds*, but as you have sent 7 shillin more, you must not pay for your frame. (The other frame will naturally form part of my small wedding present, which I am so glad to know that both you & Mr. Ward will accept, & like its subject.)

I have already written to Messrs. Foord & Dickenson, & have told them to let you know as soon as they arrive: that however will not be *quite* as soon as I had thought because I want to make the fellow or pongdonq drawing a rather particular one, for none of those I have will suit exactly. I mean to make one a'purpus, with a Campagna pine & shepherd's 'ut.

You say truly—the summer here izz delicious. My present chief=anxiety is to make some Jonah=gourdy=pumpkin= cucumber=vegetables rush up a pergola°—along with Ipo- mæas Passionflowers & Cape Jessamine. Vines is vines, it is true, & very beautiful—but they give so much bother of sulphur putting in these days that I eschew them.

Yes:—I suppose I shall go to Bombay on Octobr. 24 from Genoa. Meanwhile I work at the Tennyson paintings, of which I have 5 in hand, & as you know all the poet's works, I need not tell you where the particular quotations° are to be found.

1. Tom Moorey.
2. The Nasty crockery toll'ring falls
3. Like the wag that jumps at evening,—all along the sanded floor
4. To catch the whistling cripples on the beach
   With Topsy Turvy signs of screaming play.
5. = Spoonmeat with Bill Porter, in the hall
   With green pomegranates, & a shower of Bass.

This is frightful————but what can you expect from the Author of the Book of Nonsense?

Yrs. sincerely,
Edward Lear.

To Mrs Richard Ward

Villa Emily. Sanremo. | 25 Augt. 1873

My dear Mrs. Ward,

By today's post I send off both the drawings to Messrs. Foord & Dickenson, 90. Wardour St. | Oxford St.—where I hope they will arrive safely. On receiving this, will you kindly tell Foords where to send them when framed?,—& I will instruct them to forward them directly they are ready, when I trust you will let me have a line that I may know how you & Mr. Ward like them.

I have tried to make the pair as dissimilar as possible, yet alike in this, that I hope each may remind you of the Campagna in its own way. The subject you chose—'Evening—on the Via Appia,' is a little Temple not far from the high road to Albano—or possibly a tomb. Beyond it are the Acqueducts, & farther off Soracte, & the line of the Sabine Hills. The other view, which you have kindly accepted, is, 'Morning, near the Pinetree of Ridicicoli.' You look South East,——(in the sunset you look North West,—)—& overleaf I have made a little scratchybillity just to show you the principal localities—which happen to be interesting. The Morning view will hang well on the left—the Evening on the right, & I wishes as I was there to see them 'ung.

I am in such a Norful mess! bricks & mortar & stone—

Morning 1. Palestrina 2. town of Colonna 3. Alban Hill. 4–4, Volscian Hills. 5. Coriolanus—a smoking of a long pipe. 6. 6—site of the Lake of Gabii. 7. site of Corioli. 8. Ghost of Lucretia. 9. Ghost of Tarquin, a eating of a Nomlet & green pease.

[Evening] 1. Roons of Claudian Acqueduct. 2. Mount Soracte. 3. 4—Horace & Macænas, a playing at snowball on the top. 5 5 5—the Sabine ills 6 6—Barlams. 7 Ghost of an ancient Sabbin.

making a terrace, & a back entrance & offices as oughted to have been made long ago. Excavation also,—to keep the Elephants in as I may bring back from Ingy.

My remembrances to Mr. Ward. | Your's sincerely,

Edward Lear.

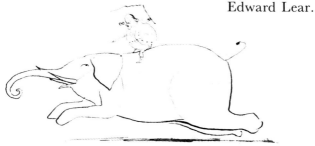

To Lord Carlingford

[In 1874 Fortescue lost his seat as Member of Parliament for Co. Louth. In Apr. he was given a peerage as Lord Carlingford.]

Poona. June 12. 1874.

My dear Fortescue,

I sent you a scrap from Simla on April 24th.—in answer to yours of March 20—but since that time I have been so constantly moving about that I have had no time to write either to you or to Milady again. At present I have come—(very unwillingly,) to an anchor for a period unknown—because all the world says it is impossible to travel in the 'Rains', & as I had perforce to stay somewhere I greatly preferred doing so here than at Simla, though I lived there in a house of Ld Northbrook's, & here am obliged to do Hotel Life—a la table d'hote,—which you may well think bores me not a little.

Yesterday I got some tin cases made, & soldered up no less than 560 drawings, large & small, besides 9 small sketch books & 4 of journals: whereby you see I have not been idle. Up to this date I have got a very good general idea of Bengal Landscape— which consists mostly of flat or plain scenery, or on [sic] big rivers, (the character of the views being chiefly pointed by detail of various kinds,)————and of Himalayan hills & vallies, of which I saw an adequate lot for my purposes at

Darjeeling, Mussoorie, & Simla. The Vegetation of Southern Bengal is delightful, as is that of the country about the high station of Darjeeling, while in the North West Provinces, Architecture & history are the main objects—& vegetation is nil nearly:—At Mussoorie & Simla, the huge mountain scenery is far less imposing than much you may see in Switzerland or Albania, owing to the gigantic heights of the Himalayas being so very far removed from the plains, & so broken into steps or ridges that you are always on too high a level to get any real sentiment of the great altitude at wh. you actually are placed. I went on for 4 days beyond Simla towards Thibet, but still failed to find any scenery whereat to screech fanatically, and as a rule my impression of all I have seen N & E. of the Ganges & Jumna is that the most delectable portion of the Landscape is that combining old Indian Temples & rivers. Nevertheless my 500 drawings in Bengal, N W. Provinces, & Punjab, form a vastly interesting mass of work & express Indian Landscape in those parts of this huge Empire——I think—as widely & fairly as a 6 months tour could well be expected to compass.

I have now decided—always with the help of Northbrook, to carry out my general views of study as far as possible all over the country, & for that end have come now to the West side of it,——which even as far as I have yet seen, pleases me extremely & is as utterly unlike Bengal is [sic] Lincolnshire is to Westmoreland. The detached mountains known as the Western Ghâts are thoroughly beautiful & interesting, & much more definite & varied in character than their giant Himalayan relatives, & the river scenery is exquisitely pretty. This place, Poonah, is so celebrated as having the coolest summer climate of India, that one hears nothing of its pictorial qualities, & I was surprised to find it as beautiful as agreeable. There are thunderstorms round the magic circle of the high Deccan plateau, but they do not seem to come near us:—albeit the people here say there will be a downfall of rain bye & bye—though I don't believe it a bit, any more than I did in Cobras, Tigers, Sunstroke & Appleplexy——all prophesied as inevitable. Thus you see I am going about my work with a method, and anyhow you & Milady will allow I am a very energetic & frisky old cove—(I was 62 last May 12,) for my age. Hitherto I am thankful to say I have been quite well, & so is my good faithful Suliot man George—whose care & help I could not have got on at all without. For, apropos of servants—of course there are numbers of good ones—natives I mean,— —but then they are drilled in a groove of exact & peculiar work for years, & such servants are not to be found out of employ. Those who want places, & who would hire themselves to a mere passing traveller, have either serious defects of character or are far too stupid to be capable of learning new ways. The old Anglo Indian bears with the routine of a multitude of slaves—each doing his part of caste=work; but hardly anybody can meet with or form a single domestic with ability for any general service.

In travelling in India, you have 3 modes open to you—Dawk Bungalows,—Hotels,—& Private Hospitality. The first is what I by far prefer. You reach a Dawk Bungalow at the end of your day's journey——it is a house belonging to Govt.—always near a high road;—containing often 2—sometimes 6 or 10 sets of rooms, the set of rooms being usually one front, one smaller behind, & a Bath room. The rooms have bedsteads, chairs, & a table—the bathrooms washing apparatus:——close by is a cooking house where the Khamsamah & one or two natives live & move & have their cooking. On arriving your luggage is placed in any vacant rooms, & old George in 10 minutes used to get both of ours into neat order—the beds (you must always carry your own,) made—& the bathroom ready for use. This would be about 6 or 7 PM, & as soon as a half hour or an hour are passed, the Khamsamah brings the dinner you have ordered—almost always chicken cutlets or a roast fowl——& you never fail to find Bass's Beer—often Claret or Sherry. By 9 or 10 I am shut up in my room & in bed——& G. in his—(though now & then only one large room is procurable with 2 bedsteads—) & next morning at 5 I rise—dress & wash—get some tea,—& by 6. G has packed up everything & we set off again. I have passed very pleasant days in these Dawk Bungalows—at Delhi 10 or 12 for instance: & their paramount good quality is that you *lose no time* while in them: nor, as I don't want the services of the people,—do I lose my temper either.

The 2d mode of travel, Hotel halts, is in 19 cases out of 20 odious & irritating, indeed I can only name 3 or 4 good Hotels as yet visited, out of dozens. Mostly the Landlords are people occupied about other matters, & leaving the visitors to the care of their own servants—most people bringing 2 or 3 or more. The hours for *meals* are at stated & often inconvenient times, & quite unsuited to my hardworking life: & the time lost by the table d'hôtes & dawdling is a frightful drawback. The rooms are neglected & dirty in many cases, & the food ostentatiously various in name & appearance, but pitifully monotonous as to its bad qualities. Your tea is brought to you cold slop ready mixed in a cup;——& with all these & many more inconveniences you have to pay double the sum which in a Dawk Bungalow would have secured you very tolerable comfort & independence. I have known instances of carelessness & impertinence on the part of Innkeepers that would be incredible in England. One, when I begged for a chamber utensil—(I grieve to say they call it 'Piss=pot' throughout this land;——'Pisspot dumpy?' you hear constantly at your door in a hotel—meaning—'do you want it emptied'?) coolly stared at me & said, walking away,——'it is plain you have not been long in this country!'——another, when I wanted to start & to pay his bill, said,——'Can't mind you Sir, till I've looked after the osses.'

But thirdly, you may have letters to people at stations, & if so, you will in almost all cases be received with the greatest kindness. Yet, say what these good people may, you cannot be master of your time in a private house as you are in a D. bungalow. You certainly *may* say to the Lady of the house, 'Maam, I want tea at 5—& cold luncheon & wine to take out with me, & dinner precisely at 7, after which I shall go to bed & shan't speak to you[']——but such a proceeding is repugnant to my way of thinking—& the result of my experience is that you *can't* do as you like in other people's Dwellings. I remember a long while ago that you used to say I always 'knew what *suited* me.'—& so I do here. Families & Hotels *don't* suit me. Dawk Bungalows *do*.

Travelling in India is as I dare say you know, very expensive—mainly on account of the immense distances you have to get over, & the necessity of moving with no end of luggage.—But Northbrook with his usual kindness supplies me with tin, advancing what I want on acct of his own & the late Mr. T. Baring's° Commissions. Otherwise I must have asked you & others to keep me afloat—but there is no occasion for this at all.

My plan—not at all as yet drawn out in detail, is to work my way south from here to Bangalore & the Nelgherry hills, & so to Madras,—& then to reach Ceylon from the end of India by Novbr.——; to pass 2 months in Ceylon, & returning thence to see the west coast—Cannara—Goa—&c & up to Bombay once more, reserving as a last tour a run through Rajpootana & Guyerât before finally quitting India in April. 1875. This I believe—all things considered,—to be my wisest plan of progress—or egress—or nogress: but of course it is susceptible of change, from unbeknown circumstances.

This place is doubtless one of the most pleasant of all those used in India as retreats from the great heats of the plains. One is not incommoded here at all, & the walks are charming, while at a little distance there are forts & other places historically interesting within a day's journey. All the Bombay world rushes here at this season, when Bombay itself becomes mouldy & wet, & Mahableshwur & Matherān are uninhabitable. (Matherān bye the bye, has most probably been the original Eden——I don't mean the first Lord Auckland,——but Paradise——at least the sculptural scantiness of the apparel worn by the natives seems to point to Adam & Eve as its originators. The people (aborigines,) of the hill are a separate tribe, & are known—naked though they be—as the most virtuous of people;—which the women's costume is this——a very short spencer just covering the upper part of the buzzim—& a narrow strip of (blue or green) cloth round the middle. Many of these worthy females are perfect in shape & very pretty—& it might be well that you should make some public suggestion that so economical & picturesque an apparel

may be brought into general use in England. To assist you in so praiseworthy a departure from modern habits, I add 3 portraits, to which you can refer ad lib. To return to Poonah & platitudes & plateau. The Govr. Sir P[hilip]. Wodehouse lives some 4 miles off at Ganeskind, & holds a levée tomorrow—to which you may conclude I don't go. He is a very amiable & kindly man,—(he recollected having met me at Ldy Wilmot Hortons° 505 years ago—) but I see the Bombay papers continually talk of is being recalled on account of the Bombay Riots°——paragraphs which may have weight where it is not so well known as in the Residency that the Editors of Bombay papers are mostly Parsees—the people who most growl at the upshot of the riots. It may however very well be that Sir P W. has not the tact & strong will of our friend N. whose statesmanlike qualities seem acknowledged as much by those who differ from him in opinion as by his friends. He writes to me from Calcutta that he is quite well—& so does Evelyn Baring: but the gt heat, & the artificial life of dark rooms & Punkah air must be no small trial, when carried on for months.

While I write, Lee Warner the Govrs. Secretary has come, & I am to go out to breakfast at Sir Philips tomorrow. His staff seem a nice lot——Col Deane (Mil: Secy—) who married a Miss Boscawen sister of Mrs. Lewis Bagot; Capt. Fawkes—grandnephew of my oldest friend Mrs. Wentworth & grandson° of Turner's Walter Fawkes of Farnley——with one Capt. Jervoise, whose father I knew° ages ago. Lady Howard de Walden cum a son & daughter were staying with them when I was at Mahableshwur.

I hope you or Mylady will write soon: please *always* address care of Captn. E Baring R A | Govt. House, Calcutta. I hope you will give me a better acct. of Ld Clermont: my kind remembrances to him & Lady C. & love to Mylady. | Your's

affectionately,
Edward Lear.

I have left no space for comments on your letter which interested me extremely. I thought & think the inhabitants of Louth, Louthsome. On the whole I am much less a liberal than I used to be in some matters.

No, I didn't went to Carlingford: does it belong to Clermont? I wonder if we shall meet in some other world to talk over past days—for alas! all the days——nearly——are past. My right eye is baddish° always. My love to Ld & Ldy Aberdare if you see them: I must write to Ldy A. soon.

To Lady Wyatt

[Villa Emily, San Remo] | 16. April. 1875.

Dear Lady Wyatt,

If I a*M inte*rupting you please excuse me
as I *mint* to have asked you a question the other day
but forgot to *mint*=ion it. Can you tell me how to make
preserved or dry *mint*? I have got a
mint of
mint in my garden, but although I
a*m int*=erested in getting some of it dried for
peasoup, I a*m in t*errible ignorance of how to dry it,
and a*m in t*orture till I know how. On cutting | the
leaves, should they be *mint*'sd up small like
mint'sd meat?—or should I put
the*m into* Gin & Tarragon vinegar? Or place them
in a jar of *Minto*n pottery, & expose them to the
ele*mint*s in a
her*mint*ically sealed bottle? If Mr. Disraeli,
who is now Prime *mint*=stir, could teach us how to stir
the *mint*,
I a*m int*ernally convinced we could manage it.
This is as plain as that the *Mint*cio is a large River in Italy, or that
Lord *Minto* was once Governor Genl. of India. Perhaps
at the rising of Parlia*mint*, he may help us. After all would the
success be com*mint*surate with the trouble?
What com*mint* can be made on this except
that Mrs. Wyatt should send T*om into* the country if he is unwell in town?
One thing is sure, all ver*mint* must be carefully excluded
from the bottle, & I a*m int*ending to get one really well
made, for I a*m int*oxicated with the idea of getting good dry
mint. Please if you have a receipt, give it me
which will be a monu*mint* of your good nature.
*Mint*ime I
a*mint*oo much haste to write any
more, so will leave off im*mint*iately.

Your's sincerely
Edward Lear.

To Mrs John Frederick Lewis

8. Duchess Street. | Portland Place | 22 June. 1875

My dear Mrs. Lewis,

Having lately returned from India & with many drawings of
almost every part of that great country,—I had thought that

Mr. Lewis,—if by chance he were passing near here,——might have been interested in looking at some of these Landscapes:—and thus it was that I wrote the enclosed envellope. But since I did so I have been grieved to hear from Foord's people that John Lewis has for some time been more or less unwell, & latterly unable to paint, so that there is no chance of my seeing him here, as he does not come to town.

So I have merely sent the envellope to you, with my kind remembrances to him, & begging you to say how sorry I am to hear of his ill health.

I bought a Catalogue of the RA. & was disappointed in not finding any of his works named there, & now I can understand the reason of their absence. There never have been, & there never will be, any works depicting Oriental life—more truly beautiful & excellent——perhaps I might say—*so* beautiful & excellent. For, besides the exquisite & conscientious workmanship, the subjects painted by JF. Lewis were perfect as representations of real scenes & people. In my later visits to England, (& it is 3 years since I was here,) I cared to go to the RA. chiefly on account of his pictures.

At present I am kept here by this exhibition of mine, but before I go back to Italy, I will try & come down to Walton, on the chance of seeing him.

Believe me, | Your's sincerely,
Edward Lear.

To Lord Aberdare

Riverhead Vicarage. 7okes. | 26. Septbr. 1875

My dear Lord Aberdare,

I meant to have answered your last—(Aug 19) before now—but have never had time—& have frequently been very unwell also. The perpetual damp of this country upsets me, & asthmatizes me horridly.

The Canvass is ordered & will soon be on its way to Sanremo: I have thought 6 feet (—frames *not* included,—) would be large enough for the space you name (making in all some 7 feet 6.) I intend that the 'Kinchinjunga' shall be so good a picture that no body will ever be able——if it is hung in your

Dining room,———to eat any dinner along of contemplating it,—so that the painting will not only be a desirable, but a highly economical object. And I shall fully trust that all future grandchildren of yours & Lady Aberdare will be Christened Kinchinjunga as an additional appellative.

I could not come to read a paper at your Society,—because I only came to know much about leeches, & these I cussed & called such bad names that I did not think the M.S.S. would be received on account of its vehement viruviolence.

I am here on my way to Phoaxtn———staying at Franklin Lushingtons—which they have a wacant Wickeridge. I wanted to walk to Knole—but it rains so hard that it has become Knoly me tangere & we can't go.

I have hired a pestilential porpuss to cross the Channel as I am too horridly afraid of the sea, & I wont go in the Castalia—as I know it would split & I should fall into the sea between the geminiferous particles.

My kindest regards to Ldy Aberdare & all. | Yrs. sincerely,
                                                    Edward Lear.

I saw P. Williams 2 days ago—& reminded him about your promise, & his wishes as to the Box:—but he seems in a *very undecided state of mind*—& so must be left.

My last days here have gone at my poor Sisters—J. F. Lewis's—Mrs. Greville Howards &c—: but I shall be glad to be off.

To W.S.

8. Duchess St. Portland Place | 25. June. 1877
Dear Sir,

On returning from Surrey just now, I find your Book of

Bosh,° & hasten to thank you for it, & for your Dedication of it
to me the Father of Nonsense.

I have not time to look at it much just now, but I thought at a
glance, the two Ladies going down into the Cellar very funny.

Believe me, | Dear Sir, | Your's very truly,
Edward Lear.

To Hallam and Lionel Tennyson

8. Duchess St. | Portland Place. | 22. Augt | 1877

Dear Hallam,

Supposing you are a tome—ask Mama & Papa if I may come
down———should I be able to do so———on Saturday next.
Perhaps you are all away: Prapps the house is full. Perhaps I
might go to Liphook, & walk over on Sunday. Prapps—più
prapps—prappsissimo.

Please send a line here. | Your's affly
Edward Lear.

If you are at Aldworth—send me word if,——(should I be
able to come down on Saturday for Sunday——which is
uncertain—) I may come for those days?

Your's affly,

Lear.

To Lord Aberdare

8. Duchess St. Portland Place. | 23d. Augt 1877.

My dear Henry Bruce,

I am in a Norfle state of sattlesphaction & delight at your & Lady Aberdare's letters just now derived. I am really immensely pleased that the Venerable the Kinchinjunga is so well placed & so much liked. After all it is better to be the means of giving armless pleasure to a limited number of people, than to be the means of slaughtering indefinite thousands——though I grant the latter function requires the greater ability.

Concerning the possibility of my picture causing travellers to progress in promiscuous & peripatetic pilgrimages to the Kinchinjungian heights,——that likewise is a refreshing consideration; but I should have preferred Napier Miles having commenced by 'extracting' a *com*mission from his paternal papa for a Himalayan Landscape, rather than a *per*mission to go & see the same in Nature. But as I was saying 2 days ago to Carlingford one of the most curious points of my Artistic Career, is the steadiness with which my friends have relied on my doing them good work, contrasted with the steadiness with which all besides my friends have utterly ignored my power of doing so. Said a foolish Artist to me°——'You can hardly be ranked as a Painter—because all you have done, or nearly all,—is merely the result of personal consideration, & you are comparatively if not wholly unknown to the public.'——Says I to he,——'that don't at all alter the qualities of my pictures— whether they are done to the commissions of Ld N[orthbrook]. or Ld A[berdare]—or Lord C[arlingford]—or Lady W[aldegrave]—or Sir F[rancis].G[oldsmid].°—or F. Lushington, or R. Bright or F. W. Gibbs—or any other friends,————or whether they are bought in a gallery by Mr. Timothy Timkins or the Duke of Popmuffin:—For the Public, says I, I have no sort of respect not none whatever————for provided pictures are cried up & well hung up—they are safe to be bought—be they by Whistler or anybody else. But the voice of Fashion whether it hissues hout of a Hart Cricket in a Paper, or hout of the mouth of a Duke or a Duchess————ain't by no means the voice of Truth. So you see o beloved growler—your ozbervations don't affect me a bit, who haven't got no ambition, nor any sort of Hiss Spree de Kor at all at all.'—

I hope the Harrogate nastinesses may benefit you, & wish I could hear you are quite well. I dine at Alfred Seymour's° today:—they, the Adml. S. Robinsons, Bertie Matthews, & E. Drummond,—are all as is left in this Meat Roppolus.

Yours affly
Edward Lear

To Sir Joseph Hooker, FRS

Villa Emily. | San Remo. | 3. June. 1878

My dear Sir James [*sic*],

I am making a set of Indian Topographical=Botanical drawings, for *Alfred Seymour*, (Ldy Rawlinson's brother,)—the 10 being studies of trees only. But I cannot get at the Botanical names of the trees,—& in one instance, am not sure of the Ordinary English one. So I have screwed up my courage to intrude on your time & kindness, to ask if you will be so good as to help me,——& to this end I have sent enclosed a list of the 10 trees, & a stamped *Envellope* to save you all possible trouble except the writing out of the names,—wh. if you can spare time to do for me I shall be really grateful. I want the Drawings to have their names properly printed below each, on the principle of 'what is worth doing at all is worth doing well'——vide copybook morals.

I hope that you & Ldy Hooker are well: I was unlucky in not seeing you last summer, but you had gone on your Wedding tour.° In my Indian notes I find a notice of the death of Sir W. Jardine, as for many years an extremely kind friend to me. I made some of my earliest drawings for him—as far back as 40 years ago!—(for I was 66 years old 2 weeks back.) I was introduced to him as a young artist by *N. A. Vigors*, then Secy. Z.S., & I have noted that the same evening I was introduced to *Daniel O'Connell*:° but the latter I only saw 3 times more, whereas Sir William, I either saw or heard from till very lately.

I shall not be in England this year—& doubt my ever going so far north again. But I may hope that you & Ldy Hooker will

be afflicted with a transient gleam of Rheumatism, & be obliged
to come to Sanremo.

Hoping you will forgive this trouble about my trees, believe
me, Dear Sir James, | Your's sincerely,
Edward Lear.

To Lord Carlingford

[On 5 July 1879 Lady Waldegrave died suddenly in London.]

Gd. Hotel Varesé, | Varésé. | Milano. | 9th. July. 1879

My dear Chichester,

I have just seen the London & Paris papers of Monday—&
know—to my great sorrow—what has happened.

At present I only write to say that I am thinking of you &
grieving for you.

God bless you. | Your's affectionately,
Edward Lear.

To James Fields

[In the autumn of 1877 the land below Lear's house was sold and a
large hotel built. This not only blocked his view to the sea, but also
destroyed his studio light. In 1880 he bought more land and built
another house, which he called Villa Tennyson, but it was many years
before he was free from worry and debt.]

Villa Emily. Sanremo. Italy. | 15. October 1879.

My dear Mr. Fields,

It is more than a year since I received a most welcome letter
from you, (the date alas! was June. 8. 1878, just after you had
received my 'Laughable Lyrics['].,° with which I am so glad
that you & Mrs. Fields were pleased. (Bye the bye, the only
attempt at Nonsense I have lately made has been,——at the
instigation of Wilkie Collins,—to conclude the History of Mr.
& Mrs. Discobbolos.° I regret to say that family dissensions
dispersed their happiness, & all the Discobboli eventually were
blown up by Dynamite=Dench——if anybody knows what
that is. If I can find the absurdity I will enclose it, & you can
publish it if you like,—only placing my name to it, & 'reserving
my rights' to republish it here.[)]

I have been unable or unwilling to write latterly from various vexatious causes:—& the last of my grievances is of so miserable a nature that I cannot bring myself to dwell on it in detail, but rather send you a statement° which I am now trying to make known as widely as possible. Having but an income of 110£ a year, the destruction of my Artist life is miserable enough,—& as I have not a chance of buying other land here (now, since 1869 greatly advanced in price,) I suppose I shall have to flee away & be heard of no more. It is however better to be sinned against than to sin, & I would rather be as I am at 68, than be the Druggist Hanbury° or Miss Shuttleworth who have worked me this misery. I cannot help laughing at one bit of advice suggested to me,——that I should stump all Europe & America & wherever the English Language is spoken, as the Writer of the Book of Nonsense, with a view to collect innumerable sixpences so as to raise 7 or 8 Thousand Pounds to buy new land & build another house!!—So look out for me & my cat some fine day—by a Boston Steamer, on my way to San Francisco.

Your account of 'Nile Note Curtis'—gives me much pleasure. Won't he ever come here?—With kind regards to Mrs.

Fields, believe me, | Your's sincerely,

Edward Lear.

We regret to learn that a serious misfortune has happened to the wellknown Artist & Author, Edward Lear, whose various works have for years been favourably noticed by the Press. Millions of English=speaking people have laughed over Mr. Lear's 'Books of Nonsense'; many have read his 'Journals of a Landscape Painter' in Italy, Albania, & Corsica: & not a few delight in his Landscapes in numerous houses throughout England. A considerable portion of the Public therefore, cannot but be interested in what affects a man who has been the cause of instruction & of infinite amusement to so many.

Some 10 years back Mr. Lear bought a piece of ground at Sanremo, on which he built a house, trusting to pass the rest of his life in quiet there, and to carry out a long=ago commenced Series of Landscape Illustrations of the Laureat's Poems. But,—through the unworthy intrigues of a few heartless persons the Land immediately below that of Mr. Lear has suddenly been sold;—and,——notwithstanding the written promise of its owner that no such outrage should be committed, an immense Hotel has been erected, which not only shuts out every particle of sea view and condemns the Garden of the unfortunate Artist to sunlessness in winter,—but—what is of far greater importance,——wholly destoys the Light of his Studio by the vast mass of glaring reflection thrown from the enormous whitewashed building opposite.

Unable any longer to use his house for Artistic purposes, we hear that Mr. Lear is preparing to abandon the place he had made so pleasant, and is about to leave Europe for New Zealand. It is sad that a person so well known & to whose talents so many are beholden should be thus cruelly treated. His departure from Sanremo will be greatly regretted; nor are the Sanremesi at all reticent in their remarks on the parties whose intrigues are about to cause it.——

To the 15th Earl of Derby

Villa Emily. Sanremo. | 13. April. 1881.

My dear Lord Derby,

I have this morning put—as far as I can see,—my last touches to your 4 remaining drawings, and in about a fortnight I think they will be sent off, so that in May—towards the end,——I hope you will receive all safely. I shall be very glad to know how you like each & all. Of the many persons who have seen them here, I may say that perhaps the Suli provokes the most envy & malignity, but to others the Parnassus & Montenegro, or the Syracuse Quarries seem the most to be desired. To myself, the Parnassus is most pleasing, because I am so fond of a flat plain: & moreover it is the most sunny—which is quite correct, for Suli & Montenegro are in themselves gloomy places enough.

I trust however that they are all tolerably correct quâ topographies, however I may have tried to poetize the scenes without altering the likeness to the originals. Arthur Stanley Dean of Westminster writing to me some short time back, says,——'Mrs. Grote, in the old days of Oxford, used to call me, "the Professor of Ecclesiastical Poetry." She might have called you, "The Painter of Topographical Poetry."['] And I suppose, with such testimony as this,—& that of A Tennyson in his 'Lines to E.L on his travels in Greece'—one ought to be proud and content, notwithstanding that nobody can be more aware than myself of the failings in all my drawings.

The above 4 views do not, nevertheless form the very last of the set I had to do for you on your so kindly helping me last year;° one circular drawing will come later, but not yet,—for now all my works, furniture &c &c &c—are being packed in hopes of getting out of my spoiled Villa in another month. The round drawing will be more poetical than topographical, though strange to say——(since it represents the 'Gromboolian Plain' & the 'Hills of the Chankly Bore'—) it is actually drawn from nature, barring the long line of the army in the foreground, which certainly I never saw;—nor will the title of the drawing 'The Passage of the Caliph Egroegts Rehcsillip° over the Gromboolian Mountains' much elucidate the matter. For all that, it is a riddle set forth by the Author of the Book of Nonsense quite capable of solution, & if for nothing else will I believe please you for its colour.

I shall not be able to get thoroughly into my new house 'Villa Tennyson'—till next Autumn, & thenceforward I hope to work hard & harder & hardest at my 300 Topographical Poetical Illustrations of A Tennyson's poems—many of which are far advanced,—but all have had to be shunted along of the abominable ShuttleworthHanbury Hotel. Some day I hope you will come along this Cornice road, & let me have the pleasure of receiving so kind a friend & patron as you have been.

Latterly I have had abundant friends to enliven my solitude——S. W. & Mrs. Clowes, Lady Wenlock° & her daughter,—W F Dawnay & Ld Adelaide, Sir Spencer & Ldy Robinson, & lastly Mrs. George Clive & Mrs. Charles Grey.

Fortescue I see will not come this year, as he has all at once turned into the Lord Privy seal,° which move, in so far as it gives him fuller occupation, I rejoice to know.

Believe me, | My dear Lord Derby | Your's obliged & sincerely,

Edward Lear.

Before the Drawings go off, I will send a Postcard.

To the Hon. Mrs James Stuart-Wortley

Villa Tennyson. Sanremo. | 26. Feby. 1882

My dear Mrs. Stuart Wortley,

In the first place observe the Envellope, for the appearance of which an oppology is kneaded, the fact being that there was only this one in the house large enough, & so, though it was originally addressed to the Hon. J. Warren, I altered it to what it now is. Secondly, I thought it so kind of you to have purchased the Mte. Generoso drawing, that I wanted you to have 2 scraps to remind you of 'Simla', & 'Ravenna forest.' Which two I enclose, hoping you may think them worth a corner in some Album. I also send 2 still smaller,—one for each of the young Ladies.

These are of singular—I may say bingular value,—as they were done in the Moon, to which I lately went one night, returning next morning on a Moonbean. As the Signorine Blanche & Katharine appreciate nonsense, I will add some few notes concerning the 2 subjects which I got with great rapidity during my visit, nothing being easier in that wonderful country than to travel thousands of miles in a minute. And these journeys are all done by means of Moonbeans, which, far from being mere portions of light, are in reality living creatures, endowed with considerable sogassity, & a long nose like the trunk of a Nelliphant, though this is quite imperceptible to the naked eye. You have only to whisper to the Moonbean what you wish to see, & you are there in a moment, & its nose or trunk being placed round your body, you cannot by any possibility fall.

The first view is of the Jizzdoddle rocks, with 2 of the many

remarkable planets which surround the moon rising or riz in the distance; these orangecoloured & peagreen orbs leaving a profound impression of sensational surprise on the mind of the speckletator who first beholds them. The second view represents the Rumbytumby ravine, with the crimson planted Buzz and its 5 Satanites on the horizon. In the foreground on the left is a Blompopp tree, so called from the Blompopp, a gigantic and gorgeous bird which builds on its summit. To the left are the tall Vizzikilly trees, the most common vegetation of the Lunar hummysphere. These trees grow to an immense height, & bloom only once in 15 years, when they produce a large crop of immemorial soapbubbles, submarine suckingpigs, songs of sunrise, & silver sixpences,—which last are ground into powder by the Lunar population, & drunk in warm water without any sugar. So little is known of the inhabitants of the moon, that a few descriptive but accurate notices relating to them may be interesting. They do not in the least resemble the people of our world,—as for instance they are all much broader than they are high; they have no hair on their heads,—but on the contrary a beautiful crest of yellow feathers which they can raise or depress at will, like that of the ordinary Cockatoo. And from the tip of their nose depends an elegant and affecting bunch of hair, sometimes extending to as much as 20 miles in length, & as it is considered sacriligeous to cut it, it is gradually wound round a silvergilt post firmly placed in the ground, but removable at pleasure. The faces of the more educated classes have a pensively perverse and placid expression,—not unlike the countenance of an oyster, while frequently a delicately doubleminded semi visual obliquity adds a pathos to their pungent physiognomy. These remarkable people, so unlike ourselves, pass 18 months of their year (which consists of 22,) in

the strictest seclusion,——suspended with their heads down-
wards, and held carefully in crimson silk bags,—which are
severely & suddenly shaken from time to time by select
servants. Thus,—exempt from the futile & fluctuating fatuity of
fashion, these estimable creatures pass an indigenous life of
indefinite duration surrounded by their admiring ancestors, &
despised by their incipient posterity. Their servants are not
natives of the Moon, but are brought at great expense from a
negative although nutritious star at a remote distance, and are
wholly of a different species from the Lunar population, having
8 arms & 8 legs each, but no head whatever;——only a chin in
the middle of which are their eyes,——their mouths, (of which
each individual possesses 8,) being one in each little toe, & with
these they discourse with an overpowering volubility & an
indiscriminatory alacrity surprising to contemplate. The
conduct of these singular domestics is usually virtuous &
voluminous, & their general aspic highly mucilagenous &
meritorious.

I have no time at present to dilate farther on other particulars
of Lunar National History;——the prevalence of 2 sorts of
gales, gales of wind and nightingales;——the general
inebriety of the Atmosphere—or the devotional functions of the
inhabitants, consisting chiefly in the immense consumption of
Ambleboff pies.

Hoping that I may see you & the 2 young Ladies on
Wednesday, Believe me, Your's sincerely,

Edward Lear.

To F. T. Underhill

[To help in preparing the Tennyson drawings for reproduction Lear
employed an impecunious artist, F. T. Underhill.]

Hotel Monte Generoso.—Mendrisio. Canton Ticino. |
Suisse. | Aug. 20 1882

Dear Mr. Underhill,

I had to go down to Sanremo for a few days;—returning here
on the 18th. I found your letter of the 9th. I am sorry you are not
getting on so well again just now. But as for 'bad times—'—&

'money scarce'—that is all bosh:—you have only to look at the Hamilton sale,° or to the prices given for Millais portraits,° to perceive that it is *fashion* rules dealers.

Meanwhile to help Miss Daisy, I send you a checque for £1/13/6 which will buy socks & biscuits for a stop gap,—till you have more children. Why don't you & Mrs Underhill have some twins? If you do, call them Buttercup & Snowdrop.

Let me know—(address as above) that you receive the enclosed. Yrs. vy truly,

Edward Lear.

To Baroness Burdett-Coutts

Villa Tennyson. | Sanremo. | Feby 7. 1883

My dear Madam,

I must first thank you for the extremely kind letter I have received by Col. Sir Edmund Henderson. And secondly I must thank you on account of Sir Edmund's friend—Sir Andrew Walker,°——having bought one of my Egyptian oil= paintings, (Philæ,) & also one of my Watercoloured drawings. Before long, I will write to Mrs. Stuart Wortley, to tell her about your letter, & its results.

It was a pleasure to me to shew my gallery to Sir Edmund & Miss Henderson & their friend, for it was at once clear that they looked at my 'Topographies' mentally & artistically, & not as wall furniture only. And as you wish to know what representa-tions I have of the Ionian Islands, I will put down a list of such as I have together with one or two other subjects which Sir Edmund Henderson & his daughter remarked & liked. I have a sort of impression that you know the Ionian Islands by a Yacht voyage—but am possibly mistaken.

I hope I am not taking a liberty in adding that I am glad to hear—as I do—from many quarters,—that you are well & very happy. Nor can this be called a flattery, since all Englishmen, to whom your large Charity & goodness are publicly known, would say the same thing.

Believe me, | My dear Madam, | Your's sincerely,

Edward Lear.

Should you wish for any of my works, they could be sent in the spring, along with Sir Andrew Walker's & others.

WATERCOLOURED DRAWINGS.

Corfù Citadel————————————	12£—or £12. 12 framed
Ditto ————————————————	8.£—or £8.. 8. do.
One Gun Battery. Corfu—————	do.————— do.———

Large unfinished drawing of Corfù from Virò: if finished, with frame, 120 Guineas. (The fellow drawings of this, Montenegro,——belongs to Earl Northbrook.)

Volume of Views of the 7 Ionian Islands—lithographed by myself from my own original drawings; now out of print—only 8 copies left. Price 5£.

A favorite drawing of Sir E. Henderson was one of the Campagne di Roma,—price 12. 12. framed.

OIL PAINTINGS

Two of the Nile——both sunsets.	35£ each framed.
Gethsemane—framed 45£.	
Two Campagna di Roma——————————each 35£ framed
Ditto of Ceylon ——————————————ditto—ditto

I have put aside the watercolor drawings, & will not hang them up until I hear from you—in case you should wish for one or more.

To John Ruskin

Villa Tennyson. | Sanremo. | 16 Feby. 1883

My dear Sir,
    Although I hesitate to take up any of your time, which is that of the public,—I cannot help sending a few lines to thank you for your kindness to a young Artist, whom at times I have tried

to help————F. T. Underhill,—who writes to me in a great state of delight at having had a letter from you about his Seppia Copies. I do not think,—if I may be excused saying so, that public writers however they may praise your works & writings, have ever paid sufficient attention to the great readiness you have ever shown to assist beginners,—for the present instance is by no means the first that has come to my notice.

Underhill, (who has at times made several good copies of Turner° for me,—also one of a large painting by myself of Damascus,° with a vast crowd of 'penning out' work, —)— is a most deserving fellow, with a fund of perseverance that has stood him in good stead in many difficulties. His having been employed by Lord Northbrook latterly, & last of all having been encouraged by you, will however I trust place him henceforward in a good path towards success.

The last time I was in England (1880) I saw at Oxford (by means of a friend at one of the Colleges—R. W. Roper,°) the wonderful Turners, in the Taylor(?) Institution. A treat for which I may also take this opportunity of thanking you, as I often do mentally for having by your books caused me to use my own eyes in looking at Landscape, from a period dating many years back.

I have also often wished that you could have seen some of the tropical Vegetation I saw in Malabar Ceylon & Elsewhere, which for 2 Years I tried to draw when in India by Lord Northbrook's kindness. I thought some of the river scenery about Calicut & Maheè more lovely than any I had before imagined, & some of the Darjeeling & Kinchinjunga scenes among the grandest conceivable.

Believe me, | My dear Sir, | Your's very truly,
Edward Lear.

To the Hon. Mrs Augusta Parker

[incomplete letter]

[Villa Tennyson, San Remo. 19 February 1883]
. . . illustrations, besides at 50 large Corsica drawings begun so far back as 1868. Whereby you may see I am not idle.

—And my garden is now admirably beautiful, & were it not for the Slugs & Snails would be inimitable. But these melancholy mucilaginous Molluscs have eaten up all my Higher-cynths & also my Lower=cynths & I have only just now found a mode of getting rid of these enemies:——which is by flattering their vanity in taking them friendly walks up & down the garden,——an inganno which blinds them to ulterior consequences. And thus, (they being of a monstrous size as you may see by the sketch below,) when I get them near the cistern, I pitch them into the water, where they justly expiate their unpleasant & greedy sins. Please write again soon. | Your's affectionately,
Edward Lear.

To Lord Carlingford

[January 1884]

RESPECT THIS!
(a special Chop.)

My dear 40scue,

It has just come into my head—(as the little charity boy said of the unexpected advent of an undesirable parasite,) that there are 2 subjects on which you,—while you continue a Phoca,——may be of use to Gt Britain in particular & to the world in general.

Of these 2 subjects, one would undoubtedly be popular & do good to your politickle repute; the other I doubt about, for it would arouse vulgar & violent opposition.

The first then is this:——if, as is not unlikely, you may again be called to open some Museum or public Institution, might you not give a help to Art & to intelligent progress by saying a word in favour of engraving & publishing——in a cheap & popular form, the Portraits exhibited in the Reynold's Collection, & those in the National Portrait Gallery? (No collection of modern art would interest me as much as those pictures of Reynolds, unless perhaps those of the N.P. Gallery.) And if you will consider that every year,—along of fires in old & great houses,——the authentic likenesses of persons known to History,—are constantly decreasing, & that when destroyed, all recovery of such invaluable matter is hopeless;——& if you will also consider that by means of good copies—& good, (by good I mean *correct*,) engravings from these copies, the said likenesses could not only be saved from all chance of obliteration, but would likewise be multiplied endlessly for the benefit of all time & peoples,——I really believe you would agree with me that one in your position might effect a most beneficial result with very little trouble to yourself & much good to others. The suggestion should be connected with *cheapness*:—Reynolds works have already been engraved, but in a style & with an expense that negative the success of the end I would propose, i.e. the widespread knowledge of portraiture connected with History. The pictures in the National Portrait Gallery would come under the same category as the Reynold's works.

As for the Second perception, I do not think——however you & I might agree as to the desirability of a move in the direction we could wish,——it could be easily managed, as the trial to reform a brutality has already more than once failed. The Brutality is the Damnation clause of the A[thanasian]

Creed.°——I don't want the Creed itself, stuff as it is,— touched,—but I think it possible that means might be found to make that particular clause hateful & ridiculous.

I wish you were here to talk over what I can ill write about. |

Your's affly

Edward Lear.

A cousin of APStanley writes to me today, that the Dean's life is to be written° by Walrond.

To the 15th Earl of Derby

Villa Tennyson | Sanremo. | 26 June 1884

My dear Lord Derby,

I believe I ought to send you a sort of Apology for your having been troubled more than enough with notices of this child's Exhibition in Wardour Street. The 4 large paintings° there were to have been put up for sale at Christies, but that Art purveyor at the last moment had neither room nor time—what with Fountain, & other collections &c. So I had to fall back on 129 Wardour St. And the annual notice of my gallery I should like to make known to all who have had my works—(& you are most certainly a large example!) that this annual notice is as much an Advertisement=universal as Eno's Fruitsalt or Epps's Cocoa, or any other;—including the public showing of crowds of Artists in Academy or W. Color Galleries—& is by no means intended to represent on my part, a persistent request to my friends that they should buy more of my work, especially when their walls are pretty well covered. Naturally I am very glad when my pictures or drawings *are* bought, for it is long, as you know, that I have lived abroad for health's sake & I have no other means of reminding people of my existence now that I no longer go to London,— —nor can I afford a shining=splendid gallery in Bond St. or elsewhere. But I confess it is an object with me that my works should be seen & talked about, by them as knows something of topographic work, poetical or literal.

It is not very likely that you have time now to go about to galleries, but if you go to Wardour St. I should be glad to know that the very slight attack of a paralytic nature wh. I had last

March, has not like Gil Blas's Archbp's, been transferred to my work. All of the 4 large latest pictures are—(nothwithstanding the illustrations of Tennyson,—) actual representations of places.

The very large painting I am now often at work on—(16 feet by 9,) is a scene in Enoch Arden's Island,° but I have yet to learn that the accuracy of my view can be contradicted,— because nobody precisely knows where the island is.

Believe me, | My dear Lord Derby, | Your's sincerely & gratefully,

Edward Lear

To Lord Carlingford

Villa Tennyson. Sanremo. | 30. April. 1885

My dear 40scue,

I should like if possible to get a letter written to you to day, though I wrote one 2 days ago, but 'torded it up' after it was bewritten.——Your last was from Aix les Bains, & you speak in it of another letter perhaps crossing mine—but that never turned up: the last I had from you was dated March 4.

You must have been glad to get back to England°—for I know Court Life is not to your taste—though a duty. As for me, I never could have mastered it even in that light; one day—after long repression of feeling, I should suddenly have jumped all round the room on one leg————or have thrown a hot potato up to the ceiling,—either of which acts would (possibly) have ruined my 'career' as G[eorge]. F[rederick]. B[owen]. used to say.

You are certainly a wonderful cove—if so be a cabinet minster is a cove,—for writing so much & so kindly to this 'dirty Landscape painter', who not seldom repents of his violent writing to a 'statesman with a well balanced mind',——as I truly believe your's to be. So far from 'not respecting' you or N[orthbrook] I endeavour to look at Poltix° from your point of view, & can well understand your both being perfectly conscientious,—though I may prefer the line of Forster & Göschen,—& (latterly even) of D Argyll. 'Let us make an Oath

& keep it, with a quiet mind, Not to write on Politics if never so inclined.' And now that the 'monstrous folly of supposing that Russia is not truthful', seems to be beaming out on many minds hitherto obstinately dark, I wish nowise to touch on that subject, to which even you allude,——though I cannot agree with you that 'the Russians have behaved abominably'—— since after Bulgaria & MidLothian, Batoum & Dulcigno & much more, it appears to me that [they] have only acted very naturally.

This leads me to write about the Admiralty horror°—& explosion. For a whole day I was really utterly miserable, as the first Telegram from Turin was only——'Explosion Admiralty—supposed Dynamite; building much destroyed: damage great—nothing yet certainly' known.'° In point of fact, the whole of our friends might have been killed——had the Devilry exploded one hour later, when all would have been at Lunch.

This mornings post brings me a long letter from N. The Barings are all so little demonstrative that—even regarding themselves I wonder at the calmness with wh. they take really awful matters. Poor Ldy Emma a little while back (after Easter) was thrown out of a carriage at Stratton, & fell among bushes, where a pointed stick pierced her ear, & went nigh to ending life. I have read the account with horror. She was driving(?)— & is a thorough 1st. class whip, & with pluck & coolness enough to set up a Regiment of soldiers: but I suppose the horse shied.

The reason of this Baring matter cropping up after the 'Politix' paragraph, is that I thought it right—to prevent N writing to me on such matters, & because I hate false colours——to tell him I was no Radical, & that I fully believed mismanagement had been the cause of all the troubles now about. Naturally I didn't run on in the Asanine way I do with you;—indeed I have never taken the least notice of what my dear good N writes on such toppix,—& I even find, looking at my diary of some time back, that when he wrote to me about the Russians having Batoūm, I replied nil—but have written regarding his remark——'I think the Russians should have Batoūm—for the greater will be their responsibility—'— —'Certainly—& such would be the case if you gave them Anglesea or the I of Wight.'

Please say nothing of this. You yourself wrote—'I sigh for the F.O—as it was under Palmerston'————but God forbid I should allude even, to your saying so.

Do you remember an incident about N. Zd—many years ago————I forget who was then your chief————but I know that owing to what (under considerable pressure,) I showed you, you yourself stated that you had got that Governor removed by demonstrating that the head of your Departmt. was not up to what was going on. And so it has been elsewhere; & one day I may tell you how I came to know of the aggrandizement of Montenegro & other matters: which I assuredly *do* know, though you wonder at how I did so.

I have been often thinking of you to day—as I have been working on elm trees—from sketches made at 'Nuneham.[']
July 27—28—29—30—1860.

Hence onward, my letter will be confused & indicative of my mucilaginous & morose mind————all more or less queer & upside down as the mouse said when he bit off his grand-mother's tail—having mistaken it for a Barley straw.

Yesterday was a very grattifying day. Principal Professr Shairp—(of St. Andrew's, & Profr. of Poetry at Oxford,) brought me a letter of introduction from Edm. Lushington (Ld. Rector of Glasgow U.[)]————He looked over all my 200 ʌ drawings with the greatest care & interest, & complimented me about them as would make the paper rosecolor if so be I wrote down his words. I am now doing the ultimate or perfect insect lot of drawings;° & I fancy it will be ordained that the whole 200 will be done only as illustrative of single poems—bit by bit—so as to stave off gt expense & labour. They will (I think,) be done in Lithography—& N advises Monochrome—or brown tint: & I believe he is right.

Tozer of Oxford sends me a charming book (wanting in dates though) by Theodore Bent° (Longmans,) all about the Cyclades. (Dearly beloved child—let me announce to you that this word is pronounced 'Sick Ladies',—howsomdever certain Britishers call it 'Sigh=claids.'

I am always reading as much of C. Lever as I can find time for. You, I imagine have no time for reading much: but 'the Martins of Cromartin' & 'Davenport Dunn'—are well worth a peroozle.

I should greatly like to know what has become of the Phoca.
Did he go to Aix les Bains with you?

Mrs. Clive comes back here from
Venice on Saty. & dines with me (I
hope) Sunday 3d. She is hurrying back
to Cannes, to pick up Mrs. Grey,
who is upset by Canadian news,° Ldy
Melgund her daughter being there.

My own health is just now—(weather warmer—) greatly
better. But I persist in drinking lots of wine—perhaps 'more
than is good for me' as a friend once said——but I don't feel
sure about that.

I have great lots of writing to do about my sister°——her
husband's nephew is the only executor who will act——&
he—naturally, prefers to communicate with her only living
relative in Europe—to acting on his own behalf without
reference to me.

Should you be injuiced by contemplating the remarkable
development of my 'Political knowledge & aspirations'——to
offer me some lucrative place under government,——be
assured that I will take nothing but the Chancellor of the
Exchequership, or the Archbishopk of Canterbury.

Various people bother me to publish my Autobiography—
—inasmuch as I have 60 volumes of Diaries:° but at present I
shan't. Some of the notes written in [days *crossed out*] [times
crossed out] years when I used to drive for days on the Campagna
with Ldy Davy° are funny enough; as are others not in that
category.

Now—if you've got so far, you've had enough. | Your's
affectionately,
Edward Lear.

And this is certain; if so be
You could just now my garden see,
The aspic of my flowers so bright
Would make you shudder with delight.

And if you voz to see my roziz
As is a boon to all men's noziz,——
You'd fall upon your back & scream——
'O Lawk! o cricky! it's a dream!'

Edward Lear.
Archbishop of Canterbury.
1886

To F. T. Underhill

[This letter is damaged.]

Villa Figini. | Barzanò. | Monza. Italia. | [19 August 1885]
Dear Mr. Underhill,

I had your letter of the 31 July, all right, & am glad that the
Cheerful Checque was pleasant to you & Mrs. Underhill.

As you say, I am always considerably worried about these ⋏
illustrations, & now I want your advice on another stage of this
everlasting bother. What paper do you recommend me to use,
on which to make the pencil drawings for possible trial? Do you
think it better to work on a *block*, (i.e. sheets of paper fastened
together,) or on separate sheets,——or on paper laid down on
panels? Foord's got me a lot of paper laid down on panels last
year—when I was all agog about Autotype°—being told that
the paper must be *quite smooth*. But this porcelain smoothness
was absolutely useless for pencil work—& all those 50 panels
were [. . .] aside. Also, what do you consider [. . .] best mode
of fixing pencil drawings [. . .]? Milk—or milk & water,—or
gum, or some sort of size?—possibly iced punch or turtle soup
would do. I really want to make the drawings most absolutely
exact & finished—which I find to my sorrow I cannot do in
washes of black & white—never having been skilful in brush
handling, but ready enough with pencil. Chalk I can't use. The
⋏ drawings would have a good deal of double B or very black
pencil for some foreground work.

I have just mounted on common paper 120 of these Chrysalisses as I call them, & as far as I can judge they are remarkable in their way; certainly the subjects are beautiful & interesting. But the rough paper I have worked on will only go so far & no farther: after alterations only sink in & produce no effect at all.

Unfortunately—not at all foreseeing the perfect quiet & comfort of this place, & the firstrate light (with no reflections—) in the large room I work in (25 feet square,)——I did not suppose I should come to the end of my original sketches (which I have to consult & work from,) so soon as I have done,——& here is [. . .] end of August & I have finished all [. . .] Chrysalis drawings here——120 in al[. . .] are still 80 to do. As I find I may stay in this delightful place as long as ever I choose, I am thinking——tho' I have not yet decided absolutely,——on sending Luigi Rusconi° into Sanremo to bring away all the rest of the drawings necessary to complete the remaining 86. If I could get those done, I could begin on the pencil ones at once, on my return. I don't like to go to Sanremo myself, as it is blazing hot there, & the fatigue would or might upset me; not to speak of the additional expense,—for under any circumstances I should have to take Luigi with me, as I am not up to the labour of lifting drawings &c.

Send me a line about the paper &c—as i ax'd about above.

Lord Northbrook has written to me, & I have sent him a long letter about all these ↑s. I wish he were here, as he has such good taste & knowledge about this sort of matter: He talks of coming out to Sanremo in the winter.

As for Mr. Arnold Congreve, I have an impression——
—not—remember—from anything you have written,——
—that he has NOT made the progress he should by this time he might have [. . .] expected to make. I do not think I shall [. . .] advice——because if he has really any [. . .] he will succeed; & if not, nothing will greatly benefit him.

In all the 50 years I have more or less lived in Italy, I never met with such a perfect climate as this of the Brianza distict——nor any summer place so everlastingly green & lovely. The view of the Lecco mountains from my windows is enough to make a blacking=brush squeak with delight; & downstairs there is a garden with the loveliest flowers.

I am thankful to say my health continues much better than it was, though I am now too infirm to walk. | Your's sincerely, Edward Lear.

Edward Lear
aet 73.$\frac{1}{2}$

His cat Foss,
aet 16.

To Amelia Edwards

Villa Tennyson | Sanremo. | 18. October. 1885.

My dear Miss Edwards,

I will begin this scribblebibble with an apology for taking up so much of your time, & indeed to write at all to one like yourself appears to me to require a distinct confession of impudence. I have never read much of your writing (once, long ago, I read Ld. Brackenbury (?)—which I liked very much;[)]—but I have gathered somehow that you are rather a placid=forgiving than a ferocious=proud person. Anyhow at the end of this letter I will tell you of a penitence I am about to practice, & whether you reply to me or knot, I shall look on the matter philosoffically.

First I want to tell you, that in 1853° I went up the Nile as far as Philæ:—& in 1867 again there & to Wady Halfeh; & during those 2 voyages (or journies,) I kept a minutely detailed diary daily from almost hour to hour, & often thought I would buplish these diaries, with small illustratiums, in a little 8vo work. It is hardly worthwhile adverting to the remarks of silly=narrow folk, who say 'Oh! the Nile! as if anything new *could* be written about that river!!——' Such remarx vos made to I in 1853, but since then various novelties have turned up on this score, leastways one of a 1000 miles by a person as is known as Miss A B Edwards. I don't say—mind,—that my 'Nile Diaries of a Landscapepainter['] would be worth the 99th part of a grasshoppers eyelash,——but they might be so if considered as a part of this child's art life, & also if orbemented by good yet small would=cuts—(say by Cooper,)——(do you know the Illustrated English Maggazeen?) be worth thinking

about. If so be as you give me the least encouragement, I would send you a copy of the sort of thing—for, say,——2 days in 1853 (at Kasres Saād)—or at Ipsambl in 1867. But if you did not axe me to do so I shoulldlt, being of a modest & retir-

ing or snaillike disposition although addicted to looking forward to active work—& unwilling to subside into muffinlike & mucilaginous monotony.

O mi i! o lor! o lork! Here is a big packet from my dear old Wilkie Collins—with a story to read!—so I suppose I shall read it at dinner time.

As for my ↟ book, I am lopping it down from *200* subjects—to a first part of *10*—but as to their eggzikusion, as yet darkness prewhales.

1   'The Dying Swan' (River Anio. Campagna di Roma[)]
2. 'The Crag that fronts the even.' (Kasr es Saād. Nile)
3. 'My tall dark pines'—(Bavella Corsica[)]
4   'Girt round with blackness'—(Marsabbas. Syria)
5   'Morn broadened on the borders of the dark' (Civitella di Subiaco[)]
6   'I will see before I die &c[']—(Cocoa Palms Maheē. Malaba[)]
7   'I will see before I die['] (Temple of Tanjore India[)]
8. 'Breadths of Tropic shade'——(Darjeeling. Hima-laya[)]
9   —'Athos—'————(Monastery of Laura[)]
10 —'on some great Plain['] (Damascus[)].

These subjects are not final, but subject to change—as the convulsed caterpillar said as he was a turning into a Chrysalis.

(Do you know anything of Rowney—a Bubblisher?)

What is curious is that in my Egyptian diaries, are various bits of description *exactly* like your's: & doubtless would be said 'Copied from Miss A M. E!!'——but that could not be as 1853 is a hurlier date nor is that of your Nile voyage.

Now for my penitence, (bye the bye a friend of mine in India, gave a Hindoo—studying English the 10 Penitentiary Psalms to copy as a punishment, wh. the youth did, but headed his paper thus, 'The 10penny Ten Sherry Sarms.') wh. I shall adopt as an atonement for taking up your time. Close by my window stands a very large basket—formerly a beehive at dear old Mr. Bell's of Selbourne,—now used as a big paper basket—; Into this I shall put my head & sit on the Terrace for an hour & a half[.]

Your's sincerely

To Mrs Hassall

Villa Tennyson. | Octbr. 21, 1885.

Dear Mrs. Hassall,

This morning's post brings me a very nice letter from Mr. Kettlewell, which I think you and Dr. Hassall may like to see, whereon I send it.

I was sorry to see so little of the Doctor yesterday, but I rise so late now and go to bed so early, that I have but very little leisure time. The best conditions of finding me now-a-days are from 12 to 1 p.m., in the garden, which I get to when it is fine.

I did not say all I might have said to Dr. H. about my health, thinking he might upbraid (or down-braid) me for doing more than I ought to do at my age, and considering how feeble I am, consequently—though I tell you in confidence—I did *not* tell him that I had climbed to the top of the tallest Eucalyptus tree in my garden and jumped thence into the Hotel Royal grounds,—nor that I had leaped straight over the outer V. Tennyson wall from the highroad,—nor that I had run a race with my cat from here to Vintimiglia, having beaten Foss by 8 feet and a half. Those facts you can impart to Dr. Hassall or knot as you like.

Yours sincerely,
Edward Lear.

To Lord Carlingford

[In Dec. 1885, Fortescue went out to stay with Lear in San Remo.]

Villa Tennyson | San Remo | 29 Decbr. 1885

My dear 40scue,

This is only to say don't make it so late before you come out. The best time is from 12 to 2.

And always put a Sill Kanterchiff in your pocket in case of change of wind:—throats is very excitable in these latitudes.

And never stay out after 4——better indoors 3.45.

I wished to tell you that the Phoca has been placed in my gt cistern, whence it can be easily out=be=got by the lower water course.

I give him 4 biscuits & a small cup of Coffee in the early dawning, & this morning I thought I would go out to sea on his back—which I did, more than half way to Corsica—for he

swims orfle quick. I had previously telegraphed to Miss Campbell at Ajaccio, & she met me half way on her Porpoise, (for she hasn't got a Phoca,) but our meeting was very short owing to the amazing number of seagulls she brought with her, who made such a d——d row that all conversation was impossible. So I came straight back & telegraphed to Ld. Harrowby's Phoca° that yours was all right.

Yrs. affly,
Edward Lear.

To John Ruskin

[In a letter to the *Pall Mall Gazette* for 15 Feb. 1886 Ruskin placed Lear's *A Book of Nonsense* as the first of his 100 favourite books.]

Villa Tennyson | Sanremo. | 19. Feby. 1886

Dear Mr. Ruskin,

Several friends have sent me by this last post—(cut from the Pall Mall of Feby. 15—) your letter about the 'Choice of Books'. And I cannot help writing a line to thank you for your most kind mention of my 'Nonsense'——& to say how proud & gratified I am by your praise.

I am now (æt 74) nearly always in bed—but can sit up now & then,—& even go on working at my 200 Tennyson illustrations begun in 1849° in Sussex in the days of old Holman Hunt—& ↑ennyson. I suppose perseverance is a virtue, even if in a foolish cause—: only one can't be sure whether the sequel will be foolishness or not. Most probably I shall die before the 200 are ready to Autotype.

With many & sincere thanks, | believe me Your's,
Edward Lear.

To the Hon. Hallam Tennyson

Villa Tennyson | Sanremo. | 24. Feby 1886

My dear Hallam,

I have to thank you for a very nice letter—date 17th—: as well as one from your dear good mama enclosed;—but I am

hardly ever out of bed now, & when I am, I have to arrange for
the total dispersion & consigning of my immense Collection of
'Topographies'°—some 12 or 15,000 in all,——so that I am
very seldom fit for writing. I thank God that I am free from
pain, & my cough is less troublesome just latterly.

Meanwhile, among other decisions, this is one. *You* (&
Audrey) are to have the large picture of Pentedatelo or
'someone pacing there alone'——wh. indeed was a matter
settled long ago—but my increasing ill health broke off an
arrangement wh. was then being carried out, i.e—of the picture
being presented to you by 30 individual parties.°

This I knocked up, & you must now kindly accept the picture
as a sort of pro=legacy, & I hope you can place it well.

I have ordered Foord's to send it down at once, with a notice
that the empty box is to be returned to 129 Wardour St.

Did you read Ruskin's letter to the Pall Mall G. (15th Feby)
(about Sir J. Lubbocks recommendation of books to read,) in
which he places ME!!! at the head of 100 authors!!

O. My!—

To John Ruskin

Villa Tennyson | Sanremo. | 1 March. 1886

Dear Mr. Ruskin,

I believe you will begin to repent having written so kindly
about my 'Nonsense', if so be your having done so entails more
interruption of your time.

I sent off (because you asked me for some notice of the ∧
work,—)—a packet with a set of Lists of all the 200—; also a
Dedication I had written to Lady Tennyson—which she &
Alfred T.—having read & approved, had sent back to
me;——likewise some *obomminably* bad specimens of repro-

duction. But I omitted to tell you a good deal I meant to have written, & finally foolishly sent off the packet without any letter—wh. I afterwards found & posted.

And now it has occurred to me—as you have taken an interest in my 'Nonsense'—that you may only hitherto have seen the first original part. And so thinking,—I write this—to tell you I have the 3 succeeding absurd volumes, which are now very rare books—& which you may never have seen, because the horrid man Bush who published them (as he did my 'Corsica') became bankrupt—& the whole machinery collapsed.

Therefore if you wish for these 3 later books of Bosh— namely—

> *1. Nonsense songs & stories*
> *2. More Nonsense*
> & *3. Laughable Lyrics*——————

you have only to say so. I do not bother you by sending them, because it may so happen that you already have them, but if otherwise only tell me & I will send the 3 copies I have here.

'E'en in our ashes live'——————

& lying as I do here, I have just now finished an absurd 'History of my aged Uncle Arly' begun long ago.° And I esteem it a thing to be thankful for that I remain as great a fool as ever I was.

I have cut & trimmed & written all the quotations to 100—(—i.e—half—)—of the ⋏ eggs—& wish I could send them to you if your time were not fully employed. It has become a question with me, whether the whole work might not be COMMENCED—(all the 200—)—in that small sketchy size, Autotyped,——& then, if needs vos—to reprojuice them bigger.

Believe me, | Your's sincerely,
Edward Lear.

To Wilkie Collins

Villa Tennyson | Sanremo. | 7. March 1886

My dear Wilkie,

'E'en in our ashes live' &c &c——so,—though I have been in bed since 14 weeks, I have none the less written an absurdity which I fancy you may like—whereby I send it.

The acute Bronchitis which I began with, Dr Hassall I am grateful to say has pretty well abolished. Not so the congestion, which with its dreadful cough—is trying enough. Yet many thousands suffer more, & I may be very thankful that only increasing weakness is my greatest drawback.

One of my old friends, Fortescue, (now Ld Carlingford) was here for two months & with me almost all day daily. And other friends come & are coming from Cannes, Hyéres—&c & I have lots of Books, (many by one Wilkie Collins,) & most attentive & able servants—to feed me, or lift me in or out of bed. Of what is called the 'Colony' here I know—I am happy to say nothing. Neither perpetual church services—(high & low——candle-stix or cursing—) are to my taste, nor are balls & Lawn Tennis among my weaknesses.

Mr. Ruskin (vide Pall Mall Gazette Feby 15—) has of late greatly exalted me, & he is now taking much interest, & writes most kind letters,—about my everlasting & never terminated Ⱥ or Alfred Tennyson illustrations—still let us hope—to come out in Autotype——about the year 4810. Meanwhile, if I go off in one of these terrible phits of coughing, this may be the last note you will ever be bothered by from, Your's affly,

Edward Lear.

To John Ruskin

Villa Tennyson | Sanremo. | [12 March 1886]

My dear Mr. Ruskin,

Only 5 minutes ago I wrote to Mrs. Severn, & the letter had only gone to the post—(together with 2 Volumes of Nonsense for her boys,) just as the postman came,——too late for me to recal [sic] my letter. So I write again.

Now—listen! You MUST NOT *bother yourself* over my *scroobious-nesses,*——which, as I already have told Mrs. Severn, I sent mainly to shew you, who had so kindly interested yourself about it,——the scope & arrangement for the ⋔ 200 work.

Nothing has come from the Autotypicals today, but directly they send, I will forward what turns up.

I am, thank you,——somewhat better today——& slept last night————thanks to Dr Hassall's never ceasing care.

Your's affly,
Edward Lear.

My cat 'Foss'. which his tail is 'far too short.'——

To the Revd. E. Carus Selwyn

Villa Tennyson | Sanremo. | 19. May or might | would could or | should be 19th. | 1886

After I sent your letter to the preconcerted predacious Poast—I remembered your wish to know about 'Uncle Arly'————of which Wilkie Collins writes to me that he thinks it the best of all 'my poetry!'——

There is another pome about the same ingividgual begun—but shunted—

> 'Accidental, on his hat,——
> 'Once my Uncle Arly sat:
> 'Which he squeezed it wholly flat.'

(Incomplete MSS—found in the brain of Mr. Edward Lear on dissection of the same—in a post mortification examination)

To Lady Tennyson

Villa Tennyson | Sanremo. | 7. December 1886.
My dear Lady Tennyson,
   Your last, date Octbr. 22, ought to have been answered long
ago. But I am so often quite disabled by rheumatism, which
now attacks my shoulders & arms, that I am frequently not at
all up to writing.
   Frank L. was with me a whole fortnight in November—& I
was very sorry when he left me. Nevertheless, you can well
understand that the depression & sadness of my life in these
days, was not much relieved by Frank who you know is often
silent for days together.
   In the present case no wonder, for he got a bad cold (by his
own folly in sitting out late without extra covering,) & was 2
days in bed. So the visit was not generally luminous so to speak.
I shall be very glad of little Michæl's Photograph:° & wish I
may get one of Elleanor his mother—
   The great ⚤ illustrative work is very much collapsed & come
to grief. For the Autotype people can't reproduce my drawings
properly—& they come all mealy=mangy=moribundy—&
just now I am having back all the 200 ⚤ s from London—tho'
what may come therefrom later I cant dream. I must stop
now—feeling like a periwinkle who has swallowed a penwiper
& 2 pounds of Cayennepepper: so goodbye. 3.30 PM. 7.
December 1886.

To the Hon. Mrs Augusta Parker

Villa Tennyson | San Remo. | 18 June 1887
My dear Gussie,
   In my last note I quite forgot to name what I have constantly
in my view & thoughts just now, i.e.—various objix given by
you to me when last here.

   1st—A paper cutter distinctly the best I ever had in all my
life.

2dly. The little volume of Wordsworth's Poems, which is a delight.

I had no idea he was so lovely a writer, & thank you heartily for having given me so much pleasure.

You will be glad to know I keep getting better, & that today I got a long walk at 7.30 A M. in the garden. Of course I have to be much assisted as yet.

My ten pigeons are a great amusement, & their punctual ways—2 hours exactly on their eggs—& then 2 hours at liberty are very curious. Giuseppi Orsini my servant° (says he) believes they have little watches under their wings, & that they wind them up at 7 P M—holding them in one foot & turning the key with t'other.

Your's affectionately,
Edward Lear.

To Lord Aberdare

Villa Tennyson | San Remo | 29 November 1887

My dear Lord Aberdare,

I have been wanting to know how your hand is now—if quite recovered, or still giving trouble? But I am little able now a days to write albeit I have a great deal of writing to get through.

For, whoever has known me for 30 years° has known that for all that time my Cat Foss has been part of my solitary life.

Foss is dead: & I am glad to say did not suffer at all—having become quite paralyzed on all one side of him. So he was placed in a box yesterday, & buried deep below the Figtree at the end of the Orange walk & tomorrow there will be a stone placed giving the date of his death & his age (31 years,)—(of which 30 were passed in my house.)

> Qui sotto è sepolto il mio buon
> Gatto Foss. Era 30 anni in casa
> mia, e morì il 26 Novembre
> 1887, di età 31 anni.

[Here lies buried my good cat Foss. He was 30 years in my house, and died on 26 November 1887, at the age of 31 years.]

All those friends who have known my life will understand that I grieve over this loss. As for myself I am much as usual, only suffering from a very bad fall I had on Novr. 5th—having risen, the Lamp having gone out, & the matches misplaced, so that I could not find them.

The effects of this fall have lasted several days—but now—THANK GOD THURSDAY 29TH are beginning to cause less worry. Salvatore has the stone for Foss, & the Inscription, & I suppose in a day or two all will be as before, except the memory of my poor friend Foss.

> Qui sotto sta seppolito il mio buon
> Gatto Foss. Era 30 anni in casa mia,
> e morì il 26 November 1887—in età
> 31 anni.

[Beneath this stone was buried my good cat Foss. He was 30 years in my house, and died on 26 November 1887—at 31 years of age.]

Let me know before long how your hand is now. I have lost many friends latterly, among these, Harvie Farquhar, brother of Mrs George Clive.

My love to all of you. | Your's affectionately
Edward Lear.

Villa Tennyson, | Sanremo. | November 29. 1887

[At the head of this letter, Lord Aberdare has written: 'Last letter from my dear old friend—who died Jan 1888.']

NOTES

1 *respiration*. The original manuscript of this letter has not survived. In the typed transcript which has survived a possible alternative reading '(recuperation?)' is suggested.

1 *indagation*. Possible alternative reading '(indication?)'.

4 *7 November 1829*. The original manuscript of this letter has not survived. The typed transcript gives the date of the letter as 7 Nov. 1829, but the dates beside each entry are transcribed as Jan. 2 Jan. 1829 was not a Monday; 2 Nov. was. The dates have therefore been changed throughout to Nov.

4 *White Horse cellar*. A post coach left the New White Horse Cellar for Arundel daily at 8 a.m.

5 *globose as a harvest moon*. The image of globular rotundity may first have been suggested to Lear by Ann, who would tease her brother Frederick by likening his circumference to that of the large round cooking apple, the Norfolk Biffin. From July 1860, Lear habitually caricatured himself as round, and in 'How Pleasant To Know Mr. Lear' said, 'His body is perfectly spherical.' (See note to p. 163.)

5 *Bury Hill*. In Nov. 1829 Lear wrote a poem subscribed 'Bury Hill'. It was published in the *Poetry Review*, 41 (Apr. 1950), 82–3.

5 *Peppering*. Peppering House, Burpham, was the home of the Drewitt family (see Biographical Register, Fanny Coombe).

5 *nephews*. Sarah had two sons, Charles and Frederick.

6 *Lyminster*. Batworth Park, Lyminster, was the home of another Jeremiah Lear, who, though a friend of Lear's father Jeremiah, was not related.

6 *Rogers' Italy*. Samuel Rogers's poem *Italy*. First published in two parts in 1822 and 1828, an illustrated edn. was published in 1830; copies were available at the end of 1829. It contained fifty-five steel engravings, of which twenty-five were after Turner and twenty after Stothard; ten were after the work of other artists. The full edn. was published by Edward Moxon, but the plates were available in portfolio or bound form without the text, published by Jennings & Chaplin.

6 *Talked of reform and Chancellor Brougham*. Henry Peter Brougham (1778–1868), Lord Chancellor, was at this time involved in a scheme of common-law reform.

6 *Wardropers—Blanches*. James Wardroper was a subscriber to *Views in Rome and its Environs* (1841), and in a letter of 15 July [1832] Lear writes of a W. Wardroper. Nothing, however, is known of their family, nor of the Blanches.

7 *Mrs George*. Mrs George Coombe of Calceto, Lyminster, was the mother of Fanny Jane Dolly Coombe (see Biographical Register).

8 *Henry Hinde.* Nothing is known of Henry Hinde.

9 *flute.* As a young man Lear played both the flute and the guitar. He took his flute with him when he went to live in Italy in 1837. He recalled playing his guitar on the terrace at Knowsley, but in 1848 he asked Ann to sell it for him. Later in life he played only the piano.

9 *the museum.* The museum of the Zoological Society in Bruton Street.

10 *the Castle.* Arundel Castle, home of the dukes of Norfolk.

10 *sprain-ancle road.* On 12 Dec. 1829 Lear wrote a poem entitled 'Peppering Roads' in which he describes the hazards of the uneven roads around Peppering. It was published in the *Sussex County Magazine* (Jan. 1936), 69–70.

11 *Mrs. Hopkins* is listed among Lear's subscribers to *Illustrations of the Family of Psittacidæ, or Parrots* (1831) as of Bank, Arundel. Nothing more is known of her.

11 *Robert.* Eliza Drewitt's brother.

12 *No. 8.* Part VIII of the *Parrots*, comprising three plates, was published on 1 Oct. 1831.

13 *Mrs Wentworth.* Mrs Godfrey Wentworth of Woolley Park, Yorkshire, was the youngest daughter of Turner's patron Walter Ramsden Fawkes. She was related by marriage to Earl Fitzwilliam who, like Lord Stanley, was an amateur zoologist and who kept a menagerie at his home, Wentworth. In 1865 Lear described the Wentworths as 'my original instigators to Artist life'; he tells us that it was through Mrs Wentworth that he became employed at the Zoological Society. Her name, with that of her daughter Mary, heads the list of subscribers to the *Parrots* (1831). Mrs Brandling was Mrs Wentworth's sister, and Mrs Clements was her daughter.

14 *turned out into the world, literally without a farthing—& with nought to look to for a living but his own exertions.* Throughout his life, Lear spoke of his early experience of having to make his own way in the world, giving the age of this independence as both fourteen and fifteen. In his autobiographical poem 'Incidents in the Life of my Uncle Arly', v. III, Lear says of himself: 'Like the ancient Medes and Persians, | Always by his own exertions | He subsisted on those hills.'

14 *Landseer's.* Lear worked with the engraver Thomas Landseer (1795–1880), son of John Landseer (1769–1852), painter, engraver, and writer, and brother of the animal painter Edwin Landseer, RA (1802–73). It is not known from which of these the autograph was to come.

15 *Mr. Yarrell.* William Yarrell (1784–1856) was one of the original members of the Zoological Society of London and treasurer of the Linnean Society. He published *History of British Fishes* (1836) and *History of British Birds* (1843).

15 *Durham.* Lear's maternal great great grandfather John Grainger, Gentleman, came from the hamlet of Sunnyside near Newcastle, county

Notes   287

Durham. In July 1826 Lear wrote a poem 'The Shady Side of Sunnyside'
(unpublished), in which his family brood on Sunnyside having passed
down through another branch of the family, and lament the 'lakes and
towers' which might have been theirs.

16 *a Zoological Work. The Gardens and Menagerie of the Zoological Society
Delineated*, ed. E. T. Bennett, vol. ii (1831), to which Lear contributed a
drawing of Blue and Yellow Macaws.

16 *Thomas Bell.* Thomas Bell, FRS (1792–1880), Vice-President of the
Zoological Society, was the author of *A Monograph of the Testudinata*
(1836–42), for which Lear prepared the lithographs, and *A History of
British Quadrupeds* (1837) (see note to p. 18). He was one of three sponsors
(with N. A. Vigors (see note to p. 52) and E. T. Bennett (see note to
p. 21) when Lear became an Associate of the Linnean Society in 1831.

16 *an India Proof.* This possibly refers to John Gould's *A Century of Birds
hitherto unfigured from the Himalaya Mountains*, which was published in parts
between Dec. 1830 and Apr. 1832.

17 *residence.* Shortly after this, Lear and Ann moved to rooms at 61 Albany
Street, close to the Zoological Gardens in Regent's Park.

17 *Niece—par adoption.* In 1870 Lear again called himself an 'Adopty
Duncle', this time to two small American children, Daisy and Arthur
Terry, whom he met in a hotel in the Italian Alps and for whom he drew
the Nonsense alphabet of *The Absolutely Abstemious Ass.*

17 *complaint in the head.* Possibly a reference to the epilepsy from which Lear
suffered from the age of 5 or 6, and which he referred to as 'the Demon'.

18 *British Quadrupeds.* Thomas Bell, *A History of British Quadrupeds* (1837), to
which Lear contributed at least four drawings, including a Hedgehog, a
Ferret Weasel, and a Greater Horseshoe Bat.

18 *Sayres.* Lear later recalled visiting Up Park with John Sayres in 1828, and
walking with him on Compton Down in 1829. He lived first in Midhurst
and then in Chichester, but nothing more is known of him.

18 *heard Paganini.* Niccolò Paganini (1782–1840), the Italian violinist and
composer, made a highly successful tour of England in 1831. The only
indication we have of Lear's musical tastes is in a letter to F. T.
Underhill of 28 Oct. 1885 in which he says, 'if you only play JIGGS I won't
have you at all at all. Even Chopin worries & fidgets me—but Mozart,
Handel (?) Mendelssohn, Haydn, Schubert & sichlike, I delight in.'

19 *the Surrey Gardens.* Later known as Chessington Zoo.

20 *original figures.* Lear contributed thirty-two plates to *Ornithology*, vol. vi,
Parrots, in the *The Naturalists' Library* series, none of them previously
published.

21 *the Giraffes.* On 24 May 1836, four giraffe arrived at the Zoological
Gardens from the Sudan. Although the first living specimens at the
Zoological Gardens, they were not the first in England. In 1827, George
IV had been presented with a giraffe which had lived in Windsor Park.

After its death in 1829, it was taken to the Zoological Gardens, where it was stuffed by the Society's taxidermist, John Gould.

21 *the Trionyx*. Nile soft-shelled turtle (*Trionyx triunguis*). The specimen, which had been brought home alive from western Africa, lived for a time at Knowsley. After it died, it was presented to the British Museum. Lear made drawings of both the top and undersides, the topside being published (as *Tyrse Argus*) as Plate XVII in *Gleanings from the Menagerie and Aviary at Knowsley Hall* (1846).

21 *The cat. Leopardus Yagouarondi*, published as Plate IV of *Gleanings* (ibid.).

21 *Mrs. Greville=Howard*. Lear first met Mrs Greville-Howard, whom he described as 'one of the finest specimens of the Grand English Lady of olden time', when he was 18. She was particularly fond of Lear to whom, when she died in 1874, she left a legacy of £100. It is not known what the lithographic drawings were.

21 *Mr. Sabine*. Joseph Sabine, FRS (1770–1837), Vice-President of the Zoological Society, who was much involved in the running of the Gardens.

21 *Mr. Bennett*. Edward Turner Bennett (1797–1836), one of the founding members and secretary of the Zoological Society, supervised the publication of *The Gardens and Menagerie of the Zoological Society Delineated*, 2 vols. (1830–1). (See note to p. 16.)

22 *Lady Maria & Sir J. Stanley*. Maria, daughter of the 1st Earl of Sheffield, married in 1796 Sir John Thomas Stanley, Bt., later 1st Baron Stanley of Alderley.

22 *Cross's garden*. William Cross of Redcar. His son John, one of Lear's closest friends, married Elizabeth, daughter of Admiral Sir Phipps Hornby and a niece of the 12th Earl of Derby.

22 *Mr. Penrhyn & Lady Charlotte*. Edward Leyster Penrhyn of East Sheen, who in 1823 married Lady Charlotte Stanley, eldest daughter of the 13th Earl of Derby.

22 *Mr. Baker*. Of Bedfordbury, near Hertford. A friend of Sabine with whom, Lear later wrote, 'I once imagined I might go out to Himalaya'.

23 *Captn. Coxon's*. In fact Coxen. Captain Henry Coxen (1771–1836) was the uncle of John Gould's wife, Elizabeth.

23 *Lizars*. William Home Lizars (1788–1859), the engraver, who worked with Sir William Jardine and Prideaux Selby, and prepared the plates which Lear contributed to *Illustrations of British Ornithology* (1821–34), *Illustrations of Ornithology* (1836–43), and *The Naturalists' Library* (1833–45).

23 *3 parts of yours*. Possibly *Birds of Europe*, of which Parts xvii and xviii were published during the summer of 1836.

24 *V. Audubon*. Victor Audubon (1809–60), son of John James Audubon (1785–1851), the American ornithologist.

24 *Mr. Hullmandel.* Charles Hullmandel (1789–1850) was the lithographer in whose studio Lear's *Illustrations of the Family of Psittacidæ, or Parrots* was prepared for publication. He subsequently printed five volumes of Lear's travel books. His definitive work, *Art of Drawing on Stone* (1824), was the established textbook for what was at that time a new method of commercial reproduction.

24 *Mrs. Warner.* Mrs T. Courtney Warner of Bath, Somerset, was a friend of Lear's family, but it is not known how they met. When she died in 1849 she left Lear a legacy of £500. Lear's sisters expected that they too might be remembered in her will, but he was the only member of the family to benefit.

24 *The Nevills.* The Nevill family lived in Upper Holloway. William, whom Lear described as 'my very earliest friend', was a contemporary of Lear. His son Allan was Lear's godson.

24 *5 pupils already.* For some years Lear had supplemented his income by teaching. He continued to do so in Florence, and when he first arrived in Rome.

24 *Knighton, (now Sir William) who used to draw at Sass's with me.* Sir William Knighton, Bt. (1812–75), of whom Lear wrote in 1885, 'He was brought up to be an artist (under Sir. D[avid]. Wilkie,) but had no talent; & finally having married a fooly Scotchwoman, she made him give up all art & artists as wulgar.' Sass's School of Art in Bloomsbury prepared students for entrance to the Royal Academy. Lear went there briefly as a student in 1834 or 1835; among his contemporaries then were William Frith (1819–1909), Douglas Cowper (1817–39), and Augustus Egg (1816–63). Lear went again to Sass's at the end of 1849 to prepare drawings for entrance to the Academy in the following Jan.

24 *Russells and Tattons.* It is not known who the Russells were. Thomas Tatton, whom Lear first met in 1836, was a first cousin of Leyster Penrhyn (see note to p. 22).

27 *all cordons are now taken off the road to Florence.* As a protection against cholera, which was raging further south.

27 *Mr. Cox.* Joseph Cox, who became a Fellow of the Zoological Society in 1835.

29 *Claude's pictures.* Claude Lorrain (1600–82), whose work Lear much admired at this time. In 1850 Lear's painting *Claude Lorraine's house on the Tiber* was the first of his works to hang in the Royal Academy.

31 *Mr. Theed and Mr. Dennew.* William Theed (1804–91), the sculptor whose work includes *Africa* on the Albert Memorial. Nothing is known of Dennew.

33 *Southampton Row.* In 1835–7 Lear and Ann had lived at 28 Southampton Row, Bloomsbury.

36 *a certain female acquaintance of mine.* Ann.

36 *Mrs. Clark's letter.* Wife of the Revd (later Archdeacon) George Clark,

who was related by marriage to Lear's boyhood friend Bernard Husey-Hunt.

37 *Prince Musignano.* Charles Lucien Jules Laurent Bonaparte (1803–57), who in 1840 became the 2nd Prince Canino on the death of his uncle. He was the son of Napoleon's brother Giuseppi, king of Spain, and the author of a number of zoological works, including *American Ornithology*, 4 vols. (1825–33).

37 *anything I might think of sending over.* Animals for the menagerie at Knowsley.

37 *Louis Philippe.* Of the house of Orleans (1773–1850), king of the French, 1830–48.

38 *Munchausenism.* A reference to the *Adventures of Baron Münchhausen*, by Rudolph Erich Raspe, first published in London in 1785, a book which described the baron's preposterous travel adventures.

38 *not a cat but hath lost all or part of her tail.* A similar fate, and for the same reason, awaited Lear's own Italian cats including both Foss and Potiphar, 'who has no end of a tail—because it has been cut off'.

40 *Captn. Hornby.* Captain Phipps Hornby, RN (1785–1867), of Little Green, was the son of Lucy, sister of the 12th Earl of Derby, and the Revd Geoffrey Hornby of Winwick. In 1838 he was sent to Woolwich as superintendent of the dockyard. He was made admiral in 1858.

40 *Lady Ellinor.* The 3rd daughter of the 13th Earl of Derby.

40 *Bishop of Norwich.* Edward Stanley (1779–1849), President of the Linnean Society and author of *Familiar History of Birds* (1836), was the father of Lear's friend Arthur Penrhyn Stanley (1815–81), later Dean of Westminster. It was with the bishop and his son that Lear travelled to Ireland in the summer of 1835. Aylmer Bourke Lambert, FRS, was one of four vice-presidents of the Linnean Society; the bishop was another.

41 *Uwins & Mr. Acland.* James Uwins, nephew of Thomas Uwins, RA (1782–1857), and possibly Peter Leopold Dyke Acland (1819–99), fifth son of Sir Thomas Acland, Bt., and later Prebendary and Sub-dean of Exeter, with whom Lear certainly travelled in 1842.

46 *a Scotch lady.* See note to p. 24.

46 *walk topsy-turvy.* Gould and his wife were in Australia, preparing *The Birds of Australia*, 7 vols. (1840–8). *A Monograph of the Macropodidæ, or Family of Kangaroos*, 2 vols. (1841–2), and *The Mammals of Australia*, 3 vols. (1845–63).

47 *now only the 4 eldest left.* In fact, five of Lear's sisters were still living—Harriett (d. 1859), Ann (d. 1861), Mary (d. 1861), Sarah (d. 1874), and Eleanor (d. 1885).

48 *Last summer I commenced oil painting.* The earliest known oil painting by Lear is dated 21 June 1838.

49 *Mrs. Gould's brother.* Charles Coxen (1808–75), also an ornithologist, had emigrated to Australia with his brother Stephen.

50 *his limb remains useless.* Shortly after succeeding to the title, Lord Derby had suffered partial paralysis.

50 *Gibson & Wyatt as sculptors—& Williams as a painter.* John Gibson (1790–1866), who had lived in Rome since 1817, revived the use of colour in sculpture. He was elected ARA in 1833, and RA in 1838. Richard Wyatt (1795–1850) studied at the RA and settled in Rome in 1821. Penry Williams (1800?–85), who also studied at the RA, was a painter of Italian genre scenes and one of Lear's closest friends in Rome. His influence can be seen in Lear's early oil painting, and Lear later spoke of 'the accuracy of Penry William's Italian peasant subjects and the correct beauty of their surroundings'.

50 *Mr. Prince.* Edwin Prince, secretary to Gould.

50 *Broad Street.* 20 Broad Street, Golden Square, Soho, was Gould's London home.

51 *you had not me by your side.* A reference to the visit which Lear and Gould made to the Continent in 1830 or 1831 while working on Gould's *The Birds of Europe.*

51 *publishing some Lithography.* During his visit to England, Lear published *Views in Rome and its Environs* (1841).

52 *Prince Canino.* See note to p. 37.

52 *your books.* Part I of Gould's *The Birds of Australia* was published on 1 Dec. 1840. Part II appeared on 1 Mar. 1841.

52 *that foolish & furious old bigot—Waterton.* Charles Waterton (1782–1865), whom Lear met in 1829 through Mrs Wentworth, published various essays on natural history. He was a staunch Roman Catholic, and Lear's criticism of him in this context reflects his dislike of all forms of extreme orthodoxy.

52 *Mr. Vigor's death.* Nicholas Aylward Vigors, FRS (1785–1840), was secretary of the Zoological Society of London. Lear made some of his parrot drawings from Vigors's birds.

52 *Mr. Eyton.* Thomas Campbell Eyton (1809–80) was the author of *A Monograph of the Antidæ, or Duck Tribe* (1838), to which Lear contributed six plates.

53 *Lord Breadalbane.* The 2nd Marquis and 5th Earl of Breadalbane (1796–1862) was President of the Royal Society of Antiquaries in Scotland, and a Fellow of the Royal Society. Lear travelled to Scotland with Phipps Hornby, and made a series of thirty-six Nonsense drawings (unpublished) illustrating their adventures there.

54 *Spectacle owl. Strix perspicillata,* of which Lear made a water-colour drawing in Aug. 1836.

54 *Stanley cranes. Scops paradisea,* named after Lord Stanley. The water-colour drawing which Lear made in Sept. 1835 was reproduced as Plate XIV in *Gleanings* (1846).

54 *Lady Charlotte Bury, & Mrs. Trollope.* Lady Charlotte Bury (1775–1861),

daughter of the 5th Duke of Argyll, was a prolific novelist. Frances Milton Trollope (1780–1863), also a prolific novelist and a travel writer, was the mother of Anthony Trollope (1815–82), whom Lear was thought by his contemporaries to resemble.

54 *a nephew of Sir Stamfd. Raffles.* Sir Stamford Raffles (1781–1826) had been one of those responsible for founding the Zoological Society, and had worked with Jardine and Selby on *Illustrations of Ornithology* (1836–43).

61 *expeditions.* To the Abruzzi. Lear had also visited the Abruzzi in the summer of 1842, travels which he described in *Illustrated Excursions in Italy* (1846).

61 *woodcutting.* Lear was pursuing this possibility for the publication of either *Illustrated Excursions in Italy* or, though this is less likely, *A Book of Nonsense*, both of which he published on his next visit to England in 1846. The first travel book in which he used wood engraving was *Journal of a Landscape Painter in Corsica*, published in 1870. Although a cheaper method of reproduction, it destroyed much of the flow of Lear's landscape. It was, however, perfectly acceptable for the Nonsense illustrations, and was the method used for the 3rd (1861) and subsequent edns.

62 *rumours of War.* The movement for Italian unification, which did not gather real momentum until 1848.

62 *Mr. White.* Revd Gilbert White, vicar of Selbourne (1720–93), whose natural history observations were published in several volumes, including *Natural History and Antiquities of Selbourne* (1789). An edn. of 1837 contained notes by, among others, Thomas Bell (see note to p. 16) and William Yarrell (see note to p. 15), and in 1872 Bell edited what was to become the classic edn. of *White's History of Selbourne*.

63 *Mr. and Mrs. Arundale.* The Arundales, with whom Ann was staying, lived in Brighton. Mrs Arundale (c. 1806–?) had gone to the Royal Academy Schools in 1829, and was a noted miniaturist. In the winter of 1846–7 she painted a miniature of Ann, possibly the one now in the National Portrait Gallery in London.

63 *one of my drawings—of Osborne House.* A pencil drawing by Lear of Osborne House is preserved in the Royal Library at Windsor.

63 *several pictures.* The painting for Mrs Earle was of *Rome, Via Cassia*; that for Dr Henry was one of two which Lear painted for him that year, of *Rome. Via Tiburtina* and *Rome. Claudian Acqueducts*; Mr Carter may have been T. Bonham Carter for whom, in 1841, Lear had painted *Olevano*—there is no record of work done for him, or for any other Mr Carter, in 1846. The large painting for no one in particular was of *Civitella di Subiaco*. It was bought in Mar. 1861 by Sir Francis Goldsmid, Bt. (see note to p. 251), and is now in the Clothworkers' Hall in the City of London.

64 *10 dollars to the Irish.* A donation made in the aftermath of the potato famine of 1845–6.

64 *Lady Gordon's.* The wife of Sir Alexander Duff-Gordon, Bt., Assistant Gentleman Usher to Queen Victoria.

65 *the Knights.* Lear met the Knight family shortly after his arrival in Rome. Isabella put together a commonplace book which contains a number of drawings by Lear, and which is now in the British Museum. Her brother Charles travelled with Lear in the Abruzzi in 1842, journeys described in the first volume of *Illustrated Excursions in Italy* (1846). A second sister, Margaret, was married to the Duke of Sermoneta.

65 *H. G. Catt.* Henry Catt of West Street, Brighton, a friend of Henry Willett, husband of Fanny Coombe (see Biographical Register).

66 *Baring.* Later the 1st Earl of Northbrook (see Biographical Register).

66 *Mrs. Sartori's.* Mother-in-law of Mary Sartoris, daughter of the 6th Viscount Barrington.

66 *Clives.* Of this list, only the Clives were more than acquaintances. A barrister and politician, George Clive was Under-Secretary of State for the Home Department, 1859–62.

66 *Lord Eastnor: Church.* Of Jacson and Clutterbuck, nothing more is heard. Lord Eastnor, later 3rd Earl Somers (1819–83), remained a friend until his death in 1883. Charles M. Church (1823–1915) was a nephew of General Sir Richard Church, who had commanded the Greek forces during their War of Independence. Lear travelled with Church in Greece later in the year. Church later became Principal of Wells Theological College and Residentiary Canon of Wells.

66 *Ldy. S. Percy.* Susannah Elizabeth Percy, sister of the 5th Duke of Northumberland, whom Lear described as 'My kind friend—the first I ever had in Rome', had died in Apr. 1847.

66 *John Wynne.* Related by marriage to Fortescue, he later became a Jesuit priest.

67 *Louth.* In the election of 1847, Fortescue had been elected Member of Parliament for Co. Louth, a seat he held until 1874. At about the same time he inherited an estate at Ardee, Co. Louth, from his uncle Mr Ruxton.

67 *one for Ld. Canning &c &c:—& one of a bigger growth for Ld. Ward.* In his list of *Pictures Painted, 1840–1877* Lear gives the date of paintings for Lord Canning of *Rome. Veii,* and for Lord Ward of *Naples,* as 1845. The first Earl Canning (1812–62) was Governor-General of India at the time of the outbreak of the Indian mutiny in 1857; Lord Ward (1817–85) later became the 1st Earl of Dudley.

67 *Bowen.* George Ferguson Bowen (1821–99), whom Lear had met through Fortescue, was in 1847 appointed President of the University of Corfu. In 1854 he became Chief Secretary to Sir John Young, Lord High Commissioner of the Ionian Islands.

68 *J. Battersby & Clowes.* Lear later preferred to travel on his own, finding that 'the quick passage of ordinary tourists is very different from my

stopping, prying, lingering mode of travel', but at this time he always
sought a travel companion. It is not known how Lear met J. Battersby
Harford whom, in 1862, he listed as no. 4 of his ten original friends (after
William Nevill, Bernard Husey-Hunt, and Robert Hornby). S. W.
Clowes, who was related to the Hornbys, is no. 6 on the same list.

68 *Simeon.* Cornwall Simeon was Fortescue's travelling companion on the
visit to Rome in 1845 when he met Lear.

70 *Lady & Miss Duncan.* See Biographical Register.

70 *Missolonghi, where Lord Byron died.* Byron was Lear's boyhood hero. In
1861 he remembered 'when I heard that Ld. Byron was dead, stupified
& crying'.

71 *Lord Seaton.* Formerly Sir John Colborne (1778–1863), who had
commanded the 52nd Foot at Waterloo.

73 *B. Husey Hunt.* Bernard Husey-Hunt (1812?–94) was one of Lear's
boyhood friends. Born Bernard Senior, he was a solicitor of 2 New Inn
Chambers, St Clements, Strand, and was executor to both Lear and
Ann. As a young man he worked for Ellis and Blackmore, the solicitors
who for a time employed Charles Dickens; his wife was a Miss
Blackmore.

73 *Sir Stratford Canning.* Canning (1786–1880), later the first Viscount
Stratford de Redcliffe, was first appointed to Constantinople as secretary
to the envoy in 1808 at the age of 21. In 1810 he was left in charge of the
embassy with the task of counteracting Napoleon's influence and
preventing war between Russia and Turkey, so leaving Russia free to
pursue its war against Napoleon. After postings in Washington and St
Petersburg, he returned to Constantinople in 1825 to seek recognition of
Greek independence. In 1842 he was appointed British ambassador.

73 *Wilmot-Horton.* An acquaintance from Rome, possibly the son of Sir
Robert Wilmot Horton (see note to p. 246), Wilmot-Horton had met
Lear again in Corfu when they had discussed the possibility of travelling
together.

79 *a friend.* Church.

80 *the last war.* The Greek War of Independence.

81 *the assistance.* This probably refers to a loan made by Fortescue.

83 *vile squash of Captn. Devereux's.* W. B. Devereux, *Views on the Shores of the
Mediterranen* (1847).

83 *Wordsworth's popular vol:.* Christopher Wordsworth, *Greece* (1839).

83 *Williams' Greece.* Hugh W. Williams, *Select Views of Greece*, 2 vols. (1829).
Williams had earlier published *Travels in Italy, Greece, and the Ionian Islands*
(Edinburgh, 1820).

83 *Baring's marriage.* On 6 Sept. 1848 Baring married Elizabeth, daughter of
Henry Charles Sturt of Crichel, Dorset.

90 *having read a description beforehand.* In his introduction to *A Leaf from the*

Journals of a Landscape Painter, a description of Lear's visit to Petra which was published in *Macmillan's Magazine* (Apr. 1897), Franklin Lushington wrote of Lear: 'Before visiting any country . . . he studied every book he could lay hands on that would give him the best information as to its physical characteristics and its history.'

95 *publish an entirely new book. Journals of a Landscape Painter in Albania, &c.* (Richard Bentley, 1851).

95 *costumes.* It was Lear's custom when travelling to buy local costumes to which he could refer in his studio when working on figures of peasants in his paintings.

95 *Mary.* One of Lear's sisters.

95 *Signora Giovanina.* Lear's landlady in Rome.

96 *the London house.* In what Lear called 'thrice odious New Street'.

97 *Lane's works.* Edward William Lane (1801–76), *An Account of the Manners and Customs of the Modern Egyptians*, 2 vols. (1836).

102 *though you did make me walk round that chimneysweeper 33 years ago.* This recalls an incident in Margate when Lear was 4, and Ann made him walk round and round a chimney sweep to make sure he was not smoking.

105 *other places as Mt. Sinai.* Scholars are unable to decide the exact route taken by the Israelites out of Egypt, and the site where the Ten Commandments were given to Moses cannot be stated with certainty. Mount Sinai is long accepted in Jewish tradition, but Mount Serbal is another suggested site.

107 *the stupid war.* Between Piedmont and Austria.

108 *he got into the Academy.* Lear was accepted for a three-month probationary period. On 26 Apr. 1850 he was accepted as a full student.

110 *Col: Leake.* Colonel W. Martin Leake (1777–1860), author of *Journal of a Tour in Asia Minor* (1824), *Travels in the Morea* (1830) and *Travels in Northern Greece*, 4 vols. (1835). Dr Holland was Henry Holland, MD, author of *Travels in the Ionian Isles, Albania, Thessaly, Macedonia, &c.* (1815).

112 *little Book I am bringing out. Journals of a Landscape Painter in Albania, &c.* (1851).

114 *middies.* Midshipmen.

115 *a series of little landscapes illustrative of some of the Poems.* The first mention of a scheme which from this time Lear kept in mind as he worked, and to which he devoted the last decade of his life.

115 *two volumes. Illustrated Excursions in Italy*, 2 vols. (1846). Lear's later volume, *Journals of a Landscape Painter in Albania, &c.* (1851), prompted Tennyson to write his poem 'To E.L. on his Travels in Greece'.

116 *today's festivity.* The christening of the Tennysons' eldest son Hallam.

119 *Thermopylæ, I trust you may yet see at the British Institution.* This picture,

which was hung at the British Institution, is now in the Bristol City Art Gallery. The painting of Reggio is now in the Tate Gallery.

119   *the Fairlight Hill Picture.* Holman Hunt's *Our English Coasts (Strayed Sheep)*, now in the Tate Gallery.

119   *Addio.* Lear's Italian was of an erratic nature, and precise translations are difficult.

119   *my sister's early quitting England.* Sarah Street and her family were leaving England to settle in Dunedin, New Zealand.

120   *the Syracuse. The city of Syracuse from the ancient quarries where the Athenians were imprisoned,* which was exhibited at the Royal Academy in 1853. The painting was bought by Henry Lygon, later Earl Beauchamp, who chose it as his Art Union Prize. Lear also exhibited a second picture, *Prato-lungo, near Rome.*

121   *S[outh] Down Sheep.* Lear was working on a painting of Windsor Castle, commissioned by Lord Derby, in the foreground of which sheep were grazing.

121   *Such a letter from Ruskin.* It is not known to what this refers.

121   *'Tiers, idol tiers'.* 'Tears, idle tears' (from *The Princess*) was one of Lear's Tennyson settings which were published by Cramer, Beale, & Co. in 1853. The others were 'Flow down, cold rivulet' ('A Farewell'), 'Edward Gray', and 'Wind of the Western Sea' (from *The Princess*). Holman Hunt painted the rolled sheet music of 'Tears, idle tears' in the bottom left-hand corner of his picture *The Awakening Conscience.*

121   *at Egg's.* Augustus Egg (1816–63), whom Lear first knew at Sass's School of Art in 1834. He had been elected ARA in 1849.

122   *at Friths.* William Frith (1819–1909), whom Lear also met at Sass's, was one of the most popular painters of his day. Among his most celebrated works were *Derby Day* and *Ramsgate Sands.* He had been elected ARA in 1845, and RA in 1852.

122   *the Bassae.* Lear's painting *The Temple of Bassae or Phigaleia, in Arcadia from the Oakwoods of Mt. Cotylium. The Hills of Sparta, Ithome and Navarino in the Distance,* was exhibited in the Royal Academy in 1853. In 1859 it was bought by subscription raised among Lear's friends, and donated to the Fitzwilliam Museum, Cambridge.

122   *I pen out: & colour old sketches.* The drawings which Lear made on his travels were generally done in pencil. In his studio he went over the pencil lines in sepia ink, a process he called 'penning out'. Water-colour washes were either laid in at the time of the original drawing, or in his studio, when he would follow the colour notes he had written on the drawing.

122   *The Hansens.* Hansen oversaw Lear's rooms in Stratford Place in the early 1850s. In 1856 he moved to 16 Upper Seymour Street, Portman Square, which Lear used as his London base for three years.

122 *sloshing & Asphaltism*. A reference to the techniques and convention of colour against which the Pre-Raphaelites had rebelled.

122 *Millais*. John Everett Millais (1829–96) was one of the three founding members of the Pre-Raphaelite Brotherhood. Lear met him in 1853 through Holman Hunt, whom he considered Millais's superior as both a man and a painter. In 1859 Lear wrote: 'I am quite aware of the qualities of his mind, which I do not apprehend are of the progressive nature, as are Holman Hunt's:—but his power & technical go I have no doubt are wonderful.' He increasingly ascribed Millais's success to the dictates of fashion (see note to p. 260). Millais was elected ARA on 7 Nov. 1853, and became President of the Royal Academy in 1896.

122 *Antony*. Henry Mark Anthony (1817–86), landscape painter and friend of Ford Madox Brown and the Pre-Raphaelites.

122 *Maddox Brown*. Ford Madox Brown (1821–93), an admirer of the German Nazarene painters, was brought into the Pre-Raphaelite circle by Dante Gabriel Rossetti. His daughter Lucy married William Michael Rossetti.

123 *I have not shaved my upside mouth for a fortnight*. An indication that Lear was about to set off on his travels. In Feb. 1854 he wrote to Ann from Egypt, 'You will be happy to hear that I shall come home with a beard like Henry 8th', a beard which he kept for the rest of his life.

123 *the Lady of Eyelashes subject as well as the night piece*. *The Awakening Conscience* and *The Light of the World*. Although *The Light of the World* was frequently known as *The Night Piece*, the 'Lady of Eyelashes' appears to have been Lear's own name for *The Awakening Conscience*.

127 *I have made a great many outlines*. Between 1853 and 1872, Lear made at least twenty oil paintings of Philae, based on these studies, which he used to illustrate the Tennyson lines 'I will see before I die | The palms & temples of the South' from 'You ask me why'.

129 *poor Frank Lushington*. Lushington's nephew, the son of Edmund Lushington and Tennyson's sister Cecelia, was dying.

130 *Watts*. George Frederick, Watts, RA (1817–1904), the historical and portrait painter and sculptor.

130 *a dish to carve*. Lear's horror at the prospect of carving dated back to an incident in 1834 when he was staying at Alderley, and was presented with a goose to carve. The situation was saved by Lady Maria Stanley, who instructed him on how it should be done.

130 *folios*. Containing Lear's water-colour drawings.

130 *Catania being utterly destroyed*. From an eruption of Etna. Bomba was King Ferdinand II of the Two Sicilies.

131 *the Pigchr*. In Feb. 1855, Fortescue bought for £23 a small painting of *Civitella di Subiaco, looking south*, which Lear saw as illustrating Tennyson's line 'Morn broaden'd on the borders of the dark' from 'A Dream of Fair Women'.

133 *Park House.* The Lushington family house near Maidstone, Kent.

133 *very old friends.* The Nevills.

133 *Beadon.* William F. Beadon, brother-in-law of Henry Bruce (see Biographical Register).

134 *by yesterday's verdict.* This refers to the trial of William Strahan, Sir John Dean Paul, and Robert Martin Bates, bankers accused of appropriating and disposing of securities entrusted to them. Although Strahan and Bates claimed to have known nothing of the transactions, all three were found guilty and sentenced to be transported for fourteen years.

135 *The war.* The Crimean War.

136 *If Ellen Lushington had come out.* Ellen had been prevented by her nephew's illness from going with Franklin to Corfu.

137 *one or 2 large paintings of Corfu.* Lear made at least thirty oil paintings of Corfu, the largest of which was more than 9 feet long and 6 feet tall. This painting of *Corfu from Ascension, Evening,* on which Lear worked during the winter of 1856–7, was sold in Aug. 1857 for 500 guineas to T. William Evans, MP, and was exhibited in the Great International Exhibition of 1862.

138 *Messrs. Huc & Gabet. Travels in Tartary, Thibet, and China, 1844–46,* trans. into English by William Hazlitt (1852).

139 *that half of our species.* No women, nor indeed any female creatures, are allowed on Mount Athos.

139 *those foolish & miserable monks.* In a letter to Fortescue, Lear described the monks as 'these muttering, miserable, muttonhating, manavoiding, misogynic, morose, & merriment=marring, monotoning, many-Mule-making, mocking, mournful, mincedfish & marmalade masticating Monx'. He added, 'it is not them,—it is their system I rail at'.

139 *my servant.* Giorgio Cocali, a Suliot by birth, had begun to work for Lear in the spring of 1856 and stayed until his death in 1883.

141 *Sir John Simeon's picture.* He chose the painting of *Nile. Kasr es Saàd* illustrating 'the crag that fronts the Even' from 'Eleänore'. Lear met Simeon through the Tennysons. After Simeon's death in 1870, Tennyson wrote 'In the Garden at Swainston', one of his poems which Lear set to music but which he did not publish.

141 *the 2 sisters Cortazzi.* Madeleine and Helena. Their mother had been a Miss Hornby.

142 *Charles Weld.* Emily Tennyson's brother-in-law.

142 *Venables'.* George Stovin Venables (1810–88), a barrister and journalist, was a friend of Tennyson.

143 *a Druid's Egg.* Emily Tennyson had told Lear of a visit they had made to north Wales, where Alfred had visited a man who owned a priceless collection of Welsh manuscripts, some Bard's beads, and 'a Druid's Egg'.

144 *I wrote 8 foolscape close pages to dear old sister Ann*. This, the longest known letter written by Lear, is more than 8,000 words.

144 *Alfred's little poem to me*. 'To E.L., on his Travels in Greece' included the line, 'Tomohrit, Athos, all things fair', although at the time it was written in 1851 Lear had not yet visited Athos.

144 *When will the next poem be out? Idylls of the King* was published in 1859. This was the first of Tennyson's works to which Lear did not wholeheartedly respond, largely because of its subject matter, 'Arthuriana, which sort of legend I dont digest easily'.

144 *'Courage—poor heart of stone—'*. Lines from *Maud* which Emily Tennyson had sent to Lear at a time of loneliness and depression in the autumn of 1855.

146 *the great picture*. Of Corfu. See note to p. 137.

146 *Mrs. Empson*. Wife of the Revd W. H. Empson, vicar of Romsey.

147 *[Stanfield's]—Cook's*. Clarkson Stanfield, RA (1793–1867), and E. W. Cooke, ARA (1811–80), both of whom regularly exhibited paintings of Venice in the Royal Academy.

148 *It is quite hard work enough to try to make them*. On 3 Sept. 1861 Fortescue wrote to Lear: 'You are a curious compound of love of Art—or at all events power of absorbing yourself in it—with hatred of the actual work.' Two days later Lear replied: 'Yes—: I certainly *do* hate the act of painting: & although day after day I go steadily on, it is like grinding my nose off.'

148 *Caroline & the Hon. Mr. Senator Jones*. Caroline Chesner was Lear's cousin. She was married to a Canadian Senator, and their son Archie travelled with Lear down the Nile in 1867.

152 *Josephus*. Flavius Josephus (AD 37/8–*c*.100). Jewish historian and author of *History of the Jewish War*.

153 *Ld. Clermont's picture*. Lear was never to get to Nazareth or Galilee, but he did do paintings of *Jerusalem*, *Mount Athos*, *Parnassus*, and *The Dead Sea* for Lord Clermont, who was Chichester Fortescue's elder brother.

153 *risk of robbery*. A few weeks earlier an American missionary and his family had been attacked, and the missionary killed, the most serious in a series of assaults by Muhammadan Arabs on Christian travellers in Syria. American consular officials had made representations to the Turkish authorities, who had been persuaded to arrest four men, but there was felt to be sympathy for the assailants among the local population. In the following weeks, stories of other attacks, both real and imaginary, were freely circulating among English-speaking travellers.

155 *Dr. Philpotts*. Dr Henry Phillpotts (1778–1869), Bishop of Exeter, was a High Church Anglican who was opposed, among many other things, to Catholic emancipation. In 1847 he refused to institute the Revd George Cornelius Gorham to a living within his diocese because of Gorham's Calvinistic views of baptismal regeneration. During the ensuing

controversy, Phillpotts excommunicated the Archbishop of Canterbury.

159 *to Mr. Harcourt, & to Mr. Milnes.* George Granville Harcourt (1785–1861) married Frances, Lady Waldegrave in 1847 as her third husband. Robert Monkton Milnes, later Lord Houghton (1809–85), the poet, and a friend of Tennyson.

161 *Blue Posts.* A hostelry frequented by Fortescue.

161 *Twickenham station.* Lear had been staying at Lady Waldegrave's house, Strawberry Hill.

162 *Nuneham.* Nuneham Park was the Oxfordshire home of Lady Waldegrave's husband George Harcourt (see note to p. 159). Lady Waldegrave had commissioned Lear to do two paintings of Nuneham, works he described in 1880 as 'the best of my very few English subjects'.

162 *Charles Braham's little one.* Constance Braham, for whom Lear made an alphabet in Aug. 1860. In 1880 she married Sir Edward Strachey, Bt., who in 1911 became the 1st Baron Strachie. She was responsible for editing *The Letters of Edward Lear* (1907) and *The Later Letters of Edward Lear* (1911), *Queery Leary Nonsense* (1911), and *The Complete Nonsense Book* (1912). Charles Braham was Lady Waldegrave's brother. Like his father, he was an opera singer.

162 *accounts of the Lebanon.* In the civil war between Druses and Christians it was reported that the Druses had carried out acts of barbarism against the Christians unrestrained by the local authorities, leading to a suggestion that there was a government-backed conspiracy to exterminate the Christians in Lebanon.

163 *The Bowl of Peace.* The illustration accompanying this caption is the first in which Lear drew himself as a sphere.

163 *Culham Station.* For Nuneham.

165 *Penrose.* Grove, who had developed a sudden interest in collecting toadstools, was at this time secretary to the Crystal Palace Company. F. Penrose was head of one of its departments.

166 *exhibited in the Brit. Institution.* The picture was accepted, and Lord Stanley, later the 15th Earl of Derby, who visited the exhibition, found it 'the only one that especially pleased me'.

167 *sad enough.* Lady Hornby, wife of Admiral Sir Phipps Hornby of Little Green, had died on Christmas Day.

167 *Pope is a vanishing.* Pope Pius IX's papal army had been defeated by Cavour in Sept. 1860 and the Papal States overrun.

167 *Cockerell.* F. Cockerell was possibly the architect Frederick Pepys Cockerell (1833–78), who was a friend of Digby Wyatt. Lear met James Edwards in Corfu in 1856, and visited Albania with him in 1857. He was the godson of Lister Parker, FRS, a friend of Lear's from the 1830s. W. Raleigh who dined with Lear on 13 Jan. 1861, he described as 'full of colonial & foreign experience for so young a man', but it is not known who he was.

168 *Mrs. Cameron.* Julia Margaret Cameron (1815–79) was the distinguished but eccentric portrait photographer who in 1860 settled near the Tennysons' home at Freshwater on the Isle of Wight. Her straightforward portrait photographs of Darwin, Tennyson, and Herschel are superb, but writing to Holman Hunt in 1865 about a series of photographs of well-known people in archaic dress, Lear said: 'They are picturesque subjects, but not likenesses—at least one may be excused for not recognizing J. Millais as Dante, or Philip in a Spanish dress—seeing they seldom walk about so attired.'

169 *the widow.* Eleanor Newsom.

171 *the Reids.* Sir James Reid was a member of the Supreme Council in the Ionian Islands, 1837–58.

171 *the Boyds.* Boyd, whom Lear described as Treasurer Boyd, lived in Corfu with his wife and son Charles. Nothing is known of the Loughman or Pagueaneau families.

172 *Aubrey de Vere.* Aubrey de Vere (1788–1846) the Irish poet, friend of Wordsworth and Tennyson. Horace de Vere, RA, was part of the garrison in Corfu. His small daughter Mary was a particular friend of Lear for whom, in Dec. 1862, he made his first known set of coloured Nonsense birds.

172 *Frank's successor.* Lushington had resigned his post in the summer of 1858.

172 *Bowen's successor.* Henry Drummond Wolfe.

172 *Ldy Young.* Wife of Sir John Young (1807–76), later 1st Baron Lesgar, Lord High Commissioner of the Ionian Islands, 1855–9. He was succeeded by Sir Henry Storks (1811–74).

172 *teach George.* In time, Lear taught Giorgio to sign his name and to keep the household accounts. His attempts to teach Giorgio to speak English, lessons which at one time involved Giorgio learning to say 'The Owl and the Pussy-Cat', were less successful.

173 *Gt. Exhibition.* The Great International Exhibition in South Kensington opened on 1 May 1862.

173 *my new Book of Nonsense.* The 3rd edn. of Lear's *A Book of Nonsense* was published early in Dec. 1861. The first two edns., published in 1846 and 1855 under the pseudonym 'Derry Down Derry', had had a limited circulation. It was this third edn. which established Lear as a Nonsense writer.

173 *A. P. Stanley's Greek Church.* Arthur Penrhyn Stanley, *Lectures on the History of the Eastern Church* (1861).

173 *Franklin's marriage.* On 21 Jan. 1862 Franklin Lushington married Kate Maria, daughter of Revd James Morgan of Corston, Somerset.

173 *Major P.* John Peel, later Lt.-Gen. His sister Alice married Robert Morier, son of David Richard Morier (see Biographical Register).

173 *the 'American Outrage'.* The American Civil War had broken out earlier in the year.

173 *Bp. Heber's widow.* Reginald Heber (1783–1826) had been Bishop of Calcutta.

174 *dedication verses.* Dedication to Prince Albert, who died on 14 Dec. 1861, which prefaced the new edn. of *Idylls of the King.*

174 *Norfolk Square.* Lushington's London house.

175 *Prince of Wales.* Between Feb. and June 1862 Arthur Stanley accompanied the prince on a tour to Egypt and the Holy Land.

175 *Brookfields.* William Brookfield (1809–74), a friend of Tennyson at Cambridge, was Chaplain in Ordinary to Queen Victoria.

175 *buzzyfuzzy.* In a letter to Ann of 22 Mar. 1857, Lear had described Corfu as 'rustymustyfustydustybustycrusty' an adjective inspired by Tennyson's epigram to the critic Christopher North who had savaged Tennyson's poetry.

175 *Luard.* The grandson of the naturalist Prideaux Selby (1788–1867), with whom Lear had worked at the age of 16 on *Illustrations of British Ornithology* (19 parts, 1821–34).

175 *John Godley.* (1814–61). Politician and writer.

175 *'my spirits falter in the mist'.* This painting, commissioned by Henry Grenfell, MP, was *Beachy Head.* Lear eventually decided that it was more suited to the lines 'Between the steep cliff and the coming wave' from *Guinevere.*

175 *Dr. Williams' case.* Rowland Williams (1817–70), an Anglican divine, who in Feb. 1860 reviewed Bunsen's *Biblical Researches,* writing of biblical criticism which took account of new scientific discoveries. The review caused immediate alarm, and the Bishop of Salisbury prosecuted him for heterodoxy. The case came before Dr. Stephen Lushington early in 1862, but judgement was deferred until the following June when it was largely, but not entirely, found in his favour. The widespread discussion which surrounded it dealt mainly with the issues of freedom to express what was believed to be true.

176 *Geoff Hornby.* Captain Geoffrey Hornby, RN (1825–95), son of Admiral Sir Phipps Hornby and himself later an admiral, whose ship called at Corfu on its way from Malta.

176 *Spring Ricy people.* Aubrey and Horace de Vere's uncle was Thomas Spring-Rice, 1st Lord Mounteagle.

176 *an ancient & polykettlejarring instrument.* The terrible piano at Farringford was a local scandal, and on one occasion in June 1860, when Lear had been invited to sing after dinner, Mrs Cameron arrived at the Tennysons' house followed by eight men carrying her own grand piano.

177 *successor of the K. of Greece.* In Feb. 1862 King Otto was deposed. He was without an heir, and a constitutional convention was summoned to select a new ruler. The first choice was Prince Alfred, second son of Queen Victoria, but he declined the offer. Edward Stanley, later 15th Earl of Derby, was suggested, but this offer was also declined. Prince Christian

of Denmark accepted the throne as George I, king of the Hellenes, and the accession was confirmed by the Treaty of London in July 1863.

177 *little tiny child.* Ruth Decie was born on 8 Sept. 1862.

177 *One of the old Greek Tragedians.* Sophocles, in *Oedipus at Colonus.*

178 *Parsondom.* Lear was in Hastings to work on a painting of Beachy Head which had been commissioned by Henry Grenfell. That day he had dined with Edgar Crake, 'who was very absurd about Orthodoxy & the Gk. church—&c. A silly but wellmeaning priest.'

179 *the Cedars.* The *Cedars of Lebanon* had been exhibited, with a painting of Corfu, in the Great International Exhibition in Kensington; both pictures were hung very high. Writing in *The Times* on 11 June 1862, Tom Taylor had suggested that Lear should be on his guard against letting himself be merely a mirror of the scene he was painting rather than recreating it and setting upon it the seal of his own mind—though he did add that the height at which the works were hung made it impossible to say if these remarks, which he had applied initially to another painter's work, were also applicable to Lear's. When first exhibited in Liverpool in the autumn of 1861 the picture had been well received, and one critic had written: 'Mr Lear has in this great picture not only achieved a professional success, but he has also conferred an obligation of the highest order on the whole Christian world.'

179 *'Letters from Palmyra'.* These publications have not been identified.

179 *The mouseplate.* A set of semicircular friezes drawn by Lear on Prescott writing paper, depicts both mice and snails. Writing to Mrs Prescott on 14 Sept. 1862, Lear said, 'Miss Perry's snail plate has come out beautifully.' The drawings were published as endpapers in *Teapots and Quails* (1953).

179 *Wolstenholme.* E. Wolstenholme, whom Lear had met at the Prescotts on 1 Nov. 1862. Of this occasion, Lear wrote in his diary, 'on showing the receipt for the Bk. of Nonsense, they seemed to think it was nil,—wh. distressed & disgusted me, & made me cross'.

179 *stamped agreements both from Routledge & from Dalziels.* Routledge was the publisher to whom, on 1 Nov. 1862, Lear sold the rights of *A Book of Nonsense* for £125. It went into twenty-four edns. in his lifetime, and has never been out of print. The Dalziel Brothers were wood engravers whom Lear commissioned to prepare the wood engravings for the 3rd edn. of *A Book of Nonsense* in 1861.

182 *Lady Shelley.* Wife of Sir Percy Shelley, Bt. (1819–89), son of the poet. Lear had set to music Shelley's lines 'O world, o life, o time!' He was unable to write music himself, and the setting was put down by Sir Percy, a link with the poet which delighted Lear.

182 *The Marriage.* Fortescue married Frances, Lady Waldegrave on 20 Jan. 1863. As after her previous marriage, she continued to be known as Lady Waldegrave.

183 *Colenso.* John Colenso (1814–83), Bishop of Natal, had published a work

which concluded that the numerous discrepancies in Genesis justified a dismissal of the entire Bible. He also questioned the doctrine of eternal punishment. He was summoned by the Bishop of Cape Town on a charge of heresy. Lear's opinion on the affair was that they should leave him alone: 'A broader creed,—a better form of worship—the cessation of nonsense & curses——and the recognition of a new state of matters brought about by centuries, science, destiny or what not,——will assuredly be demanded, & come to pass whether Bishops & priests welcome the changes or resist them. Not those who believe that God the Creator is greater than a Book, and that millions unborn are to look upward to higher thoughts than those stereotyped by foul ancient legends, gross ignorance, & hideous bigotry——not those are the Infidels,——but these same screamy ganders of the church, who put darkness forward & insist that it is light.'

183 *executed reversed.* Lear made the drawings directly on to the lithographic stones.

184 *a proximate break up in Corfù.* Corfu was ceded to the Greeks early in 1864.

184 *Maclean of the Haymarket.* Thomas McLean, lithographer, of 26 Haymarket (called by Lear both Maclean and McLean) had been associated with Lear as far back as 1831 when he subscribed to the *Parrots* (1831). He printed *Views in Rome and its Environs* (1841) and *Illustrated Excursions in Italy* (1846), and the first two edns. of *A Book of Nonsense* (1846 and 1855). In his premises at 7 Haymarket he exhibited Lear's work in the mid-1860s.

184 *Dudbrook.* One of Lady Waldegrave's homes, in Essex.

184 *New Zealand bothers.* Maori insurrections, near Plymouth in the North Island.

185 *the old House I was born in.* Bowmans Lodge, Highgate, on the corner of the Holloway Road and Seven Sisters Road.

187 *Mrs. T. Wyatt.* Wife of Thomas Henry Wyatt (1807–80), architect, President of the RIBA, 1870–3. He was the brother of Matthew Digby Wyatt (see Biographical Register).

187 *Col. Chapman.* Col. F. Chapman, whom Lear had met in 1848.

188 *4 offspring.* Lear's paintings.

189 *the 2 paintings at Clarence. Corfu, from Gastouri* and *Corfu, from Ascension,* which Lear had painted in 1862. Clarence was the Roehampton home of the Prescott family.

190 *Fairbairn's.* Thomas Fairbairn (1823–91), eldest son of Sir William Fairbairn, Bt., whose portrait Hunt was then painting. The picture on which Hunt was working was *The Children's Holiday (Portrait of Mrs Thomas Fairbairn and her Children).* An important patron of the arts, Fairbairn commissioned three paintings from Lear, *Petra. The Great Cliff* (1859), *Florence* (1862), and *Ioànnina, Albania* (1862).

190 *the Cambridge=Church=decoration=offer.* This was for work in the church

of St Michael and All Angels, Cambridge, a proposal made to Hunt by the Revd W. J. Beamont, whom he had met in Jerusalem in 1854, but which came to nothing.

190 *W. G. Clark.* William George Clark (1821–78), the Shakespearian scholar who endowed the Clark Lectures at Trinity.

190 *Water Baby.* Charles Kingsley's book has been published earlier in the year. Writing to Kingsley on 8 Nov. 1871, Lear said: 'I have often thought I should like to thank you for so much gratification given me by your many works—(perhaps above all—"Water Babies", which I firmly believe to be all true.)'

191 *Strahan.* Captain (later Sir George) Strahan who, with Baring, was aide-de-camp to Sir Henry Storks.

194 *Wade Brown.* Captain Wade Brown was part of the garrison. The poems of Thomas Hood (1799–1845) had been published in 2 vols. in 1846.

196 *Captn. Deverills 3 geese.* Captain Deverill, who was part of the garrison in Corfu, had two geese and a gander.

197 *the painting.* Lear's Greek, which was partly translation and partly transliteration, was of an idiosyncratic nature.

197 *Florence.* For Sir Thomas Fairbairn.

198 *nephew.* Frederick Street died on 15 July 1864.

199 *begins with a Nem.* In fact, Lear found rooms in Nice, and on 14 Nov. 1864 he wrote to Mrs Prescott: 'It is very degrading, having so distinctly declared that I would only go to a place beginning with an M,—to stop after all at one commencing with N:—one consolation however is that N is the next letter.'

199 *2 pickshiors I have finished. Campagna di Roma, Via Prenestina* for Sir Walter James, and *Ioànnina, Albania* for Sir Thomas Fairbairn.

203 *one of the Federals.* Two of Lear's brothers had emigrated to America, and their sons were fighting on opposite sides in the Civil War. The Federal brother was Henry, the Confederate was Frederick.

203 ⚓ *is to be made a baronet.* Early in 1865 Tennyson was offered a baronetcy, which he declined. In 1884 he accepted a peerage.

204 *Cogoletto.* Cogoleto was one of the places Lear had visited and drawn on his Corniche walk the previous winter.

204 *delusions that poor Mr. Prescott had.* On 30 Apr., William Prescott had killed himself.

206 *to Alexandria.* Lear was unable to go to Egypt until Dec. 1866.

206 *I fear you must be suffering.* Sept. had been a month of gales and heavy rain.

207 *reduction of prices.* The *Cedars* was bought in 1867 for £200 by Louisa, Lady Ashburton. Lady Lyttleton bought the *Masada.* Drummond succumbed to pressure, and bought the *Beirut* for 200 guineas.

207 *The Olympus shall be 'mended'.* Drummond's painting, *Mount Olympus, Thessaly*, had been damaged.

207 *the last drawing of the 240.* McLean had arranged to exhibit up to 250 of Lear's paintings while he was away during the winter. He began work on them on 5 Aug. and finished them on 1 Oct. These mass-produced pictures, which Lear produced in batches of up to 50 at a time, working from existing sketches made on his travels, he called his Tyrants. Between 1862 and 1884 he produced nearly 1,000 such works. They were a means of bringing in a basic income, but although they sold reasonably well their often mechanical quality contributed to the decline of Lear's reputation.

207 *Crete—Epirus—Samos &c.* Unrest against the Turkish authorities.

208 *Lord Houghton.* He had commissioned Lear to do a painting of Nazareth, and Lear had written to him from Cairo on 24 Dec. 1866 requesting half or all the money for the picture in advance. Lear was unable to get to Nazareth, and the following June he returned the loan to Lord Houghton, with a drawing of Phyle in Attica as interest on the money lent. William Langton bought a painting *Rome. Via Appia*, which Lear had painted in 1851.

208 *the Venice.* Painted in 1866, this was one of Lear's few townscapes.

208 *Fenianism.* The Irish revolutionary movement, which had been formed in 1858 among Irish immigrants in the United States, had spread to Ireland in 1865. It was active throughout the winter of 1866–7, and although denounced by the Catholic hierarchy its activities made clear to Gladstone the urgent need for a resolution of the Irish problem.

208 *C.'s letter.* A letter from Fortescue about the Irish question had been published in *The Times* on 4 Feb. 1867.

209 *Montreal cousin.* Archie Jones, the son of Lear's cousin Caroline (see note to p. 148).

209 *Ldy Duff Gordon.* The author and translator (1821–69), who had lived in Egypt from 1862.

209 *his motherless boy.* Hunt's wife Fanny (née Waugh) had died on 20 Dec. 1866, eight weeks after giving birth to a son, Cyril.

209 *the Duc D'Aumâles picture. Nile. Philæ, Sunset, looking West*, painted in 1862. The duke lived at Orleans House, Twickenham, close to Lady Waldegrave's home at Strawberry Hill.

210 *Bush the Bookseller.* Robert John Bush of 32 Charing Cross, London, published Lear's *Journal of a Landscape Painter in Corsica* (1870), *Nonsense Songs, Stories, Botany and Alphabets* (1871), *More Nonsense* (1872), and *Laughable Lyrics* (1877). In 1877 Bush became bankrupt, and no further edns. of these Nonsense books were published until after Lear's death, when Routledge and Warne, who already owned the rights of Lear's *A Book of Nonsense*, acquired the rights of these also.

210 *Mr. Romaine.* William Romaine (1815–93), who at this time was Second Secretary to the Admiralty.

210 *Chewton.* The Waldegrave home in Somerset.

211 *The J. Symonds.* The writer John Addington Symonds (1840–93) had been wintering in Cannes. His wife Catherine, whom Lear had first met in 1853, was the sister of Marianne North (see Biographical Register).

212 *Miss Campbell.* In 1868 Thomasina M. A. E. Campbell of Moniack Castle, Scotland, published *Notes on the Island of Corsica in 1868, Dedicated to those in search of Health and Enjoyment.* The frontispiece, *In The Forest of Valdaniello* [*sic*], was based on a drawing by Lear, who 'kindly contributed a sketch intended for his own work on Corsica'.

214 *the Corsica book. Journal of a Landscape Painter in Corsica* (1870), Lear's last travel book.

214 *your magazine. Our Young Folks: An Illustrated Magazine for Boys and Girls* (pub. Fields, Osgood & Co., Boston), in which three of Lear's Nonsense songs were first published: 'The Owl and the Pussy-cat' (vol 6, No. 2, Feb. 1870, pp. 111–12), 'The Duck and the Kangaroo' (vol. 6, No. 3, Mar. 1870, pp. 146–7), and 'The Daddy Long-legs and the Fly' (vol. 6, No. 4, Apr. 1870, pp. 209–12). The illustrations were not by Lear.

215 *the Lake Pipplepopple & its 7 families. The History of the Seven Families of the Lake Pipple=popple* was written in Feb. 1865 for Lady Charlotte and the Hon. Hugh and the Hon. Reginald Wentworth-Fitzwilliam, children of the 6th Earl Fitzwilliam, and was published in *Nonsense Songs, Stories, Botany and Alphabets* (1871). The manuscript is now in the British Museum.

215 *'Morn broadens'.* A small painting of *Civitella di Subiaco.*

216 *the 2 subjects he now is occupied upon. The Shadow of Death* and *The Triumph of the Innocents.* Hunt had been working on *The Shadow of Death* for some time, but *The Triumph of the Innocents* was a new project. Lear had increasing misgivings about Hunt's subject-matter, and in the autumn of 1869 had written to him, 'In what you paint I am nursing the hope that you may not have selected any subject connected with miraculous or mythical, or even traditional interest. There seems to me such a host of moral-historic truth to illustrate, that fables may nowadays be well left aside. Some parts of Jewish *History* (I don't mean traditions, speaking eagles & Lions dens,) are most touching & grand; & so also are some of the undoubtedly historic parts of the New Test. All that tends to strengthen the hands of priests—of whatever creed—the race who have preyed for ages on the foolish & helpless—should, to my fancy—be avoided.' Despite what he felt about Hunt's subject-matter, Lear's admiration for him both as a painter and as a man never wavered.

216 *J. Graham's death.* James Graham, whom Hunt had met in Jerusalem in 1854, was secretary to the Anglican mission there.

216 *the Academy.* Lear exhibited two paintings in the 1870 Academy—*Valdoniello* and *Kasr es Saad.*

216 *Foord's.* Foord and Dickenson, picture handlers and framers, who later took over from McLean the exhibiting of Lear's work.

217 *Arthur Butler.* The Revd A. G. Butler (1831–1909), who had been appointed the first headmaster of Haileybury in 1863. In 1867 his health broke down, and he was travelling abroad to convalesce.

217 *Munro.* Alexander Munro (1825–71), the portrait sculptor, who had suffered for some time from lung disease.

218 *E. Wilson.* A friend of Woolner, who had visited Italy and to whom Woolner had given a letter of introduction to Lear.

218 *the future marriage.* Lord Derby married Mary Catherine, daughter of the 5th Earl of Delawarr, and widow of the 2nd Marquess of Salisbury, on 5 July 1870.

218 *I accept your offer.* In his diary for 14 July, Lord Derby wrote, 'answered Lear, who proposed to paint for me a picture for £300, of a large size, that I have no room left for more large pictures, but would take from him either a small one, or a set of watercolour drawings, for £100, if that suited convenience. Though successful as an artist, Lear is always in want of money, and his request is quite as much an appeal for help as an offer to supply what he thinks may be wanted: I am therefore unwilling to refuse him altogether.' However, on 18 Oct. he wrote: 'Lear's picture of Corfu is come . . . It pleases me much, and the cost (£100) does not seem expensive.'

219 *2 small views. Civitella di Subiaco* and *Olevano.*

219 *the Old W/color Society.* The Old Water Colour Society, founded in 1804 by a group of painters unhappy about the treatment they received from the Royal Academy, and to which Lear was not elected a member.

220 *photographs of all my pictures.* Lear did not realize this wish. The Tennyson illustrations are a record of the composition of many of his works.

221 *The War.* The Franco-Prussian war had broken out on 19 July 1870.

221 *Carlton G[ardens].* Lady Waldegrave's London home.

222 *the Greek affair.* Earlier in the month Valaoritis had resigned as Minister of Foreign Affairs as a protest against the slowness with which the Greek authorities were investigating acts of brigandage in Greece, particularly some murders at Oropos three months before. He believed that their lack of commitment would raise doubts in Europe about the impartiality of the administration of justice in Greece. After his resignation, the king disbanded the Cabinet.

222 *publish them.* These have never been published, and the manuscript has not survived.

222 *my new Xmas book. Nonsense Songs, Stories, Botany and Alphabets* (1871), which was in the bookshops in time for Christmas. The 110 'old persons' were limericks, which were held over for publication the following year, when they were published as *More Nonsense.*

223 *Charles Roundell.* MP for Grantham and the Skipton Division of Yorkshire. Sir Roundell Palmer, Bt., later 1st Earl of Selborne, was married to Lady Laura Waldegrave, daughter of the 8th earl, who was uncle of Lady Waldegrave's husband, whom he succeeded in 1846. Lord Spencer was President of the Council. The four paintings were *Mont Blanc, Pont Pellissar* (1862), *The Dead Sea* (1862), *Cliffs of Cenc, Gozo* (1862), and *Cedars of Lebanon* (1862). He subsequently bought a fifth, *Ravenna Forest* (1872).

223 *Congreve.* Walter Congreve was Lear's neighbour in San Remo. Mrs Congreve died shortly after. His two younger sons, Hubert and Arnold, became particular friends of Lear, coming frequently to Villa Emily for painting lessons.

225 *Matt's.* Matthew Wyatt.

225 *a statue of P. Albert.* Lear had probably read reports at the end of Nov. on progress in the construction of the Albert Memorial.

226 *Ldy K. Shuttleworth.* Lady Kay-Shuttleworth was the wife of Sir James Kay-Shuttleworth, Bt., and the half-sister of Marianne North (see Biographical Register). Her son Lionel was British Vice-Consul at San Remo. Her daughter Janet was later responsible for building the hotel which blocked Lear's view to the sea and ruined his studio light.

227 *would ruin my property totally.* It was, in fact, building carried out on no. 4, Hanbury's land, which was to spoil Lear's house.

228 *Mrs. Ker.* Mrs Bellenden Ker, whom Lear met in Cannes in the winter of 1867–8. Her husband, a noted barrister and legal reformer, was the son of a botanist and one of the first private growers of orchids.

229 *'roomatizz' said the Kangaroo.* 'The Duck and the Kangaroo', v. III. 'Your feet are unpleasantly wet and cold, | And would probably give me the roo- | Matiz!' said the Kangaroo.'

229 ἀποκατόματα. Lear's meaning is obscure.

230 *Miss Edwards'.* Amelia Edwards (see Biographical Register).

230 *Mrs. G. Scrivens.* The daughter of Sir Thomas Potter, founder of the *Manchester Guardian.*

230 *my pictures in the R.A.* Lear had four paintings in the 1871 Academy—*Cattaro in Dalmatia, On the Nile near Assioot, On the Nile, Nagadeh, On the Nile near Ballas.*

233 *M[ansfield]. P[arkyns].* Mansfield Parkyns (1823–94) was a traveller and author of *Life in Abyssinia,* 2 vols. (1853).

233 *Wally.* Emma Parkyns's youngest brother, Walter.

233 *last book. More Nonsense* (see note to p. 222).

233 *the Polly Pussybite Story.* Lear wrote and illustrated *The Adventures of Mr Lear, the Polly and the Pusseybite on their way to the Ritertitle Mountains* on 23 Aug. 1866, for the children of Emma Parkyns. He had earlier written for them *The Story of the Four Little Children Who Went Round the World.* The

manuscript must have been sent to Lear, for he wrote in his diary for 7 May 1872, 'found out the Pussey Pollybite drawings'. The only known manuscript, now in the Houghton Library, is drawn on tracing paper and was probably taken from the original manuscript, which Lear would have returned to Emma Parkyns. Neither this nor the Scroobious Pip was published in Lear's lifetime; they first appeared in *Teapots and Quails* (1953). Both 'The Yonghy Bonghy Bò' and 'Mr and Mrs Discobbolos' were published in *Laughable Lyrics* (1877).

234 *Voysey.* Possibly the Revd Charles Voysey of Tadcaster.

236 *H[orace]. Walpole's letters. The Letters of Horace Walpole Earl of Orford*, ed. Peter Cunningham (1866). On the endpapers of vols. viii and ix, while ill in Apr. 1872, Lear made the first drafts of 'Some Incidents in the Life of my Uncle Arly'.

236 *Mrs. Damer.* Anne Seymour Damer (1749–1828). Sculptress, to whom Horace Walpole bequeathed Strawberry Hill for life. In 1811, according to a provision in the will, she disposed of it to the 6th Earl Waldegrave, the father of Lady Waldegrave's husband.

237 *Boards of trade.* Fortescue had been appointed President of the Board of Trade at the end of 1871.

238 *my cat.* Potiphar, who disappeared later in the year and was replaced by his twin Foss.

238 *Tozer.* Henry Fanshawe Tozer (1829–1916), author of *Researches in the Highlands of Turkey* (1869). Tozer bought and commissioned a number of paintings by Lear which are now in the Ashmolean.

239 *rush up a pergola.* On 26 Sept. 1875, Lear wrote to Sir Joseph Hooker: 'I think I prefer climbing to all other plants—they are so obligingly given to save space by growing perpendicular.'

239 *particular quotations.* 1. 'Tomorhit', and 2. 'The vast Akrokeraunian walls' both from 'To E.L., on his Travels in Greece'; 3. 'And the crag that fronts the Even, | All along the shadowing shore' from 'Eleänore'; 4. 'To watch the crisping ripples on the beach, | And tender curving lines of creamy spray', and 5. '[moonlight] on still waters between walls | Of [gleaming] granite, in a [shadowy] pass', both from 'The Lotos-Eaters'.

244 *the late Mr. T. Baring's.* Northbrook's uncle.

246 *Ldy Wilmot Hortons.* Wife of Sir Robert Wilmot Horton whom Lear had known in Rome. Sir Robert, as the representative of Lady Leigh, was responsible for destroying Byron's *Memoirs*.

246 *the Bombay Riots.* In Feb. 1874 some Muslims in Bombay had rioted, attacking members of the Parsee community. Wodehouse was reported as saying that feelings of hostility which had prevailed for a long time between the Parsees and Muslims had produced much mischief in Bombay. Some Parsees took this to mean that they were as much to blame for the riots as the Muslims, an accusation they fiercely disputed.

246 *grandson.* In fact, great grandson.

246 *whose father I knew.* Possibly Frank Ellis Jervoise, whom Lear knew in Como and Rome in 1837.

246 *My right eye is baddish.* On 27 Aug. 1872, Lear had fallen and hit his head. His right eye looked like 'a rainbow in fits' and the sight in it was permanently affected.

250 *your Book of Bosh. Bosh* by W.S., published in 1876, contained twenty-one uninspiring limericks. The dedication is to Lear, 'WITH PROFUSE APOLOGIES FOR HAVING POACHED ON HIS MANOR'. The limerick to which Lear refers is: 'There were two old Ladies of Wrexham, | Who when anything happen'd to vex 'em, | Went down to the cellar, | Each with an umbrella— | Those testy old Ladies at Wrexham.'

251 *said a foolish Artist to me.* Lear sometimes put his own thoughts into the mouths of fictitious people.

251 *Sir F[rancis]. G[oldsmid].* Sir Francis Goldsmid, Bt., MP, QC (1808–78), whom Lear met through Henry Bruce, bought four of Lear's paintings, *Civitella di Subiaco* (see note to p. 63), *Mount Athos. S. Dionisio* (1862), *Piana Rocks, Corsica* (1869), and *Bavella, Corsica* (1869). Richard Bright, MP, a friend of Aberdare's who was spending the winter of 1877–8 in San Remo, bought *Rome. Quarries of Cervara* (1860). Frederick W. Gibbs, QC, CB, whom Lear had met in Rome in the winter of 1858–9, was tutor to the Prince of Wales 1852–8; when Princess Louise was married in 1871, Gibbs presented her with a painting by Lear of the Roman Campagna.

252 *Alfred Seymour's.* Lear met Alfred Seymour when they were both students at Sass's School of Art in 1849. Admiral Sir Robert Spencer Robinson (1809–89) was Controller of the Navy, 1868–71, and Lord of the Admiralty, 1868–71. Bertie Matthews was a friend from Lear's early days in Rome.

252 *your Wedding tour.* Joseph Hooker had married for a second time in 1876. His wife Hyacinth was the widow of Lear's old friend Sir William Jardine.

252 *Daniel O'Connell.* The Irish politician and champion of Irish rights (1775–1847). It is not known where Lear met O'Connell.

253 *'Laughable Lyrics['].* The last of Lear's Nonsense books, which was in the shops in time for Christmas 1876.

253 *Mr. & Mrs. Discobbolos.* In Nov. 1880, Fields sent Lear £5 for the second part of 'Mr and Mrs Discobbolos'; the first part had been published in *Laughable Lyrics*. Fields does not appear to have published the poem, which was first published in the *Quarterly Review* of Oct. 1888, almost certainly based on a manuscript which Lear gave to Sir Edward Strachey, Bt., the husband of Lady Waldegrave's niece, in Jan. 1883.

254 *statement.* An abridged version appeared in the column *Fine Art Gossip* in *Athenaeum* of 1 Nov. 1879, p. 256, publicizing Lear's decision to go to New Zealand.

254 *Druggist Hanbury.* Hanbury had made his fortune as a chemist.

256 *your so kindly helping me last year*. At the end of 1879 Lear had approached
Lord Derby requesting a loan towards the cost of building his new house.
Lord Derby had declined to lend Lear money, believing loans to be a
mistake, but had instead offered to buy £500 worth of pictures.

256 *Egroegts Rehcsillip*. This reads Pillischer St George when reversed.
Phillischer was the name of Lear's London oculist.

256 *Lady Wenlock*. Sister of the 1st Duke of Westminster. Mrs Charles Grey
was the sister of Mrs George Clive.

257 *Lord Privy seal*. Fortescue had succeeded the Duke of Argyll as Lord Privy
Seal. The seal belongs to the family Phocidæ, and Lear played on this
zoological identity in many subsequent letters.

260 *Hamilton sale*. A huge sale of fine pictures, sculpture, furniture, and books
from the collection of the Duke of Hamilton.

260 *Millais portraits*. In Sept. 1884, Lear wrote to Lord Aberdare about his
four large unsold pictures: 'I am thankful that I have never known what
it is to envy anyone, but it cannot be otherwise than strange to me that
with all my labour I find a difficulty in getting rid of such works, while
Johnny Millais gets 1,000, 2,000, or 3000£ for what costs him hardly any
labour at all.'

260 *Sir Andrew Walker*. The Liverpool philanthropist (1824–93) who built
and donated to the city the Walker Art Gallery.

262 *copies of Turner*. Underhill made five copies of Turner paintings for Lear.
Apollo Killing the Python hung in his bedroom, and *Ulysses Deriding
Polyphemus* in the corridor. Three more hung in his library.

262 *Damascus*. A painting which had been bought by Lady Lyttleton.

262 *R. W. Roper*. Of Trinity College.

265 *The Brutality is the Damnation clause of the A[thanasian] Creed*. An issue on
which Lear had felt strongly for many years. vv. 1–2: 'Whosoever will be
saved: before all things it is necessary that he hold the Catholick Faith.
Which Faith except everyone do keep whole and undefiled: without
doubt he shall perish everlastingly.' The majority conclusion of a Royal
Commission set up in 1867 was that the creed should cease to be enforced
in public worship; the minority held that any change would give the
impression that something of the traditional faith was being surren-
dered. In the absence of a unanimous decision the creed remained
unaltered.

265 *the Dean's life is to be written*. Dean Stanley had died on 18 July 1881. *The
Life and Correspondence of Arthur Penrhyn Stanley D.D., late Dean of
Westminster*, by R. E. Prothero and G. C. Bradley, was published in
1893.

265 *4 large paintings*. These were *Argos, Gwalior, Ravenna*, and *Pentedatelo*.

266 *Enoch Arden's Island*. In Tennyson's poem 'Enoch Arden', the shipwreck-
ed mariner is washed up on an imaginary tropical island.

266 *back to England*. The Queen had spent the month of April on the Continent.

266 *Poltix*. This paragraph reflects Lear's thoughts on the Eastern question and Gladstone's part in it. Lear had developed a profound mistrust of Gladstone and his policies.

267 *Admiralty horror*. On 23 Apr. 1885 there had been an explosion in one of the rooms at the Admiralty in which one person had been injured. Northbrook was at this time First Lord of the Admiralty.

267 *certainly' known'*. Lear originally wrote 'certain'.' He later added to this, and it now reads 'certainly' known'.'

268 *insect lot of drawings*. To the various groups of Tennyson illustrations Lear gave entomological names reflecting stages in the development of a butterfly.

268 *Theodore Bent. The Cyclades: or, Life among the Insular Greeks* (1885).

269 *Canadian news*. An Indian rebellion had broken out at the beginning of Apr., but was put down within a few weeks.

269 *my sister*. Lear's last surviving sister, Eleanor Newsom, had died on 19 Mar. 1885.

269 *60 volumes of Diaries*. Of these only thirty, from 1858 to 1887, have survived.

269 *Ldy Davy*. Wife (1780–1855) of Sir Humphrey Davy, inventor of the safety lamp, and a prominent figure in Roman society.

270 *Autotype*. A patented method of reproduction.

271 *Luigi Rusconi*. Lear's Milanese servant. Giorgio Cocali had died on 8 Aug. 1883, and his son Nicola on 4 Mar. 1885.

272 *1853*. In fact 1854.

276 *Ld. Harrowby's Phoca*. The Earl of Harrowby was Lord Privy Seal, 1855–7.

276 *1849*. In fact, 1852.

277 *'Topographies'*. The drawings which Lear made on his travels, on which he based other work, and which he did not sell.

277 *30 individual parties*. Lear had hoped that Hallam's friends might subscribe towards it as a wedding present, but although he dropped hints to possible subscribers the idea was not taken up.

278 *begun long ago*. See note to p. 236.

281 *little Michæl's Photograph*. The son of Lionel and Eleanor Tennyson, born Dec. 1883.

282 *Giuseppi Orsini my servant*. Orsini had replaced Luigi Rusconi, and attended Lear until his death.

282 *30 years*. Lear acquired Foss as a kitten in Nov. 1872; he was 16 rather than 31 years old when he died. At the time of the drawing on p. 272 he was 14, not 16.

INDEX

In this selection of letters, Lear names nearly 400 towns and villages. The most important of these are indexed by name; others will be found by referring to the country in which they were located in Lear's time.